The **Rough Guide**

The Cotswolds

written and researched by

Matthew Teller

WITHDRAWN

Contents

Colour section 1

Introduction 6
Where to go 9
Things not to miss 11

Basics 17

Getting there........................... 19
Getting around......................... 21
Accommodation...................... 24
Food and drink 27
Festivals and events 29
Sports and outdoor activities... 32
Shopping 35
Travel essentials 35

Guide 41

❶ Oxford................................. 43
❷ The Oxfordshire
   countryside 87

❸ Stratford and the north
   Cotswolds........................ 133
❹ The central Cotswolds 171
❺ The west and south
   Cotswolds........................ 203

Contexts 245

Books 247

Small print & Index 251

Cotswolds food colour
section following p.120

Secret Cotswolds
colour section
following p.184

◀◀ Summer flowers in the Cotswolds ◀ Bourton-on-the-Water

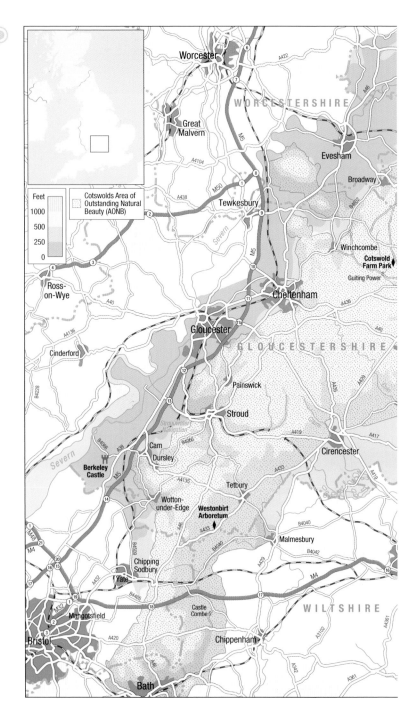

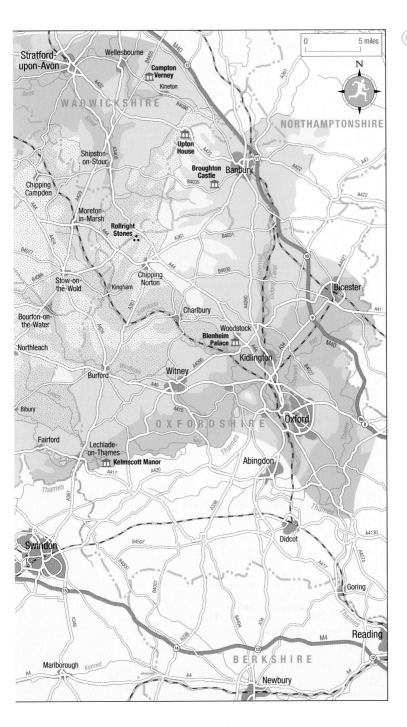

Introduction to

The Cotswolds

The Cotswold hills are special. Thatched cottages, dry-stone walls and, above all, the mellow, honey-coloured stone used in the area's buildings lend a unique warmth and unity of character to towns, villages and countryside. Sheep graze in the shadow of country churches, backwater hamlets slumber in the sunshine – catch the Cotswolds in the right place, at the right time, and you could almost imagine nothing's changed here in hundreds of years.

Except, of course, it has. Despite the appearance of natural tranquillity, this landscape, tilted gently from Oxfordshire's low-lying meadows up to the dramatic "**Cotswold Edge**", an escarpment overlooking the Severn and Vale of Evesham, has been intensively managed for centuries. Caught in the heartland of southern England, forming a rough quadrilateral between Oxford, Stratford-upon-Avon, Cheltenham and Bath, the Cotswolds first grew wealthy on the back of the **wool** trade: the local breed of sheep, sporting a distinctive shaggy mane, is known as the "**Cotswold Lion**".

By the early seventeenth century textile money was rolling in, and the Cotswolds were benefiting from the attentions of wealthy merchants. The landscape is still characterized by the grand "**wool churches**" they funded and the manor houses and almshouses they put up in the **Jacobean** style of the day – high gables, mullioned windows, tall chimney clusters and all, everything built using that rich-toned **yellow Cotswold limestone**.

The second phase of prosperity has come in our own time. Twentieth-century **tourism** – alongside an equally significant rise in **property prices**, as wealthy outsiders seek to buy into the Cotswolds' cliché of rural timelessness – has changed everything. Victorian designer William Morris was perhaps the first, taking country ways as the inspiration for his **Arts and Crafts** ideals. Today, of the 120,000 people living within the protected Cotswolds **Area of Outstanding Natural Beauty** (www.cotswoldsaonb.org.uk), 73 percent commute to jobs outside. For the first time, it has become uneconomic for many to farm. The **heritage industry** has taken over, ruthlessly marketing the region with an over-

▲ Radcliffe Camera, Oxford

reliance on twee imagery and funnelling visitors onto a tired old circuit of stately homes and gardens, tearooms and "visitor attractions".

As a consequence there's a fair amount of **money** sloshing around the Cotswolds' economy, feeding a burgeoning **service sector** but also helping to keep **traditional skills** such as thatching and dry-stone walling alive.

This is a touristy destination, but there is a very definite beaten track and it's not hard to steer clear of the crowds. Construct a visit not just around stately homes, but also around **farmers' markets**. Rather than towns, resolve to stay in **villages**: some of the Cotswolds' loveliest places to stay – and best restaurants – are out in the countryside. Tour by car if you like, but options exist for slower, more interesting ways to travel: by **bus**, **bike** and **on foot**. That's what this book is all about – an attempt to dodge the predictable and help visitors reshape their experience of this most beautiful of rural regions.

Cot's Wolds?

"Wolds" – an Old English word referring to rolling uplands – are not unique to the Cotswolds: both Lincolnshire and Yorkshire have their own. The origin of "**cot**" is trickier to pin down. Some say it has to do with a Saxon farmer named Cot or Cod, who settled near the source of the River Windrush. An alternative derivation is from the Old English term "cot", cognate with "cottage", meaning a simple rural dwelling: perhaps the Cotswolds were named for the stone shelters built on the wolds by Anglo-Saxon farmers for themselves and/or their sheep? Nobody really knows.

Celeb-free Cotswolds

From Damien Hirst to Jeremy Clarkson, Liz Hurley to Laurence Llewelyn-Bowen, Kate Winslet to Lily Allen – to name just six – celebrities galore call the Cotswolds home (or second, third or fourth home). Elton John pops by, Dom Joly lives here, Kate Moss has a mansion – and then of course there's Prince Charles at Highgrove and Princess Anne at Gatcombe... we could go on. But, aside from a mention in our Cotswold Food section for musician Alex James, now an award-winning cheesemaker, we don't. That's the last you'll hear of them.

Seasonality is key: it's no surprise that **summer** is the busiest time in the Cotswolds – and a lovely time of year to visit – but visiting out of peak season can offer great rewards. **Autumn** encompasses the grandeur of leaf-fall colours: the Cotswolds' two big arboretums, at Westonbirt and Batsford, are obvious draws, but following footpaths or back roads through wooded dells is free.

Winter is a wonderful time to explore – and not only because hotels and B&Bs drop their prices. If you thought all that honeyed Cotswold stone looked good in summer sun, wait till you see what it looks like on a clear winter's afternoon, with low, golden light pouring from blue skies, frost on the trees and your breath in the air. When you know there's a blazing log fire waiting for you at "home" – not to mention at just about every pub along the way – togging up to roam in the chill becomes an adventure. And from late January or so, **snowdrops** in their thousands adorn gardens all over the Cotswolds.

Thanks to the topography, you can even skip between seasons. Autumn can come a month early to gardens located up on the Cotswold Edge, compared with places down below: romp amid late-summer flowers in Cheltenham, then shuffle through fallen leaves in Misarden, six miles away as the crow flies, but almost a thousand feet up.

That seasonality is also expressed strongly in **food**. From the Stroud-Tetbury-Cirencester triangle all the way over to Woodstock, the last few years have seen

▼ Daffodils in the Duntisbournes

an axis of excellence developing across the Cotswolds in terms of restaurants, food producers and markets. Raising the bar benefits consumers, through innovative cooking and exemplary standards in service and design, but also creates chances for home-grown talent both in and out of the kitchen to gain high-level experience locally. Producers fuel the increased demand with high-quality seasonal ingredients, from lamb to wild boar and beer to asparagus – often also sold direct on market squares region-wide. Food is making the Cotswolds famous all over again.

▲ Punting, Oxford

Where to go

Where the Cotswolds start and end is a matter of personal opinion: there are no formally agreed boundaries. This book sets its own limits. First, we include **Oxford** – with an extraordinary history and atmosphere, it's worth a few days of anyone's time. With minor exceptions, we do not venture further east than Oxford, nor further west than the cathedral city of **Gloucester**. In the south we stick to the River Thames and then dip down to the M4, stopping short of **Bath**. The northern limit is Shakespeare's home town of **Stratford-upon-Avon**.

In the heart of the Cotswolds, three of the most visited destinations lie within twenty miles of each other: **Burford** is often dubbed the "gateway to the Cotswolds", **Bourton-on-the-Water** is a picturesque riverside village and **Broadway** forms a photogenic cluster of ex-coaching inns. All are pretty, but none is wholly satisfying – not least because everybody goes there.

The region's single most attractive town is **Chipping Campden**, a beguiling mix of golden Jacobean facades, fascinating history and thriving community spirit. Classic Cotswold landscapes abound in the villages nearby, including **Ebrington**, **Blockley** and **Stanton**, along with superb gardens at **Hidcote**, **Kiftsgate** and **Batsford**, great walking on the **Cotswold Way** and excursions to stately homes including **Snowshill** and **Stanway**.

Just to the east, past **Moreton-in-Marsh** and **Stow-on-the-Wold**, lies a gentle stretch known as the **Oxfordshire Cotswolds**, anchored by the royal town of **Woodstock** (alongside splendid **Blenheim Palace**) but best experienced in the villages – notably **Kingham** and **Charlbury**.

To the west, the Cotswolds have turned Gloucestershire into "Poshtershire": **Cheltenham** and **Cirencester** are pleasant enough, but perhaps a touch over-reliant on well-heeled locals; **Tetbury**, though similar, is smaller and better-looking. Instead, seek out lesser-known rural spots: evocative **Painswick** is on the beaten track – but **Minchinhampton**, **Nailsworth** and other hideaways in the deep **Stroud** valleys aren't. **Winchcombe** is a lovely spot, high on the hills for great walks and also on the doorstep of magnificent **Sudeley Castle**.

Wherever you go, don't think towns and A roads – think villages and B roads. The best of the Cotswolds fills the gaps on the map.

Names to conjure with

Although the region covered by this book takes in villages such as Pancakehill, Knockdown, Little Rollright and Old Sodbury, that isn't the half of it. On our travels in (and just beyond) this compact bit of countryside, we've put together a dozen **place names** to conjure with, all no doubt with eminently meaningful derivations – but all, still, truly outlandish. Savour each one with pride: this is England.

- Marsh Gibbon
- Toot Baldon
- Cold Aston
- Lower Slaughter
- Slad
- Broughton Poggs
- Kingston Bagpuize
- Poffley End
- Goosey
- Wyre Piddle
- Waterley Bottom
- Bishop's Itchington

16

things not to miss

It's not possible to see everything that the Cotswolds have to offer in one trip – and we don't suggest you try. What follows is a selective and subjective taste of the region's highlights: places to visit, top attractions and hidden gems. They're arranged in five colour-coded categories to help you find the very best things to see, do and experience. All entries have a page reference to take you straight into the guide, where you can find out more.

01 Sudeley Castle Page **210** ● Magnificent medieval castle, once home to Henry VIII's widow, worth visiting for the gardens alone.

03 Chastleton House Page 119
• Memorably handsome Jacobean mansion sporting appealingly lived-in interiors.

04 The Kingham Plough Page 115
• A lovely old village pub, now updated to a classic Cotswold hideaway for fine dining and a posh sleepover.

02 Walking Page 32
• From the 100-mile Cotswold Way to the shortest of village strolls, Shanks's pony is the only way to get under the skin of this unique region.

05 Stroud Farmers' Market Page 231
• Farmers' markets dot the Cotswolds but the oldest – and still one of the best – is the weekly event at Stroud.

06 Westonbirt Arboretum
Page **239** • Sensational gardens near Tetbury filled with colour at any season – but especially vibrant in autumn, heralded each year by the stunning late-summer Festival of the Tree.

07 Village pubs Page **27** • Cotswold village pubs hold the keys to their communities: make time to stop in for a drink, a bite to eat and/or a long, lazy afternoon.

08 Blenheim Palace Page **98** • Simply one of Britain's greatest stately homes, offering a memorable day out exploring the interiors and then roaming the park-like grounds.

09 **Chipping Campden** Page **154** • If you visit only one place in the Cotswolds, this should be it – a town of sublime architecture, fascinating history, beautiful nature and a fine choice of places to sleep and eat.

10 **Lower Slaughter** Page **186** • One of the Cotswolds' prettiest villages – popular, but not as relentlessly commercial as some of its neighbours.

11 Cotswold Farm Park Page **184** • A family day out on a working farm that also gives great insight into the region's agricultural past (and present) through their presentation of rare breeds.

13 Gloucester Cathedral Page **222** • Rambling, absorbing old cathedral with perhaps England's most beautiful cloisters.

12 Oxford Covered Market Page **72** • Drop into this noisy, busy enclave in the city centre for fresh-baked bread, local cheeses and deli items galore.

14 Stratford-upon-Avon Page **136** • Shakespeare's home town – but dodge the heritage hype in favour of a good meal and some world-class theatre.

15 Oxford colleges Page **58** • Packed with atmosphere, and often displaying stunning architecture, Oxford's colleges offer a fascinating glimpse of academic life.

16 Painswick Page **228** • From its yew-studded churchyard to its delis and country walks, this tiny, historic village embodies Cotswold charm.

Basics

Basics

Getting there 19

Getting around 21

Accommodation 24

Food and drink 27

Festivals and events 29

Sports and outdoor activities 32

Shopping 35

Travel essentials 35

Getting there

The Cotswolds lie midway between London, Bristol and Birmingham. Internationally, it's easy to fly into Heathrow or Birmingham airports and pick up direct transfers by road or rail. Domestically, rail and motorway links are excellent.

From around the UK

By **car**, aim for the **M40**. Junction 8 (or, coming from the north, junction 9) feeds into Oxford and also serves the A40 heading west to Witney and Cheltenham, and the A44 heading northwest to Chipping Norton, Moreton-in-Marsh and Evesham. However, traffic at both Oxford junctions and on the Oxford ring road (see p.49) can be hellish at peak times: if you're aiming for the villages, it might be less stressful to come off instead at junction 10 and use minor roads. See p.49 for details of Oxford's park-and-ride scheme. Further north, M40 junction 11 is good for Banbury, Chipping Norton and Stow-on-the-Wold, while the quickest access to Stratford is from junction 15.

Elsewhere, the **M4** skirts the southern edge of the Cotswolds – junction 15 is useful for Lechlade and Cirencester – or, if you're approaching from the west/southwest, come off the **M5** at junction 13 for Stroud and Cirencester, junction 11 for Gloucester, Cheltenham, Northleach and Oxford, or junction 9 to pick up routes to Stow.

If you're coming from the south coast, avoid London by aiming for Winchester: from there (M3 junction 9), join the quick and convenient **A34** dual carriageway (signed Newbury) which cuts north directly to Oxford.

From the north, the **M6/M5** gives access to Cheltenham and the western Cotswolds, and (via the **M42**) Stratford and the northern Cotswolds. Alternatively, stay on the **M1** down to junction 15A (Northampton) to pick up the fast, easy **A43** dual carriageway towards Oxford.

By train

From London there's a choice of First Great Western from Paddington to Oxford (55min) or Cheltenham (2hr 10min) – or Chiltern

Railways from Marylebone to Banbury (1hr) and Stratford (2hr). Some FGW trains continue past Oxford onto the Cotswold Line towards Worcester, serving village stations including Charlbury, Kingham and Moreton-in-Marsh (more info on p.22), while FGW trains towards Cheltenham serve the little station at Kemble (useful for Cirencester and Tetbury) as well as Stroud. A new line from Marylebone to Oxford is expected to open in 2013; details at www .chiltern-evergreen3.co.uk.

From southern England Cross Country has regular trains to Oxford from Bournemouth, Southampton, Winchester and Basingstoke. Each of those has links from around Surrey and Sussex, or you could aim instead to join Cross Country or FGW trains at Reading – which has connections from Redhill, Guildford and Clapham Junction. **From the southwest** a separate Cross Country route runs from Plymouth and Exeter to Cheltenham.

From the north, opt for Cross Country trains from Manchester, Stoke, Derby, Sheffield, Leeds, York, Newcastle and Edinburgh direct to Banbury, Oxford or Cheltenham. They're slower than mainline Virgin services, but you can sit tight all the way without having to change at Birmingham New Street. Another method is to change instead at Wolverhampton onto a Wrexham & Shropshire train to Banbury – pleasant, comfortable and rarely packed.

For information on routes, timetables and fares contact **National Rail Enquiries** (☎0845 748 4950, www.nationalrail.co.uk).

By coach

There are two specific routes where **coaches** beat the train. The first is to Oxford **from Central London** (1hr 40min) – the UK's highest-frequency service, with more than

150 coaches a day in each direction: **Oxford Tube** (☎01865 772250, ⓦ www.oxfordtube .com) and **Oxford Espress** (☎01865 785400, ⓦ www.espress.info) operate day and night from Victoria, Marble Arch and elsewhere, with departures every ten minutes at peak times. Both offer luxury seating, free wi-fi and other commuter perks. An open return (valid 3 months) costs £20.

The other is the east-west route to Oxford – notoriously difficult to do by train – **from Cambridge** (3hr 15min), **Bedford** (1hr 55min)

and **Milton Keynes** railway station (1hr 10min), served half-hourly by coach **X5** (☎01604 676060, ⓦ www.stagecoachX5 .com). An open return from Cambridge (valid 3 months) is £18.

Otherwise coaches are much slower than trains. **National Express** (☎0871 781 8181, ⓦ www.nationalexpress.com) has direct links to Oxford, Gloucester, Cheltenham, Banbury and Stratford – as well as, usefully, Cirencester, which has no train service – from, for example, central London, the south coast

International arrivals: airports and transport links

London Heathrow (LHR) ⓦ www.heathrowairport.com.
London Gatwick (LGW) ⓦ www.gatwickairport.com.
London Stansted (STN) ⓦ www.stanstedairport.com.
London Luton (LTN) ⓦ www.londonluton.com.
Birmingham (BHX) ⓦ www.bhx.co.uk.
Bristol (BRS) ⓦ www.bristolairport.co.uk.
East Midlands (EMA) ⓦ www.eastmidlandsairport.com.
Oxford (OXF) ⓦ www.oxfordairport.co.uk.

From London Heathrow
From Heathrow you don't need to head into London: the best connections are by **bus** (or, to use the more common term for long-distance bus services, **"coach"**). Oxford Bus runs frequent "Airline" coaches (ⓦ www.theairline.info) nonstop to Oxford (1hr) for £25 return. National Express (ⓦ www.nationalexpress.com) has coaches direct to Banbury (1hr 15min), Cirencester (1hr 55min), Cheltenham (2hr 30min) and Gloucester (3hr). Thandi (ⓦ www.thandicoaches.com) also serves Banbury. A convenient alternative is the Stow Shuttle minibus (☎01993 705993, ⓦ www.stowshuttle.com; £70 return; advance booking essential), which runs several times a day from Heathrow to Witney and Stow-on-the-Wold. Otherwise, trains to London Paddington are run by Heathrow Express (ⓦ www.heathrowexpress.com) – fast but very expensive (£32 return) – and slightly slower Heathrow Connect (ⓦ www.heathrowconnect.com), at £16 return. From Paddington, frequent trains serve Oxford and the Cotswolds.

From London Gatwick
From Gatwick, the "Airline" **coach** (ⓦ www.theairline.info) heads nonstop to Oxford (2hr 30min) for £35 return – or you could take a **train** from Gatwick airport station to Reading (1hr 15min) and change there for Oxford, Banbury, stations on the Cotswold Line, Stroud, Gloucester or Cheltenham.

From other airports
From **Birmingham airport** station (known as "Birmingham International") Cross Country trains go direct to Banbury (40min) and Oxford (1hr). From **Stansted airport** take a National Express coach to Oxford (3hr 30min); from **Luton airport** do the same (1hr 55min). From **Bristol airport** take the "Flyer" bus (£6; 30min) – either to Bristol bus station for a National Express coach to Gloucester (55min), Cheltenham (1hr 25min) and Stratford (2hr 35min), or to Bristol Temple Meads station for a train to Cheltenham (40min) or Gloucester (50min). From **East Midlands airport** take the "Skylink" bus to Derby station (£3.20; 35min), from where Cross Country trains serve Banbury (1hr 25min), Oxford (1hr 45min), Cheltenham (1hr 25min) and Gloucester (1hr 45min). For **Oxford airport**, see p.49.

(Torquay, Weymouth, Portsmouth and others), and the north (Glasgow, Newcastle, Liverpool, Leeds and others). Their sole attraction is price: booking ahead could net you a "funfare" on certain routes of £3–6 each way.

Megabus (℡0900 160 0900, ⓦwww .megabus.com) has even cheaper fares. If you can accept their restrictions about only boarding specific coaches at specific points, and always booking in advance, you could pay as little as £1.50 for a seat on the Oxford Tube, the X5 or their coaches to Oxford from Portsmouth, Southampton, Manchester and Leeds, or to Cheltenham and Gloucester from London.

From the US and Canada

From the US take your pick of dozens of scheduled and charter flights into London from New York, Washington DC, Boston, Chicago, Atlanta, Miami, Las Vegas, San Francisco, Los Angeles, and other cities. Return fares from New York start around US$400, from Los Angeles US$500–600.

From Canada, look for nonstop routings from mainly Toronto, Montréal, Calgary and Vancouver, with return fares roughly covering the range C$500–900.

As well as checking for deals on the usual airlines, look for low fares on unusual carriers. Air India, for instance, flies nonstop between Toronto and London at bargain rates, as does Kuwait Airways out of Kennedy.

From Australia & NZ

Routes **from Australia and New Zealand** to London are highly competitive, with return fares out of Sydney, Melbourne or Perth usually A$1500–2500, or NZ$2000–3000 out of Auckland. Check out the obvious carriers first, such as Qantas, British Airways and Air NZ – but then explore options on, for instance, Emirates, Etihad or Qatar via the Gulf, Air Asia via Kuala Lumpur, or even take a low-cost hop on a budget airline to, say, Bangkok or Singapore from where you can pick up super-cheap deals on scheduled carriers to London.

From Europe

For **flights** the best advice is to check the website of your preferred arrival airport, to find out who flies there from your country.

Trains serve London St Pancras from Lille (1hr 20min), Paris (2hr 15min) and Brussels (2hr), with connections coming into those cities from all around Europe. Eurostar (ⓦwww.eurostar.com) sells tickets for journeys from certain stations in western Europe (see website for list) to any UK station; otherwise consult a rail agent in your country.

By **ferry** Portsmouth is the Cotswolds' nearest Channel port, 86 miles from Oxford – served mainly from Le Havre (ⓦwww .ldlines.com), Caen or Santander (ⓦwww .brittany-ferries.com).

Getting around

Although trains and buses are fine for moving between towns, and for accessing specific points in the countryside, public transport in the Cotswolds just isn't good enough to do any serious touring. To cover decent ground you'll need your own wheels – four or, perhaps, two. That said, main roads in summer can get busy with holiday traffic (though minor roads remain quiet) – and visitors from outside the UK should be prepared for high rental and fuel costs.

For public transport, two information sources are key. For trains, **National Rail Enquiries** (℡0845 748 4950, ⓦwww.nationalrail.co.uk) is the fount of all knowledge, if not wisdom, while the impartial official service **Traveline**

(℡0871 200 2233, ⓦwww.traveline.info) has full details and timetable information for every bus, train, coach and ferry route in the UK.

Much more convenient, though, are the area-specific **timetable booklets** published twice a year by the Cotswolds Area of Outstanding Natural Beauty (ⓦwww.cotswoldsaonb.org.uk), covering trains and buses in three regions (North Cotswolds, Central Cotswolds and South Cotswolds), as well as one specifically for walkers on the Cotswold Way. All are available free at tourist offices, and downloadable from the AONB website.

By train

Train lines mostly skirt the edges of the Cotswolds, serving larger towns such as Oxford, Banbury, Stratford, Gloucester and Cheltenham; full details on p.19.

The **Cotswold Line** – part of the London–Worcester main line, run by First Great Western – has approximately hourly trains serving a string of villages between Oxford and Evesham including Hanborough, Charlbury, Kingham, Moreton-in-Marsh and Honeybourne. This is supplemented by the Railbus service (ⓦwww.railbus.co.uk), which has buses coordinated to meet arriving trains at Charlbury and Kingham to shuttle passengers to/from nearby rural areas. Most routes are for commuters, operating in peak hours only and/or requiring advance booking, but the handy X8 bus to Chipping Norton runs all day from Kingham station, with through-ticketing possible. The website has details.

First Great Western trains from London to Cheltenham cut across country after Swindon, following the **Golden Valley Line** to Kemble – well placed for Cirencester and Tetbury – and Stroud. FGW also runs a few stopping trains on the **Oxford Canal Line** between Oxford and Banbury, accessing canalside scenery and country walks around Tackley, Heyford and King's Sutton villages.

For bridging the last few miles from the station to your final destination check **Traintaxi** (ⓦwww.traintaxi.co.uk), a useful database of local cab numbers for every railway station in the country.

Another useful adjunct to train services is **Plusbus** (ⓦwww.plusbus.info), a discounted bus pass which you buy with your train ticket. This allows unlimited bus travel for one day, seven days or longer in and around selected rail hub towns, including Oxford, Banbury, Gloucester, Cheltenham and Stroud. Their prices are invariably lower than an equivalent bus pass bought on the spot from local operators. Children under 16 and railcard holders (see below) get further discounts. Their website has full details.

Rail fares and passes

For point-to-point travel, "**advance**" tickets are cheapest: these cannot be bought on the day of travel and come with several restrictions. "**Off-peak**" fares can be bought in advance or on the day of travel, but are only valid at quieter times (generally after 9.30am Monday to Friday, all day at weekends). Most expensive are "**anytime**" tickets, which permit travel on any train. You can **buy** a ticket for any journey in person at any station, or by phone or online from any train operator (all of which are listed on the National Rail Enquiries website). Sometimes two singles are cheaper than a return.

Check ⓦwww.railcard.co.uk for details of the **16-25 Railcard**, **Senior Railcard** and **Family & Friends Railcard**, which bring good discounts. Many other options exist to cut the cost of rail travel. If you're in a group of three or four adults, ask about **GroupSave**, whereby you can travel together off-peak for the price of two adults (with up to four children paying only £1 each). First Great Western offer the **Cotswold Line Railcard** (£7.50), giving discounts for a year's off-peak travel between Oxford and Worcester, and the **Oxfordshire Day Ranger** (£13), giving unlimited off-peak travel between Reading, Oxford, Banbury and Moreton-in-Marsh. Chiltern Railways have the **Shakespeare Explorer** (one/four days £30/£45), valid from London for trips to and around Stratford-upon-Avon. If you're touring the Cotswolds by train from a starting-point in London or Surrey, the **Thames Rover** (three/seven days £40/£75) could save you money – as could the **Heart of England Rover** (three/seven days £65/£85) from the Midlands.

Rail contacts

In the UK

Chiltern Railways ☏0845 600 5165, ⓦwww.chilternrailways.co.uk.

Cross Country ☏0844 811 0124, ⓦwww.crosscountrytrains.co.uk.

First Great Western ☏ 0845 700 0125, ⓦ www.firstgreatwestern.co.uk.

National Rail ☏ 0845 748 4950, ⓦ www.nationalrail.co.uk. The official source for UK train information, with timetables, maps, links for purchasing and more.

Seat 61 ⓦ www.seat61.com. Top resource for rail travel, including a detailed section on travelling around Britain, with plenty of information, tips and links.

Worldwide

Britain on Track US & Canada ☏ 1-888/667-9734, ⓦ www.britainontrack.com.

BritRail US & Canada ☏ 1-866/BRITRAIL, ⓦ www.britrail.com.

Rail Europe US ☏ 1-800/622-8600, Canada ☏ 1-800/361-RAIL; ⓦ www.raileurope.com.

Rail Plus Australia ☏ 03/9642 8644, ⓦ www.railplus.com.au; New Zealand ☏ 09/377 5415, ⓦ www.railplus.co.nz.

By bus

Public transport in the Cotswolds mostly means **buses**. Services are run by dozens of companies, some national enterprises, others tiny local firms. You don't really need to know which is which – we've identified bus numbers, routes and options at each relevant point throughout this book. For **timetable** info check Traveline (see p.21) or the booklets published by the Cotswolds Area of Outstanding Natural Beauty (described opposite).

Beware: many villages (including relatively well-known places such as Broadway or Winchcombe) have limited bus service – perhaps only two or three a day, often with none on Sundays – while others have no buses at all. Some prominent attractions, such as the Cotswold Farm Park, are inaccessible on public transport.

Each bus operator issues its own **tickets and passes**, which makes for a horribly confusing patchwork of options. The soundest advice is to have a chat with tourist office staff: they'll know what's best for your particular travel plans. Apart from local one-day tickets, worthwhile passes covering larger areas include the **Stagecoach Oxfordshire** DayRider Gold (£7/day) or MegaRider Gold (£22/week), valid across their network. The MegaRider Country (£15/week) covers Oxfordshire villages only, excluding Oxford and Banbury. **Stagecoach Warwickshire** has its own MegaRider Gold (£20/week), valid on buses between Oxford, Chipping Norton, Banbury and Stratford, plus local villages. Just to confuse matters, **Stagecoach West** also has a MegaRider Gold (£18/week) for bus travel around Oxford, Cirencester, Cheltenham and Gloucester. Full details are at ⓦ www.stagecoach.com.

By car or motorbike

The easiest and, for most people, best way to tour the Cotswolds is by **car**. Scenic drives abound: tourist offices like to tout specific routes but, in truth, just about any road between Oxford, Stratford and Cheltenham sooner or later offers up picturesque honeystone villages and gentle views over rolling fields. Some of the loveliest driving can be on ordinary back routes between untouristed villages.

Traffic on some main roads such as the A40 and A429 can be heavy over the summer – especially bad at weekends – and cars are being firmly given the squeeze in the town centres across the region, most notably central Oxford. That said, back roads are invariably quiet.

Parking in villages is rarely a problem, but in towns and popular tourist spots it can be limited – and often expensive. If you're driving to Oxford, Stratford, Gloucester, Cheltenham or Bath for the day (or longer), you'd do best with **park-and-ride** (ⓦ www.parkandride.net), whereby you park for free at signposted car parks on the outskirts and take a cheap bus to the centre. Return fares are around £2.50 or £3 – there are often discounts for families and groups of two or more adults – and you rarely have to wait longer than ten minutes for a bus.

Car rental is usually cheaper arranged in advance through one of the global chains. If you rent locally, expect to pay around £30 per day, £50 for a weekend or from £120 per week. Book well in advance for the cheapest rates. Few companies will rent to drivers with less than one year's experience and most will only rent to people between 21 and 75 years of age. Cotswold Campers (☏ 01386 423009, ⓦ www.cotswoldcampers.co.uk) and Comfy Campers (☏ 01242 696774, ⓦ www.comfy campers.co.uk) rent well-equipped retro VW **campervans** sleeping up to four people for self-drive adventures. Prices range from about £375 to £650 a week, with weekend-only deals often available. Just Go (☎01582 842888, ⓦwww.justgo.uk.com) rents modern **motorhomes** for up to six people for £300–1000 per week.

Cycling

Although the Cotswolds is renowned for its rolling hills, don't let that put you off **cycling** – not merely as a recreational activity, but as a viable method of getting about. The "A" roads can be a bit busy, but the quieter "B" roads and country lanes see little traffic, and are boosted by a network of rural cycleways.

For more details of local options, including cycling routes and specialist tour operators offering cycling holidays, turn to p.32.

Accommodation

Accommodation in the Cotswolds ranges from roadside lodges to old-fashioned country retreats, and from budget guesthouses to chic boutique hotels. Well-turned out properties in towns and villages alike offer heaps of historic atmosphere.

Nearly all tourist offices will **book rooms** for you on request (by email, phone or in person), generally charging a booking fee of about £3–5, as well as taking a non-refundable deposit – usually ten percent – that is later deducted from your final bill. Official tourism websites ⓦwww.cotswolds.com and ⓦwww.oxfordshirecotswolds.org – as well as most of the others listed on p.39 – offer online booking.

Two bodies inspect accommodation nationwide and award star ratings: Quality in Tourism, acting for Visit Britain's "Enjoy England" brand (ⓦwww.enjoyengland.com), and the AA (Automobile Association; ⓦwww .theaa.com). They both use the same criteria to grade properties from one to five stars,

within separate schemes: **Serviced Accommodation** – which includes hotels in various categories, as well as B&Bs, guesthouses, inns and farmhouses – **Self-Catering**, **Hostels** and **Holiday Parks**. **Campsites** are rated by the AA on a five-pennant scale. Rated properties will have a sticker or signboard displaying the star rating – either a blue sign with Enjoy England's red rose logo or a yellow and black sign with the AA logo.

However, the star-ratings are only a guide: bear in mind that there is no absolute correlation between rating and price – and official listings of rated accommodation may exclude otherwise excellent places which have either been left unrated, or which are awaiting inspection.

Accommodation price codes

All accommodation in this book has been given a **price code**, indicating the lowest you could expect to pay per night for a **double room in high season**. Breakfast is included unless otherwise stated.

❶ £39 and under	❹ £80–99	❼ £150–174
❷ £40–59	❺ £100–124	❽ £175–199
❸ £60–79	❻ £125–149	❾ £200 and over

Bear in mind that this is only a guide: establishments graded as ❸ may also have better rooms at ❹ rates. Single rooms, where available, tend to cost roughly sixty to eighty percent of the double-room rate.

Hotels

Hotel prices in the Cotswolds start at around £50 per night for a simple double/twin room, breakfast included. Two- and three-star hotels can cost £90–100 a night, while four-and five-star properties may start at £150–180 or more. Character comes in spades: places at all budgets may occupy historic properties, often in Cotswold honey-coloured limestone, bedecked with ivy and/or sporting floral window boxes, offering classic views of village or countryside scenes.

Despite the Cotswolds' conservative reputation, don't imagine that chintzy drapes and fusty interiors prevail: lots of competition and a constant flow of visitors keep standards high, and you can expect good attention to detail across the board on interior styling, bathroom accessories and high-tech features such as flat-screen TVs and wi-fi. At the top end, besides the traditional country estates you might expect, the Cotswolds can also offer world-class boutique hotels, replete with contemporary styling and a sense of artful chic.

Cotswolds Finest Hotels (ⓦwww.cotswoldsfinesthotels.com) is a grouping that includes some of the region's best luxury properties. **Cotswold Inns and Hotels** (ⓦwww.cotswold-inns-hotels.co.uk) draws together a handful of attractive but less stratospherically priced options.

B&Bs and guest houses

At its most basic, a **B&B** (bed-and-breakfast) is an ordinary private house with a couple of

Over 100 award-winning camp sites

If you love camping as much as we do, you'll love staying on one of The Camping and Caravanning Club's 108 UK Club Sites. Each of our sites are in great locations and are an ideal base for exploring.

There's just one thing: once you've discovered the friendly welcome, the excellent facilities and clean, safe surroundings, you'll probably want to join anyway!

To book your adventure or to join the Club call **0845 130 7633** quoting code **2857** or visit **www.thefriendlyclub.co.uk**

The Camping and Caravanning Club
The Friendly Club

bedrooms set aside for paying guests. Larger establishments with more rooms may style themselves **guesthouses**, but they are pretty much the same thing. Either way, these are a great option for travellers looking for charm and a local experience: the best – with fresh, house-proud rooms, hearty home-cooked food and a wealth of local knowledge – can match or beat a hotel stay at any price.

In countryside locations some of the best accommodation is found in farmhouses, while many village **pubs** (termed "**inns**" in listings) offer B&B. You may also come across the self-explanatory concept of a "**restaurant with rooms**".

Single travellers should be aware that many B&Bs and guest houses don't have single rooms, and sole occupancy of a double/twin room may be charged at seventy or eighty percent of the standard rate.

Tourist offices across the region list B&Bs, inns and the rest as part of their accommodation listings, and offer a booking service as described above. Nationwide schemes also cover properties within the Cotswolds area, including the following:

Budget hotel chains

All the following budget chains have hotels in the region covered by this book, generally located on the outskirts of larger towns and/or beside main roads. Their style is generic and without character – but special advance offers can bring en-suite room rates down to an unbeatable £20–30.
Holiday Inn Express ⓦwww.hiexpress.com.
Ibis ⓦwww.ibishotel.com.
Premier Inn ⓦwww.premierinn.com.
Travelodge ⓦwww.travelodge.co.uk.

B&B My Guest ☏0870 444 3840, ⊛www.beduk .co.uk. Online bookings at traditional or historic B&B properties.

Distinctly Different ☏01225 866842, ⊛www .distinctlydifferent.co.uk. Unusual buildings converted into accommodation, including an Oxfordshire dovecote and an old windmill near Bath.

Farm Stay UK ☏024 7669 6909, ⊛www .farmstay.co.uk. The UK's largest network of farm-based accommodation.

Wolsey Lodges ☏01473 822058, ⊛www .wolseylodges.com. Superior B&B in inspected properties, from Elizabethan manor houses to Victorian rectories.

Self-catering

Cotswold **self-catering** accommodation runs the gamut from purpose-designed new builds to historic, converted barns or **cottages**. The minimum rental period is usually a week: depending on the season, expect to pay around £250 a week for a small cottage in an out-of-the-way location, maybe three or four times that for a larger property in a popular spot. We've listed some agencies below; tourist boards also keep full details of self-catering rentals in their area.

Broadway Manor Cottages ☏01386 852913, ⊛www.broadwaymanor-cottages.co.uk. Highly rated enterprise in Broadway, with a fistful of awards, that offers several good options.

Campden Cottages ☏01386 593315, ⊛www .campdencottages.co.uk. Local agency in Chipping Campden with a good choice of properties.

Cottage in the Country ☏01608 646833, ⊛www.cottageinthecountry.co.uk. Another local firm, based in Chipping Norton, offering cottages and holiday self-catering throughout the Cotswolds.

Cottages Direct ☏0845 268 0947, ⊛www .cottagesdirect.com. Massive choice of properties, offering direct booking.

Cottages4You ☏0845 268 0760, ⊛www .cottages4you.co.uk. Wide range of graded properties all over the Cotswolds.

Country Accom ⊛www.countryaccom.co.uk. A grouping of local self-catering (and B&B) properties, dubbing themselves "Oxfordshire and Cotswolds Farm and Country House Accommodation".

HomeAway ☏020 8827 1971, ⊛www .homeaway.co.uk. Hundreds of Cotswold properties, from luxury apartments in central Oxford to thatched countryside cottages.

Landmark Trust ☏01628 825925, ⊛www .landmarktrust.org.uk. A preservation charity

handling historic properties converted into holiday accommodation, including Jacobean banqueting halls in Chipping Campden.

Manor Cottages ☏01993 824252, ⊛www .manorcottages.co.uk. Based in Burford, offering a broad choice of holiday cottages and houses across the Cotswolds.

National Trust ☏0844 800 2070, ⊛www .nationaltrustcottages.co.uk. The NT owns more than 350 cottages, houses and farmhouses, most set in their own gardens or grounds.

Rural Retreats ☏01386 701177, ⊛www .ruralretreats.co.uk. Upmarket accommodation, often in restored historic buildings. Especially strong on the Cotswolds.

Sykes Cottages ☏01244 356869, ⊛www .sykescottages.co.uk. Dozens of options throughout the Cotswolds.

Hostels and student halls

The **Youth Hostel Association** (YHA; ☏01629 592700, ⊛www.yha.org.uk) has three properties in the area covered by this book, in Oxford, Stratford and Stow-on-the-Wold; the last is the only hostel within the Cotswolds proper. Depending on the season, expect to pay around £15–25 for a bed, with some private twin/double and family rooms available. Meals – breakfast, packed lunch or dinner – are good value (around £5). The YHA is affiliated to the global Hostelling International network (⊛www.hihostels.com).

In Oxford, two **independent** "back-packer" hostels (⊛www.independenthostels uk.co.uk) add a bit of choice and **student halls** can offer great value over the summer (July–Sept), plus at Easter and Christmas, generally in single rooms or self-catering apartments. See p.56 for details.

Camping

Campsites vary from rustic, family-run places to large sites with laundries, shops and sports facilities: charges can be from about £5 per adult up to around £20 per tent. Many sites also offer accommodation in permanent **caravans**, mostly large, fully-equipped units. Check ⊛www.campingand caravanningclub.co.uk – and take a look at ⊛www.ukcampsite.co.uk and ⊛www .theaa.com for listings and reviews. **Farmers** and friendly pub owners may offer pitches for a nominal fee, but setting up a tent without asking first will not be well received.

Food and drink

Changing tastes have transformed England's food and drink over the last decade. Much importance is being placed on "ethical" eating – sourcing products locally, and using organic, humanely produced, high-quality ingredients. This is being felt strongly in the Cotswolds, too, where locally farmed produce is celebrated at dozens of village markets and hundreds of rural restaurants.

There's little doubt that the area's proximity to London has had an impact: second-home-owners, who bring big-city expectations with them, are one factor – but transport links are also key. Urban foodies can finish work, take the train from Paddington for a lavish meal in the sticks at (for instance) the critically acclaimed *Kingham Plough* – and still be back in central London before midnight. Critical mass is another issue: there are now enough Cotswold restaurants seeking high-quality ingredients that it has become viable for – to take one example – Cornish suppliers to make frequent, perhaps even daily, deliveries of fresh-caught fish and seafood, thereby fuelling a spiral of supply and demand which raises standards across the board.

Memorable, often award-winning, food is just as common nowadays in Cotswold village pubs as in the poshest of Oxford's or Cheltenham's formal restaurants. Sourcing quality products from local farmers, showcasing seasonal cooking – often with creative takes on traditional recipes – and taking pride in presentation and service have become articles of faith wherever you go.

For more on local specialities (and local beers), see this book's *Cotswold food* colour section.

Useful websites

Aside from **Cotswold Food** (Ⓦ www .cotswoldfood.co.uk), which lists and reviews local restaurants and producers, one way to keep pace with local foodie news is to follow chef James Benson's blog **The Cotswold Food Year** (Ⓦ www.thecotswold foodyear.com): Benson's company is based in Broadway, and his site is packed with anecdotes and local knowledge as well as recipe ideas.

For unique insight into local food culture, make contact with **Rob Rees, "The Cotswold Chef"** (Ⓦ www.thecotswold chef.com), who offers bespoke, upmarket food tours of the area and runs a Food Centre in Cirencester, hosting courses and showcasing the work of local producers. Many of the region's most acclaimed restaurants feature at **Cotswolds Finest Hotels** (Ⓦ www.cotswoldsfinesthotels.com).

Markets and farm shops

Many towns around the region have a **market** at least once a week – often a commercialized affair for bric-a-brac and cheap bananas (Ⓦ www.country-markets .co.uk has nationwide listings) – though lots of places also host weekly, fortnightly or monthly **farmers' markets** where local food producers sell homegrown goods direct to the public: see Ⓦ www.farmersmarkets.net for details. We've highlighted farmers' markets at relevant points throughout this book: they are often worth making a special journey for, and the best (such as Stroud, Deddington or Stratford) define their communities. Oxford's famous Covered Market – a permanent feature, open daily – is another draw, hosting butchers, bakers, fishmongers, cheese sellers and more.

You'll find similarly authentic local items in **farm shops**, often marked with a rudimentary sign propped by the side of rural roads. Don't be shy of turning off and following a bumpy track onto what may look like private farm property – the best of these farm shops are a revelation, selling country essentials and hard-to-find specialist products to those in the know. Take a look, for instance, at Ⓦ www.thebuttsfarm shop.com, an award-winning farm shop

The Wychwood Brewery Store

BRAKSPEAR OXFORD GOLD

HOBGOBLIN — Traditionally Crafted Legendary Ruby Beer

BRAKSPEAR BITTER

Open 10am–5pm Monday to Saturday*

Enjoy a warm welcome & browse our legendary selection of bottled & cask conditioned beers, gifts & merchandise.

Beers available by the: •Bottle •Case •Jug (4Pt)

Perfect for parties & special occasions: •Piggin (17Pt) •Polypin (35Pt) •Firkin (72Pt).

Firkins available by pre-order only. Please call:

01993 890 800

Why not join us for a Weekend tour?
Visit us online at: www.wychwood.co.uk
for further details & to book online.

Wychwood Brewery, Eagle Maltings,
The Crofts, Witney, Oxon OX28 4DP.
*Excluding public holidays

near Cirencester, or contrast sophisticated ⓦ www.wellsstores.co.uk south of Oxford with down-to-earth ⓦ www.waysidefarm shop.co.uk outside Evesham. There are dozens more; we've highlighted special ones throughout this book, and ⓦ www.farm shopping.net pinpoints those that are members of the industry association FARMA.

Food and drink festivals

British Asparagus Festival (Evesham) April–June ⓦ www.britishasparagusfestival.org.
Wild Thyme Food Festival (Chipping Norton) April ⓦ www.wildthymerestaurant.co.uk.
Fairford & Lechlade Food & Drink Festival May ⓦ www.fairford-lechladefoodanddrink.co.uk.
Cheltenham Food & Drink Festival June ⓦ www.garden-events.com.
Foodies Festival (Oxford) August ⓦ www .foodiesfestival.com.
Stroud Food & Drink Festival September ⓦ www.stroudfoodfest.com.

Stratford Food Festival September ⓦ www .stratfordfoodfestival.co.uk.

Beer festivals

Winter Ales Festival (Tewkesbury) February ⓦ www.tewkesburycamra.org.uk.
Banbury Beer Festival May ⓦ www .banburybeerfest.org.uk.
Cirencester Beer Festival May ⓦ www .cirencester-beerfestival.co.uk.
Chadlington Beer Festival June ⓦ www .chadlingtonbeerfestival.com.
Stratford Beer Festival June ⓦ www .stratfordbeerfestival.org.uk.
Cotswold Beer Festival (near Winchcombe) July ⓦ www.gloucestershirecamra.org.uk.
South Cotswold Beer Festival (Chipping Sodbury) July ⓦ www.bs37.com/beer.
Hook Norton Festival of Fine Ales July ⓦ www .hookybeerfest.co.uk.
Frocester Beer Festival (near Stroud) August ⓦ www.dursleylions.com.

Festivals and events

With its location in the middle of England, and its proximity to the innovation-loving urbanites of London, Bristol and Birmingham, the Cotswolds hosts a surprising quantity of annual festivals and events. Some are out-and-out touristy, others are more authentic expressions of local life – and a fair few are plain daft, rollicking remnants of a less self-conscious age.

What follows is only a selection of events; for detailed local listings contact tourist offices or search online. Two good sites to keep an eye on are **Oxford Inspires** (ⓦ www.oxford inspires.org) and **Cotswolds Culture** (ⓦ www.cotswoldsculture.com).

January to May

King's Sutton Literary Festival (early March; ⓦ www.kslitfest.co.uk). Bookish gathering that can draw leading authors to this village outside Banbury.
Cheltenham Gold Cup (mid-March; ⓦ www .cheltenham.co.uk). Centrepiece of England's top steeplechase (fence-jumping) horse race meeting.
St George's Day (April 23; ⓦ www.stgeorges holiday.com). England's patron saint is feted with traditional music and Morris dancing on village greens

around the region. The same day, by happy chance, is also the birthday of William Shakespeare: expect parades, folk dancing and special events at Stratford-upon-Avon (ⓦ www.shakespearesbirthday.org.uk).
Oxford Literary Festival (early April; ⓦ www .oxfordliteraryfestival.com). World-class book festival, featuring ten days of lectures, events and talks.
Stratford Literary Festival (late April; ⓦ www .stratfordliteraryfestival.co.uk). Renowned event, with talks, readings and workshops.
Stroud International Textiles Festival (May; ⓦ www.stroudinternationaltextiles.org.uk). Celebration of contemporary textile design, centred around exhibitions and talks.
Oxfordshire Artweeks (May; ⓦ www.artweeks .org). Artists and craftspeople open their homes and studios to the public.

Music festivals

England has gone **music festival** crazy, with every weekend from June to September now seeing some kind of musical happening. Here are some Cotswold events to choose from; check ⓦ www.efestivals.co.uk for details of many more.

Cheltenham Folk Festival (mid-Feb; ⓦ www.cheltenhamtownhall.org.uk). A weekend of folk music to banish the winter chill.

Oxford Folk Festival (mid-April; ⓦ www.oxfordfolkfestival.com). Three days of gigs at venues across the city.

Cheltenham Jazz Festival (late April; ⓦ www.cheltenhamfestivals.com). High-profile week, including free events and big-name stars.

Wychwood Festival (early June; ⓦ www.wychwoodfestival.com). Family-friendly weekend of music, comedy and cabaret, held at Cheltenham racecourse.

Cornbury (early July; ⓦ www.cornburyfestival.com). Cheerful, easygoing music festival near Charlbury, supplemented by folk performers, craft stalls and more.

WOMAD (late July; ⓦ www.womad.org). Acclaimed three-day world music event at Charlton Park, outside Malmesbury.

Truck (late July; ⓦ www.thisistruck.com). Much-loved independent festival held at Steventon, south of Oxford.

Global Gathering (late July; ⓦ www.globalgathering.com). A weekend of electronic dance music at Long Marston Airfield near Stratford.

Cropredy (mid-Aug; ⓦ www.fairportconvention.com). Genial weekend for a crusty crowd at Cropredy, near Banbury, always headlined by 1970s supergroup Fairport Convention.

Greenbelt (late Aug; ⓦ www.greenbelt.org.uk). A celebration of Christian music, entertainment and talks, held at Cheltenham Racecourse.

Banbury Folk Festival (Oct; ⓦ www.banburyfolkfestival.co.uk). Lively folk weekend which takes over Banbury with gigs and sessions.

Classical music festivals

Oxford May Music (early May; ⓦ www.oxfordmaymusic.co.uk). Concerts and lectures in central Oxford.

Gypsy Horse Fair (mid-May). A week of travellers' stalls and horse-trading, held in fields near Stow-on-the-Wold.

Levellers' Day (mid-May; ⓦ www.levellers.org.uk). Burford hosts a day of debates, music and entertainment, linked to the seventeenth-century Levellers movement.

Eights Week (late May; ⓦ www.ourcs.org.uk). Raucous rowing competitions on the Thames in Oxford.

Nailsworth Festival (late May; ⓦ www.nailsworthfestival.org.uk). Varied choice of poetry, music and theatre.

Cheese Rolling (late May; ⓦ www.cheese-rolling.co.uk). Mass pursuit of a cheese wheel down Cooper's Hill in Gloucestershire.

Tetbury Woolsack Races (late May; ⓦ www.tetburywoolsack.co.uk). Men and women race up and down a steep hill carrying a giant sack of wool, while the town celebrates with a street fair.

June, July and August

Cotswold Olimpick Games (early June; ⓦ www.olimpickgames.co.uk). Traditional sporting endeavour on Dover's Hill near Chipping Campden dating back to 1612, celebrated with bands, cannon fire and shin-kicking. The day after sees the crowning of the Scuttlebrook Queen, followed by dancing round the maypole.

Ramsden Fete (mid-June; ⓦ www.ramsdenvillage.co.uk). Village fete at Ramsden, near Witney, featuring tug o' war, egg-throwing, jousting, strong man competitions and more.

Deddington Festival (mid-June; ⓦ www.deddingtonfestival.org.uk). Two weeks of community fun at Deddington, north of Oxford, featuring music, poetry competitions, willow-weaving and guided walks.

Fresh Air (late June; ⓦ www.freshair2011.com). Open-air contemporary sculpture event at Quenington near Cirencester, held every two years: 2011, 2013, 2015.

Cowley Road Carnival (early July; ⓦ www.cowleyroadcarnival.com). Oxford's buzzing, multicultural Cowley Road district gets

Spring Sounds (May; ⓦ www.springsounds.co.uk). Old favourites and premieres of new works at venues in and around Stratford-upon-Avon.

Chipping Campden Music Festival (May; ⓦ www.campdenmusicfestival.co.uk). Prestigious cycle of evening and lunchtime concerts.

English Music Festival (late May; ⓦ www.englishmusicfestival.org.uk). Celebration of English music from Tallis to Britten, mostly staged in Dorchester Abbey, south of Oxford.

Garsington Opera (June; ⓦ www.garsingtonopera.org). Month-long season of opera, formerly at Garsington Manor outside Oxford, now based at Wormsley near Watlington.

Bledington Music Festival (June; ⓦ www.bledingtonmusicfestival.co.uk). Three nights of concerts and recitals.

Dean & Chadlington Festival (late June; ⓦ www.chadlingtonfestival.co.uk). High-quality recitals and concerts at venues near Chipping Norton.

Longborough Festival Opera (June & July; ⓦ www.lfo.org.uk). Small-scale productions at this mansion near Moreton-in-Marsh.

Cheltenham Music Festival (July; ⓦ www.cheltenhamfestivals.com). Major classical event, concentrating on chamber and orchestral music.

Bampton Opera (July; ⓦ www.bamptonopera.org). Charming summer opera productions in an Oxfordshire garden, filled out with concerts and recitals during the autumn in various venues.

Guiting Festival (late July; ⓦ www.guitingfestival.org). A week of classical music (with a spot of jazz) in Guiting Power, near the Slaughters.

Tetbury Music Festival (late Sept; ⓦ www.tetburymusicfestival.org.uk). Modest festival that nonetheless draws world-renowned soloists and performers.

Stratford Music Festival (Oct; ⓦ www.stratfordmusicfestival.com). Week-long showcase of classical and jazz.

costumed up for parades, music and dancing in the streets.

Eynsham Carnival (early July; ⓦ www .eynshamcarnival.com). Family-oriented shindig in Eynsham village, near Witney, featuring a craft fair, Morris dancing, pram-racing and more.

Hobby Horse Festival (early July; ⓦ www .hobbyhorsefestival.co.uk). Quirky event in Banbury, with costumed parades, folk dancing and lots of hobby horses.

Cotswold Show (early July; ⓦ www.cotswold show.co.uk). Cirencester hosts a weekend of child-friendly parades and events, from sky-diving to horse-whispering, along with a food market and fairground rides.

Royal International Air Tattoo (mid-July; ⓦ www.airtattoo.com). The world's largest military air show, held at RAF Fairford in Gloucestershire.

Football in the River (late Aug). Two teams play a half-hour football game in the River Windrush at Bourton-on-the-Water, in a nutty (but hundred-year-old) tradition.

September to December

Moreton-in-Marsh Show (early Sept; ⓦ www .moretonshow.co.uk). Gloucestershire's largest agricultural show, with livestock competitions and country events.

Woodstock Literary Festival (mid-Sept; ⓦ www .woodstockliteraryfestival.com). Blenheim Palace and venues around Woodstock host events with leading writers, academics and journalists.

Charlbury Street Fair (mid-Sept; ⓦ www .charlbury.info). Town fair and knees-up to raise funds for Charlbury's historic buildings.

Clypping Ceremony (mid-Sept). St Mary's Church in Painswick is "clypped", or embraced, by local parishioners, who join hands to encircle the building in a ceremony dating back to 1321.

Heritage Open Days (mid-Sept; ⓦ www .heritageopendays.org.uk). A once-a-year opportunity to peek inside hundreds of historic buildings which don't normally open their doors to the public.

Cheltenham Literature Festival (Oct; www .cheltenhamfestivals.com). Prestigious event drawing world-renowned authors, with talks, readings, workshops and more.

Gypsy Horse Fair (late Oct). Fun and horse-trading in fields outside Stow-on-the-Wold.

Halloween (Oct 31). All Hallows' Eve – and Samhain, last day of the Celtic calendar. Now swamped by commercialized US-style costumes and trick-or-treating, although druidic ceremonies survive at a few sites, such as the Rollright Stones near Chipping Norton (www.rollrightstones.co.uk).

Bonfire Night (Nov 5). Fireworks and bonfires held in village communities nationwide to commemorate the foiling of the Gunpowder Plot in 1605.

New Year's Eve (Dec 31). Expect plenty of jollity in town and village pubs alike.

Sports and outdoor activities

With its rolling landscape, bucolic scenery and networks of paths and country trails, the Cotswolds is classic walking country – but there are also many other ways to enjoy the great outdoors, from cycling to canal trips to horse-riding.

Walking

Two of England's long-distance **National Trails** (www.nationaltrail.co.uk) pass through the region. Best known – and, by all accounts, best – is the **Cotswold Way** (www.nationaltrail.co.uk/cotswold), which leads for 102 miles along the highest points of the Cotswold escarpment from Chipping Campden in the north to Bath in the south, giving panoramic views over the Severn Vale much of the way. Walking the whole route takes, on average, seven days – but it's easy to tackle shorter stretches, and the website gives details of a dozen half-day circular walks at various points. We highlight the best of them throughout this book – as do the Cotswolds Area of Outstanding Natural Beauty (www.cotswoldsaonb.org.uk) on their excellent website, which is packed with ideas and route descriptions. A tougher test combines the Cotswold Way with an 86-mile stretch of the **Macmillan Way** (www .macmillanway.org) between Banbury and Bath, known as the "Cross-Cotswold Pathway", to form the epic 217-mile **Cotswold Round** circular route.

Then there's the **Thames Path** (www .nationaltrail.co.uk/thamespath), which stretches 184 miles from the source of the river near Kemble, outside Cirencester, to end at Woolwich in southeast London; some of its prettiest sections are around Lechlade and Oxford, again highlighted in this book – and at the excellent British Waterways website (www.waterscape.com).

Hundreds of miles of other footpaths crisscross the area: we've noted the best of the shorter walks at relevant points. Ones to look out for include the **Windrush Way** and **Warden's Way**, sister trails connecting Bourton-on-the-Water with Winchcombe – the former a hill route, the latter passing between villages; the **Gloucestershire Way**, which includes a looping section between Stow-on-the-Wold and Gloucester; the **Glyme Valley Way**, a riverside path between Chipping Norton and Woodstock; numerous pretty walks along the **Oxford Canal** between Kidlington and Cropredy; and a host of others.

Winchcombe in particular has set itself up as "walking capital of the Cotswolds": its website **Winchcombe Welcomes Walkers** (www.winchcombewelcomeswalkers.com) has loads of tips and links, as does the **Long Distance Walkers Association** (www.ldwa.org.uk) and the tourist office sites www.cotswolds.com and www .oxfordshirecotswolds.org. Trail **maps** are widely available online; see p.37 for some information about Ordnance Survey maps.

Cycling

Several sections of the **National Cycle Network** (see www.sustrans.org.uk) pass through the Cotswolds, including Route 45 (Gloucester to Stroud, Nailsworth and Cirencester), Route 41 (Gloucester to Cheltenham, Evesham and Stratford) and Route 5 (Oxford to Woodstock, Banbury, Chipping Campden and Stratford). As with walking, there are countless other trails to follow, gentle ones for leisure cyclists and tougher routes alike. We've picked out the best throughout this book.

You can take a bike free of charge on most **trains**, apart from certain peak-hour weekday services. From a starting-point at, say, Banbury or Stratford stations you could be cycling in open countryside within a few minutes. Arriving at stations on the Cotswold Line or Oxford Canal Line, or at Kemble (for all of these, see p.22), deposits you directly in the heart of the countryside. Of circular routes with easy rail access, the **Cherwell Valley Ride** is a loop from Tackley station, north of Oxford, which passes through Woodstock; the **Kingham Route** covers ten easy miles from and to Kingham station; and one of the six Cotswold Cycling Routes, developed by Cotswold District Council and

the Gloucestershire Rural Transport Partnership, includes a section from the station at **Moreton-in-Marsh** to Chipping Campden and back. All these – and others – are downloadable, with trail maps and descriptions, at ⓦwww.cotswolds.com and ⓦwww.oxfordshirecotswolds.org, with extra info at ⓦwww.cotswoldsaonb.org.uk. If you want to cycle on a **canal towpath**, you must first obtain a free cycle permit from British Waterways, downloadable (along with loads of useful information) at ⓦwww.waterscape.com.

If you're around in October, look out for the **Bike Blenheim Palace** charity day (ⓦwww.bikeblenheimpalace.com), the only occasion when cyclists are permitted to ride through the Blenheim grounds.

Serious cyclists should take a look at ⓦwww.ctc.org.uk for more ideas and/or consider entering the "sportive" events **Cotswold Spring Classic** (ⓦwww.cotswoldspringclassic.co.uk) or **Circuit of the Cotswolds** (ⓦwww.circuitofthecotswolds.org) – or the tougher **Cotswold Audax** (ⓦwww.beaconrcc.org.uk).

Activity holiday operators

Blakes Holiday Boating ☎0845 604 3985, Ⓦ www.blakes.co.uk. All kinds of boating holidays, including narrowboats on the Oxford Canal.

Capital Sport ☎01296 631671, Ⓦ www.capital -sport.co.uk. Gentle self-guided cycling tours in the Cotswolds, in either B&B or "fine" accommodation.

Celtic Trails ☎01291 689774, Ⓦ www.celtrail .com. Tailor-made walks along the Cotswold Way.

Compass Holidays ☎01242 250642, Ⓦ www .compass-holidays.com. Quality firm offering walking and cycling short breaks and longer holidays throughout the region.

Contours ☎017684 80451, Ⓦ www.contours.co.uk. Major operator with short breaks or longer walking holidays and self-guided hikes around the region.

Cotswold Country Cycles ☎01386 438706, Ⓦ www.cotswoldcountrycycles.com. Cycle tours, advice, accommodation bookings and luggage transfer.

Cotswold Walking Company ☎01242 604190, Ⓦ www.thecotswoldwalkingcompany.com. Small firm offering guidance, advice and walking holidays.

Cotswold Walking Holidays ☎01242 518888, Ⓦ www.cotswoldwalks.com. Good selection of guided and self-guided walks – some featuring unique itineraries – with tailor-made options available.

Cotswolds Discovery ☎07718 660070, Ⓦ www .cotswoldsdiscovery.net. Personal guiding for historical walks through the area.

Cotswolds Riding ☎01386 584250, Ⓦ www .cotswoldsriding.co.uk. Horse-riding lessons, as well as guided and private "hacking" in the countryside, at this rural B&B near Broadway.

Discovery Travel ☎01904 632226, Ⓦ www .discoverytravel.co.uk. Wide range of self-guided walking and cycling itineraries.

Footpath Holidays ☎01985 840049, Ⓦ www .footpath-holidays.com. Excellent selection of guided, self-guided and tailor-made itineraries.

HF Holidays ☎020 8732 1250, Ⓦ www .hfholidays.co.uk. Co-operative-run company offering a wide range of guided and self-guided walking and cycling trips, including specialist themes such as medieval architecture or gardens.

Oxfordshire Narrowboats ☎01869 340348, Ⓦ www.oxfordshire-narrowboats.co.uk. Based at Lower Heyford wharf on the Oxford Canal, offering day rental, short breaks and complete holidays afloat.

Ramblers Holidays ☎01707 331133, Ⓦ www .ramblersholidays.co.uk. Sociable guided walking tours: scenic, themed or special interest.

Rob Ireland Activity Days ☎01386 701683, Ⓦ www.robireland.co.uk. One-off special day events, such as quad-biking, tractor-driving, helicopter treasure hunts, shooting, archery and more.

Saddle Skedaddle ☎0191 265 1110, Ⓦ www .skedaddle.co.uk. Biking adventures nationwide, including leisurely Cotswold tours.

Sherpa Van Project ☎01748 826917, Ⓦ www .sherpavan.com. Luggage transfer service for independent walkers and cyclists along the Cotswold Way. Accommodation booking also available.

Talking Walks ☎01608 641839, Ⓦ www .talkingwalks.co.uk. Expert-led thematic walks through the north Cotswold countryside, part of Gloucestershire University's public outreach programme. Scheduled walks run once or twice a month year-round – with tailor-made options and local B&B accommodation available.

Walk the Landscape ☎01295 811003, Ⓦ www .walkthelandscape.co.uk. Family-run business near Banbury offering acclaimed guided, self-guided and tailor-made walks, many with a historical and/or botanical angle. Also affiliated to *Talking Walks* (see above).

Walking Holiday Company ☎01600 718219, Ⓦ www.thewalkingholidaycompany.com. Tailor-made, self-guided walks along the Cotswold Way.

Xplore Britain ☎01740 650900, Ⓦ www. xplorebritain.com. Escorted and independent walking and cycling holidays.

Shopping

Although shopping is now one of the chief leisure activities of the English, it can be a rather soulless experience. High streets in towns up and down the country feature the same bland chain stores selling similar ranges of mass-produced items. Sleepy Cotswold villages can offer a good deal more local choice.

Antiques are the "traditional" stock-in-trade of Cotswold retailers – in some places, it seems that almost every shop is selling furniture, ceramics and/or craft items from a bygone age – but you'll also find that the Cotswolds nurtures a surprisingly healthy independent, often locally owned, retail sector. Specialist **food** outlets are a favourite, from cheesemongers and bakers to urban-style delis and coffee shops. This is also where the nineteenth-century Arts and Crafts movement flourished (see p.112) and there's no shortage of **potteries** turning out local styles, upmarket

home furnishing outlets for locally designed textiles and homeware, wood-turners, glass-makers, jewellers and more. You may, in more popular locations, have to wade through a proliferation of twee trinkets and scented candles to find anything truly original – but there's some good stuff out there. It's heartening to remember, too, that even in this most touristy of areas, many **independent retailers** have little direct reliance on tourist trade – not least the family-run butchers, shoeshops, florists and greengrocers which survive across Cotswold towns.

Travel essentials

Costs

Once you move away from the most heavily touristed towns, the Cotswolds represents fairly decent value for money. Nonetheless, even if you're camping or hostelling, using public transport, buying picnic lunches and eating in pubs and cafés your minimum expenditure is likely to be around £35/US$55/€40 per person per day. Couples staying in B&Bs, eating at unpretentious restaurants and visiting some attractions should expect roughly £70/US$110/€80 per person, while if you're renting a car, staying in hotels and eating well, budget for £120/US$185/€135 each. Double that figure if you choose to stay in stylish boutique hotels or grand country houses.

Many of England's **historic attractions** – from castles to stately homes – are owned and/or operated by either the **National Trust** (℡0844 800 1895, ⓦwww.nationaltrust.org .uk) or **English Heritage** (℡0870 333 1181, ⓦwww.english-heritage.org.uk). Both usually charge entry fees (roughly £5–10), though some sites are free. You can join online or in person at any staffed attraction: annual membership is around £40.

Throughout this book, admission prices quoted are the **full adult rate**, unless otherwise stated. Concessionary rates – generally half-price – for **senior citizens** (over 60), under-26s and **children** (aged 5–17) apply almost everywhere, from tourist attractions to public transport; you'll need official ID as proof of age. Full-time students are often entitled to discounts too. Children under 5 are rarely charged.

Students can benefit from an ISIC (International Student Identity Card), people under 26 can get an IYTC (International Youth Travel Card) and full-time teachers qualify for the ITIC (International Teacher Identity Card). Each costs around £10/€14/US$22 and is valid for special air, rail and bus fares and discounts at attractions; see ⓦ www.isic.org for details.

Crime and personal safety

Inspector Morse and *Midsomer Murders* are, of course, fantasy: in the real world, Cotswold villages don't see body counts on a par with Detroit. Oxford does have some tough estates where **crime** flourishes, but as a holidaymaker you won't be visiting them. Village life remains placid: the worst trouble you're likely to see is a bit of late-night drunkenness at weekends in town centres. If you're the victim of any sort of crime, report it straight away to the police: your insurance company will require a crime report number.

Electricity

The current is 240v AC. North American appliances may need a transformer and adaptor, those from Europe only an adaptor.

Entry requirements

EU citizens can travel to – and settle in – the UK with just a passport or identity card. US, Canadian, South African, Australian and New Zealand citizens can stay for up to six months without a visa, provided they have a valid passport. Many other nationalities require a visa, obtainable from the British consular office where you live. Check with the UK Border Agency (ⓦ www.ukvisas.gov .uk) for up-to-date information.

Health

No vaccinations are required for entry into Britain. Citizens of all EU and EEA countries are entitled to free medical treatment within the UK's National Health Service (NHS), on production of their **European Health Insurance Card (EHIC)**. The same applies to Commonwealth countries with reciprocal arrangements – for example Australia and New Zealand. Everyone else will be charged: definitely take out health insurance before you travel.

Pharmacies (also known as **chemists**) can dispense some drugs without a doctor's prescription. Most are open standard shop hours; check signs in the window for which local chemists are due to be staying open late and/or at the weekend. For medical advice 24 hours a day, call **NHS Direct** (☎ 0845 4647, ⓦ www.nhsdirect.nhs.uk). The website is packed with useful information, and also has directories of doctors' surgeries and walk-in centres nationwide.

Otherwise, minor issues can be dealt with at the surgery of any local **doctor**, also known as a **GP** (General Practitioner); get directions from NHS Direct or your hotel. For serious injuries, go to the "**A&E**" (accident and emergency) department of the nearest hospital. In a life-or-death situation, call for an ambulance on ☎ 112 or ☎ 999.

Insurance

Always take out an insurance policy before travelling to cover against theft, loss and illness or injury. A typical policy will provide cover for loss of baggage, tickets and – up to a certain limit – cash or travellers' cheques, as well as cancellation or curtailment of your journey. **Medical cover** is strongly advised. Keep receipts for medicines and medical treatment, and in the event you have anything stolen you must obtain an official statement from the police.

Main hospitals with 24-hour A&E

Banbury Horton Hospital, Oxford Road ☎ 01295 275500.
Cheltenham General Hospital, Sandford Road ☎ 0845 422 2222.
Gloucester Royal Hospital, Great Western Road ☎ 0845 422 2222.
Oxford John Radcliffe Hospital, Headley Way ☎ 01865 741166.
Warwick Warwick Hospital, Lakin Road ☎ 01926 495321.
Worcester Royal Hospital, Hastings Way ☎ 01905 763333.

Mail

Post offices (@www.postoffice.co.uk) open Monday to Friday 9am to 5.30pm, Saturdays 9am to 12.30pm. Main offices in larger towns stay open all day Saturday, while small branches sometimes close on Wednesday afternoons. In villages you may find that postal services are provided at a branded counter within a shop. Note that you can also buy **stamps** at a wide variety of ordinary shops, supermarkets and filling stations. Check @www.royalmail.com for postal rates worldwide.

Maps

Some of the clearest road maps are produced by Geographers' A–Z (@www .a-zmaps.co.uk): their 1:150,000 *Cotswolds & Chilterns Visitors' Map* is perfect for most needs. If you're intending to explore minor roads and byways, opt for county atlases produced by A–Z, Philips (@www.philips-maps.co.uk) and others at scales either side of 1:20,000. The most detailed maps are produced by Ordnance Survey (OS; @www.ordnance survey.co.uk): their Landranger series (1:50,000) is fine for most walkers and cyclists, while their Explorer series (1:25,000) has detail down to individual farm buildings. Both have several sheets covering the Cotswolds. The OS website lets you buy paper maps, download digital maps to an iPhone and even create your own map, centred at any point in Britain. **Stanfords** (@www.stanfords.co.uk), the UK's premier map and travel bookshop, can order any product and will ship worldwide.

Money

UK currency is the **pound sterling** (£), divided into 100 pence (p). Coins come in

denominations of 1p, 2p, 5p, 10p, 20p, 50p, £1 and £2. Notes are in denominations of £5, £10, £20 and £50.

Every sizeable town and village has a branch of one or other of the retail, or "high street", **banks**, along with smaller "building societies" (which operate in roughly the same way). The easiest way to get hold of cash is to use your **debit card** in a "cash machine" (ATM); check in advance with your home bank whether you will be subject to a daily withdrawal limit. **ATMs** are ubiquitous, but beware that a charge of about £1.50 or £2 may be levied on cash withdrawals at stand-alone ATMs in out-of-the-way places: the screen will notify you if so and give you an option to cancel.

Outside banking hours, you can change travellers' cheques or cash at post offices and **bureaux de change** – the latter tend to be open longer hours and are found in most town centres, airports and railway stations. Avoid changing in hotels, where the rates are normally poor.

Credit and debit cards are widely accepted – MasterCard and Visa are almost universal – **charge cards** such as American Express and Diners Club less so. A few smaller establishments may accept cash only. Paying by plastic involves inserting your card into a "**chip-and-pin**" terminal beside the till, then keying in your secret PIN number to authorize the transaction: the only person handling your card is you. (Many restaurants use wireless chip-and-pin handsets: your waiter will bring it to your table when it's time to pay.) At establishments which have older swipe systems – susceptible to fraud – never let your card leave your sight: take it yourself to the till and watch while staff are doing the swiping. At supermarkets and some other shops, you may be asked at the checkout if you want "**cash back**": they let you pay (by card) for up to £50 more than the cost of your goods and give you the change in cash – very handy.

Opening hours and public holidays

Opening hours for most businesses, shops and offices are Monday to Saturday 9am to 5.30 or 6pm, with many shops also open on

England's public holidays

New Year's Day (Jan 1)

Good Friday

Easter Monday

Early May Bank Holiday (1st Mon in May)

Spring Bank Holiday (Last Mon in May)

Summer Bank Holiday (Last Mon in Aug)

Christmas Day (Dec 25)

Boxing Day (Dec 26)

If Jan 1, Dec 25 or Dec 26 fall on a Saturday or Sunday, the next weekday becomes a public holiday.

Sundays, generally 10.30am to 4.30pm. Big supermarkets have longer hours. Some towns have an **early-closing day** (usually Wednesday) when most shops close at 1pm. **Banks** are usually open Monday to Friday 9am to 4pm, and Saturday 9am to 12.30pm or so.

We've quoted full opening hours for specific museums, galleries and other attractions throughout this book.

Phones

British phone numbers are a mess. Most have eleven digits, including a prefix beginning ☎01, 02 or 03 which generally denotes a fixed landline, or ☎07 which almost invariably denotes a mobile phone/cellphone. However those eleven digits can be sliced numerous ways: some are composed of three-digit area codes with eight-digit numbers, several are four-digit area codes with seven-digit numbers, most are split five and six, and a few are split six and five. Some are only ten digits long, split five and five.

Numbers beginning ☎0800 and ☎0808 are free to call if you're using a landline, but expensive if you're calling off a mobile; ☎0844 and ☎0845 are cheap if you're with one phone company but expensive otherwise; ☎0870 and ☎0871 are pricey whatever you do. "Premium rate" ☎09 numbers, common for pre-recorded information services (used by some tourist authorities), can cost anything up to £1.50 a minute.

Of those public **pay phones** (or "phone boxes") which survive, most accept coins (minimum charge 40p) and credit cards; some are card-only. You can make international calls from any phone box, though it's cheaper to buy a **phonecard**, available from many newsagents.

Mobile phone coverage is universal in towns and cities, but rural areas often have blind spots.

UK **directory enquiries** on the phone is expensive; instead look online at ⓦwww .bt.com. Business and service numbers are searchable at ⓦwww.yell.com.

Time

From the last Sunday in March until the last Sunday in October, the UK is on GMT+1, known as "British Summer Time" (**BST**). For the rest of the year, it follows **GMT** ("Greenwich Mean Time", or Coordinated

Useful numbers

Domestic operator ☎100
Police/fire/ambulance ☎112 or ☎999

International operator ☎155

Calling England from home
Dial your international access code, then **44** for the UK, then the area code (excluding the zero), then the number.

Calling home from England
Australia 0061 + area code (excluding the zero) + number.

New Zealand 0064 + area code (excluding the zero) + number.

US and Canada 001 + area code + number.

Republic of Ireland 00353 + area code (excluding the zero) + number.

South Africa 0027 + area code (excluding the zero) + number.

Universal Time, UTC). England is always one hour behind most of Europe and, apart from short periods around the changeovers, five hours ahead of New York. Full details at ⓦ www.timeanddate.com.

Tipping

Although there are no fixed rules for tipping, a ten to fifteen percent tip is anticipated by restaurant waiters. Tipping taxi drivers is purely optional. Some restaurants levy a "discretionary" or "optional" service charge of 10 or 12.5 percent, which must be clearly stated on the menu and on the bill. You are not obliged to pay it, and certainly not if the food or service wasn't what you expected. You don't usually tip in a pub; if you want to, you could offer the bar person a drink – and

then give them enough money to cover it. In fancy hotels, porters and bell boys expect (and usually get) a pound or two.

Tourist information

The body promoting inbound tourism to the UK is **VisitBritain** (ⓦ www.visitbritain.com) – it has a comprehensive website, packed with useful tips and ideas. Its partner agency VisitEngland operates under the branding "**Enjoy England**" (ⓦ www.enjoyengland .com) – another excellent source of information. Within England, responsibility for promoting particular areas is in the hands of regional tourism boards (see below) and smaller local bodies.

The Cotswolds straddles administrative boundaries: Oxfordshire counts as part of

---

Tourism websites

English regions
Heart of England ⓦ www.visittheheart.co.uk.
Southeast England ⓦ www.visitsoutheastengland.com.
Southwest England ⓦ www.visitsouthwest.co.uk.

Cotswolds promotion
Cotswolds Tourism ☏ 01242 864171, ⓦ www.cotswolds.com. Official promotional body, part of Gloucestershire County Council, based in Cheltenham. Its annual visitor guide is encyclopedic – and is also promoted by Cotswold District Council (for Cirencester and nearby villages; ⓦ www.cotswold.gov.uk), Stroud (ⓦ www. visitthecotswolds.org.uk), Tewkesbury (ⓦ www.visitcotswoldsandsevernvale.gov.uk) and others. It also runs ⓦ www.the-cotswolds.org – targeted at Japanese visitors – and ⓦ www.cotswoldsculture.com.
Oxfordshire Cotswolds ☏ 01993 775802, ⓦ www.oxfordshirecotswolds.org. Brand name for the tourism promotion division of West Oxfordshire District Council, based in Witney – an excellent source of information for the area between Woodstock, Burford and Chipping Norton.
Cotswolds AONB ☏ 01451 862000, ⓦ www.cotswoldsaonb.org.uk. Cotswolds Conservation Board, the body overseeing the Cotswolds "Area of Outstanding Natural Beauty", based at Northleach.

Other tourism bodies
Enjoy Warwickshire ☏ 01926 412210, ⓦ www.enjoywarwickshire.com. Includes Stratford-upon-Avon and villages around Shipston-on-Stour.
Visit Cheltenham ☏ 01242 522878, ⓦ www.visitcheltenham.info.
Visit North Oxfordshire ☏ 01295 753752, ⓦ www.visitnorthoxfordshire.com. Includes Banbury.
Visit Oxford ☏ 01865 252200, ⓦ www.visitoxfordandoxfordshire.com.
Visit Wiltshire ☏ 0845 602 7323, ⓦ www.visitwiltshire.co.uk. Includes Castle Combe and Malmesbury.
Visit Worcestershire ☏ 01905 728787, ⓦ www.visitworcestershire.org. Includes Broadway and Evesham.

Ten ideas for families

Alice Day p.75. Whimsical fun in Oxford.
Berkeley Castle p.227. Storm the ramparts and admire the armoury.
Blenheim Palace p.98. Tons of family-friendly activities.
Cotswold Farm Park p.184. Rare breeds on a proper working farm.
Cotswold Wildlife Park p.111. Penguins, rhinos, giraffes and more.
Giffords Circus ⓦ www.giffordscircus.com. Traditional local touring circus.
Gloucestershire & Warwickshire Railway p.168. Ride on a real-life steam train.
Harry Potter film locations. Famously in Oxford (p.75) and Gloucester (p.222).
Natural History Museum, Oxford p.79. Full-size dinosaur skeletons.
Walks on Wheels ⓦ www.cotswoldsaonb.org.uk. Downloadable PDFs describing 15 short country walks suitable for parents pushing buggies.

Southeast England, but Gloucestershire and Wiltshire are **Southwest England** and – to make matters worse – Warwickshire and Worcestershire are the Midlands (which, for tourism purposes, is retitled "**Heart of England**"). Responsibility for promotion is split across several bodies, public and private.

Many towns (and some villages) have a **tourist office**, called a Tourist Information Centre ("**TIC**") or Visitor Information Centre ("**VIC**"). They tend to follow standard shop hours (Mon–Sat 9am–5.30pm), sometimes also open on Sundays. Hours are curtailed in winter (Nov–Easter). Staff will nearly always be able to book accommodation, reserve space on guided tours, and sell guidebooks, maps and walk leaflets. They can also provide lists of local cafés, restaurants and pubs, and though they aren't supposed to recommend particular places you'll often be able to get a feel for the best local places to eat.

Travellers with disabilities

Aside from the obvious difficulties with hilly terrain and historic buildings (gravel drives, uneven footpaths and the like), the Cotswolds generally caters well for travellers with disabilities. All new public buildings – including museums and galleries – must provide wheelchair access, public transport is fully accessible and dropped kerbs and signalled crossings are widespread. The number of accessible hotels and restaurants is also growing, and reserved parking bays are available almost everywhere. If you have specific requirements, it's always best to talk first to your travel agent, chosen hotel or tour operator.

Access-Able ⓦ www.access-able.com. US-based resource for travellers with disabilities.
Door-to-Door ⓦ dptac.independent.gov.uk /door-to-door. Travel website offering information and advice.
RADAR ⓦ www.radar.org.uk. Campaigning organization with links and advice.
Tourism for All ☏ 0845 124 9971, ⓦ www .tourismforall.org.uk. Excellent resource, with advice, listings and useful information.

Travelling with children

If you're travelling with children, facilities in England are comparable with those in most other European countries. Breastfeeding is legal in all public places, including restaurants, cafés and public transport, and baby-changing rooms are available widely, including in malls and railway stations. Under-5s aren't charged on public transport or at attractions; 5–16-year-olds usually get a fifty-percent discount. Children aren't allowed in certain licensed (that is, alcohol-serving) premises – though this doesn't apply to restaurants, and many pubs have family rooms or beer gardens where children are welcome. Check ⓦ www.travellingwithchildren.co.uk and ⓦ www.babygoes2.com for tips and ideas.

Guide

Guide

1 Oxford 43

2 The Oxfordshire countryside.. 87

3 Stratford and the north Cotswolds 133

4 The central Cotswolds 171

5 The west and south Cotswolds 203

Oxford

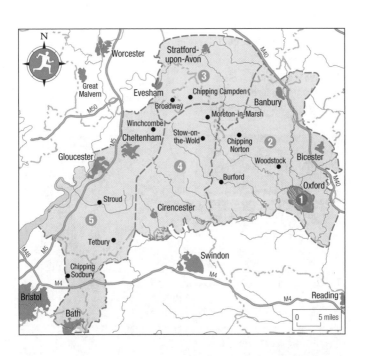

CHAPTER 1   # Highlights

* **Bodleian Library** One of the world's great libraries, notable for the stunning Divinity School interior. See p.64

* **New College** Seclusion, medieval architecture and a magnificent chapel. See p.65

* **Punting** Take to the water and indulge in a lazy riverbank picnic to boot. See p.70

* **Covered Market** A blast of commercial reality, with old-style butchers, bakers and fishmongers laying out their wares. See p.72

* **Christ Church College** Take in the splendour of Oxford's biggest, grandest college. See p.74

* **Oxford Castle Unlocked** Fascinating insight into the city's past. See p.77

* **Ashmolean Museum** World-class art and historical collections. See p.78

* **Jericho** A village within the city, perfect for aimless strolling. See p.80

▲ Gargoyles on St Mary's church

Oxford

That sweet city with her dreaming spires...

Matthew Arnold, from *Thyrsis* (1865)

When visitors think of **OXFORD**, they almost always imagine its **university**, revered as one of the world's great academic institutions, inhabiting honey-coloured stone buildings set around ivy-clad quadrangles. The image is accurate enough, but although the university dominates central Oxford both physically and spiritually, the wider city has an entirely different character, its economy built chiefly on heavy industry.

This small city of just 150,000 presents as impressive a collection of Gothic, Classical and Revival **architecture** as anywhere in Europe, set amid a vivid, engaging urban environment that is both compact and easily navigable. The leading colleges – **Christ Church**, **Merton**, **Magdalen**, **St John's** – are fascinating to explore; marry them with the dozen or more others which pack the city centre, plus the university's showpiece buildings such as the **Bodleian Library**, **Sheldonian Theatre**, **Radcliffe Camera** and extraordinary **Ashmolean Museum**, and few national capitals can keep pace.

Losing yourself in the splendid architecture and evocative isolation of the colleges is seductively easy. It takes something of an effort to subvert Oxford's obvious narrative and instead access the equally rich, and often quite separate, history and outlook of the surrounding city, represented most tangibly for visitors by the fine **Museum of Oxford**, the **castle** remains, the commercial *joie-de-vivre* of the **Covered Market** and outlying community neighbourhoods such as **Jericho**. Oxford was where Britain's first mass-produced cars were manufactured in the 1920s and, although there have been more downs than ups in recent years, the plants at **Cowley**, southeast of the centre, are still vitally important to the area. The fact that the **Mini** – a national icon – is still produced in Oxford to this day is a source of huge local pride.

Farmers' markets

Oxford's main **farmers' market** (Ⓦ www.sketts.co.uk) is held at Gloucester Green on the first and third Thursdays of every month (9am–3pm), featuring local produce from all over the Cotswolds. If you can't make that, try the smaller farmers' markets – hosting many of the same stallholders – in outlying districts: Cowley Road (every Sat 10am–1pm; Ⓦ www.eastoxfordmarket.org.uk), Wolvercote (every Sun 10am–1pm; Ⓦ www.wolvercotefarmersmarket.co.uk) or Headington (4th Fri 8am–12.30pm; Ⓦ www.headingtonmarket.net). Deddington's excellent market (see p.131) is not far away. More information at Ⓦ www.farmersmarkets.net.

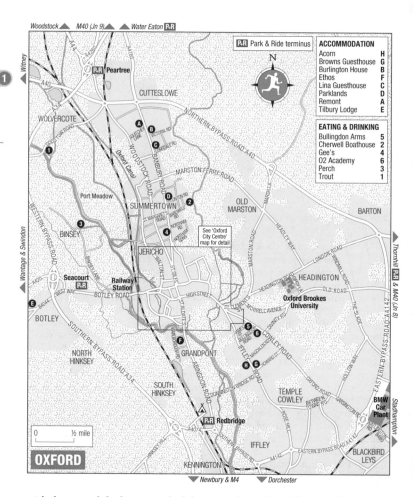

P·R Park & Ride terminus

ACCOMMODATION

Acorn	H
Browns Guesthouse	G
Burlington House	B
Ethos	F
Lina Guesthouse	C
Parklands	D
Remont	A
Tilbury Lodge	E

EATING & DRINKING

Bullingdon Arms	5
Cherwell Boathouse	2
Gee's	4
O2 Academy	6
Perch	3
Trout	1

See 'Oxford City Centre' map for detail

OXFORD

0   ½ mile

▼ Newbury & M4   ▼ Dorchester

It's that to-and-fro between what's known as **"town" and "gown"** (that is, the city and the university) which makes a stay here unique – that, and the fact that more than half of the city's population is under thirty. The shopping streets are buzzing, pubs – many of them historical curiosities – are packed, restaurateurs and hoteliers search for innovative, creative ways to make their mark… it's quite a whirl. Yet **Magdalen Bridge** still represents something of a border. To the west is the city centre, dominated by college grandness in both architecture and mindset, while to the east – notably in **Headington** and along the **Cowley Road** out towards the **Blackbird Leys** estate – lies ordinary, working Oxford, unusually ethnically diverse and harbouring pockets of poverty and deprivation which entirely counter the Oxford stereotype. As throughout the city's history, those "dreaming spires" stand for only part of the story.

Some history

Although some tales date the establishment of a settlement near the confluence of the Thames and Cherwell rivers as early as 1000 BC, it seems more likely that

Oxford was founded after the Romans had departed, probably during the **Saxon** era in the eighth century AD. One legend has it that the oxen ford which gave the town its name may have been the work of Offa, king of Mercia from 757 to 796, though the town's foundation is most persuasively linked with **St Frideswide**, an Anglo-Saxon princess who miraculously restored the sight of a blinded suitor with water from a holy well. The priory she founded, located on a tongue of land near where the Cherwell meets the Thames, was destroyed by fire – along with its records – in 1002 but was refounded 120 years later under the **Normans** to house her relics, subsequently becoming a focus for pilgrimage. (Frideswide's well survives today in the grounds of St Margaret's church in Binsey, roughly a mile northwest of Oxford, while the site of her priory now falls within the walls of Christ Church College.)

Around this time **Henry I** (1069–1135) chose Oxford as the royal residence: both Richard the Lionheart and King John were born in the palace of **Beaumont**, located near where the Ashmolean Museum stands today. Henry, known as "Beauclerc" ("Good Scholar"), also hosted formal study at Beaumont during his reign – augmented in the decades following, when English clerical scholars, expelled *en masse* from the University of Paris in 1167, returned home. They gravitated towards Oxford, pursuing a form of academic monasticism: their custom of living, dining, praying and studying together under the guidance of a master, in halls founded mostly by wealthy bishops, was the forerunner of college life. As the number of halls and colleges grew, a committee developed to administer them – and Oxford's **university** was born.

Aided by royal patronage, and the development of the wool trade across the Cotswolds during the thirteenth century, Oxford's prosperity grew alongside its academic reputation, sparking the first conflicts between the city and the university – "**Town**" and "**Gown**". In 1209, two scholars were executed for the murder of a local woman. Many students subsequently departed, some heading east to found a new university in Cambridge. The notorious **St Scholastica Day Riot**, of February 10th, 1355, saw an argument about beer escalate to armed conflict between students and townsfolk, in which more than ninety people died. Yet, mutual resentment notwithstanding, town and gown had become co-dependent, with a host of trades from weaving and shoemaking to stone-masonry supporting academic life. Money continued to pour into the university (and thus the town) from the Church and the aristocracy, both of which were equally keen to foster the creation of an educated elite for, respectively, holy orders and royal service.

The sixteenth to nineteenth centuries

Henry VIII's dissolution of the monasteries in 1536 briefly threatened the university – then still, chiefly, an ecclesiastical entity. Monastic orders were expelled and their property taken over by the colleges, but Henry had a personal stake in the university's survival: four years earlier he had taken over Cardinal College, founded by Wolsey in 1525 on the site of St Frideswide's Priory, and renamed it Henry VIII's College. (As part of the reorganization within the Church of England it was shortly afterwards refounded as Christ Church College.)

Oxford survived, but maintained a reputation for religious turbulence. In 1555 Henry's daughter, **Mary**, chose the city for the heresy trial of three influential Protestant clerics. Bishops Hugh Latimer and Nicholas Ridley and archbishop Thomas Cranmer – the "**Oxford Martyrs**" – were all found guilty and burnt at the stake on what is now Broad Street, Latimer famously remarking, "Be of good comfort, Master Ridley: we shall this day light such a candle in England as I trust shall never be put out." At his trial Cranmer, who had previously confessed to heresy, rounded on his accusers and re-confirmed his Protestant faith, an action which stunned Mary and gave new heart to her religious opponents.

During the **Civil War**, Charles I, expelled from London, set up court in Oxford: the university backed the Royalist cause, while much of the town supported the Parliamentarians. Charles remained for almost five years, slinking out in disguise during the 1646 Parliamentarian **Siege of Oxford** – following which, the restoration of the monarchy heralded a golden age of university expansion, with the Sheldonian Theatre, Clarendon Building and iconic **Radcliffe Camera** all going up.

The eighteenth and nineteenth centuries saw progress on two fronts. **Canals** and, later, **railways** put Oxford on the industrial map as a commercial hub between London and Birmingham – and **academic reform** sealed the university's reputation for excellence, with examinations introduced, professors finally permitted to marry in 1877 and, shortly afterwards, women admitted as undergraduates (though it was not until 1920 that women were awarded degrees). Religious controversy persisted, though: the **Oxford Movement** of the 1830s and 1840s, led by Cardinal Newman, caused a split within High Church Anglicanism which spurred the creation of Anglo-Catholicism. Newman was beatified by Pope Benedict XVI in 2010.

Modern Oxford

The last century has seen, if anything, a deepening of the gulf between town and gown. Aided by **William Morris**, who launched mass production of cars at his works in Cowley, as well as other Oxford industries (notably printing and brewing), town prosperity grew exponentially in the first half of the twentieth century, even while Edwardian attitudes at the university – portrayed in Evelyn Waugh's 1945 novel *Brideshead Revisited* – ossified into **elitism**. Postwar civic development, as well as student disaffection and reform after 1968 (and the success of a new, more egalitarian university, **Oxford Brookes**), helped restore some balance, but attitudes remain entrenched on both sides. Eight hundred years of mutual resentment is unlikely to dissipate overnight.

Arrival

Oxford is not the easiest city for new **arrivals** to negotiate. Public transport drops off in locations that are either inconvenient – the railway station – or unpredictable: buses and coaches have a variety of termini around the central area, depending on the operator and route. Driving in the centre can be difficult: using the "park-and-ride" options around the city perimeter is a better idea for drivers.

Wherever you arrive, an efficient – and very green – option for getting you and/ or your bags to your hotel is to book **Oxon Carts** (℡07747 024600, ⓦwww .oxoncarts.com), a cycle-rickshaw firm charging roughly £6–8 for a trip across the city centre.

By train

Trains come into Oxford from around the UK; there's a brief rundown of major routes on p.19. The **railway station** is at the western edge of the city centre: exit the station forecourt onto traffic-heavy Frideswide Square, and then it's an unromantic ten-minute walk left past the Said Business School and along busy Hythe Bridge Street (and its continuation George Street) into the centre. Plenty of **taxis** wait outside the station, or you could take half-hourly bus 14 or 14A to Magdalen Street (opposite the *Randolph* hotel), or – better – bus 5, which runs

Oxford airport

Oxford's tiny **airport** (☎01865 290600, ⓦwww.oxfordairport.co.uk), six miles north of the centre in Kidlington – and ambitiously retitled "London Oxford Airport" – mainly handles private jets, plus a few short-hop scheduled flights. To reach Oxford city centre, take **bus** 2/2A/2B, book ahead for the **shuttle** (£10; ☎0845 644 7099, ⓦwww.oxfordairportshuttle.com), or grab a **taxi** (about £15). From the airport Woodstock (see p.94) is nearer than Oxford – only a couple of miles west.

every five minutes to Castle Street, up St Aldates to Carfax, along the High Street (stopping by St Mary the Virgin) and then out along the Cowley Road.

By bus and coach

Two companies operate most **buses**: Stagecoach (☎01865 772250, ⓦwww.stagecoachbus.com/oxfordshire) and Oxford Bus (☎01865 785400, ⓦwww.oxfordbus.co.uk) – though there are several smaller firms as well. A few routes terminate at the railway station, but most end up in the city centre: the **bus station** on Gloucester Green in the town centre is the terminus for many, including Espress and Oxford Tube **coaches** from London (details on p.20), Airline coaches from Heathrow and Gatwick airports (see p.20) and National Express coaches from around the UK. Other buses arrive on one or other of the main streets, most commonly Magdalen Street, George Street, St Aldates or St Giles.

By car

See p.19 for a basic idea of approaching Oxford by **car**. From whichever direction you arrive, you'll sooner or later be cajoled into joining the **Oxford ring road**, a poorly engineered dual carriageway punctuated by too many roundabouts and notorious for its heavy traffic, especially in the morning and evening peak hours.

Negotiating the ring road is made doubly confusing by its lack of consistent numbering: you can't just follow one "A" road all the way round. Running anticlockwise, in the east and north the ring road is formed from the **A40**, on its way in from the M40 junction 8. In the north of Oxford at the Wolvercote roundabout, ring-road signs direct you away from the A40 (which branches westwards to Witney) and onto a bit of the **A44** to the horribly confusing Pear Tree interchange, in order to join the **A34**, on its route in from the M40 junction 9. The A34 forms the western half of the ring road, running south past Botley (where the A420 Swindon road arrives) before leaving Oxford at the Hinksey Hill interchange to plough on towards Newbury and the M4. Ring-road signs will instead bring you off at Hinksey for a 1.3-mile stretch of the **A423** (which many maps wrongly label as the A4074) east to the Heyford Hill (Sainsbury's) roundabout, where the A4074 arrives from Reading. The southeastern stretch of the ring road is completed by the **A4142** round to its meeting-point with the A40. In short, the whole thing's a mess.

Wherever you join the ring road, the best advice is to venture no further into the city and instead take advantage of excellent park-and-ride facilities, outlined in the next section. Central Oxford is not car-friendly and the city council is deliberately giving traffic the squeeze: many streets are pedestrianized and parking (see p.55) is both limited and expensive.

Park and ride

Oxford has five huge **park-and-ride** car parks (ⓦwww.parkandride.net), clearly signposted at strategic points around the ring road. All offer **free parking** as well

OXFORD

1

Green Templeton

RADCLIFFE
OBSERVATORY
QUARTER

Radcliffe
Infirmary

OBSERVATORY ST

JUXON STREET

MOUNT STREET

NEWTON ST
JEUNE ST
HART ST
ALBERT ST

CRANHAM STREET
CRANHAM TERR

JERICHO

CLARENDON STREET

RICHMOND ROAD

WALTON STREET

1 2 3 4 5 6

St Giles'

Somerville

Keble

KEBLE ROAD

PARKS ROAD

BANBURY ROAD

WOODSTOCK ROAD

A 7

Oxford
University Press

LITTLE CLARENDON STREET

9 8
10

11
12
13

WELLINGTON
SQUARE

St Barnabas

GREAT CLARENDON STREET
WELLINGTON STREET
ALBERT STREET
CARDIGAN STREET
CRANHAM STREET

NELSON STREET

16 B

WALTON LANE

WORCESTER PLACE

Ruskin
College

Oxford Canal

REWLEY ROAD

P

Railway
Station

F

Said
Business
School

BOTLEY ROAD

HYTHE BRIDGE STREET

D C 18
E 19

PARK END STREET

17

P

HOLLYBUSH ROW

G

ST THOMAS STREET

OSNEY LANE

OSNEY LANE

OXPENS ROAD

P

Ice Rink

⊠ Public entrance
to college

0   100 yards

RICHMOND ROAD

WALTON CRESCENT

BEAUMONT BLDGS

WALTON STREET

ST JOHN STREET

BEAUMONT STREET

PUSEY STREET

St Cross

PUSEY LANE

Worcester

Bus
Station

GLOUCESTER GREEN

GEORGE STREET

WORCESTER STREET

Nuffield

NEW ROAD

ST MICHAEL'S STREET

NEW INN HALL STREET

BULWARKS LANE

St Peter's

Oxford
Castle

CASTLE STREET

BONN SQ

PARADISE STREET

River Thames

PARADISE SQ

Westgate
Shopping
Centre

NORFOLK STREET

OLD GREYFRIARS STREET

St Ebbe's

CASTLE STREET

BECKET STREET

LAMB
& FLAG
PASSAGE

14

WELLINGTON
PLACE

15

MUSEUM ROAD

St John's

BLACKHALL ROAD

PARKS ROAD

Ashmolean
Museum

BEAUMONT STREET

Oxford
Playhouse

P

GLOUCESTER STREET

FRIARS' ENTRY

MAGDALEN STREET

ST GILES'

MAGDALEN ST EAST

Trinity

Balliol

BROAD

ℹ

SHIP STREET

Jesus

TURL STREET

MARKET STREET

Oxford
Union

Clarendon
Centre

CORNMARKET

Covered
Market

CARFAX

QUEEN ST

Town
Hall

BLUE

⊠

ST ALDATE'S

PEMBROKE STREET

Pembroke

BREWER STREET

ROSE PLACE

ST ALDATE'S

Alice's Shop

SPEEDWELL STREET

THAMES STREET

BLACKFRIARS RD

BREWER'S CT

TRINITY STREET

FRIARS WHARF

SPEEDWELL STREET

BEEF LANE

PEMBROKE STREET

River Thames

Punts

OXFORD CITY CENTRE

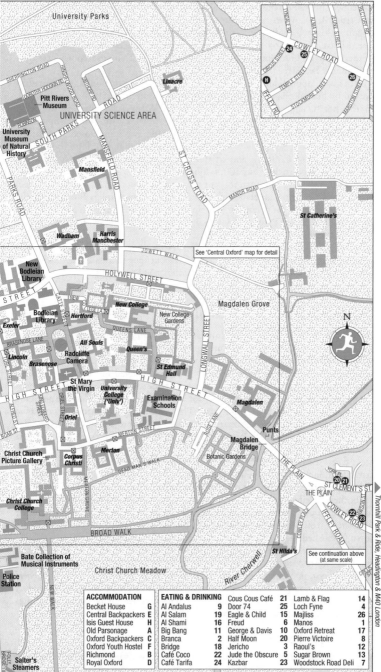

Banbury

University Parks

University Science Area

Pitt Rivers Museum

University Museum of Natural History

Mansfield

Wadham

Harris Manchester

New Bodleian Library

HOLYWELL STREET

Bodleian Library

Exeter

New College

New College Gardens

Hertford

All Souls

Lincoln

Brasenose

Radcliffe Camera

Queen's

St Edmund Hall

St Mary the Virgin

University College ('Univ')

HIGH STREET

Examination Schools

Oriel

MERTON STREET

Corpus Christi

Merton

Christ Church Picture Gallery

Christ Church College

Magdalen Grove

St Catherine's

Magdalen

Punts

Magdalen Bridge

Botanic Gardens

DEAD MAN'S WALK

BROAD WALK

St Hilda's

See continuation above (at same scale)

Bate Collection of Musical Instruments

Police Station

Christ Church Meadow

River Cherwell

Salter's Steamers

See 'Central Oxford' map for detail

JOWETT WALK

N

COWLEY ROAD

24
25

H

26

THE PLAIN

ST CLEMENT'S ST

20 21

22
23

COWLEY ROAD

IFFLEY ROAD

Thornhill Park & Ride, Headington & M40 London

ACCOMMODATION		EATING & DRINKING		Cous Cous Café	21	Lamb & Flag	14
Becket House	G	Al Andalus	9	Door 74	25	Loch Fyne	4
Central Backpackers	E	Al Salam	19	Eagle & Child	15	Majliss	26
Isis Guest House	H	Al Shami	16	Freud	6	Manos	1
Old Parsonage	A	Big Bang	11	George & Davis	10	Oxford Retreat	17
Oxford Backpackers	C	Branca	2	Half Moon	20	Pierre Victoire	8
Oxford Youth Hostel	F	Bridge	18	Jericho	3	Raoul's	12
Richmond	B	Café Coco	22	Jude the Obscure	5	Sugar Brown	13
Royal Oxford	D	Café Tarifa	24	Kazbar	23	Woodstock Road Deli	7

Redbridge Park & Ride & Abingdon

51

as frequent **buses** into the city centre (usually every 8–15min: Mon–Sat from 6am, Sun from 8am). A return bus fare is £2.20 (£2.50 before 9am Mon–Fri), with discounts for two adults travelling together. Up to three children under 16 travel free. All five sites stay open late (Mon–Sat until 11.30pm, Sun until 7pm), but four of them have no buses into town after about 7.45pm: if you're arriving later than that aim for Pear Tree (see below).

In the east, approaching from London via the M40 junction 8, is **Thornhill** (served by bus 400; last bus into central Oxford Mon–Sat 7.50pm, Sun 6.50pm). In the north, approaching from Woodstock, Witney, Banbury or the M40 junction 9, choose from **Pear Tree** (bus 300; last bus in Mon–Sat 11.15pm, Sun 6.45pm) or **Water Eaton** (bus 500; last bus in Mon–Sat 7pm; closed Sun). In the west, coming from Swindon or Wantage, is **Seacourt** (bus 400; last bus in Mon–Sat 7.50pm, Sun 6.50pm), and in the south, approaching from Newbury or Abingdon, is **Redbridge** (bus 300; last bus in Mon–Sat 7.45pm, Sun 6.45pm).

If you're intending to return to your car after 8pm, note that all (bar Pear Tree) operate different bus timetables, bus numbers and pick-up points during the evenings; see online for details, or pick up a leaflet at any of the park-and-ride sites. Thornhill and Water Eaton allow parking for up to 72 hours; all the rest have a 24-hour maximum.

Caravans and motorhomes have secure parking zones at Redbridge (☎01865 815865) and Water Eaton (☎0845 337 1138) – but they're usually kept locked, so check with staff onsite or phone ahead to confirm access details.

Information and tours

Oxford's friendly, well-equipped **tourist office** is plumb in the centre of town at 15 Broad Street (Mon–Sat 9.30am–5pm, Sun 10am–4pm; ☎01865 252200, Ⓦ www.visitoxfordandoxfordshire.com). As well as trinkets and Alice-themed souvenirs (Lewis Carroll, author of the *Alice* books, lived in Oxford; see p.75), staff can offer a wealth of information about the city and its sights – though virtually nothing is free: expect to pay for a map, for their "What to See and Do" brochure, and almost everything else. The handy **listings booklet** *In Oxford* (Ⓦ www.inoxford.com) is an exception, as is the "Where To Stay" accommodation brochure. At the back of the shop is an area with racks of (free) tourist pamphlets covering attractions in and around the city, as well as neighbouring areas across the Cotswolds. Staff also sell **discounted tickets** for a range of nearby attractions, including Blenheim Palace and the Cotswold Wildlife Park, as well as tickets for Espress and Airline coaches to London.

Another excellent source of listings and information is **Daily Info** (Ⓦ www .dailyinfo.co.uk), the continually updated online version of Oxford's student newssheet. You'll spot the paper version pinned up in colleges and cafés around town (published Tues, Thurs & Sat in term-time; otherwise Fri only).

Otherwise, pick up a copy of *The Guide*, the Thursday entertainment pullout in the daily *Oxford Mail* (Ⓦ www.oxfordmail.co.uk) or the leisure magazine *Oxfordshire Limited Edition*, published on the first Thursday of the month in the weekly *Oxford Times* (Ⓦ www.oxfordtimes.co.uk). Monthly magazine *Oxford Life* (Ⓦ oxford.great britishlife.co.uk) has local lifestyle features and reviews. Useful independent websites include Ⓦ www.oxfordcityguide.com and Ⓦ www.viewoxford.co.uk.

Walking tours

The tourist office runs dozens of excellent **guided walking tours**, starting from their premises. The best bet for an introduction to the city centre and colleges is

A weekend in Oxford

Friday night

Toast your weekend with a **champagne cocktail** in the Randolph's *Morse Bar* and a slap-up **dinner** at, say, *Al Shami*, *Gee's* or *Jamie's Italian*.

Saturday

Start the day with a visit to the **Covered Market**, to relax with a coffee while getting a flavour of town life and watch the butchers and fishmongers lay out the new day's wares. Extend the theme by dropping into the **Museum of Oxford**, or join one of the introductory **walking tours** offered by the tourist office. Grab lunch on the hoof and then devote the afternoon to "gown" life: choose two or three of the **colleges** (Christ Church, Merton and New would make a fine hat-trick) and pick up the atmosphere of the old city-centre streets (Broad, Merton, Turl) – or the water meadows behind Christ Church – as you go. End the day with a **punt**, before setting off down the **Cowley Road** to sample Oxford's lounge bars and ethnic restaurants, and perhaps stumble across a gig or a club.

Sunday

Begin with a lazy brunch in one of **Jericho**'s taverns and cafés – or, if you prefer, a genteel 11.15am "coffee concert" at the Holywell Music Room – before tackling the wonder that is the **Ashmolean Museum**. Sample more history at **Oxford Castle Unlocked**, or opt for a country walk in the deer park of **Magdalen College** – then either slope off to the *Half Moon* for their regular Sunday folk session or settle in at *Quod* for live early-evening jazz followed by dinner.

the **University and City Tour** (daily 10.45am & 2pm; also 11am & 1pm if there's sufficient demand; 2hr; £7) – but you could pick from more than a dozen other specialist themed walks which run regularly, including Alice in Wonderland, the English Civil War, American Roots, Gargoyles and Grotesques, Tolkien and C.S. Lewis. The most popular by miles are the **Inspector Morse tour** (Sat 1.30pm; 2hr; £7.50) and the **Harry Potter tour** (July & Aug every 2 weeks, rest of year monthly; 2hr; £11). Everything is detailed on the website, which also includes an option to **book in advance** – advisable for all tours.

Nearby, the **Blackwell bookshop** at 53 Broad Street (℡01865 333606, Ⓦwww.blackwell.co.uk) also runs guided walks (April–Oct only; all 1hr 30min): a **Literary Tour** (Tues 2pm, Thurs 11am; £7), an **"Inklings" Tour** focused on C.S. Lewis and Tolkien (Wed 11.45am; £7) and **Chapels, Churches and Cathedrals** (Fri 2pm; £9).

Separately, **Oxford Walking Tours** (℡07790 734387, Ⓦwww.oxfordwalking tours.com) has introductory tours of the city and colleges (Easter–Oct Mon–Fri 11am, 1pm & 3pm, Sat & Sun hourly 11am–4pm; rest of year Mon–Fri noon & 2pm, Sat & Sun hourly 11am–3pm; 1hr 30min; £7.50) as well as evening **ghost tours** (June–Aug daily 7.30pm; April, May, Sept & Oct Fri & Sat 7.30pm; Nov–March daily 4pm plus Fri & Sat 7.30pm; 1hr 30min; £7). Both depart from outside Trinity College gates in Broad Street, diagonally opposite the tourist office.

Another fine option is **Bill Spectre's Oxford Ghost Trail** (℡07941 041811, Ⓦwww.ghosttrail.org), an entertaining walk around the city centre led by a guide dressed as a top-hatted Victorian undertaker, which starts from outside the gift shop at Oxford Castle Unlocked (Fri & Sat 6.30pm; additional tours in July & Aug; 1hr 45min; £6). For a shorter walk, you can join at 7pm outside the tourist office, as the tour passes by.

Other tours

The tourist office has details of dozens more private tours – both **tailor-made walks** with a personal guide and more unusual options.

Oxon Carts (☎07747 024600, ⓦwww.oxoncarts.com) – half a dozen students who've set up a Jericho-based firm offering **cycle rickshaw** transport – has a great itinerary through the medieval lanes of the city centre, covering more ground than most walks. The rickshaws can seat one or two people only. Book in advance: tours run on demand (1hr; £25).

Another option is a **cycling tour** through the city and out into nearby country-side, run by Capital Sport (June–Aug Sat 10am; 3hr; £25; ☎01296 631671, ⓦwww.capital-sport.co.uk) – the price includes rental of a bike for the whole day. Book at least three days ahead.

City Sightseeing (☎01865 790522, ⓦwww.citysightseeingoxford.com) runs an open-top **bus tour** around the edges of the medieval city centre (every 10–15min daily 9.30am–6pm; Oct–April ends 1hr earlier; £12.50). Tickets are valid all day: you can board at any of twenty pick-up/drop-off points (including Broad Street opposite the tourist office) and then hop on or off as you like. Also available are two-day tickets, family discounts and good-value combo deals with Oxford Castle and Oxon Carts rickshaws.

Getting around

The easiest way to get around central Oxford – indeed, the only way to get under the skin of the place – is to **walk**. For an idea of distance, just about the longest walk you're likely to do in one go might be from the rail station to Magdalen Bridge; this is roughly a mile and a quarter, and you would pass almost everything of interest in the city centre on the way.

For all but the narrowest lanes, **cycling** is a good second-best, and a bike will also get you to outlying districts more easily and often more quickly than a **bus**. Alternatively, you could sit back and let someone else do the pedalling for you: Oxon Carts (see "Arrival" p.48) offer transport around town by **cycle-rickshaw**.

By bike

As you'll see from the racks of bicycles on just about every street corner – and the numerous signs warning "Bikes attached to these railings will be removed" – **cycling** is how a fair few Oxford residents get about. Several of Oxford's many bike shops offer **bike rental** and repairs, including Bainton Bikes, 6 Bainton Road (☎01865 365658, ⓦwww.baintonbikes.com), about two-thirds of a mile north of the centre off Woodstock Road. They charge £7 for a day, £15 for three days or £22 a week; the price includes lights, a lock, a city map, free delivery to anywhere in Oxford and full backup support. Always book ahead. Others, with broadly comparable prices, include Bike Zone (ⓦwww.bikezoneoxford.co.uk) – who have a central outlet on Market Street (☎01865 728877) and another at Summertown Cycles, 200 Banbury Road (☎01865 316885) – and the mobile back-of-a-van service Back on Trax (☎07773 325552 or 07919 445464, ⓦwww.backontrax.co.uk). Cycloanalysts, 150 Cowley Road (☎01865 424444, ⓦwww.cycloanalysts.com), have classier bikes for higher rates. Ask at the tourist office for the very useful, free **Oxford Cycle Map**, also downloadable at ⓦwww.oxfordshire.gov.uk/cycling.

By bus

We've given contact details on p.49 for Stagecoach and Oxford Bus, who operate the majority of **city buses** – but you're unlikely to need to use them. The exception might be if you're staying at a hotel or B&B on one of the approach roads (Banbury Road or Woodstock Road in the north, Botley Road in the west, Abingdon Road or Iffley Road in the south, or Headington Road in the east), in which case you'll probably need to use buses to get to and from the city centre: reception staff will be able to tell you which – or you could check routes and fares online. Stagecoach and Oxford Bus tickets are not interchangeable, but there is the multi-operator **Pulse Pass** (£6 for 24hr), buyable from any bus driver and valid city-wide.

By car

As gridlock on Beaumont Street and Hythe Bridge Street can testify – not to mention jams at other pinchpoints around the city, notably during the morning and evening commute – **driving** in Oxford is often a frustrating and time-consuming endeavour. Most of the city-centre streets are **pedestrianized**; those that aren't have time restrictions or deliberately obstructive one-way rules. Four "bus gates" ring the central area, monitored by cameras: drive through the ones on Magdalen Street, George Street or Castle Street at any time, or the one on the High Street between 7.30am and 6.30pm daily, and you'll get a £60 fine.

If you have to drive in, aim for the largest **car park** in town (see Ⓦwww.oxford .gov.uk), alongside the Westgate shopping mall, accessed off Thames Street. Expect to pay £10–15 for half a day. The railway station car park (Ⓦwww.apcoa.co.uk) is only for rail users. **On-street parking** (locations specified at Ⓦwww.oxfordshire .gov.uk) is limited to two hours during the day (Mon–Sat 8am–6.30pm £2–2.50/hour, Sun 9am–6.30pm free), with unlimited parking every day after 6.30pm (free). The only secure, public **overnight parking** is in the underground car park at Gloucester Green – but at an eye-watering cost of roughly £30 for 24 hours, more at the weekend (advance booking essential ☎01865 252489).

If you have a reservation at a city-centre hotel and want to drive in to unload, check with hotel staff beforehand about access restrictions. Several central hotels offer parking for guests (generally £10–20 a night; always book ahead).

Accommodation

With supply struggling to keep pace with demand, Oxford's central **hotels** can be expensive. There are one or two more affordable hotels in or near the centre, but at the budget end of the market you're better off choosing a **guest house** or **B&B**, which are plentiful if usually some distance out. As usual, though, the divisions between these are fuzzy: in terms of price, facilities and service a good B&B can easily trump a mediocre hotel – and staying in a B&B doesn't automatically expose you to swirly carpets and lopsided pelmets. Oxford's demanding, cosmopolitan clientele (and their high rate of repeat bookings) means that standards are, on the whole, satisfyingly high.

You might also consider **self-catering**. Oxstay (Ⓦwww.oxstay.co.uk) is one of several agencies offering short-stay, serviced apartments in the city centre: less than £120 a night could net you a modern studio or one-bedroom flat (with parking). The tourist office has details of other options.

Wherever you stay, **book ahead** – either direct or (for a £5 fee) through the tourist office.

Your ivory tower awaits

For an overnight stay that is light on service but rich in atmosphere – and *very* Oxford – check ⓦwww.oxfordrooms.co.uk and ⓦwww.budgetstayuk.com for details about staying in a **college room** on a B&B basis. Expect little (or no) hotel-style service, but you may score with a view over a historic quad, and are free to soak up the college ambience and roam the grounds at will. Breakfast is generally served in the wood-panelled college dining-hall. This is also a great option if you're **travelling solo**: although there are some twins and doubles, the vast majority of rooms are singles (not all of them en suite). Historic colleges in the scheme – which runs mainly during the summer months (mid-June to mid-Oct), with some availability at Easter and Christmas – include Balliol, Jesus, Keble, Magdalen and Queen's. Depending on dates, rates for single rooms hover either side of £50 (some as low as £30); doubles from roughly £110.

All the places reviewed here are keyed on the maps on p.46, p.50 or p.60.

Hotels

Central

Bath Place 4 Bath Place ☎01865 791812, ⓦwww.bathplace.co.uk. This unusual hotel comprises a handful of higgledy-piggledy medieval cottages around a tiny cobbled courtyard off Holywell Street. There are seventeen creaky rooms, each individually decorated in attractive, antique style – canopied beds, exposed beams and so forth. Some rooms feel a touch compact; the hotel labels these "smaller doubles" and prices them lower. By contrast, steep spiral stairs lead to room 11 ("superior king"), with rooftop views and a huge carpeted bathroom. The central location is excellent, though the famous *Turf Tavern* is round the corner: the courtyard does see foot traffic to and from the pub. Secure parking nearby (£10/night). Map p.60. ❺

Eastgate 73 High St ☎01865 248332, ⓦwww.mercure.com. Modern four-star chain hotel insinuated into an ex-coaching inn. Public areas feature sleek, contemporary styling and the hotel's *High Table* brasserie has developed a good reputation. Rooms are blandly modern, but this is still a reliable choice with warm, efficient service and a very central location. Map p.60. ❹–❺

🏃 **Malmaison** Oxford Castle, New Rd ☎01865 268400, ⓦwww.malmaison.com. Classy and atmospheric designer hotel occupying what was a Victorian prison, part of the Oxford Castle complex. Rooms – which take up three cells, knocked through – are nothing short of glamorous, featuring contemporary bathrooms and hi-tech gadgets: being walked along the (now carpeted) catwalks through the *Porridge*-style prison hall is quite an eye-opener. Head through to C wing for bigger mezzanine suites. Book ahead for bargain rates. Parking £20/night. Map p.60. ❺

Old Bank 91 High St ☎01865 799599, ⓦwww.oldbank-hotel.co.uk. Great location for a slick and sleek boutique hotel in a Georgian edifice plumb on the High Street, converted from (you guessed it) an old bank. All forty-plus bedrooms are decorated in crisp, modern style – pastel shades and whites – and some have great views over All Souls College opposite. Map p.60. ❽

Old Parsonage 1 Banbury Rd ☎01865 310210, ⓦwww.oldparsonage-hotel.co.uk. Lovely upmarket hotel occupying a charming, wisteria-clad stone building dating from 1660 near the church at the top of St Giles. The thirty-odd rooms are tastefully furnished in a bright modern manner and the location is nigh-on perfect, across the road from the parks but only a stroll from the hustle and bustle of Jericho and/or the city centre. Free walking tours for guests on request. Map p.50. ❽

Randolph 1 Beaumont St ☎0844 879 9132, ⓦwww.randolph-hotel.com. Oxford's most famous hotel, long the favoured choice of the well-heeled visitor, occupying a well-proportioned neo-Gothic brick building opposite the Ashmolean Museum with a distinctive, nineteenth-century interior – the carpeted staircase is especially handsome. Now part of the *Macdonald* chain, but with impeccable service, well-appointed bedrooms and a distinguished club atmosphere. Top-floor rooms are quietest. Limited parking (£26.50/night). Map p.60. ❾

Royal Oxford Park End St ☎01865 248432, ⓦwww.royaloxfordhotel.co.uk. Convenient three-star, occupying a posh-looking building facing onto Frideswide Square, two min walk from the railway station and right by a stop for buses from Thornhill and Seacourt park-and-ride car parks. Chiefly a business hotel – the 26 bedrooms are clean and functional, service is smooth and efficient – but the location and modest prices make it worth considering. Some traffic noise. Map p.50. ❹

Further out

Ethos 59 Western Rd, Grandpont Ⓦ 01865 245800, Ⓦ www.ethoshotels.co.uk. Chic and perhaps slightly pretentious boutique hotel in a residential district just over the Thames, about a 15min walk south of Carfax. The styling is upmarket contemporary, very swish, but the service ethic is hands-off. Each room – some of which open directly from the street – has a fridge and kitchen area, with basic supplies, and no breakfast is served: you're instead given a "breakfast basket" of muffins, juice, cornflakes and yoghurt to eat alone in your room. Great for design-lovers who prefer an independent life – but a touch chilly for others. Map p.46. ❹–❺

Guest houses and B&Bs

Central

Becket House 5 Becket St ☎ 01865 724675, Ⓦ www.beckethouse.co.uk. Modest but proficient bay-windowed guesthouse in a plain terrace close to the railway station. Most rooms en suite. Map p.50. ❷–❸

Buttery 11 Broad St ☎ 01865 811950, Ⓦ www.thebutteryhotel.co.uk. Slap-bang central location for this sixteen-room guest house-cum-hotel, with modest rooms (including one single), mostly on the large side, plainly but decently decorated. Service from the student waiting-staff at the café downstairs is friendly if a bit clueless. You're paying over the odds for the location – but choose a back room to avoid the noise of carousing students on Broad Street late at night. Stairs are narrow and steep. Map p.60. ❹–❺

Richmond 25 Walton Crescent ☎ 01865 311777, Ⓦ www.the-richmond-oxford.co.uk. Small B&B attached to the excellent *Al-Shami* Lebanese restaurant (see p.84) in Jericho. Expect few frills – rooms are plain and unrenovated – but prices are remarkably low, the welcome is warm, the location is very quiet and you get a choice of breakfasts: English or – uniquely for Oxford – Lebanese (hummus, olives, white cheese, pitta bread and more). Map p.50. ❷

🏃 **St Michael's Guest House** 26 St Michael's St ☎ 01865 242101. Often full,

this friendly, well-kept B&B, in a cosy three-storey terrace house, has unsurprising furnishings and fittings, but a charming location on a pleasant old street in the very heart of the city centre. A snip. Map p.60. ❷

Further out

Acorn 260 Iffley Rd ☎ 01865 247998, Ⓦ www.oxford-acorn.co.uk. Huge Edwardian house a couple of miles southeast of the centre offering a friendly, efficient welcome and a well-kept interior. The fourteen guest rooms are fresh and pretty, all en suite (bar a single and small twin), with quiet ones overlooking the rear garden. Good value. Map p.46. ❸

Browns Guest House 281 Iffley Rd ☎ 01865 246822, Ⓦ www.brownsguesthouse.co.uk. Well-maintained guesthouse in a pleasing Victorian property with fourteen rooms, mostly en suite. Just under two miles southeast of the centre. Map p.46. ❸

🏃 **Burlington House** 374 Banbury Rd ☎ 01865 513513, Ⓦ www.burlington-house.co.uk. Excellent, very high quality boutique-style B&B in the upmarket North Oxford suburb of Summertown. Twelve large bedrooms fill a Victorian house, built in 1889, now rejuvenated with a thoroughly modern ambience and superb attention to detail – luxurious fabrics, feature walls, bright designs. Sumptuous breakfasts and generous service exemplify the approach. Map p.46. ❹–❺

Isis Guesthouse 45 Iffley Rd ☎ 01865 248894, Ⓦ www.isisguesthouse.com. Ten minutes' walk southeast of the centre – and a short stroll from both Magdalen Bridge and the bars of Cowley Road – this big old Victorian house serves most of the year as lodgings for students at St Edmund Hall, but over the summer months morphs into a congenial, well-run B&B, with en suite and shared-bath rooms. For the location, and the quality, it's a bargain. July–Sept only. Map p.50. ❸–❹

Lina Guesthouse 308 Banbury Rd ☎ 01865 511070, Ⓦ www.linaguesthouse.com. Spotless, well-maintained establishment occupying a Victorian house in Summertown, a short bus ride north of the centre, with great service. All rooms are en suite and stylishly appointed. Free parking. Map p.46. ❸–❹

Parklands 100 Banbury Rd ☎ 01865 554374, Ⓦ www.parklandsoxford.co.uk. Pleasant fourteen-room B&B in a large Victorian house with a garden and bar. Attention to detail is sometimes a bit lacking, but it's a cheerful enough choice. Map p.46. ❹

Remont 367 Banbury Rd ☎ 01865 311020, ⓦ www.remont-oxford.co.uk. Very classy hotel-style B&B in Summertown, a couple of miles north of the centre. The approach throughout is of a chic boutique hotel, with black leather, dark wood, vivid fabrics, contemporary eco-friendly bathrooms and speedy wi-fi. Service is warm and accommodating, and breakfast is fantastic, in terms of both the food and the airy, modern buffet-style dining area. Map p.46. ❺–❻

Tilbury Lodge 5 Tilbury Lane ☎ 01865 862138, ⓦ www.tilburylodge.com. Unpretentiously modern guest house in Botley, well west of the centre, that offers unusually good value for money. The rooms are comfortable, but nothing to write home about – unlike the mighty breakfasts and the genuinely outgoing, friendly owners, for whom nothing seems too much trouble. A great find. Map p.46. ❹

Hostels and camping

Hostels

Central Backpackers 13 Park End St ☎ 01865 242288, ⓦ www.centralbackpackers.co.uk. Award-winning hostel, independently owned and operated, with fifty beds in 4-, 6-, 8- and 12-bed dorms (including female-only), 24-hour access, a good range of facilities and a friendly can-do

attitude. Located on a lively street midway between the railway and bus stations: expect late-night noise from nearby bars and clubs. Beds £18–21 including breakfast and wi-fi. Map p.50.

Oxford Backpackers 9a Hythe Bridge St ☎ 01865 721761, ⓦ www.hostels.co.uk. Independent hostel with 120 beds in 4-, 8-, 10-, 14- and 18-bed dorms (including female-only) and 24-hour access – but a touch scruffier and more make-do than its near-neighbour. Similarly handy location. Beds £14–17 including breakfast. Map p.50.

Oxford Youth Hostel 2a Botley Rd ☎ 0845 371 9131, ⓦ www.yha.org.uk. In a clumpy modern block behind the railway station, with 24-hour access, this popular YHA hostel has 187 beds in four- and six-bedded dorms plus nine double rooms, with good facilities and a decent café and restaurant. Beds £16–20 including breakfast (YHA non-members pay £3 supplement). Map p.50. ❷

Campsite

Oxford Camping & Caravan Club 426 Abingdon Rd ☎ 01865 244088, ⓦ www.campingand caravanningclub.co.uk. Fully equipped site a mile or so south of the centre beside a busy road, with tent pitches and hookups for caravans and motorhomes. Map p.46.

The City

The compact **centre** of Oxford is wedged in between the rivers Thames and Cherwell, just to the north of the point where they join. The old Saxon ground-plan is still discernible, with the east–west **High Street** ("the High") cut by the north–south **Cornmarket** at the busy junction of **Carfax**. To the east of Cornmarket lies the heart of the university, with **Broad Street**, **Turl Street** and the High Street flanked by grand college architecture, culminating in the iconic **Radcliffe Camera** at the centre of the city. Further east, High Street continues to **Magdalen Bridge** over the Cherwell, beyond which lie the workaday districts of St Clement's and Cowley Road. South of Carfax, **St Aldates** heads down to the Thames, passing the majestic **Christ Church College** – within whose grounds stands **Oxford Cathedral** – on the way. To the west rises the mound of now-vanished **Oxford Castle**, while to the north the broad avenue of **St Giles** leads past the vast **Ashmolean Museum** to exit the city towards Woodstock and Banbury.

Visiting the colleges

Colleges operate restricted public **opening hours** – often just a couple of hours in mid-afternoon, and sometimes less than that during the exam season (late April to early June). Some impose an **admission charge**. For details check the "Visitors and Friends" pages of the university website (ⓦ www.ox.ac.uk), or phone the relevant college.

Oxford University – a rough guide

So where, exactly, is **Oxford University**? Everywhere – and nowhere. The university itself is nothing more than an administrative body, setting examinations and awarding degrees. Although it has its own offices (on Wellington Square), they are of no particular interest. What draws all the attention are the university's constituent **colleges** – 38 of them (plus another six religious foundations known as Permanent Private Halls), most occupying historic buildings scattered throughout the city centre. It is they which hold the 800-year-old history of the university, and exemplify its spirit.

The university operates a **federal** system: all the colleges are independent and self-governing, in most cases selecting their own students and remaining responsible for them throughout their time in Oxford. It's the colleges who teach, not the university, mainly through weekly one-to-one or small-group **tutorials**. Students keep the same college tutor for the duration of their course (three years in most instances), live in college accommodation, use the college library, meet in the college "common room" and compete in college sports teams. Their only contact with the university, other than at **exam** time, may be if they choose to attend lectures or seminars – which students from different colleges attend together – or if they use facilities in a university library or laboratory.

What does a college look like?
There's no standard ground-plan, but most Oxford colleges – and all the most interesting historic examples – look similar, and are generally shielded from the street behind high stone walls: it's impossible to tell the character of the place from outside. The college **porter**, sitting in a **lodge** (an office beside the main entrance gate), controls access. Beyond, college buildings are arranged around a quadrangle, or "**quad**". Doorways from the quad access numbered **staircases** within each building, off which lie the residential rooms of tutors and other teaching staff (known as "**dons**") and students. Passageways may lead through to other quads beyond.

Two buildings are normally open to visitors. The **hall** is where students and academics eat breakfast, lunch and dinner. Generally a grand, high-ceilinged chamber, often with wood panelling, vaulting and perhaps a stone fireplace, it is invariably hung with portraits of notable **alumni** (past students) or prominent figures associated with the college. Students take their food from a self-service buffet and sit communally at long tables, often on wooden benches, while staff are served separately at "**high table**", raised on a dais at the back of the hall beneath a portrait of the college founder or benefactor. Every college also has a **chapel**, which – unusually – are all T-shaped: there is no nave, and instead transepts serve as an antechapel leading into the choir, where stalls face each other across an aisle. Behind the altar often rises a wall of statues in ornate niches, known as a reredos.

Why visit a college?
• For the **architecture**. Each college has its own atmosphere, characterised by Gothic, Classical, Victorian, even contemporary architecture: to find examples of such original styles so well maintained, and rubbing shoulders with each other so harmoniously, is very rare.

• For the **sense of discovery**. Colleges do not advertise: there are no signs on the street indicating which college is which. You make your own enquiries, follow your own path, and are free to discover what you will.

• For a slice of **real life**. Colleges are not tourist attractions: despite their somewhat rarefied atmosphere and appearance, they are places of work, offering a glimpse into the daily lives of people of diverse backgrounds from all over Britain and the world.

In short, colleges are the repository of the city's history and character. In Florence, visit churches. In Damascus, visit souks. In Oxford, visit colleges.

▲ Cowley Road

CENTRAL OXFORD

ACCOMMODATION
Bath Place	B
Buttery	C
Eastgate	F
Malmaison	G
Old Bank	E
Randolph	A
St Michael's	D

0 — 100 yards

N

EATING & DRINKING
Ashmolean Dining Room	1	George & Danver	20	News Café	10
Bear	19	Gloucester Arms	6	Pie Minister	12
Ben's Cookies	17	Grand Café	15	Quod	14
Chiang Mai Kitchen	18	Jamie's Italian	8	Rose	14
Chocology	16	Kings Arms	2	Turf Tavern	4
Edamame	3	Missing Bean	13	Vaults & Garden	11
Fire and Stone	9	Morse Bar	3	White Horse	5
		Mortons	9		7

Banbury Road & Woodstock Road ▲

Jericho ▲

WALTON ST

Bus Station

GLOUCESTER GREEN

Nuffield

BEAUMONT STREET

Ashmolean Museum

Oxford Playhouse

ST GILES

Martyrs' Memorial

St Mary Magdalen

MAGDALEN ST

Oxford Union

BROAD STREET

Balliol

Trinity

Blackwell's Bookshop

Museum of History of Science

Exeter

Sheldonian Theatre

New Bodleian Library

PARKS ROAD

HOLYWELL STREET

Holywell Music Room

New College

Hertford

Bridge of Sighs

Radcliffe Camera

Bodleian Library

RADCLIFFE SQUARE

Brasenose

All Souls

CATTE STREET

QUEEN'S LANE

New College Gardens

MANSFIELD RD

St Edmund Hall

Queen's

University College ('Univ')

St Mary the Virgin

Oriel

MAGPIE LANE

LONGWALL STREET

Magdalen

Magdalen Grove

ROSE LANE

Magdalen Bridge

Botanic Gardens

Merton

Corpus Christi

MERTON STREET

ORIEL STREET

HIGH STREET

Examination Schools

MERTON GROVE

BROAD WALK

NEW WALK

Folly Bridge ▼

Christ Church College

Oxford Cathedral

Christ Church Picture Gallery

Tom Tower

ST ALDATE'S

War Memorial Gardens

Museum of Oxford

Town Hall

Covered Market

Jesus

Lincoln

TURL STREET

SHIP STREET

CORNMARKET

CARFAX

QUEEN ST

Clarendon Centre

Modern Art Oxford

St Aldate's

Pembroke

St Ebbe's

Westgate Shopping Centre

NEW INN HALL STREET

GEORGE STREET

NEW ROAD

Oxford Castle

Oxford Castle Unlocked

St George's Tower

River Thames

CASTLE STREET

NORFOLK STREET

OLD GREYFRIARS STREET

PARADISE SQUARE

WORCESTER ST

HYTHE BRIDGE ST

Worcester

P

Railway Station ▼   ▼ Railway Station   ▲ Railway Station

⊠ Public entrance to college

P

St Peter's

GLOUCESTER STREET

ST JOHN ST

However, regardless of published hours, it's always worth trying your luck and asking at the **porter's lodge**, located beside the main college entrance: porters have ultimate discretion and if you ask they may let you wander in. On the other hand, they may tell you that the college is closed that day for a function or conference – and if you're *very* unlucky, you might pay for admission only to discover during your visit that, say, the college chapel is closed for choir practice or the dining hall is off-limits because of an event that evening. You're unlikely to get your money back in these situations.

We've described many of the colleges in the pages following, but you'd need Olympic stamina and dedication to visit all 38. If there is a single "must-see" it would be Christ Church, for its cathedral and magnificent dining hall; otherwise, dropping into more or less any college can make for an atmospheric quarter-hour. A speculative, subjective checklist for beginners, in no particular order, might run as follows:

• **Five should-sees**: Christ Church, Merton, New, All Souls, Magdalen
• **Five could-sees**: Brasenose, St John's, Queen's, Lincoln, Jesus
• **Five might-sees**: Exeter, University, Pembroke, Trinity, Keble

Broad Street

Marking what was the town ditch, just beyond the now-vanished northern walls, **Broad Street** is one of Oxford's most handsome thoroughfares, a quiet, spacious street festooned with parked bicycles. On one side rise Balliol College and gates shielding views to the lawns of Trinity College; on the other jostles a line of higgledy-piggledy shop facades which include the **tourist office**, at number 15. Two doors down, number 17 houses what was the first-ever **Oxfam** charity shop when it opened in 1948: the "Oxford Committee for Famine Relief", founded during World War II, continues its work today from head offices in Cowley. Nearby, grab an espresso or a sandwich at *Morton's* café (see p.81), at number 22, to view a section of the city wall – dating from the early thirteenth century – which survives overlooking their rear terrace. At the corner of Turl Street, look up: gazing out from a vantage point atop the roof of Exeter College (see p.72) stands the 2009 **Antony Gormley sculpture** *Another Time* – a seven-foot figure in iron of a naked man.

Broad Street is perhaps best known as the home of **Blackwell**, Oxford's leading bookshop, founded by Benjamin Blackwell in 1879 and now a global concern. The original outlet, at number 50, still forms part of the main shop, a creaky, lopsided warren which now spreads from 48 to 53 (flanking the old *White Horse* pub; see p.86) and reaches both above and below ground: its immense, subterranean Norrington Room, extending beneath the adjacent quadrangle of Trinity College, has three miles of shelving. Across the road, Blackwell has a separate music shop at 23 Broad Street and art bookshop at number 27.

Turl Street, which runs south off Broad Street, is covered on p.72.

Balliol and Trinity colleges

Sporting a fine Victorian Gothic frontage opposite the tourist office, designed in 1868 by Alfred Waterhouse, **Balliol College** (no set hours; £2; ☎01865 277777, ⓦwww.balliol.ox.ac.uk) is one of the university's oldest, founded in 1263 (or thereabouts) by Scottish noble John de Balliol as penance for insulting the bishop of Durham. Nevertheless, despite its antiquity, Balliol has little to offer architecturally: remodelled and rebuilt in the nineteenth century, it presents an unexceptional assembly of buildings, haphazardly gathered around two quads.

Oxford: college by college

A list of all 38 Oxford colleges, ordered by their date of foundation, with a few notable alumni.

• **University** 1249 – Shelley, V.S. Naipaul, Stephen Hawking, C.S. Lewis, Bill Clinton
• **Balliol** 1263 – Graham Greene, Aldous Huxley, Peter Snow, Boris Johnson
• **Merton** 1264 – John Wycliffe, Max Beerbohm, Roger Bannister, T.S. Eliot
• **St Edmund Hall** c.1278 – Terry Jones, Sir Robin Day, Amitav Ghosh
• **Exeter** 1314 – Martin Amis, Alan Bennett, Richard Burton, J.R.R. Tolkien, Philip Pullman
• **Oriel** 1326 – Sir Walter Raleigh, Cardinal Newman, Beau Brummell, Ian Hislop
• **Queen's** 1341 – Edmund Halley, Jeremy Bentham, Tim Berners-Lee, Rowan Atkinson
• **New** 1379 – Tony Benn, Hugh Gaitskell, Rick Stein, Dennis Potter, Rageh Omaar
• **Lincoln** 1427 – John Wesley, John Le Carré, Theodore Geisel ("Dr Seuss")
• **All Souls*** 1438 – T.E. Lawrence, Isaiah Berlin
• **Magdalen** 1458 – Cardinal Wolsey, Oscar Wilde, C.S. Lewis, Sir John Betjeman
• **Brasenose** 1509 – John Buchan, Michael Palin, William Golding, David Cameron
• **Corpus Christi** 1517 – John Ruskin, David Miliband, Vikram Seth
• **Christ Church** 1546 – Lewis Carroll, W.H. Auden, Albert Einstein, Sir Christopher Wren
• **Trinity** 1555 – William Pitt the Elder, Terence Rattigan
• **St John's** 1555 – Philip Larkin, Robert Graves, Kingsley Amis, Tony Blair
• **Jesus** 1571 – T.E. Lawrence, Harold Wilson
• **Wadham** 1610 – Sir Thomas Beecham, Cecil Day-Lewis, Melvyn Bragg, Monica Ali
• **Pembroke** 1624 – Samuel Johnson, King Abdullah of Jordan
• **Worcester** 1714 – Thomas de Quincey, Rupert Murdoch, Anthony Seldon
• **Hertford** 1740 – John Donne, Jonathan Swift, Evelyn Waugh, Fiona Bruce
• **Harris Manchester** 1786 – Sir Oliver Popplewell, Lord Nicholas Windsor
• **Keble** 1870 – Imran Khan, Chad Varah, Giles Coren
• **Lady Margaret Hall** 1878 – Gertrude Bell, Benazir Bhutto, Nigella Lawson
• **Somerville** 1879 – Indira Gandhi, Margaret Thatcher, Shirley Williams, Iris Murdoch
• **Mansfield** 1886 – Pamela Sue Anderson, Stephen Pollard
• **St Hugh's** 1886 – Joanna Trollope, Barbara Castle, Aung San Suu Kyi
• **St Anne's** 1893 – Edwina Currie, Susan Sontag, Martha Kearney
• **St Hilda's** 1893 – Barbara Pym, Wendy Cope, Susan Greenfield
• **St Peter's** 1929 – Ken Loach, Hugh Fearnley-Whittingstall
• **Nuffield**** 1937 – Manmohan Singh
• **St Antony's**** 1950 – Thomas Friedman, Rashid Khalidi, Alvaro Uribe Velez
• **Linacre**** 1962 – Yasmin Alibhai-Brown, Terry Eagleton
• **St Catherine's** 1963 – Joseph Heller, Sir Matthew Pinsent, Jeanette Winterson
• **St Cross**** 1965 – Hermione Lee
• **Wolfson**** 1966 – Dame Kay Davies, Nigel Hitchin
• **Kellogg**** 1990 – Umberto Eco (honorary fellow)
• **Green Templeton**** 2008 – Crispin Tickell (fellow)

*Admits fellows only. **Admit graduate students only.

Just outside Balliol, a cross set into the road marks the spot where the "**Oxford Martyrs**" (see p.47) were burnt at the stake for their Catholicism – Hugh Latimer and Nicholas Ridley in October 1555, Thomas Cranmer five months later. The event is also commemorated by the **Martyrs' Memorial**, a Victorian monument round the corner in Magdalen Street.

Beside Balliol, wrought-iron gates reveal the splendid Front Quad of **Trinity College** (daily 2–4pm, sometimes also 10am–noon; £2; ☎01865 279900, ⓦwww.trinity.ox.ac.uk). Entry is alongside, beside three seventeenth-century lodge-cottages. Behind them the manicured lawns stretches back to the richly decorated **chapel**, awash with Baroque stuccowork. Its high altar is flanked by an exquisite example of the work of master wood-carver Grinling Gibbons – a distinctive performance, with cherubs' heads peering out from delicate foliage. The chapel and stone-flagged **hall** are entered from amid an attractive ensemble of late seventeenth-century buildings around **Durham Quad**: Trinity was originally named Durham College, founded in 1286, purchased by Oxfordshire landowner Sir Thomas Pope during the dissolution of the monasteries and refounded in 1555.

The collegiate neighbours are, as you might expect, arch-rivals, living out a grudge which goes back 750 years to John de Balliol's dispute with Durham's bishop. This has become ritualized with the singing of *The Gordouli*, a scatological verse yelled over the wall by Balliol students at their adversaries, usually at unsociable hours of the night. It includes the lines: "I'd rather be a bastard than a bloody Trinity man / Bloody Trinity! / Trinity's burning, pour on petrol / Bloody Trinity!" Trinity's response is not recorded.

Museum of the History of Science

The east end of Broad Street showcases much of Oxford's most monumental architecture, not least the fine seventeenth-century building opposite Blackwell's bookshop. Originally home to the Ashmolean collection (see p.78), it now houses the fascinating **Museum of the History of Science** (Tues–Fri noon–5pm, Sat 10am–5pm, Sun 2–5pm; free; ⓦwww.mhs.ox.ac.uk). Start on the entrance level, which features cases crammed with antique microscopes and astrolabes, as well as a diverting collection of early spectacles. Against the back wall stands one of the world's oldest pendulum clocks, an elegant piece made in the early 1660s by one Ahasuerus Fromanteel. As you make your way up the creaky staircase, don't dismiss the huge, intricately detailed depiction of the moon as a recent NASA image: it is, in fact, a pastel by English artist John Russell dating from 1795. This extraordinary work was rehung in 2007 when a visiting astronomer noticed that it was upside down – whereupon Russell's signature, lurking unnoticed for decades in the top left corner, was rediscovered at bottom right.

The upper gallery has more cases packed with dizzyingly complex mathematical instruments, from a Roman sundial and an "equatorium", used to establish the position of the planets, to a surveying sextant used by Isambard Kingdom Brunel and Elizabeth I's astrolabe. Venture down to the basement for Lewis Carroll's photography kit and, amazingly, a blackboard used by Albert Einstein during a lecture in Oxford on May 16, 1931: it remains as he left it, scrawled with a series of equations in chalk that – apparently – show the density, radius and age of the universe.

Sheldonian Theatre

Beside the Museum of the History of Science, a curving set of railings with stone steps leading up mark an enclave of buildings connected with the university (rather than with individual colleges). Adorning the tops of pillars between the railings are thirteen glum, pop-eyed Classical-style busts, all curly locks and togas, usually known as the **Emperors**. (Four more reside in front of the Museum of the History of Science.) They've been there in one form or other for almost 350 years – the current crop were unveiled in 1976 after a Victorian set had worn smooth

– though nobody knows who they represent or what the point of them might be. Some maintain, plausibly, that they depict the history of beards.

The Emperors guard access to the curving rear of the **Sheldonian Theatre** (Mon–Sat 10am–12.30pm & 2–4.30pm; Nov–Feb closes 3.30pm; £2.50; Ⓦ www .sheldon.ox.ac.uk). One of the first buildings designed by Sir Christopher Wren, in 1663, it was intended to be a reworking of the Theatre of Marcellus in Rome, though Wren – then a 31-year-old professor of astronomy – had not visited Italy at the time and his design is timid in comparison. The exterior, particularly the magnificent southern facade of the D-shaped building, is the best of it; inside, though the column-less space, spanning more than twenty metres, is impressive, there's not much sense of drama. The theatre sometimes stages lectures and concerts but it was designed principally for university ceremonies – notably matriculation, graduation and the June event *Encaenia*, where honorary degrees are awarded. You can make your way up to the cupola, an 1838 replacement of Wren's original, for some striking views over Oxford's rooftops.

Bodleian Library

Christopher Wren's pupil Nicholas Hawksmoor designed the **Clarendon Building**, a domineering, solidly symmetrical edifice topped by allegorical figures that lies immediately east of the Sheldonian, completed in 1713 to house the Oxford University Press. It now forms part of the **Bodleian Library**. Founded by scholar Sir Thomas Bodley in 1602, the Bodleian is now the UK's largest library after the British Library in London, with an estimated 117 miles of shelving. Yet despite its nine libraries spread across Oxford – which include the rather refreshingly modernist 1930s **New Bodleian** directly opposite the Clarendon, designed by Sir Giles Gilbert Scott and linked to the main building by tunnels beneath Broad Street – plus a host of off-site storage facilities from a Swindon warehouse to a Cheshire salt mine, space remains tight. As one of the UK and Ireland's six copyright libraries, the Bodleian must find room for a copy of every book, pamphlet, magazine and newspaper published in Britain.

Behind the Clarendon and across a gravel courtyard – note the diagonal line in the paving by the Clarendon's south facade, which shows the former line of the medieval city wall – you enter the Bodleian's beautifully proportioned **Old Schools Quadrangle**, completed in 1619 in an ornate Jacobean-Gothic style and offering access to all of the university's academic faculties, or schools: the name of each is lettered in gold above the doorways which ring the quad. On the east side rises the handsome **Tower of the Five Orders**, which gives a lesson in architectural design, its tiers of columns built according to the five classical styles – in ascending order Tuscan, Doric, Ionic, Corinthian and Composite.

The highlight, though, is opposite. A statue of William Herbert, 3rd Earl of Pembroke, stands before the elegant facade of the **Divinity School** (Mon–Fri 9am–5pm, Sat 9am–4.30pm, Sun 11am–5pm; £1). Begun in 1424, and sixty years in the making, this exceptional room, reached via the Proscholium vestibule, is a masterpiece of late Gothic architecture, featuring an extravagant vaulted ceiling adorned with a riot of pendants and 455 decorative bosses. Built to house the university's theology faculty, it was, until the nineteenth century, also where degree candidates were questioned in detail about their subject by two interlocutors, with a professor acting as umpire. Few interiors in Oxford are as impressive.

Bodleian tours

An **audio-guide** is available for self-guided tours of the quad and Divinity School (40min; £2.50) – or otherwise there's a host of **guided tours** to those few areas of the Bodleian open to the public. It's always advisable to **book in advance** with the tours office (☎01865 277224, ⓦwww.bodley.ox.ac.uk), located beneath the Tower of the Five Orders at the Great Gate on Catte Street. The **mini tour** (Mon–Sat 1pm, 4pm & 4.30pm; Sun 12.30pm, 4pm & 4.30pm; fewer in winter; 30min; £4.50) takes in the Divinity School and atmospheric **Duke Humfrey's Library** immediately above, distinguished by its superb beamed ceiling and carved corbels. The **standard tour** (daily 11.30am, 2pm & 3pm, Mon–Sat also 10.30am; 1hr; £6.50) includes both these and the **Convocation House** alongside the Divinity School, a sombre wood-panelled chamber where parliament sat during the Civil War, which now sports a fancy fan-vaulted ceiling completed in 1759. Finally, the Bodleian's **extended tour** (Sun 11.15am; in summer also some Weds & Sats 10am; 90min; £13) takes in all of the above plus, most notably, the interior of the Radcliffe Camera (see p.66).

A stroll north of the Clarendon Building and Bridge of Sighs, on Parks Road, lies **Wadham College**, covered on p.80.

Beneath the Bridge of Sighs

From the courtyard between the Bodleian and the Clarendon Building, a gate opens east onto **Catte Street** (once known as Mousecatcher's Lane, then Cat Street, before Victorian gentrification as Catherine Street; it reclaimed its feline origins last century, though with the affectation of medieval spelling). A short walk south brings you to the Radcliffe Camera (see p.66), but almost directly opposite, spanning **New College Lane**, you can't miss the iconic **Bridge of Sighs**, an archway completed in 1914 to link two buildings of **Hertford College**. In truth it bears little resemblance to its Venetian namesake but nonetheless has a certain Italianate elegance, despite, prosaically, having been designed purportedly in order to give residents of the older buildings to the south covered access to newfangled flushing toilets being installed across the road.

Atmospheric, traffic-free **New College Lane**, a favourite cyclists' rat-run, extends east beneath the bridge, flanked for the most part by high, medieval stone walls. Squeeze down narrow **St Helen's Passage** – decorously renamed from its original title, Hell's Passage – on the left to reach the famed *Turf Tavern* (see p.86) and the seventeenth-century cottages on Bath Place, insinuated into kinks of the medieval city walls. Just past St Helen's Passage, the modest house on the left, topped by a mini-observatory, was the home of astronomer Edmund Halley (1656–1742), discoverer of the comet which bears his name.

New College

New College Lane jinks a couple more times between blank walls before reaching the tall, rather sinister gate-tower of **New College** (daily: Easter to early Oct 11am–5pm, £2; rest of year 2–4pm, free; ☎01865 279555, ⓦwww.new.ox .ac.uk). Note that access in winter is usually via the gate in Holywell Street instead. Founded in 1379, the college was built rapidly under the guidance of founder William of Wykeham, bishop of Winchester, whose statue adorns the gatehouse beside that of the Virgin Mary. The buildings surrounding the attractive **Front Quad** date mostly from the last quarter of the fourteenth century, though their splendid Perpendicular Gothic architecture was somewhat tempered by the addition of an extra storey in 1674.

Round to the left a passage leads through to the tranquil **cloisters**, home to an ancient holm oak, while nearby a door gives access to the **chapel**, one of the finest in Oxford, for its contents as much as its design. The antechapel contains some superb fourteenth-century stained glass and the west window – of 1778 – holds an intriguing (if somewhat unsuccessful) nativity scene based on a design by Sir Joshua Reynolds. Beneath it stands the 1951 sculpture *Lazarus* by Jacob Epstein; Khrushchev, after a visit here, claimed that the memory of this haunting work kept him awake at night. The chapel itself, with a hammerbeam ceiling by George Gilbert Scott, is dominated by a magnificent nineteenth-century floor-to-ceiling stone **reredos**, consisting of about fifty canopied figures, mostly saints and apostles, with Christ Crucified as the centrepiece. A dim portrait of St James, on the north wall, is by El Greco.

Across the Front Quad, a set of 21 stone steps lead up to the **hall**, a beautiful room featuring sixteenth-century linenfold panelling. An archway nearby leads through to the modest **Garden Quad**, flanked by Palladian architecture, with the flowerbeds of the **College Garden** beckoning beyond tall wrought-iron gates. Wedged into the northeast corner of the city walls (which survive in plain view) the garden was a cemetery during the Black Death, revamped in later centuries with the addition of a conspicuous grassed **mound** to afford views over the grounds.

Back on New College Lane, you could continue the walk left beneath another arch – the street becomes **Queen's Lane**, leading to St Edmund Hall (see p.74) and the High Street – or return to Catte Street and turn left for Radcliffe Square.

Radcliffe Square

Radcliffe Square, nestled amid the most splendid of "gown" architecture, is Oxford's great theatrical set-piece. Standing with your back to the Decorated Gothic steeple of the great university church of St Mary the Virgin (see opposite), the view is exceptional, taking in the Perpendicular facade of All Souls College chapel on the right, the Gothic frontage of the Bodleian Library ahead, the mixed Gothic and Renaissance architecture of Brasenose College to the left and, dominating the centre of the square, the **Radcliffe Camera**. This mighty rotunda, built between 1737 and 1748 by James Gibbs, architect of London's St Martin-in-the-Fields church, displays no false modesty. Dr John Radcliffe, royal physician (to William III), was, according to a contemporary diarist, "very ambitious of glory": when he died in 1714 he bequeathed a mountain of money for the construction of a library. Gibbs was one of the few British architects of the period to have been trained in Rome and his design is thoroughly Italian in style, its limestone columns ascending to a delicate balustrade, decorated with pin-prick urns and encircling a lead-sheathed dome. Taken over by the Bodleian Library in 1860, it now houses a reading-room, accessible to the public only on the Bodleian's "extended tour" (see p.65).

Brasenose and All Souls colleges

Reached directly from Radcliffe Square, **Brasenose College** (daily 2–4.30pm; £1.50; ☎01865 277830, ⓦwww.bnc.ox.ac.uk) offers something of a haven: its elegant Tudor **Old Quad**, dating from 1516, remains more or less untouched, bar the addition of dormer windows in the seventeenth century. Look in the hall porch for a panel describing how to decipher the large **sundial** of 1719, which adorns the quad's north wall. In the **hall**, hanging over the high table, you'll spot a bronze door-knocker in the shape of a nose, from which the college got its name. Made sometime in the twelfth century – or perhaps earlier – the brazen nose was stolen in 1330 by a group of students, who took it to Stamford in Lincolnshire with the aim of founding a new university. Their caper fizzled out, but the

Oxford University – quick facts (2010)

- Total students: 20,928 (undergraduates 11,766)
- Total non-UK students: 7,505 (undergraduates 1,715)
- Total applications for entry in 2008: 13,388 (ratio of men to women 51:49)
- Total numbers admitted in 2008: 3,170 (ratio of men to women 53:47)
- UK students: ratio of state sector to independent sector 55:45
- Undergraduate college with most students: St Catherine's (741)
- Undergraduate college with least students: Harris Manchester (194)

OXFORD | The City

knocker stayed in Stamford until the building with the door to which it had been attached came up for sale in 1890. Brasenose bought the entire building in order to reclaim their emblem. Stroll through to the **Chapel Quad** to climb the stairs of a barrel-vaulted porch into the college **chapel**, designed in the 1650s in a striking blend of Gothic and Renaissance styles, and housing an eye-popping painted plaster ceiling of fan vaulting. Emerging onto Radcliffe Square, turn right and you'll spot, flanking the wooden door of a side entrance, two wonderful **gilded fauns**; C.S. Lewis noticed them, too, and used them as the inspiration for Mr Tumnus in his *Narnia* books.

Running the entire east side of Radcliffe Square, its immense chapel windows the epitome of the Perpendicular Gothic style, **All Souls College** is one of the quietest places in central Oxford: it has no undergraduates. Uniquely, it admits only "fellows" – that is, distinguished scholars – either by election of existing fellows, or by an exam reputed to be the hardest in the world. Each year two graduates, at most, are awarded fellowships. There is no teaching: fellows may pursue their research in Oxford or elsewhere, the only requirement being occasional attendance at formal weekend dinners. The result is that All Souls is generally silent. Sightseers gather at the elaborate gates on Radcliffe Square, wondering how to gain access to the lovely quad beyond: turn right and walk around the corner onto High Street to reach the **college entrance** (Mon–Fri 2–4pm, closed Aug; free; ℡01865 279379, ⓦwww.all-souls.ox.ac.uk). This gives onto the modest Front Quad, location of the spectacular fifteenth-century **chapel**, with its gilded hammerbeam roof and neck-cricking reredos (though all its figures are Victorian replacements). Move through to the spacious **North Quad**, the object of all that admiration: Hawksmoor's soaring Gothic twin towers face the Radcliffe Square gates, while ahead, the Codrington Library – also Hawksmoor – sports a conspicuous, brightly decorated sundial designed by Wren.

From the All Souls gate on the High Street, directly opposite the *Quod* brasserie (see p.83), turn left to walk towards Queen's College (see p.71) – or pop into the church of St Mary immediately on your right.

St Mary the Virgin

Midway along the High Street just behind Radcliffe Square, **St Mary the Virgin** (daily 9am–5pm, July & Aug until 6pm; free; ⓦwww.university-church.ox.ac.uk) is a hotchpotch of architectural styles, but mostly dates from the fifteenth century. Its distinctive Baroque **porch**, flanked by chunky corkscrewed pillars, was installed in 1637 with the approval of William Laud, Archbishop of Canterbury and religious adviser to Charles I. Shortly afterwards, when Parliament tried Laud for high treason, this porch was cited as evidence of excessive Catholicism. Laud was finally executed at the height of the Civil War in 1644.

The church's interior is disappointingly mundane, though the carved poppy heads on the choir stalls are of some historical interest: the tips were brusquely squared off when a platform was installed here in 1555 to stage the heresy trial of Cranmer, Latimer and Ridley, the "Oxford Martyrs" (see p.47). The church's other diversion is its **tower** (same hours; £3): as recompense for climbing 127 steps, you gain stupendous views over Radcliffe Square, the spires of All Souls and much of central Oxford.

_7_## South to Merton Street

The hulking presence of the **Rhodes Building**, a 1911 bequest to Oriel College by diamond tycoon Cecil Rhodes (1853–1902), overshadows the High Street directly opposite St Mary's. Duck down Oriel Street, on its right (western) flank, to reach the entrance to **Oriel College** on Oriel Square (generally groups only; ☏01865 276555, ⊛www.oriel.ox.ac.uk), with a beautiful seventeenth-century Jacobean-Gothic Front Quad and a small, narrow chapel which includes some contemporary stained glass and an oratory dedicated to Cardinal Newman (1801–1890), a leading figure in the Oxford Movement (see p.48).

Oriel Square ends on the corner with medieval **Merton Street**, still cobbled and offering one of Oxford's most picturesque views. Just past the corner on the right is the gateway to **Corpus Christi College** (daily 1.30–4.30pm; free; ☏01865 276700, ⊛www.ccc.ox.ac.uk), smaller than most, with a paved Front Quad focused on a pillared sundial of 1581 topped by a gilded pelican.

Merton College

A few metres further along Merton Street rise the buildings of **Merton College** (Mon–Fri 2–5pm, Sat & Sun 10am–5pm; £2; ☏01865 276310, ⊛www.merton.ox.ac.uk), historically the city's most important college. Balliol and University colleges may have been founded earlier, but it was Merton – established in 1264 by Thomas de Merton, Lord Chancellor and the bishop of Rochester – which set the model for colleges in both Oxford and Cambridge, being the first to gather its students and tutors together in one place. Furthermore, Merton retains a good deal of its original medieval architecture.

Entry is via the fifteenth-century **gatehouse**, above which a stone-carved panel shows Walter de Merton kneeling before the "Book with Seven Seals" of Revelation, observed by a lamb, unicorn, woodland animals and John the Baptist. The cobbled **Front Quad** feels rather disordered; opposite stands the **hall**, rebuilt by George Gilbert Scott but retaining its ornate thirteenth-century door. Head right down a narrow passage to reach the compact but charming **Mob Quad**, Oxford's oldest (completed in 1378), ringed by mullioned windows and Gothic doorways: the layout is familiar but developed here organically, with buildings added over the course of a century to form an enclosed space.

Merton's atmospheric **library**, on the south side of Mob Quad, uniquely permits public access (usually on guided tours only). Completed in the 1370s, it was the first library in England to store books upright on shelves, rather than in piles. Much of the woodwork, including the panelling, screens and bookcases, dates from the Tudor period, but some fittings are original.

On the north side of Mob Quad, an archway leads through to the **chapel**, which dates from 1290. Walter de Merton's intention was that this hugely grand space would form merely the choir and transepts for a much larger, naved church; standing here today, the scale of that imagined building boggles the mind. Funds ran out before his vision could be realised, and the truncated T-shaped form which survives served as the model for all future college chapels. The antechapels house numerous monuments to benefactors, including Thomas Bodley, founder of the Bodleian, whose funerary plaque shows him surrounded, oddly, by ungainly-looking allegorical ladies. The chapel's stained glass is largely original

x_7_OXFORD | The City

77_7_77

thirteenth-century work; the stunning east window, with seven lancets and a rose, is especially beautiful.

From the Front Quad, wander south into the seventeenth-century **Fellows' Quad**, venue for the self-consciously weird **Merton Time Ceremony**. On the last Sunday in October, at exactly 2am – the moment when the clocks go back one hour, marking the end of British Summer Time – college members, in full gowned regalia, link arms and walk backwards around the quad, drinking port and toasting "good old times". The ceremony ends after an hour, at 2am Greenwich Mean Time.

Around Merton College

From Merton College, narrow **Magpie Lane** cuts north to the High Street. To the east on Merton Street, alongside the medieval Postmasters' Hall, gates on the left give access to Merton's **Real Tennis Court**, an indoor space for playing this ancestor of lawn tennis – still with racquets and a net, but using a solid ball and featuring squash-like rebounds off the interior walls. You might be lucky and catch a game in progress.

Another pleasant walk begins at the wrought-iron gates on the south side of Merton Street, just past the chapel tower: these give access (daylight hours only) to **Merton Grove**, a footpath – punctuated by a turnstile – which opens onto expansive views across Christ Church Meadow to the tree-lined riverbanks beyond.

From here, turn left (east) to follow **Dead Man's Walk** beside the walls of Merton, with broad views on your right across the lawns of Merton Field; this was originally the funerary route to Oxford's Jewish cemetery, which fell into disrepair after the expulsion of the Jews from England in 1290 and was refounded in the seventeenth century as a botanic garden (see below). Alternatively, head straight on (south) to meet the grand **Broad Walk**, which gives access left to the banks of the River Cherwell and right to the lovely, tree-shaded **New Walk**, progressing further south to the Thames.

Bounded by a graceful curve of the Cherwell, the university's **Botanic Garden** (daily 9am–6pm; March, April, Sept & Oct closes 5pm; Nov–Feb closes 4.30pm; £3.50, free Nov–Feb Mon–Fri only; ⓦwww.botanic-garden.ox.ac.uk) is the oldest of its kind in England, established in 1621. Still enclosed by its original high wall, it comprises several different zones, from a lily pond, a bog garden and a rock garden through to borders of bearded irises and variegated plants. There are also six large **glasshouses** housing tropical and carnivorous species.

In summer, a walk along the banks of Cherwell here is lovely, with punts passing and friends picnicking. It's a short stroll out along Rose Lane onto the High Street, with Magdalen College directly opposite.

Magdalen College

Its stone buildings clustering together on the north side of the High Street, and its chunky sixteenth-century bell tower dominating the views over this part of town, **Magdalen College** (pronounced *mawdlin*; daily: July–Sept noon–7pm, rest of year 1–6pm or dusk; £4.50; ⓣ01865 276000, ⓦwww.magd.ox.ac.uk) sprawls across a large site, also taking in a swathe of riverside meadow. Founded in 1458 by William Waynflete, bishop of Winchester, it served during the Civil War as a fortified redoubt for Royalist troops – and is the focus for Oxford's **May Day** festivities. Choristers sing Latin hymns from the top of the bell tower at 6am every May 1, to the accompaniment down below of Morris dancing, much revelry and, once Magdalen Bridge reopens to traffic, the occasional splash as reckless types pursue the tradition of jumping off – a ten-metre drop into a metre or so of water. Hospitalizations are common.

Taking to the water

Punting is a favourite summer pastime among both students and visitors, but handling a **punt** – a flat-bottomed boat ideal for the shallow waters of the Thames and Cherwell – requires some practice. The punt is propelled and steered with a long pole, which beginners inevitably get stuck in riverbed mud: if this happens, let go of it and paddle back, otherwise you're likely to be dragged overboard. The Cherwell, though narrower than the Thames and therefore trickier to navigate, provides more opportunities for pulling to the bank for a picnic, an essential part of the punting experience.

There are two central **boat rental** places: Magdalen Bridge boathouse (☏01865 202643, ⓦwww.oxfordpunting.co.uk), beside the Cherwell at the east end of the High Street; and Salter's Steamers (☏01865 243421, ⓦwww.salterssteamers.co.uk) at Folly Bridge, south of Christ Church. Opening times vary: call for details, or try and arrive early (around 10am) to avoid the queues which build up on sunny summer afternoons. At either expect **to pay** about £16–20 per hour plus a deposit of about £50; ID is required. Punts can take a maximum of five people: four sitting and one punting. Both boathouses also rent out **chauffeured punts** (about £50–60/hr) and cheaper **pedaloes**. Another option is the Cherwell Boathouse (☏01865 515978, ⓦwww.cherwellboathouse.co.uk), a bit further out – north of the centre on Bardwell Road – but in a lovely location and also slightly cheaper.

Alternatively, Salters Steamers runs **passenger boats** along the Thames from Folly Bridge downstream to Abingdon, about eight miles south, between late May and late September. There are two boats daily in each direction; the return trip takes four hours and costs £16.40. Oxford River Cruises (☏0845 226 9396, ⓦwww.oxfordriver cruises.com), based at the *Perch Inn* on Binsey Lane, a mile or so northwest of the rail station, have punts and pedaloes but are a better bet for their short cruises (July–Sept only) upstream on the Thames: prices and schedules for their "lunchtime picnic trips" and "afternoon river experiences" – as well as occasional longer jaunts – are given online.

From the college's High Street entrance, you emerge into **St John's Quad**, named for the twelfth-century hospital of St John the Baptist which occupied the site: high on the right-hand wall is a pulpit from which a sermon is preached every June 24, John's feast day. Below it, a narrow arch gives into the triangular **Chaplain's Quad**, at the base of the soaring bell tower. Back in St John's Quad, turn right and right again to discover the door into the **chapel**, which has a handsome reredos, though you have to admire it through the windows of an ungainly stone screen. The adjacent fifteenth-century **cloisters**, perhaps the finest in Oxford, are adorned by standing figures, some biblical and others folkloric, most notably a tribe of grotesques. At the southeastern corner, stairs rise to the **hall**, where two Magdalen alumni confront each other in silence: a bust of Lord Denning above the fireplace, directly opposite another of Oscar Wilde.

Passages on the opposite (northern) side of the cloisters face the Neoclassical **New Building**, completed in 1733 to be part of a grand new quad which never materialized. To the left, a fence bars access to the **Grove**, Magdalen's own deer park – you might spot the sixty-strong herd roaming – while to the right a little bridge over the River Cherwell connects with **Addison's Walk**, a lovely footpath which encircles a water meadow; rare wild snake's-head fritillaries flower here in spring and the deer often graze this way during the summer and autumn. In the far (northeastern) corner, cross two wooden bridges to reach the secluded **Fellow's Garden**.

West along the High Street

Oxford's **High Street** – universally abbreviated to "The High" – runs in a graceful curve west from Magdalen Bridge to Carfax, lined with buildings of interest all the way along, and marking a transition from "gown", at its western end, to "town" around Carfax. The roadway's new, ugly coating of black asphalt detracts from the view only slightly.

Past Magdalen's bell tower, traffic is diverted north up Longwall Street; this was where the east gate of the city stood until its demolition in 1772. Just past the ornate **Examination Schools** building on the left – especially busy in June, when students sit their exams here dressed in the obligatory "subfusc" garb of dark suit, white shirt and gown – two cafés face each other across the street, both claiming to be **England's oldest coffee house**. On the left, the *Grand Café* (see p.81) occupies the site of a coffee house opened by a Lebanese Jew named Jacob in or just after 1650; opposite, the *Queen's Lane Coffee House* stands where a Syrian Jew named Cirques Jobson launched a competing enterprise at roughly the same time. Either way, Oxford's gentlefolk were drinking coffee – and also hot chocolate – well ahead of London.

Queen's Lane, to the right, makes for an attractive detour: a short way up on the right is the entrance to **St Edmund Hall** (no set hours; free; ℡01865 279000, Ⓦwww.seh.ox.ac.uk). Though a fully-fledged college only since 1957, "Teddy Hall" can trace its history back to the thirteenth century: it's the only survivor of the medieval halls which predated the formation of colleges. Its attractive sixteenth-century Front Quad, centred on an ancient well, leads through to **St Peter-in-the-East**, originally Saxon, now deconsecrated to serve as the college library. The only part open to the public is its vast **crypt** (ask about access at the porter's lodge), but the yew-shaded churchyard is one of the loveliest hideaways in central Oxford. Queen's Lane continues north to New College (see p.65) and Catte Street.

Queen's and University colleges

Beside Queen's Lane, and entered from the High Street, stands **Queen's College** (no set hours; ℡01865 279120, Ⓦwww.queens.ox.ac.uk), whose handsome Baroque buildings cut an impressive dash. Erected in a single period (1682–1765), Queen's benefited from the skills of several talented architects, most notably Wren and Hawksmoor. Crossing straight across its expansive, cloistered **Front Quad** leads to the entrance of the most diverting building, the unusually spacious **chapel**, designed – or at least influenced – by Wren, with a ceiling filled by cherubs amid dense foliage.

Continuing west on this (north) side of the High brings you to All Souls College (see p.67) and St Mary the Virgin. Opposite, the long facade and twin gateway towers of **University College** (no set hours; ℡01865 276602, Ⓦwww .univ.ox.ac.uk) rise above the south side of the High. "Univ" spuriously claims Alfred the Great as its founder, but – that aside – it is still Oxford's oldest college, endowed in 1249. Nothing, though, remains from that period. The attractive Jacobean-Gothic buildings around the **Main Quad** conceal, in the northeastern corner, a shrine-like domed chamber housing a white marble sculpture of **Shelley**, who was expelled from Univ in 1811 for writing a pamphlet entitled *The Necessity of Atheism*. Guilt later induced the college to accept a memorial: Edward Onslow Ford's sculpture of the limp body of the poet (who drowned in Italy in 1822), borne by winged lions and mourned by the Muse of Poetry shows pathos or melodrama, depending on your taste.

Continue left (west) along this side of the High, past the Rhodes Building (see p.68) to the University of Oxford Shop (Ⓦwww.oushop.com), in order to admire the splendid Victorian frontage of Brasenose College directly opposite – gables, oriel windows, gate-tower, battlements and all.

A few metres further west, at the end of the High Street, is **Carfax**.

Turl Street

Leading north between the High Street and Broad Street, **Turl Street** – named for a long-demolished twirling turnstile gate at its northern end, designed to keep cattle out of the town – is one of Oxford's most atmospheric streets. Modest, narrow and pedestrianized, shaded at its northern end by a huge chestnut tree, it nonetheless hums with activity, straddling as it does "town" and "gown" – shoppers at the Covered Market mixing with students and dons passing between the street's three colleges: Lincoln, Jesus and Exeter.

Marking the corner with the High, the *Mitre* is one of Oxford's oldest inns, in existence for more than 700 years, chiefly as a coaching inn owned by nearby Lincoln College. The current incarnation dates from around 1630, now, sadly, run by an unimaginative restaurant chain: step into the old bar for a swift half, but step out again before you get hungry.

Opposite rises the distinctive circular spired tower of All Saints Church, rebuilt after the original collapsed in 1700. The church, now deconsecrated, serves as the library for **Lincoln College** (Mon–Fri 2–5pm, Sat & Sun 11am–5pm; free; ℡01865 279800, ⓦwww.linc.ox.ac.uk), founded in 1427 and presenting a charming, ivy-clad Front Quad that has remained largely untouched since then. Its chapel sports unusual enamelled – rather than stained – glass and a host of richly carved woodwork. Lincoln backs directly onto Brasenose; the single door between the two colleges is opened only once a year, at noon on Ascension Day, when members of Brasenose are invited through to sup free beer at Lincoln's expense, in commemoration of some half-remembered inter-collegiate slight. Long ago, Lincoln took to tainting the ale with ivy, Brasenose say in order to discourage excessive consumption, but Lincoln maintain merely as continuance of a brewing tradition – before hops arrived in England – which used herbs such as ground ivy as a flavouring agent. Brasenose partakes regardless.

Diagonally opposite Lincoln, **Jesus College** (daily 2–4.30pm; free; ℡01865 279700, ⓦwww.jesus.ox.ac.uk), makes for an attractive stop: its two small, sixteenth-century quads are gentle on the eye and the atmospheric hall sports portraits of Elizabeth I – founder of the college in 1571 – and T.E. Lawrence ("of Arabia"), Jesus's most famous alumnus. Across the road stands **Exeter College** (daily 2–5pm; free; ℡01865 279600, ⓦwww.exeter.ox.ac.uk), another medieval foundation, with an elaborate Gothic Revival chapel conceived by Gilbert Scott in the 1850s. It contains a fine set of **stained-glass windows** illustrating biblical stories – St Paul on the road to Damascus, Samson bringing down the pillars of the Philistine temple – as well as a superb Pre-Raphaelite tapestry, the *Adoration of the*

Covered Market

For refreshment on the hoof – as well as a fascinating glimpse into the everyday life of Oxford away from all the pomp and history of the colleges – drop into the **Covered Market** (Mon–Sat 9am–5.30pm, Sun 10am–4pm), wedged between High Street, Turl Street and Market Street. Opened in 1774, it remains full of atmosphere, home to butchers, bakers, fishmongers, greengrocers and cheese sellers as well as a welter of excellent cafés, patisseries and even some clothes boutiques and shoe shops. Whatever you do, don't miss the *Ben's Cookies* stall (reviewed on p.81), where sensational cookies are baked continuously throughout the day and sold by weight.

Magi, a collaboration between William Morris and Edward Burne-Jones, both former students.

Broad Street, which abuts Turl Street, is covered on p.61.

Carfax and around

At the western end of the High Street, the busy **Carfax** crossroads is a fulcrum, where chiefly "gown" architecture to the east is balanced by the distinctly "town" atmosphere of Cornmarket and Queen Street to the west. This has been a cross-roads for more than a thousand years: roads from north, south, east and west met here in Saxon times, and the name "Carfax" derives from the Latin *quadrifurcus* ("four-forked"). The junction is overlooked by an interesting remnant of the medieval town, a square thirteenth-century **tower**, adorned by a pair of clocktower jacks, which is all that remains of St Martin's church, demolished in 1896 to ease traffic access. You can **climb** it (daily 10am–5.30pm, winter closes 3pm; £2.20) for wide views over the centre, though other vantage points – principally St Mary's (see p.67) – have the edge.

Oxford's main pedestrian shopping street, **Cornmarket** (see p.77), storms its way north of Carfax, while **Queen Street** runs west of Carfax to Oxford Castle, covered on p.77.

Museum of Oxford

Spreading **south of Carfax** down St Aldates, Oxford's **Town Hall**, an ostenta-tious Victorian confection, reflects a municipal determination not to be overwhelmed by the university. On its south side, a staircase gives access to the fine **Museum of Oxford** (Tues–Sat 10am–5pm; free; ⓦ www.museumofoxford.org .uk) – often ignored, though it does a great job of telling the history of the city. Start downstairs with displays on prehistory and the Roman and Saxon eras, including a grave slab tentatively identified as that of St Frideswide (see p.47) and the city's 1191 charter. Reconstructions of period interiors, such as the parlour of a sixteenth-century inn, are particularly absorbing. The ground-level galleries cover intricate exhibits on Victorian Oxford, including a reconstruction of a Jericho kitchen of the 1880s, and take the story through to the rise of twentieth-century industry, from cars to marmalade. Well worth an hour or two.

A little south of the museum, in plain view, rises the squat Tom Tower of Christ Church College – see p.74 for details – while beside the museum, Blue Boar Street leads to what is often claimed as **Oxford's oldest pub**, *The Bear*, recorded as early as 1242, though its current incarnation dates from the seventeenth century. We review it on p.85.

Modern Art Oxford and Pembroke College

Opposite the Museum of Oxford, the Victorian main post office leads to Pembroke Street, where you'll find the outstanding **Modern Art Oxford** gallery (Tues & Wed 10am–5pm, Thurs–Sat 10am–7pm, Sun noon–5pm; free; ⓦ www .modernartoxford.org.uk), hosting an excellent programme of temporary exhibi-tions. Accessed from tree-shaded Pembroke Square, alongside the Victorian church of St Aldates, **Pembroke College** (no set hours; free; ⓣ 01865 276444, ⓦ www.pmb.ox.ac.uk) is little-visited, but was eulogized by John Betjeman in his verse autobiography *Summoned by Bells* (1960):

> How empty, creeper-grown and odd
> Seems lonely Pembroke's second quad

Still, when I see it, do I wonder why
That college so polite and shy
Should have more character than Queen's
Or Univ, splendid in the High.

If Betjeman's words appeal, you'll enjoy the atmosphere of Pembroke's seventeenth- and eighteenth-century buildings. Make your way through a passage from that "second quad" (Chapel Quad) into the New Quad, formed in 1962 when adjacent Beef Lane was closed off and a row of houses incorporated into the college grounds.

Christ Church College

Fronting St Aldates south of Carfax is the main facade of **Christ Church College** (Mon–Sat 9am–5pm, Sun 2–5pm; £6; ☏01865 276492, ⓦ www.chch.ox.ac.uk), whose distinctive Tom Tower lords it over the main entrance of what is Oxford's largest and most prestigious college. Visitor access, though, is further south, a signed five-minute walk away – continue down St Aldates, turn left through the tiny War Memorial Gardens and onto **Broad Walk**, a tree-lined path which leads across **Christ Church Meadow** (see p.76 for more). You'll see the college entrance on the left.

Albert Einstein and no fewer than thirteen British prime ministers were educated at Christ Church and the college also claims the distinction of having been founded three times, first by Cardinal Wolsey in 1525, then by Henry VIII after the cardinal's fall from favour and finally, after the Reformation – when the second college was suppressed – in 1545, when it assumed its present name. Overlooking the confluence of the Thames and the Cherwell, Christ Church occupies the site of the eighth-century priory founded by St Frideswide, which was destroyed by Danish invaders in 1002 and refounded by the Augustinians. The college chapel, uniquely, is also the cathedral for the Oxford diocese.

In addition to the standard self-guided itinerary described below, you could book ahead with the college for a **"Behind the Scenes Tour"**, taking in areas normally off-limits to visitors. These cost £2 per person on top of the standard admission fee, with a minimum charge of £25 per tour.

Tom Quad and around

Entering the college from the south, through the Victorian Gothic **Meadow Building**, the numbered trail leads you through to the tranquil, fifteenth-century **cloister**, part-demolished by Wolsey to clear space for his grand new quad (see below). Move on to one of Oxford's most impressive spaces, the hall **staircase**, laid

---

Oxford time

One of the oddest of Oxford's many idiosyncrasies is that it keeps its own **time**. Before the railways most British towns followed their own local time, but the adoption of London time as the national standard in the 1840s and 1850s erased the differences – barring Oxford. Located just over one degree of longitude west of the Greenwich Meridian, the city is officially 5 minutes and 2 seconds behind London time. To this day, Christ Church College's "Great Tom" bell rings out every night at 9.05pm (it tolls 101 times, to mark the number of students at the college's foundation), and all services in the Christ Church cathedral begin five minutes after the advertised time. Lewis Carroll adopted the oddity into his *Alice* books: the White Rabbit (who was modelled on the contemporary Dean of Christ Church) was perpetually late despite always checking his pocket-watch – presumably because it was set to Oxford time.

out in the 1820s beneath a stupendous fan-vaulted ceiling installed in 1640. A door on the right has the words "No Peel" studded into it – student political graffiti from 1829, objecting to the plans of Home Secretary (and Christ Church alumnus) Sir Robert Peel for reform of anti-Catholic laws.

Head up to the **Hall**, the largest and grandest college refectory in Oxford – famously featuring as Hogwarts Hall in the *Harry Potter* films – its three long tables, seating about 250, swathed by dark wood panelling beneath a superb hammerbeam roof. Charles I held court here when the Parliamentarians were in control of London. It's a hugely atmospheric space, hung with portraits of past scholars by a roll-call of well-known artists, including Reynolds, Gainsborough and Millais. Lewis Carroll, author of *Alice's Adventures in Wonderland* (who, under his real name **Charles Dodgson**, was a mathematics tutor at Christ Church), is commemorated with a portrait by the door; images of characters from his books are set into the fifth stained-glass window on the left, and as you pass the fireplaces you'll see long-necked figures flanking the grates, looking remarkably similar to how Alice ended up after she sampled the hookah-smoking caterpillar's mushroom.

From here, it's a short step out to the southeastern corner of the striking **Tom Quad**, at eighty-odd metres square the largest in Oxford, so large in fact that the Royalists penned up their mobile larder of cattle here during the Civil War. The quad's soft, honey-coloured stone makes a harmonious whole, but it was actually built in two main phases, with the southern side dating back to Wolsey, the north finally finished in the 1660s. Opposite – and fronting onto St Aldates – rises **Tom Tower**, added by Christopher Wren in 1681 to house the seven-ton "Great Tom" bell, named for Thomas Becket, which was recovered from Osney Abbey near Oxford during the Dissolution.

Oxford Cathedral

From Tom Quad, the trail directs you to the right, to reach the college chapel, otherwise known as **Oxford Cathedral**. The Saxon priory of St Frideswide, located on this site, was rebuilt in the twelfth century but suppressed in 1524; its church survived and was granted cathedral status soon afterwards by Henry VIII, during his ecclesiastical reforms following the break with Rome.

Architecturally, it's unusually discordant, with all sorts of bits and bobs from different periods – not helped by the fact that Wolsey demolished the west end to make space for Tom Quad. The dominant feature is the sturdy circular columns and rounded arches of the Normans, but there are also early Gothic pointed arches and the chancel ceiling is a particularly fine example of fifteenth-century stone vaulting. The battered **shrine of St Frideswide**, in the Latin Chapel – to the far left (northeast) of the entrance – was destroyed during the Dissolution, but the pieces were found down an old well and gamely assembled by the Victorians. Today, it exhibits some of the earliest natural foliage in English sculpture, a splendid filigree of leaves dating from around 1290. The shrine is overlooked by an equally rare, two-storey, stone and timber **watching loft**, from where custodians would keep a close eye on the tomb of the saint. Also here is a deeply coloured **stained–glass window** by Edward Burne-Jones, crammed with biblical bodies; it was completed in 1858, long before Jones got into his Pre-Raphaelite stride, but there are three examples from his later period along the rest of the back of the chancel, with the **St Catherine Window**, in the right-hand corner of the church, being the finest. A stained-glass image of the martyrdom of Thomas Becket survives nearby, created in 1320 and defaced during the Reformation, though still discernible: the saint kneels while his four knightly killers lurk behind.

Christ Church Picture Gallery

The trail returns to lead around two sides of the cloister and the length of Tom Quad before turning right into **Peckwater Quad**, dominated by the whopping Neoclassical library. A few paces more and you're standing on the cobbles of the pocket-sized **Canterbury Quad**; through a gateway ahead stands Oriel Square, with Merton College (see p.68) just beyond, or you could return through Christ Church grounds to the Meadow Building to exit onto St Aldates or to stroll in Christ Church Meadow.

On one side of Canterbury Quad – and also accessible directly from the Oriel Square gate – is the **Christ Church Picture Gallery** (May–Sept Mon–Sat 10.30am–5pm, Sun 2–5pm; Oct–April Mon–Sat 10.30am–1pm & 2–4.30pm; £3, or £1.50 if you show your Christ Church admission ticket; ⓦ www.chch.ox.ac.uk/gallery). Designed in 1968 behind the original frontage, it displays a surprisingly impressive array of works by many of Italy's finest artists from the fifteenth to eighteenth centuries, including Veronese and Filippino Lippi. There's also a good showing by the Flemish and Dutch – Van Dyck, Frans Hals and so forth. The gallery's collection of Old Master drawings is world-class, taking in examples by Leonardo, Michelangelo, Raphael and Rubens, displayed in temporary, themed exhibitions.

South to Folly Bridge

From the southern entrance to Christ Church College, the **Broad Walk** footpath runs east and west along the edge of **Christ Church Meadow**. Popular with strollers, the meadow fills in the tapering gap between the rivers Cherwell and Thames and offers lovely views over the sports pitch of Merton Field and back to the towers of both Christ Church and Merton colleges. Head east along Broad Walk towards the Cherwell, or cut south along the similarly tree-lined (and perhaps prettier) **New Walk** to reach the Thames. Partway along Broad Walk, **Merton Grove** (see p.69) heads north to reach Merton Street, Dead Man's Walk and the Botanic Garden.

Otherwise, back out on St Aldates, more or less opposite the War Memorial Gardens stands the quaint little **Alice's Shop** at no. 83 (daily 9.30am–6.30pm; Sept–June 10.30am–5pm; ⓦ www.aliceinwonderlandshop.co.uk), now crammed full of Alice souvenirs but in Victorian times a sweet-shop, known to Lewis Carroll; it makes an appearance in *Through the Looking-Glass*, staffed by a spectacled sheep, and described by Alice as "the queerest shop I ever saw!"

Opposite, signposted within the university's Faculty of Music, you'll find the **Bate Collection of Musical Instruments** (Mon–Fri 2–5pm; free; ⓦ www.bate .ox.ac.uk), displaying over a thousand instruments of all kinds and styles, including the earliest surviving double-keyboard harpsichord, made in 1700, and a Javanese gamelan.

Continue south down St Aldates to reach **Folly Bridge** over the Thames, likely location for the Saxon-era oxen ford which gave the city its name. The current bridge, busy with traffic, is nineteenth-century; just to one side stand the famous *Head of the River* pub and a boat-rental station. This stretch of river is where many

Name your river

Two rivers embrace Oxford, meeting at a point just south of the city centre. To the west is the **Thames**, en route from its Cotswolds source to London. Most maps rename the stretch of the river within Oxford as the "Thames or **Isis**", but the latter name is an affectation stemming from disdain for Celtic terminology (*tamesas* means "dark water"). Sixteenth-century scholars thought to instil more lofty Classical associations by subtly adapting part of the old name to evoke the Greco-Roman goddess Isis; it was also about this time that someone decided to stick a Greek-looking "h" into the Celtic name for the river, thus creating "Thames". The machinations stuck, though in truth few Oxford locals today, other than university types, use the term Isis; it's become a cartographer's fancy.

Oxford's other river, to the east, is the **Cherwell**, whose name, inexplicably, is pronounced by a certain sector of society as "charwell".

---

college **rowing** teams practise (ⓦ www.ourcs.org.uk): the college boathouses are a short way south at the confluence of the two rivers, venue for both the Torpids races in February or March and the more prestigious Summer Eights, in late May.

Oxford Castle

From the base of Carfax tower, shop-heavy **Queen Street** bustles westwards past the bland, paved **Bonn Square**, named for Oxford's twin city in Germany; this was once the graveyard of the medieval St Peter-le-Bailey church and much controversy surrounded its 2008 redevelopment, which saw trees felled and skeletons reburied. Opposite looms the 1970s-vintage **Westgate shopping centre**, a none-too-pretty lump.

Alongside, on New Road, is the former site of **Oxford Castle**, a classic motte-and-bailey fortress dating from 1071. In December 1142 it was besieged by King Stephen, who had usurped the throne after the death of Henry I; Henry's daughter Matilda only escaped by dressing in white as camouflage against the snow and fleeing over the frozen river. The motte (mound) survives, though the buildings atop it were demolished after the Civil War. In later centuries a cluster of stern Victorian edifices beside the mound served chiefly as Oxford's prison. The prison was decommissioned in 1996; today, the restored complex (ⓦ www .oxfordcastle.com) takes in shops and restaurants gathered around the luxurious *Malmaison* hotel (see p.56), which occupies the old prison buildings.

Through a passage to the right of the hotel – and also accessed through a gate (daily 9am–6pm) on Tidmarsh Lane – is the excellent heritage centre **Oxford Castle Unlocked** (daily 10am–5pm) offering memorable forty-minute **guided tours** (every 20min, last at 4.20pm; £7.75; ⓦ www.oxfordcastleunlocked.co.uk), during which costumed warders lead you up the Saxon-era **St George's Tower**, show you medieval prison cells and take you down into the Romanesque crypt beneath **St George's Chapel**, telling tales of wars, executions and hauntings along the way.

North of Carfax

Storming north of Carfax, **Cornmarket** is now a busy pedestrianized shopping strip lined with familiar high-street stores. There's precious little here to fire the imagination – the *Crown Tavern*, once at 3 Cornmarket (not to be confused with the current *Crown* across the road, beside *McDonald's*), was where William Shakespeare lodged on his regular visits to Oxford, but it has long since vanished. Further north on the left, pleasant **St Michael's Street** is the location of the

Oxford Union (no public access), the university debating society, where scores of budding politicians have flexed their oratorical muscles, while directly opposite on the corner of **Ship Street** is a splendid old wood-framed building, probably fifteenth-century; once the *Ship Inn* it is now occupied by a mobile phone outlet and a sandwich bar.

On the same side stands **St Michael-at-the-Northgate**, a church recorded in the Domesday Book, with a late fourteenth-century font where Shakespeare's godson was baptized in 1606. The church's Saxon **tower** (daily 10.30am–5pm, Nov–March closes 4pm; £2; Ⓦwww.smng.org.uk), built in 1050, is Oxford's oldest surviving building; as well as rooftop views you can see the door of the cell in which Latimer, Ridley and Cranmer were imprisoned (for more, see p.47) and a modest treasury, including an eleventh-century sheela-na-gig.

The top of Cornmarket is central Oxford's busiest corner, streets clogged by buses and pavements crammed with shoppers. To the east is **Broad Street** (see p.61), north is truncated **Magdalen Street**, best known for the imposing *Randolph Hotel* (see p.56), while to the west **George Street** fights a path through to **Gloucester Green**, a pedestrianized clearing in the shops which serves partly as the venue for open-air markets (see p.86) and, on one side, as a bus station.

Beside the *Randolph*, the Martyrs' Memorial (see p.63) gazes north up **St Giles**, a broad, tree-lined boulevard with a graceful air about it. On the left, look out for the seventeenth-century *Eagle & Child* pub, favoured haunt of the "Inklings" literary group which included C.S. Lewis and J.R.R. Tolkien; they met here from the 1940s until Lewis's death in 1963. You can pop in to see the old front rooms of the pub (see p.85), which include the fireplace nook where the writers sat to share ideas and discuss their work, now hung with memorabilia.

Opposite, if you can run the gauntlet of crossing St Giles at its widest point, a passage beside the *Lamb & Flag* pub cuts east to Keble College and the University Museum of Natural History (see opposite).

St John's College

Occupying splendid buildings on the east side of St Giles, **St John's College** (daily 1–5pm or dusk; free; ☎01865 277300, Ⓦwww.sjc.ox.ac.uk) is reputedly the richest in Oxford: it is said that one could walk from St John's College Oxford to St John's College Cambridge – perhaps 80 or 90 miles – and remain on St John's-owned land the whole distance. The college was founded in 1555 on the site of a pre-existing Cistercian monastery; the statue of St Bernard above the gatehouse and much of the splendid **Front Quad** date from the earlier, fifteenth-century foundation. The hall, on the left of Front Quad, is not open to visitors, and the chapel, alongside, was ruined with Victorian "improvements", but through the passage between them lies **North Quad**, overlooked by the intriguing, Modernist **Beehive Building** of 1960, named for its hexagonal bedrooms. From Front Quad, a fan-vaulted passage opposite the gatehouse leads to the glorious Italianate Renaissance architecture of **Canterbury Quad**, featuring scalloped niches holding bronze statues of Charles I and, opposite, his wife Henrietta Maria. Straight ahead, another passage ducks through to the extensive college **gardens**.

Ashmolean Museum

Occupying a mammoth Neoclassical building on the corner of St Giles and Beaumont Street, opposite the *Randolph Hotel*, the **Ashmolean Museum** (Tues–Sun 10am–6pm; free; Ⓦwww.ashmolean.org) grew from the collections of the magpie-like **John Tradescant**, gardener to Charles I and an energetic traveller. During his wanderings, Tradescant built up a huge assortment of artefacts and natural specimens, which became known as Tradescant's Ark. He bequeathed everything to his friend and sponsor, the lawyer Elias Ashmole, who in turn gave it to the university. Today the Ashmolean possesses a vast and far-reaching collection, second in the country only to the British Museum in London, and showcased to superb effect in bright, uncluttered contemporary galleries. Allow at least half a day to scratch the surface, a full day (or more) to dig a little deeper.

The **Egyptian** rooms are not to be missed: in addition to well-preserved mummies and sarcophagi, there are unusual frescoes, rare textiles from the Roman and Byzantine periods and several fine examples of relief carving, such as those on the Taharqa shrine. Look out, too, for the superb Islamic ceramics in the **Islamic art** collection, while the **Chinese art** section boasts some remarkable early Chinese pottery with the simple monochrome pots of the Sung dynasty (960–1279) looking surprisingly modern. The archeologist Arthur Evans had close ties with the museum and he gifted it a stunning collection of **Minoan** finds from his years working at Knossos in Crete (1900–06): pride of place goes to the storage jars, sumptuously decorated with sea creatures and marine plants. A further highlight is the extraordinary **Alfred Jewel**, a tiny gold, enamel and rock crystal piece of uncertain purpose. The inscription translates as "Alfred ordered me to be made" – almost certainly a reference to King Alfred the Great.

The museum is very strong on **European art**. Amongst the **Italian** works, watch out for Piero di Cosimo's *Forest Fire* and Paolo Uccello's *Hunt in the Forest*, though Tintoretto, Veronese and Bellini feature prominently as well. **French paintings** make a strong showing too, with works by Pissarro, Monet, Manet and Renoir hanging alongside Cézanne and Bonnard, and there's a representative selection of eighteenth- and nineteenth-century **British artists**: Samuel Palmer's visionary paintings run rings around the rest, though there are lashings of Pre-Raphaelite stuff from Rossetti and Holman Hunt to assorted cohorts.

Finally, don't miss the basement display of treasures from **Tradescant's Ark**. A particular highlight is **Powhatan's mantle**, a handsome deerskin wall-hanging which belonged to the father of Pocahontas. Other items down here with the wow factor include Guy Fawkes' lantern, Elizabeth I's gloves and the death mask of Oliver Cromwell.

Further north

From the Ashmolean, it's a brief walk north up St Giles to the *Lamb & Flag* pub, beside which an alley cuts through to the **University Museum of Natural History** (daily 10am–5pm; free; Ⓦwww.oum.ox.ac.uk) on Parks Road. The building, constructed under the guidance of John Ruskin, looks like a cross between a railway station and a church – and the same applies inside, where a High Victorian-Gothic fusion of cast iron and glass features soaring columns and capitals decorated with animal and plant motifs. Exhibits include some impressive dinosaur skeletons, though the museum's natural history displays are outdone by the **Pitt Rivers Museum** (Mon noon–4.30pm, Tues–Sun 10am–4.30pm; free; Ⓦwww.prm.ox.ac.uk), reached through a door at the rear of the ground-floor level. Founded in 1884 from the bequest of Grenadier Guard-turned-archeologist Augustus Henry Lane Fox Pitt Rivers, this is one of the world's finest ethnographic museums and an extraordinary relic of the Victorian age, arranged like an exotic junk shop with each intricately crammed cabinet labelled meticulously by hand. The exhibits were brought to England by, amongst others, Captain Cook, and range from totem poles and mummified crocodiles to African fetishes and gruesome shrunken heads.

Opposite the museums, you can't miss **Keble College** (daily 2–5pm; free; Ⓣ01865 272727, Ⓦwww.keble.ox.ac.uk) – it looks like an overgrown gingerbread house. The college was founded in 1870, in memory of Tractarian cleric John Keble. Its architect, William Butterfield, has bequeathed a *tour-de-force* of Gothic Revival, complete with turrets, pinnacles, ornamental chimney clusters, steeply pitched gables – the whole nine yards, done not in gentle Oxford stone but in vivid red brick, interspersed with polychromatic patterning in decorative white and blue brick. It tends to evoke strong reactions. Venture through to the main **Liddon Quad**; on the right looms the gigantic **chapel**, covered rather exhaustingly with ornament both inside and out, and hosting in a side-chapel Holman Hunt's Pre-Raphaelite masterpiece *The Light of the World*.

From Keble, the long Parks Road heads south back into the centre; just before you reach Broad Street (see p.61), pop into the harmonious quads of **Wadham College** (daily 1–4.15pm; free; ☎01865 277900, Ⓦwww.wadham.ox.ac.uk) on the left, built in the 1610s and virtually unchanged since.

Jericho

For a pleasant stroll away from the dreaming spires – and a flavour of workaday residential Oxford to boot – aim for **JERICHO**, just northwest of the centre.

This was Oxford's first suburb, originally little more than a cluster of cottages around a travellers' inn: the origin of the name is uncertain, perhaps deriving from the biblical idea of Jericho as a place on the fringes. As Oxford grew in the nineteenth century, workers arrived to service industries including the canal and a local iron foundry, but it was the **Oxford University Press**, which moved into grand Neoclassical premises on **Great Clarendon Street** in 1830, that spurred development. Hardy characterized the area as a cholera-ridden slum in *Jude the Obscure*. Today, Jericho retains a quite different feel from the city centre – quiet, almost village-like, with a strong community atmosphere, its ragtag population of students and young professionals mixing with local families and old-timers who've been here all their lives.

Walton Street is where the daily dramas are played out, a long, curving thoroughfare of some character, still largely residential. Just past **Ruskin College**, an adult-education centre known for its social activism, Richmond Road on the left leads to the modest **synagogue**. Oxford's Jewish community is unique in Britain for its independence, remaining unaffiliated with any of the national Jewish organizations – and for conducting both conservative Orthodox and liberal Progressive services at the same time in the same building. They publish an excellent online history of the Jews in Oxford, and occasionally run Jewish tours of the city; see Ⓦwww.oxfordjewishheritage.co.uk for details.

Continue along Nelson Street and turn right on Canal Street to dig into the heart of Jericho. Above looms the white campanile of **St Barnabas**, a large church built in 1868 on canalside land newly drained for development. Modern housing here breaks the atmosphere, and the old **Castle Mill boatyard** – which was forcibly closed in 2005, in the face of local protests – has stood derelict since plans to build luxury flats on the site were quashed. Follow lanes back onto Walton Street; the *Jericho Tavern*, on the corner of Jericho Street, stands on the site of the district's original inn. A stroll north leads to an alley on the left giving into **St Sepulchre's cemetery**, opened in 1850 on the site of an abandoned farm as overflow to handle victims of the cholera epidemic. Full since 1945, and now without a chapel, the semi-overgrown graveyard makes for an atmospheric interlude before a return to the buzz of city life – or extend your walk out onto Port Meadow and beyond (see box, p.85). Otherwise stroll back down Walton Street and turn left along **Little Clarendon Street**, one of Oxford's liveliest restaurant strips, which meets Woodstock Road just north of St Giles.

Eating

With so many students and tourists to cater for, Oxford has a wide choice of **places to eat**. Lunchtimes tend to be very busy, especially during the week, though there's no shortage of options – we've listed some of the better **cafés** and delis below, but you'll have no difficulty finding somewhere congenial and affordable for a midday bite. The Covered Market in particular offers rich pickings.

Oxford's **restaurant** scene has skyrocketed recently and now takes in fine-dining restaurants to match those in London (on both quality and price), as well as a diverse range of more affordable outlets for high-quality, seasonal cooking, often using locally sourced ingredients. A diverse palette of ethnic restaurants also helps to keep interest levels high. For the best choice, avoid the city centre and instead stroll either northwest to the engaging district of **Jericho**, where Walton Street and Little Clarendon Street offer a string of pleasant restaurants, or southeast to the **Cowley Road**, buzzing with after-work lounge bars and ethnic food of all kinds.

All places reviewed below are marked on the maps on p.46, p.50 or p.60.

Cafés

Ben's Cookies Covered Market ⓦ www .benscookies.com. Not strictly speaking a café, this hole in the wall – the first outlet in the Ben's Cookies chain – has been churning out the best cookies in Oxford, perhaps England (and some say the world) since 1984, from ginger to peanut butter to triple chocolate chunk. They bake different varieties constantly: it's pot luck what's hot when you turn up. Either way, it's a must-try. Map p.60.

Chocology Covered Market ⓦ www.chocology .co.uk. Sensational hot chocolate in this little indoor café, along with luxury chocs and other sweeties, plus teas and coffees. Map p.60.

George & Davis 55 Little Clarendon St ⓦ www .gdcafe.com. Great café offering everything from (delicious) ice cream to bagels and full breakfasts. The cow mural is good fun too. Also try "brother" establishments *George & Danver* (94 St Aldates, near Carfax) and *George & Delila* (104 Cowley Road). Daily till midnight. Map p.50.

Grand Café 84 High St ⓦ www.thegrandcafe .co.uk. Vies with the *Queen's Lane Coffee House*, directly over the road, for which is older – both opened around 1650. This is the more glamorous of the two, with marble pillars, gold leaf and an Art Deco-style mirrored interior. The food is posh, and not cheap – smoked salmon and scrambled eggs £7, cream tea £7.50 – yet, regrettably, quality is variable. Pop in to be seduced by the surroundings more than the cuisine. Map p.60.

Missing Bean 14 Turl St ⓦ www.the missingbean.co.uk. Plate-glass windows look out onto this pleasant old street, as conversation swirls and reputedly the best coffee in Oxford goes down. A fine, friendly spot. Map p.60.

Mortons 22 Broad St ⓦ www.mortonsatwork.co .uk. Long-standing Oxford café and sandwich bar, easily missed from the street but with upstairs seating (well, a room lined with stools) and a rear garden. All their coffee is Fairtrade, and all their milk is organic. Also at 22 New Inn Hall Street, 39 Little Clarendon Street and the Covered Market. Map p.60.

News Café 1 Ship St. Breakfasts, bagels and daily specials, plus beer and wine in this brisk and efficient café. Plenty of local and international newspapers are on hand too. Daily till 10pm. Map p.60.

Rose 51 High St ⓦ www.the-rose.biz. Lovely independent tearoom with an ethical bent: free-range eggs, organic flour and meat, locally sourced clotted cream. Sociable, lively and pleasant, with the added bonus of fresh-baked scones daily. Closed Mon. Map p.60.

Vaults & Garden Radcliffe Sq ⓦ www.vaultsand garden.com. Occupying the atmospheric stone-vaulted chambers of the university's old congre-gation house, built in 1320 beside the church of St Mary the Virgin, this café serves up good-quality organic, locally sourced wholefood, as well as coffee and cake. A small outside area gazes up at the Radcliffe Camera. Cash only. Map p.60.

Woodstock Road Deli 15 Woodstock Rd ⓦ www.oxfordfinefood.com. A stroll along St Giles lies this fabulous little locals' deli and café (affiliated to the Oxford Cheese Company in the Covered Market), with a range of veggie and vegan salads and mains – all organic, prepared daily. Map p.50.

Restaurants

British

🍴 **Big Bang** 124 Walton St ☎ 01865 511441,
Ⓦ www.thebigbangrestaurants.co.uk.
Friendly, much-loved little independent Jericho
restaurant that concentrates on sausages, serving
"bangers and mash" to die for, gourmet Cumber-
land sausages, wild venison sausages and more
(including veggie options). The style is eclectic:
menus are pasted into antiquarian cloth-bound
novels which the waiters lug around like librarians,
the shabby-chic furniture is mix-and-match, and
there's live jazz in the cellar on Tuesdays. Book for
a table in their lovely upstairs room. Mains £9–12.
Map p.50.

Cherwell Boathouse Bardwell Rd ☎ 01865
552746, Ⓦ www.cherwellboathouse.co.uk. Popular
rustic restaurant on the banks of the River
Cherwell, just north of central Oxford, serving
classic British cuisine – rack of lamb with spring
vegetables, fillet of trout with rainbow chard, and
so forth – alongside an especially highly regarded
wine list. Mains £16–24 – or midweek two-course
set lunch £12.50. Book well ahead. Map p.46.

Door 74 74 Cowley Rd ☎ 01865 203374, Ⓦ www
.door74.co.uk. Relaxed little hideaway in the heart
of the Cowley Road bustle, serving outstanding
seasonal contemporary British cuisine to an appre-
ciative, foodie clientele. The signature dish is their
organic beef burger with onion marmalade (£9), or
you could try dishes such as braised shoulder of
lamb, or semolina gnocchi with roasted veg. Mains
£8–13. Map p.51.

Gee's 61 Banbury Rd ☎ 01865 553540, Ⓦ www
.gees-restaurant.co.uk. A well-established formal
restaurant occupying chic Victorian conservatory
premises in North Oxford. The inventive menu
takes in British seasonal dishes such as asparagus
and locally reared spring lamb, aided by steaks,
fish dishes and more Continental cuisine – lobster
linguine, bouillabaisse, duck confit. Mains £16–24,
though they do a two-course evening set menu for
£23. Book ahead. Live jazz on Sun eve. Map p.46.

Loch Fyne 55 Walton St ☎ 01865 292510,
Ⓦ www.lochfyne.com. Jericho outlet for this highly
regarded nationwide chain of fish and seafood
restaurants, serving a range of ethically sourced
dishes from poached Scottish haddock to Cromer
crab. Steaks and veggie options (such as goat's
cheese with roasted beetroot) add variety. The
interior stretches far back – airy and spacious, with
skylights and smart contemporary styling – and the
bar area is perfect for a light lunch on the go. Most
mains are £12–17; cheaper stand-bys include fish
pie, mussels and chips or salmon fishcakes, all for

under £10. Set menus feature at lunch and on
weekday evenings (Mon–Thurs). Map p.50.

Oxford Retreat 1 Hythe Bridge St ☎ 01865
250309, Ⓦ www.oxfordretreat.com. Independently
owned restaurant in an unusual setting, in the fork
between two busy streets but set down in its own
tree-shaded gardens, with an unexpectedly
tranquil feel. It styles itself a "boutique pub" – the
building is original but the interior feels more like
a contemporary, upmarket dining club, with white
leather sofas, a log fire and candlelit tables. As
well as pub grub – they're proud of their burger –
the menu also takes in seasonal fish and game,
with daily specials chalked up on a board. Mains
£8–16. Map p.50.

🍴 **Pie Minister** Covered Market ☎ 01865
241613, Ⓦ www.pieminister.co.uk. Your
nose will lead you to this fantastic little pie shop
inside the Covered Market, with a counter for take-
aways and a sit-down restaurant section. The wide
choice includes porky pie (outdoor-reared pork and
apple), moo pie (beef and ale), heidi pie (goat's
cheese, sweet potato and spinach), and so on, all
substantial items accompanied by creamy mashed
potato, gravy and minty peas for around £5–6.
Unmissable. Open daily, daytimes only. Map p.60.

European

Al Andalus 10 Little Clarendon St ☎ 01865
516688, Ⓦ www.tapasoxford.co.uk. Congenial
tapas bar with fresh, contemporary decor, a good
selection of Spanish wines, great tapas (around £5,
with plenty for vegetarians) and live flamenco on
weekend nights adding to the buzz. Map p.50.

🍴 **Branca** 111 Walton St ☎ 01865 556111,
Ⓦ www.branca-restaurants.com. Large and
informal brasserie-restaurant offering a wide-
ranging menu, though Italian dishes predominate.
Much-loved spot for those seeking a casual, buzzy
get-together or a romantic tête-à-tête, with atmosphere for both and amiable service. À la carte
starters are £5–7 and mains £8–15 – or go for the
great-value two-course lunch or early dinner, at
£10.45 including a glass of wine or beer (served
noon–7pm, Sat until 5pm). Map p.50.

Fire and Stone 28 George St ☎ 0844 371 2552,
Ⓦ www.fireandstone.com. Wood-fired pizzas
served in a bright, designer-ish interior – think
"The Marrakech" (pizza with cumin-spiced lamb),
"The Sydney" (pizza with smoked bacon), and so
on. Mains around £9. Map p.60.

🍴 **Jamie's Italian** 24 George St ☎ 01865
838383, Ⓦ www.jamieitalian.com. Flagship
Italian restaurant under the Jamie Oliver banner –
always busy, featuring a laid-back interior of
exposed bricks, graffitied walls and hams hanging

above the salad station. The rustic-style food is exquisite, marked by Jamie's trademark informality: mixed antipasti arrive on a plank of wood, the pasta menu takes in "beautiful bucatini" and old-school spaghetti bolognese, while mains include "flash steak" and "lamb chop lollipops". Mains £10–15. Book well ahead. Map p.60.

Manos 105 Walton St ℡01865 311782, ⊛www .manosfoodbar.com. Family-run Greek deli and restaurant on a sunny Jericho corner, offering budget meals of salads and wraps (£2–4) alongside delicious Mediterranean mains such as butter beans in tomato sauce, spinach and feta tart or wine-and-pork sausages (£6–8) and, of course, coffee and pastries. Mon–Wed 9.30am–9pm, Thurs–Sat 9.30am–10pm, Sun 11.30am–8pm. Also hosts beer and whisky tastings from one of Oxford's artisan brewers – see ⊛www.compass brewery.com for dates. Map p.50.

Pierre Victoire 9 Little Clarendon St ℡01865 316616, ⊛www.pierrevictoire.co.uk. Independently owned French brasserie on this popular restaurant street that consistently comes up trumps in both food and service. Start with snails, roquefort soufflé or black pudding and move on to rib-eye steak, chicken with goat's cheese, roast rabbit or Cornish mussels – or dip your way through a Savoyard-style cheese fondue. Mains are £10–15, but take advantage of sub-£10 set menus at lunch and dinner. Map p.50.

Indian and East Asian

Chiang Mai Kitchen 130a High St ℡01865 202233, ⊛www.chiangmaikitchen.co.uk. Oxford's best Thai restaurant, a smart little place in a seventeenth-century timber-framed house off the High Street. All the classics are served – and then some – and it's particularly strong on vegetarian dishes. Mains around £8. Closed Sun eve. Map p.60.

Edamame 15 Holywell St ℡01865 246916, ⊛www.edamame.co.uk. Regularly voted as one of the best Japanese restaurants in Britain, this tiny canteen-style place, tucked away opposite New College, enjoys a flawless reputation among town, gown and Japanese tourists for authenticity, pristine fresh food and a friendly welcome. No bookings are taken, so you may have to queue (and then share a table) – but it's worth it. Sample the salted edamame beans – popped fresh from the pod – as an appetizer, then tuck into ramen noodle soup with pork, chicken or tofu, for instance, or salmon *teriyaki*. There's plenty for vegetarians. Thursday night is sushi night – hugely popular, so turn up early. Mains £5–8. Opening hours are idiosyncratic, tied to specific menus: lunch menu (Wed–Sat 11.30am–2.30pm, Sun noon–3.30pm), sushi menu (Thurs only 5–8.30pm), evening menu (Fri & Sat 5–8.30pm). Closed Mon & Tues all day, Wed & Sun eve. Map p.60.

Majliss 110 Cowley Rd ℡01865 726728, ⊛www .majliss.co.uk. Although the acclaim for Oxford's best curry has long been directed at *Aziz*, further down the Cowley Road, *Majliss*, which opened in early 2009, has rapidly won plaudits for its fresh outlook, super-efficient service and simply delicious cooking. There's an impressive buzz about the place: the interior is tasteful, with contemporary decor, and the menu takes in a range of unusual Bangladeshi fish and seafood curries and South Indian *dosa* (savoury pancakes), in among familiar biryanis and kormas. Booking recommended at the weekend. Mains £5–12. Map p.51.

International

Ashmolean Dining Room At Ashmolean Museum, Beaumont St ℡01865 553823, ⊛www .ashmoleandiningroom.com. Contemporary, open-plan restaurant occupying a stunning space on the museum's rooftop level, with an outside terrace. Cuisine runs from chorizo, crêpes and squid to lamb and sea bream, alongside a range of cheeses and charcuterie. Mains £11–17. Also a fine spot for posh afternoon tea (£25 for two). Has its own opening hours, independent of the museum: Tues–Sat 10am–10pm, Sun 10am–6pm. Map p.60.

Café Coco 23 Cowley Rd ℡01865 200232, ⊛www.cafe-coco.co.uk. Award-winning informal bar-cum-restaurant plumb on the Cowley Road – something of an Oxford institution, serving pizzas and vaguely Continental-style dishes, plus comforting American desserts like pecan pie and waffles, to a frequently packed house. The volume goes up as the beers (and cocktails) go down. Mains £8–10. Map p.51.

Quod 92 High St ℡01865 202505, ⊛www.quod .co.uk. Landmark brasserie in a perfect central location. Once the solemn hall of an Oxford bank, it's been transformed, along with the *Old Bank* hotel above: the spacious, stone-flagged interior now offers picture windows onto the High Street and cheery, colourful contemporary art. Plump for the bargain two-course set lunch (£10) – think devilled kidneys on toast or minty courgette soup, followed by steak *béarnaise* or mushroom tagliatelle. The à la carte dinner menu is a pricier affair, with mains such as salmon fishcakes with warm sorrel or gourmet burgers around £12–15. There's a nice bar to one side, and live jazz on Sunday evening (5–7pm) – or drop in for breakfast (daily from 7am) or afternoon tea (3–5.30pm). Map p.60.

Lebanese and North African

Al Salam 6 Park End St ☎01865 245710. Busy, informal Lebanese restaurant on an always-buzzing street. The food doesn't quite match up to *Al Shami* (see below) but is still very good, with a long choice of authentic hot and cold mezze (£2–3) and good variety of expertly prepared kebabs and grills (£7–8). The difference comes in the atmosphere: this is a great place for a mid-budget romantic dinner, or a fun night out being guided through the flavours and textures of an unfamiliar cuisine – service is unfailingly warm and outgoing. They sometimes lay on the Oriental kitsch a bit thick, going so far as to bring in a bellydancer on Saturday nights, but it's all part of the fun. Map p.50.

Al Shami 25 Walton Crescent ☎01865 310066, ⓦwww.al-shami.co.uk. Splendid family-run Lebanese restaurant on a placid Jericho back street – coincidentally, opposite Oxford's synagogue – serving authentic mezze, grills and kebabs to a knowledgeable local clientele. Its calm, undramatic interior, which features windows spanning the curve of the building, also includes a magnificent back room sporting Syrian-style inlaid wood panelling. Mezze cost £2–3, mains £6–8 – or go for the extensive set menu at £15 per person. There's plenty for veggies and vegans. Wash it down with a choice from the extensive selection of Lebanese wines – and make sure you sample their high-quality Lebanese arak (aniseed-flavoured spirit), traditionally served to accompany mezze. Map p.50.

Cous Cous Café 19 St Clement's ☎01865 722350. Cheery little Moroccan deli and casual restaurant serving delicious, authentic nosh at low prices – lentil soup, hummus, salads, lamb tagines, baklava, mint tea – in a relaxed Moorish-style setting. Mains roughly £3–7. Closes Mon–Sat 8pm, Sun 6pm. Map p.51.

Drinking and entertainment

As you'd expect, Oxford has plenty of **pubs** and **bars** – not all of them student dives. We pick out several below, notable for their atmosphere and/or their beer. The city's buzzing **live music** scene spawned Radiohead and Supergrass, among others, and continues to unearth new discoveries at a clutch of venues around town. Devotees of **classical music** are also well catered for, with halls and some college chapels – primarily Christ Church and Merton – offering concerts and recitals. Live **theatre** is another option, with high-quality productions supplemented by more casual open-air Shakespeare in summer. For **listings**, consult *In Oxford*, available free from the tourist office, or check ⓦwww.dailyinfo.co.uk.

All places reviewed below are marked on the maps on p.46, p.50 or p.60.

Bars

Café Tarifa 56 Cowley Rd. Atmospheric lounge bar in Moorish/Arabian style, with cocktails and cushions, also hosting a variety of generally chilled live music and DJ nights. Map p.51.

Freud 119 Walton St ⓦwww.freud.eu. Occupying a nineteenth-century former church, this fashionable café-bar is an upmarket spot for cocktails and chit-chat, along with good Italian/Mediterranean food (mains from £6). Live music some nights too – but the architecture and the interiors are the main attraction. Map p.50.

Kazbar 27 Cowley Rd ⓦwww.kazbar.co .uk. Eye-poppingly beautiful lounge bar-cum-restaurant in a hippyish/Moorish style – adobe, incense, lanterns, bar stools in cracked tan leather and bartenders in embroidered jackets. Food and cocktails are great, and there's always a buzz. Mon–Fri 4pm till late, Sat & Sun noon till late. Bar-hop your way down the road to the similarly alluring *Café Tarifa* (see above). Map p.51.

Morse Bar At *Randolph Hotel*, Beaumont St. Traditional hotel bar – roaring fire, club armchairs, wood panelling – which featured so often in *Inspector Morse* that the hotel renamed it to match. Specializes in whisky and champagne cocktails. Map p.60.

Raoul's 32 Walton St ⓦwww.raoulsbar.co.uk. Award-winning Jericho cocktail bar, with a retro 70s theme, great tunes and a devoted clientele who know (and love) their drinks. Daily 4pm till late.

Sugar Brown 30 Walton St ⓦwww.baby-bar.co.uk. Funky neighbour to *Raoul's* which manages to hold its own, with cocktails (including an original 1931 mojito), comfy sofas and decent bar food. Mon–Thurs 4pm till late, Fri–Sun 11am till late. Map p.50.

From Trout to Perch

This leisurely half-day **walk** leads from the city centre to two of Oxford's best-loved pubs and back again. Start on Walton Street in Jericho (see p.80): just past the alley for St Sepulchre's cemetery, Walton Well Road leads left over the railway tracks onto **Port Meadow**, a large stretch of common parkland between the Thames and the canal which has had free and open access for at least a thousand years. Follow paths (and the river) northwards for roughly an hour's ramble to the village of **WOLVER-COTE** – also accessible on bus 6 (every 15–20min; £2) from Magdalen Street in central Oxford.

In Wolvercote village, the Godstow Road heads left (west) across a stream before bumping into the legendary **Trout** pub (℡01865 510930, ⓦ www.thetroutoxford.co .uk; see map on p.46). Made famous by *Inspector Morse* – though an Oxford favourite long before television – this rambling, seventeenth-century riverside inn, bedecked in ivy, enjoys a picture-perfect location alongside the old Godstow Bridge, with its own wooden footbridge just downstream and a broad, south-facing terrace overlooking the water. The interiors have been done up: beer is the main draw, but this now doubles as a decent restaurant for good Modern British cooking (honeyed gammon, calves' liver and onions, rack of lamb, and so on, as well as stone-baked pizzas and more, including veggie options), though it can get phenomenally busy, especially on sunny weekends, when service can suffer. Mains £7–17, or two-course set menu £12. If you intend to eat, book in advance.

From the *Trout*, cross the river and follow the Thames Path southwards along the western bank for about half an hour to reach a little path leading right (west) to the **Perch** (℡01865 728891, ⓦ www.the-perch.co.uk; see map on p.46), set 100m back from the riverbank in **BINSEY** village. Another historic, thatched pub dating from the seventeenth century (though with its origins going back another five hundred years or so), this was a favourite of Lewis Carroll and C.S. Lewis, and still offers a generally peaceful, well-pulled pint, as well as a lovely beer garden and upmarket French cuisine in its restaurant (mains £13–18). Oxford River Cruises (see p.70) have punts and pedaloes nearby, while around 750m north on Binsey Lane stands St Margaret's Church, location of St Frideswide's well (see p.47).

From the *Perch*, you can follow the Thames Path south into the city centre – or take Binsey Lane, which joins the main Botley Road about 600m west of Oxford rail station. Both the *Trout* and *Perch* are accessible by road, though to drive between them you'd have to go the long way round via the bypass.

Pubs

Bear 6 Alfred St. Tucked away down a narrow side street in the centre of town, this tiny old pub (the oldest in Oxford, founded roughly 800 years ago) has not been themed up – and a good job too. Offers a wide range of beers amid its traditional decor, which includes a collection of ties, framed on the wall. Map p.60.

Eagle & Child 49 St Giles. Dubbed the "Bird & Baby", this was once the haunt of J.R.R. Tolkien and C.S. Lewis. The beer is still good and the old wood-panelled rooms at the front are great, but the pub is no longer independently owned – and feels it. The food (and atmosphere) are corporate, and the modern rear extension is a travesty. Pop over the road to the *Lamb & Flag* (see below) to compare. Map p.50.

Jericho 56 Walton St ⓦ www.thejericho.co.uk. Much-loved Jericho tavern which doubles up as a leading indie music venue. Map p.50.

Jude the Obscure 54 Walton St. Comfortable Jericho pub with bookish decor, pleasant outdoor seating and a refreshingly down-to-earth attitude that is rather atypical for the area. Map p.50.

Kings Arms 40 Holywell St ⓦ www.kingsarms oxford.co.uk. Pleasant seventeenth-century pub on the crossroads with Broad Street, Catte Street and Parks Road, offering great people-watching from its front terrace. Snug rooms at the back and a decent choice of ales at the congenial atmosphere – though beware: it's also one of Oxford's most popular student pubs. Map p.60.

Lamb & Flag 12 St Giles. Generations of university types have relished this quiet old tavern, which comes complete with low-beamed ceilings and a series of cramped but cosy rooms in which to enjoy hand-drawn ale and genuine pork scratchings. Cash only. Map p.50.

Turf Tavern Bath Place, off Holywell St ⓦwww .theturftavern.co.uk. Small, atmospheric medieval pub, reached via narrow passageways off Holywell Street or New College Lane, with a fine range of beers, and mulled wine in winter. Abundant seating outside. Typical pub grub on offer includes Sunday roast from £8. Map p.60.

White Horse 52 Broad St ⓦwww.whitehorse oxford.co.uk. A tiny old pub beside Blackwell's bookshop in the town centre with snug rooms, pictures of old university sports teams on the walls, real ales and good food. Map p.60.

Clubs and music venues

Bridge 6 Hythe Bridge St ⓦwww.bridgeoxford .co.uk. Popular bar and club with smooth DJing on three floors. Open 10pm till late (student nights Mon–Thurs). Closed Sun. Map p.50.

Bullingdon Arms 162 Cowley Rd ⓦwww.famous mondayblues.co.uk. Lively pub and venue that is well known for its long-running Monday night blues sessions, as well as regular gigs and comedy nights. Map p.46.

Café Tarifa See "Bars" on p.84.

Gloucester Arms Friars Entry. Grungy back-alley pub off Gloucester Green showcasing rock and punk acts in a suitably downbeat setting. Map p.60.

Half Moon 18 St Clements ⓦwww.halfmoon oxford.com. Legendary Irish pub that hosts live folk every Sunday, in amongst a regular timetable of jazz and other music. Map p.51.

Jericho See "Pubs" on p.85.

O2 Academy 190 Cowley Rd ⓦwww.oxford -academy.co.uk. Oxford's biggest indie,

mainstream and dance venue, with a good programme of live bands and guest DJs. Map p.46.

Theatre and classical music

Creation Theatre ⓦwww.creationtheatre.co.uk. Unattached troupe, best known for its summer season of Shakespeare at unusual venues around town – Headington Hill Park, the roof of the Said Business School, on the factory floor of BMW's Mini production plant, and so on.

Holywell Music Room 32 Holywell St ⓦwww .musicatoxford.com. This small, plain, Georgian building was opened in 1748 as the first public music hall in England. It offers a varied programme, from straight classical to experimental, with occasional bouts of jazz. Sunday morning "coffee concerts" (ⓦwww.coffeeconcerts.co.uk) run year-round. Map p.60.

New Theatre George St ☏01865 320760, ⓦwww.newtheatreoxford.org.uk. Popular programme of theatre, dance, pop music, musicals and opera.

North Wall South Parade ☏01865 319450, ⓦwww .thenorthwall.com. Arts centre located in Summer-town, a mile or so north of the centre, hosting small-scale theatre and workshops.

Oxford Playhouse 11 Beaumont St ☏01865 305305, ⓦwww.oxfordplayhouse.com. Profes-sional touring companies perform a mixture of plays, opera and concerts at the city's leading theatre. Map p.60.

Sheldonian Theatre Broad St ☏01865 277299, ⓦwww.sheldon.ox.ac.uk. Seventeenth-century edifice that is Oxford's top concert hall, despite rather dodgy acoustics, with the Oxford Philomu-sica symphony orchestra in residence (ⓦwww .oxfordphil.com). Map p.60.

Listings

Bookshops The leading university bookshop is Blackwell: see p.61. Be sure to drop into the relaxed Albion Beatnik Bookstore, 34a Walton Street in Jericho, for "interesting twentieth-century books", as well as readings, events and jazz evenings.

Hospital See p.36.

Markets Weekly food market at Gloucester Green (Wed 8am–4pm). For farmers' markets, see box, p.45; for the daily Covered Market, see p.72. Arts and crafts market at Oxford Castle (Fri & Sat 11am–5pm).

Pharmacy Boots, 6 Cornmarket ☏01865 247461.

Police St Aldates ☏01865 841148, ⓦwww .thamesvalley.police.uk.

Post office 102 St Aldates.

Taxis There are taxi ranks at Carfax, Gloucester Green, St Giles and the railway station. Otherwise try Radio Taxis (☏01865 242424, ⓦwww .radiotaxisoxford.co.uk) or Royal Cars (☏01865 777333, ⓦwww.royal-cars.com).

The Oxfordshire countryside

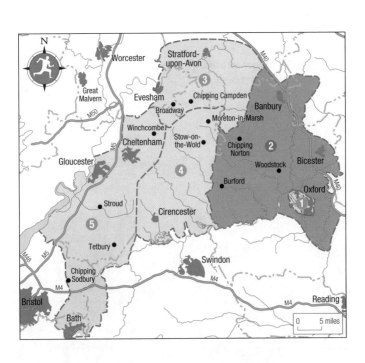

CHAPTER 2 # Highlights

* **Woodstock** Handsome, historic little town within a stone's throw of Blenheim. See p.94

* **Blenheim Palace** One of England's great stately homes, displaying taste and hubris in equal measure. See p.98

* **Burford** Busy little place marketing itself as the "Gateway to the Cotswolds". See p.108

* **Kelmscott Manor** Isolated Thames-side farmhouse preserving superb Victorian Arts and Crafts furnishings. See p.112

* **Kingham** Lovely Cotswold village that manages to combine fine pubs, fine views and fine walks. See p.115

* **Chastleton House** Glorious Jacobean architecture combined with an endearing air of neglect. See p.119

* **Rollright Stones** Prehistoric stone circle in fields overlooking Warwickshire. See p.120

* **Great Tew** Backwater village hosting one of Oxfordshire's best-loved pubs. See p.121

▲ Woodstock

2

The Oxfordshire countryside

I n Cotswold terms often playing second fiddle to Gloucestershire next door, **Oxfordshire** nonetheless hosts much that is most beautiful about the region – rolling, hilly landscapes chiefly given over to agriculture, crossed by ancient roads and dotted with similarly ancient villages of honey-coloured ironstone. Oxfordshire's difference, if one can be discerned at all, stems perhaps from its position closer to the centre of national events. A key battleground throughout the Civil War, and tightly bound into the later rush of economic development – thanks, chiefly, to the canals and railways serving towns at the fringes of the high ground – Oxfordshire has long found itself serving as a trunk route for both ideas and conflicts moving between Birmingham and London. In truth the wider county has less to do with its academic city-capital than most observers suppose.

Royal patronage has also played its part. The ancient hunting forest of Wychwood once covered the hills northwest of Oxford: one of the county's most attractive small towns, **Woodstock**, developed as an adjunct to a royal hunting lodge nearby. That lodge, destroyed during the Civil War, was rebuilt in the eighteenth century as **Blenheim Palace**, a monument to the glory of the dukes of Marlborough and, in 1874, the birthplace of Winston Churchill. Otherwise, it's mainly a case of getting as far away from main roads as possible – down, for example, to **Kelmscott Manor**, the remote farmhouse where Victorian designer William Morris developed his hugely influential "Arts and Crafts" ideas.

Although Oxfordshire's borders stretch far to the south and east of Oxford, across to Thame, Henley and the high downs above Wantage, most of that terrain falls

Farmers' markets

- **Banbury** 1st Fri of month 8.30am–1.30pm Ⓦwww.tvfm.org.uk.
- **Bicester** 2nd Thurs of month 8.30am–2pm Ⓦwww.tvfm.org.uk.
- **Charlbury** Quarterly on 2nd Sat 9am–1pm Ⓦwww.tvfm.org.uk.
- **Chipping Norton** 3rd Sat of month 8.30am–1.30pm Ⓦwww.tvfm.org.uk.
- **Deddington** 4th Sat of month 9am–12.30pm Ⓦwww.deddington.org.uk.
- **Witney** 3rd Wed of month 8.30am–1.30pm Ⓦwww.tvfm.org.uk.
- **Woodstock** 1st Sat of month 8.30am–1pm Ⓦwww.tvfm.org.uk.
Dates may change around Christmas and New Year. See also Ⓦwww.farmersmarkets .net and Ⓦwww.local-food.net.

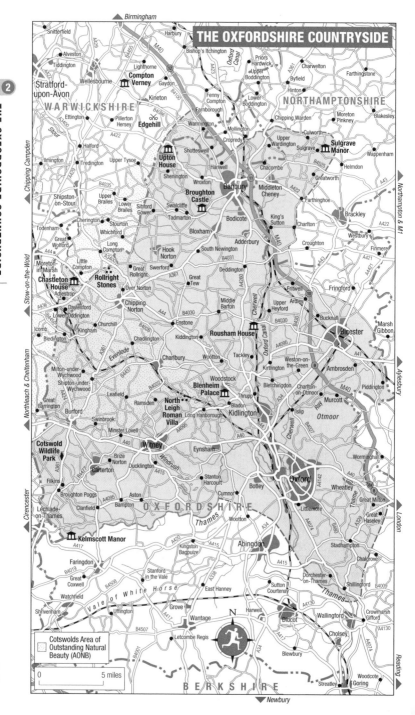

beyond the remit of a Cotswolds guidebook. We've instead focused our coverage on the area bounded by the Thames in the south and the M40 motorway in the east, a large part of which falls within the Cotswolds Area of Outstanding Natural Beauty (Ⓦwww.cotswoldsaonb.org.uk). Within that, there is a fairly well-developed rural infrastructure – **Burford** is often cited as the "Gateway to the Cotswolds", but you don't really need a gateway. Opt, instead, for the Cotswold Line railway, which gives direct village-by-village access to otherwise little-known rural gems such as **Kingham** and **Charlbury**, or meander from pillar to post on buses plying between the market towns of, for instance, **Chipping Norton** and **Banbury**. Further out, stately homes at **Chastleton** and **Broughton** have atmosphere to entice even the most jaded history-hater – and everywhere, of course, there are long, lonely **walks** to tackle and heart-warming village **pubs** to offer succour and refreshment.

Southeast of Oxford

Although much of Oxford's hinterland to the east and south lies beyond the remit of this book, if you're driving to or from the M40 motorway you could plan a diversion or two. Dominating the picturesque Thames-side village of **DORCHESTER**, eight miles south of Oxford, **Dorchester Abbey** (daily 8am–6pm; free; Ⓦwww.dorchester-abbey.org.uk) was built in the twelfth century to replace earlier Saxon foundations; it is truly magnificent, sporting exquisite stained glass. A shade further south, just over Shillingford Bridge, drop in for tastings and sales at the award-winning **Brightwell Vineyard** (Fri–Sun noon–6pm; ☎01491 832354, Ⓦwww.brightwellvineyard.co.uk).

The wonderful *Mole Inn* (☎01865 340001, Ⓦwww.moleinntootbaldon.co.uk) in tiny **TOOT BALDON**, off the B480, is much-loved by Oxford cognoscenti for its cuisine – or drop into the well-stocked **farm shop** of the wacky *Crazy Bear* hotel/restaurant (☎01865 890714, Ⓦwww.crazybeargroup.co.uk) at nearby **STADHAMPTON**.

Taking top billing, though, is *Le Manoir aux Quat'Saisons* (☎01844 278881, Ⓦwww.manoir.com), the country restaurant and hotel of renowned chef Raymond Blanc, on the edge of **GREAT MILTON** village, eight miles southeast of Oxford. It's everything you might wish for: a sixteenth- and seventeenth-century manor house, beautifully preserved outside and tastefully updated inside, set in seven acres of lavish, naturalistic gardens. We couldn't possibly do justice to the food here; suffice it to say that it's world-class. À la carte mains cost £40–45, set menus start from £100 a head or a daily three-course lunch menu is £58. Book at least two months in advance. Both the service and the rooms (❾) are exceptional.

North of Oxford

North of Oxford, once you're free of the ring road, the county's character reasserts itself in a series of quiet, rural villages worthy of gentle exploration. Beyond busy **Kidlington**, you could put your feet up with a pint in **Thrupp** – or aim for gentle **Islip**, on the edge of misty, desolate **Otmoor**. Just to the west, **Woodstock** makes for a lovely base, within a stone's throw of majestic **Blenheim Palace**.

Kidlington

KIDLINGTON, five miles north of central Oxford, though once famed for its apricots, is now renowned for sternly insisting that it is still a village, despite having a population topping 17,000. It has resisted all attempts at redefinition and

A Kidlington walk

An easy **circular walk** of about three and a half miles starts at the church in Kidlington, crosses the fields past Hampton Poyle to a ruined Elizabethan manor house at Hampton Gay, heads along the River Cherwell (watch for kingfishers, deer, even foxes) and then back from Thrupp through riverside woods to Kidlington again. Download a full route description and map at Ⓦ www.oxfordshire .gov.uk/kidlingtonwalk.

thus currently qualifies as pretty much the largest village in Britain, though, in truth, Kidlington looks like a town, walks like a town and quacks like a town – a pretty mundane one, at that. Some character persists in the streets around the thirteenth-century **St Mary's Church**, located about 750m east of the main A4260 road via High Street, where many Georgian town houses also survive – as does *Warsborough House*, 52 Mill Street (Ⓣ 01865 370316, Ⓦ www.warsborough house.com; ◐; no cards), a good **B&B** with spacious rooms in a former farmhouse – but otherwise you can press on with impunity.

Thrupp

A mile north of Kidlington, served by Stagecoach **bus** 59 (not Sun) between Oxford and Banbury, **THRUPP** – an end-of-the-road hamlet watching over the Oxford Canal – deserves a lazy afternoon. Pretty cottages aside, its standout feature is the 🍴 *Boat Inn* (Ⓣ 01865 374279, Ⓦ www.theboatinnthrupp.co.uk), occupying a sixteenth-century canalside farmhouse: great atmosphere, great beer and unusually good **food** (mains £10–17; no food Sun eve), modern British in style with fresh, seasonal ingredients and a pride taken in careful presentation. Sit back on the terrace and gaze over the water, often fringed with wildflowers and spanned just to the east by an elegant lift bridge. Over the bridge, *Annie's Tea Room* offers refreshment (winter closed Tues–Fri), and there's also an outpost of Oxford-shire Narrowboats (Ⓣ 01869 340348, Ⓦ www.oxfordshire-narrowboats.co.uk), with both **boat rental** (£135–199/day, depending on season) and **cycle rental** (£15/day): cycle paths head from here to Blenheim Palace and Woodstock, or along the towpath south to Oxford or north towards Heyford Wharf (see p.132). It's a canalside **walk** of about seven miles into central Oxford – especially scenic as you cross Port Meadow (see p.85) in front of the "dreaming spires".

Islip

Only fifteen minutes by train from Oxford and a couple of miles east of Kidlington, **ISLIP** (pronounced "eye-slip") makes for a lovely counterpoint to the urban pace of its bigger neighbours. There's not much here – a couple of pubs, a handful of streets lined by seventeenth- and eighteenth-century cottages (most of them updated to suit the monied lifestyles of their twenty-first-century residents) – but the calm and sense of timelessness are rather alluring. The poet and novelist Robert Graves lived in Islip in the early 1920s; his meetings here with Siegfried Sassoon fuelled his First World War memoir *Goodbye To All That*, published in 1929.

But it is Islip's status as the birthplace of **Edward the Confessor** – England's last Anglo-Saxon king, bar Harold – in around 1004, which has most resonance. Although Edward's church is no more, the arcade that separates the nave from the north aisle within the current **Church of St Nicholas** dates from just after, in the twelfth century. As you walk into this wonderfully atmospheric building, behind the fifteenth-century font ahead of you – and flanking a modern portrait of

Edward – leer a stone-carved lion and hunting dog, gifts from Westminster Abbey in London, itself founded by Edward in 1065. Take time, too, to walk the **Confessor's Way** path, waymarked around the village: from the church it heads down to the *Swan* (℡01865 372590), a fine eighteenth-century inn (with space to park a car), across the bridge over the leafy River Ray – scene of a Roundhead victory in April 1645 – and between the fields to cross the River Cherwell, re-enter the village and end at the church. The whole thing is only a mile, but it encapsulates both the beauty of Oxford's countryside and the mood of Islip's long history. Download a map with notes at Ⓦwww.bicesterlink.info – or buy a booklet at the village hall-cum-shop (Mon–Fri 10am–noon & 3–6pm, Sat 10am–noon, Sun 3.30–5pm; closed Wed am; Ⓦwww.islip.org.uk), behind the church.

Otmoor

Some four thousand acres of fenland stretching from Oxford to Bicester, **Otmoor** is a world apart – misty, boggy and largely uninhabited. It is thought that Lewis Carroll visited: Otmoor's patchwork appearance, divided by ditches and hedges, made its way into *Through the Looking Glass*, described by Alice as a landscape "marked out like a large chessboard". This sliver of fame helped when, in 1980, the government proposed building the new M40 motorway across the moor: environmental campaigners bought a nondescript field, renamed it **"Alice's Meadow"**, divided it up into three thousand tiny parcels of land and sold each one off to its supporters. This was effectively sabotage: it meant the government would have been forced to fight each new "landowner" in the courts over compulsory purchase orders. The motorway was built on an alternative route, skirting the moor to the east – and the laws on land purchase were changed to ensure such a thing could never happen again. **Walking** isn't easy here, partly because of the boggy ground and partly because a chunk of the moor is taken up by a Ministry of Defence rifle range – seek advice before venturing onto open ground, or check with the RSPB (Ⓦwww.rspb.org.uk), who administer a wetland reserve on the moor.

A narrow road strikes east from Islip for a few miles to **CHARLTON-ON-OTMOOR**, which has a fine medieval church with a characteristic square tower and sixteenth-century carved rood screen – as well as the quiet *Crown* pub (℡01865 331783; closed Mon–Fri lunchtimes). The main reason to come this way, though, lies in silent **MURCOTT**, the next village but one. Here, almost dropping off the edge of the world, the tumbledown 🍴 *Nut Tree Inn* (℡01865 331253, Ⓦwww.nuttreeinn.co.uk; closed Mon) makes the journey worthwhile: as well as being the core of its community, this fifteenth-century pub doubles as one of the finest rural **restaurants** in Oxfordshire. Located alongside the village duck-pond – the ducks will greet you when you arrive – the low-beamed thatched building has been lovingly spruced up inside: alongside the cosy bar, there is a contemporary feel to the dining area, which spreads into a stone-flagged rear extension. The owners (awarded a Michelin star) keep Gloucester Old Spot pigs and also grow their own vegetables: expect seasonal, local, ethically sourced food prepared with panache. Mains, which might include slow-roasted belly of Oxfordshire pork or risotto of summer vegetables, range from £16 to £25 – or you could opt for the eight-course tasting menu, at £50 a head (plus £32 for wine), or the daily changing set menu (available Tues–Thurs plus Fri lunch) at £15 for two courses. Service is warm and relaxed, to suit the ambience.

Kirtlington and around

Three otherwise unremarkable villages northeast of Oxford offer stand-out lodging and dining. The first is **KIRTLINGTON**, where you'll find the *Dashwood*

Say again?

Just a reminder not to mix up Kirtlington with its larger neighbour of Kidlington to the south – nor Kiddington a few miles west, Piddington a few miles east or Oddington in between, let alone Kennington, Shenington, Cassington, Cuddesdon, Headington, Deddington, Tredington, Bledington, Bletchingdon, Chadlington or Ducklington, which are all within spitting distance.

(☎01865 352707, ⓦwww.thedashwood.co.uk; ❺), a friendly boutique hotel within a historic inn: inside, contemporary furniture in wood and dark leather complements the rusticity of gnarled beams and light stonework. The twelve bedrooms are airy, featuring that same whiff of urban chic – bold fabrics, feature walls – while the restaurant covers modern British staples (mains £14–20).

Down the road in **HAMPTON POYLE**, the *Bell* (☎01865 376242, ⓦwww .thebellathamptonpoyle.co.uk; ❹–❺) is another independent boutique hotel worked into the village's only pub. Its style is a touch more restrained than the *Dashwood*, with fresh, tasteful bedroom interiors and a darker, more traditional feel to its restaurant, which serves more international cuisine – pizzas, salads, seafood grills, and so on (mains £12–18).

More traditional hospitality is on offer at **WESTON-ON-THE-GREEN**, where resides the splendid *Weston Manor* (☎01869 350621, ⓦwww.westonmanor .co.uk). Concealed by beech trees at the end of a long driveway, and set in twelve acres of lovely gardens, this is a country house hotel from the old school, dating largely from a rebuilding in 1587 by Henry Lord Norreys, Elizabeth I's ambassador to France. Its Baronial Hall dining room is a hugely atmospheric place to eat, with a vaulted ceiling, oak linenfold panelling, stained glass, iron chandeliers, a stone fireplace and a minstrels' gallery; the quality of the food doesn't always match up, but you may be prepared to overlook that for the setting and relatively modest prices (two-course menus £19–24). If you choose to stay, be sure to get a room in the main house (❺): they are adequate, though not luxurious – but better than those in the adjacent Coach House (❸), which was put up in the 1980s.

If all this sounds too fancy, opposite the manor stands *Weston Grounds Farm* (☎01869 351168; ❷), offering cosy, midrange B&B – or head to the next village, **BLETCHINGDON**, for the *Diamond Farm Caravan Park* (☎01869 350909, ⓦwww.diamondfarmcaravanpark.co.uk), which has pitches for caravans, motorhomes and tents, plus a swimming pool and kids' play area.

From all of these, the **Oxford Canal** (see p.132) is only a couple of miles away. Within easy reach are **Woodstock** to the west (see below) – and central Oxford, only about ten minutes' drive south via the A34.

Woodstock

WOODSTOCK, eight miles northwest of Oxford, has royal associations going back to Saxon times, with a string of kings attracted by the excellent hunting in the Wychwood Forest, which formerly covered the area. Henry I built a royal lodge here and his successor, Henry II, enlarged it to create what is thought to have been a manor house-cum-palace, where Edward, the Black Prince, was born in 1330, where Henry VIII dallied with Catherine of Aragon and where the future Elizabeth I was imprisoned by her half-sister Mary in 1554. During the Civil War, Woodstock was a Royalist base: the manor house was badly damaged by Roundhead attacks in 1646 but Cromwell never got around to razing the ruins, which were only swept away by the Duke of Marlborough when work started on the construction of Blenheim Palace on the same site in 1704 (see p.98 for more).

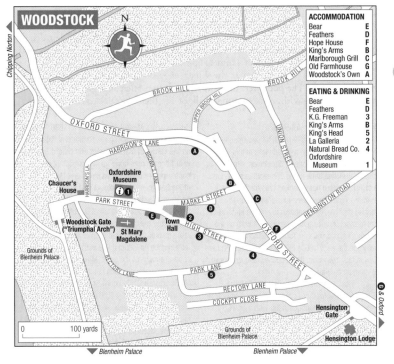

Long dependent on royal and then ducal patronage, Woodstock is now both a well-heeled commuter town for Oxford and a provider of food, drink and beds for visitors to Blenheim. Historic, dignified and attractive, it has Oxfordshire character in spades.

Arrival, information and accommodation

Stagecoach **bus** S3 heads to Woodstock from Oxford railway station and Gloucester Green, as well as from Chipping Norton and Charlbury. Bus 242 (not Sun) arrives from Witney. Street parking is free, but often full: turn off the main road beside the *Punch Bowl* pub to find a signed car park (also free) on Hensington Road. The Oxfordshire Museum (see below) doubles as the **tourist office** (Mon–Sat

---

Oxford Bus Museum

Barely three miles from Woodstock, the **Oxford Bus Museum** (Wed & Sun 10.30am–4.30pm, Easter–Oct also Sat; £4; ⓦ www.oxfordbusmuseum.org.uk) comprises a giant warehouse crammed with vintage buses and coaches, many open for onboard exploration, along with memorabilia, models and ephemera – plus evocative whiffs of engine grease and waxed bodywork. At 3pm on the first Sunday of the month (March–Oct) they do free rides on one of their old buses. Alongside is a separate exhibition on Morris Motors, the historic Oxford car maker. The museum is located on the A4095 Woodstock–Witney road beside **HANBOROUGH** station: get there by train from Oxford (one stop), or on bus 242 (not Sun) between Woodstock and Witney, which drops off outside.

10am–5pm; ℡01993 813276, ⓦwww.oxfordshirecotswolds.org), well-stocked with Cotswolds maps and information as well as some fascinating books on local history. One useful local website is ⓦwww.wakeuptowoodstock.com. For details of the **farmers' market**, see p.89. Local historian Andrew Webster leads a **guided walk** around town (Tues–Sun 11am & 6pm; 90min; £7) – always book ahead on ℡01993 812164 or in person at the *King's Head* on Park Lane, where the walk begins and ends. The pub offers discounted meals to participants. All **accommodation** in town lies within five minutes' walk of the Blenheim Palace entrance gate.

Hotels and B&B

Bear Park St ℡0844 879 9143, ⓦwww.macdonald hotels.co.uk. Behind the ivy-clad walls of this former coaching inn in the centre of Woodstock, whose history stretches back to the thirteenth century, lurks a stylish, modern hotel, packed with traditional features. From oak-carved four-poster beds to roaring log fires, bay windows to antique furniture – not to mention outstanding service – it ticks all the boxes. Plump, if you can, for the Marlborough Suite, where in the early 1960s Elizabeth Taylor and Richard Burton hid, away from their spouses (and the press), to conduct an affair. ❺

🏃 **Feathers** Market St ℡01993 812291, ⓦwww.feathers.co.uk. A discreet, attractive little independent boutique hotel with just 21 bedrooms, worked into seven adjacent seventeenth-century town houses. Although traditional elements remain – a grandfather clock here, an oak bookcase there – the style is definitely upscale contemporary, with designer textiles, tastefully vivid wallpaper, modern lighting and swanky bathrooms. Member of the "Cotswolds Finest Hotels" group (see p.25). ❼

Hope House Oxford St ℡01993 815990, ⓦwww.hopehousewoodstock.co.uk. Eighteenth-century town house with just three super-luxurious suites – all of them enormous and kitted out to the highest standards: antique furnishings, king-size four-poster beds, contemporary designer decor, Italian linen sheets, handmade silk duvets, heated marble floors in the bathrooms, Bulgari toiletries, and so forth. Service is caring, attentive, intelligent and individually tailored, while the breakfast (all local and organic) comes on Royal Doulton china. One suite is for two people only, the others are both two-bedroom suites sleeping up to four people. Minimum two-night stay applies at weekends (April–Oct). ❾

King's Arms Market St ℡01993 813636, ⓦwww.kingshotelwoodstock.co.uk. Rather chic little hotel on the corner of Market Street and Oxford Street, with fifteen rooms done up in a fresh, appealing contemporary style – bowl sinks and Molton Brown in the bathroom, pale colours and light wood in the bedroom. Beware, though: like the other hotels on Oxford Street (*Marlborough Grill*, *Punch Bowl* and others), the bar/restaurant area at ground level remains busy until 11pm or later and traffic noise may also be an issue: if you want an early night, choose a room at the back. Minimum two-night stay applies at weekends (June–Sept). ❻

Marlborough Grill Oxford St ℡01993 811657, ⓦwww.marlboroughgrill.co.uk. Formerly the *Marlborough Arms*, this ex-coaching inn is a more modest option than others in this list – rooms are less huge, decor is less snazzy, attention to detail sometimes not quite up to scratch. Service is good but, as above, late-night noise from the bar can be an issue. ❹

Old Farmhouse Station Hill, Long Hanborough ℡01993 882097, ⓦwww.countryaccom.co.uk. Farmhouse B&B located three miles from Woodstock, on the Witney road. The building is seventeenth-century – think stone floors, beams, inglenook fireplace – and has three guest rooms, one of which is en suite: it's not fancy, but the welcome is warm, the breakfast is good and it's only five minutes' walk from Hanborough railway station. ❸

Woodstock's Own Oxford St ℡01993 810040, ⓦwww.woodstocksown.co.uk. Keep walking for a couple of minutes past the *King's Arms* to find this little B&B on a tree-shaded curve in the road, above a café-cum-interiors shop. Four en-suite bedrooms do the job nicely – and weekend discounts are a cheery bonus. ❸

The Town

An extremely pretty little place, Woodstock is characterized by handsome stone buildings gathered around a little knot of streets on the western side of the A44 Oxford–Evesham road, which passes through the town centre as **Oxford Street**, lined once with coaching inns and now with upscale fashion and crafts shops flanking the Woodstock Bookshop (ⓦwww.woodstockbookshop.co.uk). Buses stop at the *Marlborough Grill*, an eighteenth-century inn on Oxford Street updated to a boutique hotel; across the road, either follow **Market Street** into the centre or stroll along to the *Crown Inn*, marking the corner with **High Street**. Opposite the *Crown*, elegant, bay-windowed **Hope House** is said to have been designed by Vanbrugh, architect of Blenheim; it, too, now holds a boutique hotel.

A stroll along High Street, invariably bustling with commerce, takes you to the Palladian **Town Hall**, standing at the apex of the triangle where Market Street joins. Gracious, tree-lined **Park Street** leads away; on the left is the famous *Bear Hotel*, whose origins go back to the 1250s, while opposite, reproduction stocks have been set up in front of an acacia-shaded Elizabethan building housing the **Oxfordshire Museum** (Tues–Sat 10am–5pm; Sun 2–5pm; free; ⓦ www.tomocc .org.uk), a well-composed review of the county's archeology, social history and industry. Part of the museum's lovely rear garden shelters original megalosaurus footprints, recovered from a local quarry and displayed amid a Jurassic garden of ferns, pines and redwoods.

A step further along Park Street stands **Chaucer's House**, named for Thomas Chaucer, son of Geoffrey, who owned a house on this spot (the current building is seventeenth-century), while across the road, the church of **St Mary Magdalene** sports a Norman doorway with zigzag carving, an eighteenth-century square tower and an atmospheric yew-shaded churchyard – but a disappointingly bland Victorian interior.

Park Street continues to the end of the town, where a peremptory notice fixed to the wall warning fishermen to be quiet heralds a courtyard offering the exceptional sight of Nicholas Hawksmoor's Classical-style **Woodstock Gate** (sometimes known as the Triumphal Arch) into the grounds of **Blenheim Palace**. If the officials in the ticket booth will let you, nip through to take a peek at the spectacular panorama just beyond: Blenheim Palace in the distance, Capability Brown's landscaped grounds, Vanbrugh's Grand Bridge over the lake – what Randolph Churchill termed "the finest view in England". A full account of Blenheim starts on p.98.

Walks around Woodstock

Woodstock lies at the heart of the former royal hunting forest of Wychwood, long since cleared for agriculture or settlement and now reduced to isolated woods here and there, most notably a stretch of forest at Cornbury Park, a private estate between Leafield and Charlbury. In an effort to preserve links with pre-industrial culture and encourage greater understanding of the landscape, rural activists and Oxfordshire council formed the Wychwood Project (☎01865 815423, ⓦ www.wychwoodproject .org), which has included the establishment of the 37-mile **Wychwood Way** circular trail. This forms a rough quadrilateral, waymarked from Woodstock and heading through Stonesfield, Chadlington, Ascott-under-Wychwood, Leafield, Ramsden, North Leigh, East End, Combe and back to Woodstock. The route bypasses Charlbury, but short-cuts connect to and from Charlbury railway station, facilitating half- and full-day walks: full details are in the Wychwood Way guidebook (£4.95), available online and at local tourist offices.

Another long-distance route worth tackling is the **Glyme Valley Way**, a full-day route running 16 miles from Chipping Norton to Woodstock; for more, see p.117. This is best tackled in a downhill (southerly) direction: if you're starting from Woodstock take the hourly bus S3 to Kiddington, from where it's a gentle eight miles back, around farm buildings, past a medieval church at Glympton and then along the River Glyme past Wootton to end at the Woodstock museum. Full details, with maps and descriptions, at ⓦ www.oxfordshire.gov.uk.

THE OXFORDSHIRE COUNTRYSIDE | North of Oxford

97

Eating and drinking

With its long tradition of hospitality – a century and a half ago twelve stagecoaches a day were stopping here, served by dozens of inns – Woodstock still has plenty of places to **eat**. However, with the quantity of holidaymakers passing through, quality at some of the tearooms can be patchy. For a hearty lunch on the hoof, or to put together a picnic, stop in at *K.G. Freeman*, a family butcher at 10 High Street selling freshly made pies and pasties and hefty "doorstop sandwiches" (£2.50). At 30 High Street, the *Natural Bread Company* (ⓦ www.naturalbreadcompany.co.uk; closed Sun & Mon) bakes its own loaves and also has a few tables for coffee and buns.

Bear Park St (see p.96). Traditional charm in the restaurant of this old coaching inn. Try to grab a table by the big bay window for classic, upscale, country-house hotel-style food – Gressingham duck, corn-fed chicken, Scottish beef and all. Two-course menus around £28.

Feathers Market St (see p.96). Lovely, award-winning restaurant in this boutique hotel. Expect minimalist portions, artfully presented, encompassing seasonal, organic ingredients – spring lamb or Cornish brill or mackerel, scallops in sherry or quail. Two-course menus are £39, or opt for the six-course Tasting Menu at £55 (plus £43 for wine to accompany). Afterwards – or before – repair to the Gin Bar, which offers over fifty gins from around the world, as well as the Ultimate Gin and Tonic (£16.75): Shetland dry gin from a numbered bottle, tonic made with hand-picked Peruvian quinine and ice cubes of Blenheim Palace's own spring water.

King's Arms Market St (see p.96). Lively bar and restaurant, very popular with a local, rather posh set who pack in on Wednesdays in particular, when all champagne is half-price. The relaxed restaurant is a reliable, relatively affordable choice for modern British cooking, such as steak with blue cheese, organic salmon with rocket mash, free-range chicken breast with field mushrooms, and the like. Mains are £12–23 (most around £15) – the desserts are particularly special.

King's Head Park Lane ☏ 01993 812164, ⓦ www .kingsheadwoodstock.co.uk. Purportedly Woodstock's oldest standing pub: above the door is a stone marked "1735". Tucked away slightly off the main drag, this is a more down-to-earth establishment than others in town, with decent, uncomplicated food: haddock fishcakes, chicken and mushroom pie, cheeseburgers and so on (mains £9–14) – plus local Cotswold ice cream and a board of all-Oxfordshire cheeses. Closed Sun eve & Mon.

La Galleria Market Place ☏ 01993 813381, ⓦ www.lagalleriawoodstock.com. Accomplished little Italian with an appealingly fresh interior of flowers set on white tablecloths, its terrace tables spilling out onto the cobbled "Shambles" – formerly the butchers' market – behind the Town Hall. Always popular, with a buzz of conversation inside and out. There are few surprises on the menu, but everything is cooked perfectly and served with grace: pastas are £8.50–10, mains – including grilled Dover sole (£22.50) – are mostly £13–18.

Oxfordshire Museum Park St ☏ 01993 811456, ⓦ www.tomocc.org.uk. If you need to let the kids run free on a sunny day while you refuel with tea and cakes, aim for the garden café at the rear of the museum. It's nothing fancy, but the lawns are lovely and this is one of central Woodstock's quietest retreats – oddly, more local than touristy.

Blenheim Palace

Nowadays, successful British commanders get medals and titles, but in 1704, as a thank-you for his victory over the French under Louis XIV at the Battle of Blenheim (a small town on the Danube in Bavaria, pronounced "blennim"), **Queen Anne** gave **John Churchill**, Duke of Marlborough (1650–1722), the royal estate of Woodstock, along with the promise of enough cash to build himself a palace. Marlborough was a brilliant general, but the gift had more to do with Anne's fear of Louis XIV – and the relief she felt after the battle – than a recognition of his genius, as events were to prove.

Work started promptly on **Blenheim Palace** under the guidance of **John Vanbrugh**, architect of Castle Howard in Yorkshire. However, Marlborough's formidable duchess wife, Sarah – who, it is said, had wanted Christopher Wren as architect – was soon at loggerheads with Vanbrugh, while the queen had second thoughts about the whole scheme. Treasury money dried up and, in 1712, construction work halted altogether. The Marlboroughs went into self-imposed exile and only returned to Britain after Anne's death in 1714. With George I refusing to stump up any more cash, Marlborough decided to finish the house at his own expense, and reinstated Vanbrugh and his architectural assistant **Nicholas Hawksmoor**. Building work restarted in 1716 but creative differences persisted: Marlborough couldn't or wouldn't pay the going rate, meaning that skilled designers who had worked on the house previously, such as **Grinling Gibbons**, refused to return. Before the end of the year, the Duchess had fallen out again with Vanbrugh, who departed in high dudgeon and never returned. Marlborough died in 1722, whereupon the Duchess brought Hawksmoor back to complete the palace, paying the bills out of her own pocket (and thus reportedly designing some interiors herself and using lower-quality materials). Within a couple of years the house was finished, though wrangling about some of the interior fittings continued into the 1730s.

As impressive is Blenheim's large, rolling estate, through which passes the River Glyme. During the house's construction period Vanbrugh had altered the river's flow and built his Grand Bridge, and the Duchess had had the Column of Victory (see p.103) installed in 1730 shortly after the 1st Duke's death, but it was only when the 4th Duke commissioned master landscaper **"Capability" Brown** in 1764 that the estate was transformed. Brown created the lake which exists today by damming the Glyme, and shaped the land with undulations and naturalistic tree-planting. Later dukes added follies and ornamental gardens.

The end result is England's grandest example of Baroque architecture, an Italianate palace of finely worked yellow stone, designed chiefly as a national monument to the military exploits of the 1st Duke and only secondarily as a

Churchills, Spencers and Vanderbilts

The history of the dukes of Marlborough is a complicated tale entwining three families. **John Churchill**, an English general, was made Earl of Marlborough by William III in 1689 – and then elevated to **Duke of Marlborough** by Queen Anne in 1702. He died in 1722 without surviving sons: it took a special Act of Parliament to allow his title to pass to his eldest daughter, **Henrietta**. On her death in 1733, the title reverted to the male line, passing to the 1st Duke's grandson, **Charles Spencer** (an ancestor of Lady Diana Spencer, Princess of Wales in the 1980s and 1990s). For two generations the dukes of Marlborough bore the Spencer surname, until the 5th Duke obtained the right in 1817 to reinstate "Churchill": to this day, the family is **Spencer-Churchill**. Winston Leonard Spencer-Churchill – who preferred to be known as **Winston Churchill** – was born in Blenheim Palace in 1874, grandson of the 7th Duke.

By the time the 9th Duke, **Charles**, inherited in 1892, the family was virtually bankrupt after decades of poor financial management. In a bid to inject new money into the estate, in 1895 Charles married the American railroad heiress **Consuelo Vanderbilt**. It was a loveless match of convenience: the Vanderbilts were simply paying for access to the British aristocracy, to the tune of, in today's money, several hundred million dollars – enough to ensure the survival of the Blenheim estate. Two sons were born in rapid succession, then Vanderbilt left her husband in 1906; they divorced in 1921.

The current owner of Blenheim, who still lives in the palace, is John George Vanderbilt Spencer-Churchill (born 1926): he inherited the title **11th Duke of Marlborough** in 1972. He has effectively disowned his eldest son and direct heir, Charles (born 1955), the **Marquess of Blandford** – who goes by the name Jamie Blandford, and who has twice been jailed, for forgery, criminal damage and dangerous driving. Blandford will inherit the ducal title, but ownership of Blenheim will skip over him to his son, George (born 1992).

home. Around it stretches some of the finest landscaping in the country. Everything is intended to wow.

Blenheim Palace practicalities

Blenheim Palace (☎01993 811091, ⓦwww.blenheimpalace.com) and its formal gardens are **open** from 10.30am to 5.30pm in two distinct seasons: from mid-February to the end of October (daily) and from early November until mid-December (Wed–Sun only). The surrounding park is open daily all year round from 9am to 6pm or dusk. Last entry is at 4.45pm.

Blenheim has two **entrances**, both admitting cars, pedestrians and cyclists: the **Hensington Gate** lies just south of Woodstock town centre on the A44 Oxford Road, a few minutes' walk from the *Punch Bowl* pub, while the quieter **Woodstock Gate** (described on p.97) is at the far end of Park Street in the centre of Woodstock. Stagecoach **bus** S3 stops at the Hensington Gate, on its route between Oxford (train station and Gloucester Green) and Chipping Norton or Charlbury, as does bus 242 (not Sun) from Witney.

There are two **ticket** types: "park and gardens" (£10.30) or "palace, park and gardens" (£18). Both include **car parking** and both are discounted for families, students and seniors. You can buy in person when you arrive, or in advance via the website. A long-running scheme, which might still be operating when you visit, allows you to convert your one-day ticket into an **annual pass** without further payment: see staff onsite for details.

Note that several public **rights of way** pass through far-flung areas of the park, including stretches of the Wychwood Way and Oxfordshire Way near the Column of Victory. These are **free** to use; the easiest access is from a signed path opposite the *Black Prince* pub, down the hill from Woodstock town centre. **Anglers** can fish part of the lake for trout, under strict conditions (£35/day; booking essential).

Check the website for details of Blenheim's many **annual events**, including horse trials, jousting, charity bike rides and more, as well as occasional **themed tours** on – for instance – "The Unknown Winston" or "Ladies of Blenheim" (£4.50; book in advance).

Touring Blenheim Palace

From the car parking area, the main entrance to the palace complex is the massive, top-heavy **East Gate**, topped by a flagstaff. Stroll on across an enclosed courtyard, past the **Orangery** on the left (usually open only at Sunday lunchtimes when a rather posh lunch is served, from £20pp; booking essential), and pass beneath the chunky, dense **Clock Tower Arch**, carved by Grinling Gibbons with English lions nonchalantly tearing chunks out of squawking French cockerels. You emerge into the **Great Court**, an expanse of stone paving and gravel paths: to the right opens a majestic vista over the park, centred on an arrow-straight axis climbing to the **Column of Victory** (see p.103), while to the left soars the imposing **north front** of the palace itself.

The facade is designed to be daunting – and it is. A broad mass of pillars and stonework and towers and finials claws its way upwards, reaching a cluster of roofs topped with heroic Classical statues in the Renaissance style. Squat, spiky and utterly impenetrable, it encloses the courtyard on three sides. As you face the main entrance, its columns and pediment reminiscent of a Roman temple, the **private apartments** of the current Duke and Duchess of Marlborough are to the left (east). On the right a marked passageway beneath the colonnade leads through to the **café** and **Water Terraces** beyond. Dead ahead, climb the steps to the palace doors – but pause at the top to turn round: perfectly aligned on the horizon rises the Column of Victory.

The Great Hall and Churchill Exhibition

As you enter the stunning **Great Hall**, staff will explain how to tour the interior (and whether the private apartments are open that day; see p.102). Free **guided tours** (35min) around the palace's display rooms depart about every quarter-hour (or when enough people have gathered), though you're free to opt out and stroll at your own pace. On Sundays or when the palace is very busy, the tours are replaced by guides stationed in every room, who give details of the collections as you move through.

To the left around the hall's perimeter, you could start upstairs with the "**Untold Story**", a forty-minute audiovisual trot through Blenheim's history, with interactive panels and video characterizations – or you could turn right for the self-guided Churchill Exhibition and to begin touring the palace's display rooms.

Before you do either, take in the hall itself – an extraordinary spectacle, with its vast marble floor, double rows of arches, high windows and carved Corinthian capitals. Opposite the door looms the main arch, topped by the arms of Queen Anne, with, behind, a bust of the 1st Duke above the entrance to the Saloon (which is visited later on the tour; On the ceiling twenty metres overhead, the 1st Duke kneels in victory before Britannia, in a heroic painting of 1716 by Sir James Thornhill.

The **Churchill Exhibition** comprises a half-dozen rooms in the west wing of the palace, housing fascinating displays on Winston's life, from the room where he was born in 1874 – admire his baby vest and a lock of his hair – to letters, paintings and the "US Honorary Citizen's Document" awarded by John F. Kennedy in 1963.

It returns you to a corridor of the Great Hall, alongside a cabinet with a collection of lead soldiers given to the current duke in 1935. This is the spot from where the guided tours depart; you could pause here to join the next one – or just stroll onwards.

The drawing-rooms and writing-room

First comes the **China Anteroom**, lined with cabinets displaying Sèvres and Meissen porcelain including – at the far end on the right, bottom shelf – a soup tureen with handles made to look like sliced lemons and asparagus spears. At the back of the anteroom stands the Blenheim Bureau, designed by Viscount Linley to celebrate the millennium and set with a fine marquetry panel.

Winston Churchill and Blenheim

Winston Churchill, Britain's Prime Minister during most of World War II – and the "Greatest Briton of All Time" according to a public vote for a 2002 BBC TV show – once wrote: "At Blenheim I took two very important decisions: to be born and to marry. I am happily content with the decisions I took on both those occasions." The room where Churchill was born is preserved in the palace, along with memorabilia both personal and public: he often returned to Blenheim over his lifetime, proposing here (see p.103), painting views of the house and gardens and researching the life of the 1st Duke for the biography *Marlborough, His Life and Times*, published in four volumes (1933–38). Churchill died in 1965 and, at his request, was buried in the family plot at St Martin's Church in **BLADON**, just outside the Blenheim estate. His grave can be visited today: narrow lanes climb steeply through Bladon village, on the south side of the A4095 road a mile or so outside Woodstock, to the modest little church, quiet and atmospheric. Perhaps coincidentally, the axis line which runs from the Column of Victory over Vanbrugh's bridge to Blenheim Palace can be extended to finish exactly at the Bladon churchyard.

Alongside, the **Green Drawing-Room** sports a stunning ceiling in 24-carat gold leaf by Nicholas Hawksmoor. The furniture is Louis XV, while over the fireplace hangs a portrait of the 4th Duke; on the north wall, his wife, Caroline, dandles her baby in a painting by Joshua Reynolds. In the contrasting **Red Drawing-Room** – very English in style, with Chippendale chairs – two huge paintings face each other. On the right is the 4th Duke and family, by Reynolds (1778); on the left, the 9th Duke and family, by John Singer Sargent (1905). In the latter, Consuelo Vanderbilt wears a dress which deliberately echoes that worn by Lady Killigrew in a painting by Van Dyck which also hangs here.

The **Green Writing-Room** – with another Hawksmoor gilded ceiling – features the first of a series of Flemish tapestries in wool and silk commissioned while the palace was being built. Left of the fireplace is the victory scene from the Battle of Blenheim: the French commander Tallard is doffing his hat in surrender to the Duke of Marlborough, while, behind, mills blaze and French troops flee. To the right hangs a vigorous portrait of the duke at the age of 25, in black armour.

The saloon and state rooms

Focal point of the palace and, in truth, the entire estate, is the **Saloon** or State Dining-Room, designed so that when the duke was seated in prime position, all the landscaping of the park – focused around the axis from the Column of Victory to this room – and all the architecture of the palace, also centred on this room, served to glorify his person. Around the walls are depictions of the peoples of the world, as if gazing into the room, by French artist Louis Laguerre (who left a self-portrait in the far right-hand corner). The ceiling, showing the 1st Duke in victory, held back by the hand of Peace, is also by Laguerre. Today, the saloon is used by the family only once a year, on Christmas Day, when the table is extended to seat about forty.

Beside, three lavish state rooms house more tapestries. The **First State Room**, with a radiant portrait of Consuelo Vanderbilt at 17 over the fireplace, displays a copy of the Blenheim Dispatch, a note scribbled on the back of a tavern bill by the 1st Duke to inform Queen Anne of "a glorious victory". In the **Second State Room**, the tapestry on the left shows a rare artistic blunder: a dog with horse's hooves. The **Third State Room** was originally the duke's bedchamber, full of furniture from Versailles, including beautiful marquetry cabinets of ebony, overlaid with brass on tortoiseshell.

The Long Library and chapel

These lead to the palace's largest room, the **Long Library**, which runs the length of the west wing. Originally planned by Vanbrugh to be a gallery, though for the most part executed by Hawksmoor (his stucco ceiling is exceptional), it is 56 metres long and ten metres high. Ten thousand books line its walls, while at the far end looms an elaborate organ, installed in 1891. Stroll down the room, past family photos and a collection of ermine ceremonial robes, and exit behind the organ onto the honeystone colonnade above the Great Court. Signs lead down some stairs into the adjacent **Chapel**, a long, slender room with mostly Victorian furniture that is overwhelmed by a gigantic marble monument to the 1st Duke. Tellingly, the high altar is demoted to an inconsequential – and heterodox – position on the west wall to make space for it.

The private apartments

On days when the duke and his family are absent, their **private apartments** in the east wing are sometimes opened for **guided tours** (£4.50 extra; 30min): to book, consult staff in the Great Hall. You enter outside, at an anonymous door off the

Great Court; this gives into what was the palace undercroft. Highlights include a billiard room and, alongside the kitchens, a functioning panel of Victorian bells – 47 of them – connected to rope-pulls in rooms all over the palace. Upstairs, you pass through the duchess's **Sitting Room**, hung with portraits by Lady Diana Spencer (1734–1808), daughter of the 3rd Duke, to the **Smoking Room**, which has views over the splendid **Italian garden** and a miniature painting of a packet of Marlboro cigarettes – a little pun on the family title. The twelve bedrooms upstairs and the servants' dorms in the attic (dubbed "Housemaids' Heights") are off-limits.

Blenheim's gardens and park

Most people start their exploration of Blenheim's **formal gardens** by riding the little narrow-gauge **railway** (April–Oct every 30min; free) from the "Palace Station", located by the car parking area outside the main East Gate entrance, on a short, looping journey to the **Pleasure Gardens** a few hundred yards to the east (also an easy walk). Here, as well as a café, you'll find a **butterfly house**, **lavender garden**, the **Marlborough Maze** – a huge hedge-maze – and other diversions.

Between the palace and the Pleasure Gardens, the **Secret Garden** – a twentieth-century creation – is a lovely place to sit, surrounded by bamboos, succulents, Japanese maples and more.

Otherwise, aim for the west side of the house, where fountains in the gorgeous **Water Terraces** spout beside the terrace of the palace café. Paths lead down to the lake on a long, circular route past the **Cascades** – part of Capability Brown's designs – the **Arboretum**, planted with cedar, beech and willow, and the vivid **Rose Garden** (with a picturesque **Temple of Diana**, where Winston Churchill proposed to his wife-to-be in 1908) and back to the palace: reckon on an hour or more in total. Rent an **audio-guide** (£3) for the walk from the small bookshop beside the palace chapel.

Blenheim's open **park** is at least as enticing, with the path from the front of the house leading you down to Vanbrugh's **Grand Bridge** over the artificial lake – beside a strategically placed island of poplar trees – and up the other side to the hilltop **Column of Victory**, topped by a heroic statue of the 1st Duke. It's said that Capability Brown laid out the trees and avenues to represent the Blenheim battlefield.

For coverage of Charlbury and villages north of Woodstock, turn to p.116.

West of Oxford

West of Oxford you start to knock on the door of the Cotswolds proper. The A40 zooms past humdrum **Witney** and some evocative rural destinations – notably the ruined manor at **Minster Lovell** and the remains of a Roman villa in open fields outside **North Leigh** – on its way towards the Cotswolds "gateway" town of Burford (described on p.108). If you have the time, allow yourself to be tempted off the beaten track by some fine country pubs scattered through Thames-side villages south of Witney.

Witney

A busy little town of about 25,000, located on the River Windrush twelve miles west of Oxford, **WITNEY** doesn't pay much attention to the tourism going on all around it. The town centre revolves around Corn Street, approaching from the west, and High Street, coming in from the north (where the A4095 is carried on the town's only bridge over the Windrush). Where they meet stands the **Butter-cross**, an open-sided ex-dairy market building of about 1600. To the south, the long Church Green extends to **St Mary's Church**, with Norman elements surviving in what is chiefly early Gothic. In the other direction, past the seventeenth-century arcaded **Town Hall**, Witney's wonky **High Street** bustles away down the hill, lopsided (its west side higher than the east) and closely shaded by tree cover. Strolling this way, past bits of Georgian and bits of Jacobean on either side, everything and everyone occupied with cafés and commerce, takes you to the **museum** (April–Oct Wed–Sat 10am–4pm, Sun 2–4pm; £2; ⊛www.westoxford shiremuseum.co.uk). This has a working loom, old photographs and displays on Witney's historic **blanket-making** industry, which sustained the town from the thirteenth century right through until the last mill closed in 2002.

Otherwise, an enticing reason to visit might be the **Wychwood Brewery**, located on The Crofts behind Corn Street. Begun in the 1980s as an independent concern, but now – like its sister company on the same site Brakspear's – controlled by the national brewer Marston's, Wychwood flies the flag for Oxfordshire's grand old brewing tradition, with its best-selling "Hobgoblin" leading a range of highly acclaimed craft-brewed beers. It opens for **brewery tours** (Sat 2pm, 2.30pm, 4pm & 4.30pm, Sun 2pm & 2.30pm; £6.50; booking essential ⊤01993 890800, ⊛www.wychwood.co.uk), which take 45 minutes to lead you through the brewing process before letting you loose to sample Hobgoblin and other beers.

Practicalities

Partway down the High Street near the museum is the well-stocked **tourist office**, 3 Welch Way (Mon–Thurs 9am–5.30pm, Fri 9am–5pm, Sat 9.30am–5pm; ⊤01993 775802, ⊛www.oxfordshirecotswolds.org). Most of the **hotels** are business-oriented: one good central **B&B** is *Corncroft*, 69 Corn Street (⊤01993 773298, ⊛www.corncroft.co.uk; ❸), with nine en-suite rooms done up in antique style. Three miles south beside Standlake, *Lincoln Farm Park* (Feb to mid-Nov; ⊤01865 300239, ⊛www.lincolnfarmpark.co.uk) was named the UK's **Best Campsite of the Year** for 2010 by the AA: as well as five-star amenities, it has an on-site leisure centre with two indoor swimming pools and spa.

Pay the t(r)oll

A few miles east of Witney, to the south of **EYNSHAM** village, the B4044 road crosses the River Thames via **Swinford Bridge**, a beautiful Georgian structure opened in 1769. By a quirk of English law, the bridge is an investment opportunity: its own Act of Parliament states that the owner can charge a **toll** – fixed at 5p per vehicle – without paying any taxes on the income. Since the next bridge upstream is about twenty miles away, and the next bridge downstream is the Oxford ring road – not exactly renowned for free-flowing traffic – about four million vehicles use Swinford Bridge each year, generating a tidy £200,000 or so, tax-free.

Needless to say, the locals aren't happy. Every rush-hour, tailbacks of a mile or more build up through Eynsham as people pause on the bridge to hand over their 5p. In addition, the argument runs, why should people be paying £20-odd a year on top of road tax for the privilege of driving to and from work? Nobody has a decent answer. In 2009, after the death of the previous owner, locals campaigned for Oxfordshire County Council to step in and abolish the toll. Instead, an anonymous buyer splashed out almost £1.1 million at auction to buy the bridge – and the tolls are still flowing in. The rich are getting richer, while the tailbacks (and pollution) grow. Track the protests at ⊛www.eynsham.org and ⊛www.scrapthetoll.blogspot.com.

Witney's standout options for **eating and drinking** include the *Hollybush Inn*, 35 Corn Street (☎01993 708073, ⦿www.hollybushwitney.co.uk), a renovated pub with a nice rear terrace and accomplished down-the-line pub grub (mains £10–16). The *Fleece*, 11 Church Green (☎01993 892270, ⦿www.fleecewitney .co.uk), is a step up in both ambience – it's a lovely Georgian building near the church – and quality: go for a mix of cheeses, charcuterie, smoked fish and crudités as a starter, then try dishes such as roast lamb with a Moroccan salad or baked trout with almonds (mains £10–18). It's open from 8am (Sun 9am), serving food all day.

North of Witney

The most scenic road out of Witney is the B4022, a lovely drive climbing north up out of the Windrush Valley, over the tops and down again into the Evenlode Valley at Charlbury (see p.116). RH Transport **bus** X9 (not Sun) follows this road on its hourly run between Witney and Chipping Norton, dropping off along the way. Past the turn for Poffley End, beside rolling fields at **WHITEOAK GREEN**, you'll pass the *Bird In Hand* (☎01993 868321, ⦿www.birdinhandinn.co.uk), a lovely old pub newly renovated inside, with an excellent restaurant and comfortable, modern rooms (⑤). Quieter still, with yet higher culinary accomplishment, is the *Royal Oak* (☎01993 868213, ⦿www.royaloakramsden.com) in the peaceful old village of **RAMSDEN**, just off the main road. Download a map and notes at ⦿www.cotswoldsaonb.org.uk for "Step Into The Cotswolds: Walk 5", an easy **walk** from the *Royal Oak* through Ramsden and across rolling countryside in a circuit of a mile and three-quarters back to the pub.

North Leigh Roman villa

Parts of an early-fourth-century **Roman villa**, indicating impressive prosperity in what would have been dense, riverside forest, survives outside the village of **NORTH LEIGH**, off the A4095 Witney–Woodstock road. Before you reach the bus museum at Hanborough (see p.95), turn off left at the signs, drive through the outlying hamlet of **EAST END** and park in a marked layby. From here, the only approach is **on foot**, 550m down a stony track into the valley of the River Evenlode. What survives (see ⦿www.english-heritage.org.uk) is modest: a course or two of foundation stonework, with the remnants of a hypocaust system for underfloor heating. An explanatory panel explains the layout of the villa – which was substantial, with kitchens, baths and dozens of other rooms set around a courtyard. To one side, a **mosaic floor** in browns and reds lies protected by a modern shelter. What's just as evocative, though, are the sense of discovery, the setting – surrounded by hills echoing with bleats – and, for good measure, the occasional train passing on the Cotswold Line laid yards away, beside the Evenlode. As a mute counterpoint to Blenheim, another, younger, bolder, country palace barely two miles distant, it couldn't be more perfect.

Minster Lovell

Hooked into a corner of the River Windrush, a couple of miles upstream (west) of Witney, tiny old **MINSTER LOVELL** will, sooner or later, take your breath away. There's no hurry, though: the village has been here since the Domesday Book (1086), which recorded it as Minster – its suffix came later in honour of the landowning Lovell family – and it may have been around much longer, since Akeman Street, the Roman road between St Albans and Cirencester, ran nearby. Either way, what survives is an alluringly rural cluster of thatched cottages, medieval inns and a strong sense of undisturbed history.

You approach down a slope off the main road (B4047) to an old, narrow bridge over the bubbling River Windrush; on the right stretches Wash Meadow, absurdly picturesque when a cricket match is going on. At a fork by the *Old Swan*, turn right and head along the village street between cottages. Further up, bear right again for **St Kenelm's Church** (Mon–Sat 9.30am–sunset, Sun 7.30–8.45am & 10.30am– sunset), rebuilt in 1450 by William Lovell – beautiful, but still not the culmination of the village's charms. That lies immediately behind the church, where Lovell also built a large **manor house** on a stretch of meadow beside the river. The house does not survive, largely dismantled in the 1740s, yet its **ruins**, open to the elements with crumbling towers and toothless windows, are picture perfect. A cobbled pathway leads to the entrance porch, vaulted inside, while beyond is the great hall, now roofless; by the river stand remnants of a tower, marking the far corner of what was a vast interior courtyard, giving an idea of the size of the house when complete. If you have any breath left, a first glimpse of these old stones in their riverside setting will banish it.

Back in the village, the *Old Swan and Minster Mill* (℡01993 774441, Ⓦwww .oldswanandminstermill.com) – the pub on one side of the road, the converted mill on the other – was taken over by new owners in 2010. The mill will remain what it has been for some years – a modern, rather unromantic conference centre – but the *Old Swan* is slated for a makeover, turning it from a dowdy pub with midrange rooms into an upmarket rural **restaurant** and boutique **hotel**. Check the website for the latest details.

Practicalities

For a vivid retelling of Minster Lovell's history, along with a dash of legend and perhaps a snatch of song, drop into the **Minster Lovell Experience** (Mon–Fri 10am–1pm & 2–5pm; £2; Ⓦwww.minsterlovell.com), run by Graham Kew out of his picture-framing business on the main B4047 road, not far from a **bus stop** at the *White Hart* served by, among others, Stagecoach bus S2 from Oxford (Gloucester Green) and Witney (Mon–Sat every 30min), and Swanbrook bus 853 between Oxford (St Giles) and Cheltenham/Gloucester (Mon–Sat 3 daily, 1 on Sun). On Sundays, Stagecoach bus 233 serves Minster Lovell from Chipping Norton, Kingham railway station and Burford.

Swinbrook (see p.111) lies a mile or so west of Minster Lovell, with Burford (p.108) a couple of miles further.

Bampton and around

A couple of stand-out pubs along a boggy stretch of the Upper Thames could entice you south of Witney. Aim first for Bampton, five miles southwest: drive direct, or detour slightly in order to gape at military aircraft taxiing within the giant **RAF Brize Norton** airbase nearby – the minor road south of Brize Norton village runs alongside the perimeter fence, yards from the runway. A shade north of Brize Norton, on the Burford road, the **Foxbury Farm Shop** (Ⓦwww .foxburyfarm.co.uk; closed Mon), stocks a wide range of local produce – perfect for a picnic.

BAMPTON (Ⓦwww.bamptonoxon.co.uk) was once important enough to merit its own castle, demolished in the eighteenth century, though its fine **church**, with a thirteenth-century spire and slightly later stone reredos, survives in what is a rather handsome village, with a Georgian air to its broad streets and, in the centre, **West Ox Arts** (Tues–Sat 10.30am–12.30pm & 2–4pm, Sun 2–4pm; free; Ⓦwww.westoxarts.org), a gallery displaying local art in the old town hall. Across the way stand a couple of old pubs, including the attractively veranda'd *Romany Inn* (℡ 01993 850237, ⓦ www.theromanyinnbampton.co.uk). If you're around on the last Monday in May, don't miss Bampton's **Day of Dance**, featuring live music and morris dancing, and look out for **Bampton Opera** (ⓦ www.bamptonopera.org) in July. Download "Bampton Footpaths", comprising maps and detailed notes for walks in the area, at ⓦ www.oxford shirecotswolds.org.

A mile east near **ASTON**, the **Aston Pottery** (Mon–Sat 9am–5pm, Sun 10.30am–5pm; ⓦ www.astonpottery.co.uk) has become a leading visitor attraction, with a showroom, café and gardens. The popularity of their comfortingly countryfied ware, made on site and exported worldwide, means they remain a key village employer, keeping two dozen people in rural work. A minor road heads south to the Thames-side hamlet of **CHIMNEY**, where a **nature reserve** on the floodplain offers walks among flower meadows and wet woodlands – see ⓦ www .bbowt.org.uk for details.

A couple of miles south of Bampton, where Tadpole Bridge crosses the Thames, stands the lovely 🍴 *Trout Inn* (℡ 01367 870382, ⓦ www.trout-inn .co.uk), named by the AA as England's 2009 **Pub of the Year**. Doubling as a rural restaurant and an honest village local – with well-kept cask ales, including several Oxfordshire pints – this is a stand-out experience in every way, from the warm welcome and the superb setting to the courteous, efficient service. The food is classic English, prepared with style: expect local pork, rack of lamb, saddle of wild rabbit and the like, as well as the special Thursday "Sausage Club" menu, from venison to black pudding. Mains cost £11–19. The pub is also a member of the "Cotswolds Finest Hotels" group, offering six spacious **rooms** (❻), decorated in contemporary style. Room prices go up at the weekend, when half-board is compulsory and a two-night minimum stay is imposed. Note, too, that the pub is **closed in the afternoon** (Mon–Sat 3–6pm) and on Sunday evening.

Aston and Bampton are both served by Stagecoach bus 18 (not Sun), running hourly from Oxford (George Street), and 19 (not Sun), hourly from Witney.

Clanfield and Radcot Bridge

West of Bampton at **CLANFIELD**, the 🍴 *Plough* (℡ 01367 810222, ⓦ www .cotswoldsploughhotel.com) offers fine country-pub atmosphere: the building sets the scene, with its Jacobean gables and mullioned windows – a mood sustained inside, where the part-stone-flagged, part-parquet-floored bar is updated with modern sofas and rich red walls. Duck through to the dining room, laid with mix-and-match antique furniture; the menu has meat and veg options though concentrates on fish and seafood (mains £11–18, or two-course lunch menu £11). If you **stay** (❺–❻) – prices rise at weekends – ask for one of the four traditionally styled bedrooms in the main house, rather than the newer options in the extension. Stagecoach bus 19 (not Sun) runs to Clanfield hourly from Witney, as do two evening services (not Sun) on route 18 from Oxford.

A mile south of Clanfield, **RADCOT BRIDGE** is the oldest (some say second-oldest) crossing of the River Thames, perhaps thirteenth-century, comprising three brief, humpback bridges in quick succession. This is a popular mooring-point; alongside stands the *Swan* (℡ 01367 810220, ⓦ www.swanhotelradcot.co .uk), which has a self-steer narrowboat for rent (£175/day). Just before the bridge, a turnoff leads west to **Kelmscott Manor** (see p.112). An easy circular **walk** entitled "Heaven on Earth in the Oxfordshire Cotswolds" (5 miles; 2hr) runs from Radcot across the water-meadows to Kelmscott and back along the riverside Thames Path; download details at ⓦ www.ruralways.org.uk.

The Oxfordshire Cotswolds

Although many of the attractions in the Oxfordshire countryside tag themselves as Cotswolds, the official **Cotswolds Area of Outstanding Natural Beauty** (Ⓦ www.cotswoldsaonb.org.uk) occupies a stretch of terrain in the northwest of the county, from the gateway town of **Burford** in the south, northwards to **Chipping Norton** and beyond. That said, there are no formal boundaries and, in truth, the beauty is porous: Minster Lovell, covered previously (on p.105), falls within the AONB, whereas **Kelmscott Manor**, covered below, lies far beyond it. You'll also see and feel no difference crossing from Oxfordshire into the adjacent counties of Gloucestershire and Warwickshire, where the AONB extends. The tourism authorities oblige, slapping more or less everything west of Oxford and south of Banbury with the **Oxfordshire Cotswolds** name (Ⓦ www.oxfordshire cotswolds.org).

Highlights are all **rural**: the fulcrum of the area is the titchy **River Evenlode**, which winds west–east, from its source across the county border in Gloucestershire, past the gorgeous village of **Kingham** – tiny, but with a railway station offering direct Oxford/London trains and replete with places to stay, eat and walk – around the remnants of the ancient Wychwood forest near **Charlbury**, also on the rail line, and onwards to meet the Thames. Its gentle valley offers the most perfect of Cotswolds scenery. But most visitors, unsure how to handle all that open countryside, home in instead on the only significant town, **Burford** – which is pretty, but now rather fancy and very busy, not unlike its Gloucestershire near-neighbour Bourton-on-the-Water (p.185). If Burford is a five-star Cotswolds gateway, **Chipping Norton** further north is its midrange counterpart – less accomplished but also less packaged. A final note: the hugely atmospheric Jacobean country mansion **Chastleton House**, way out west on Moreton-in-Marsh's doorstep, is worth going a long way out of your way to see.

Burford

Twenty miles west of Oxford, many visitors get their first real taste of the Cotswolds at **BURFORD**, where the long and wide **High Street**, which slopes down to a bridge over the River Windrush, is magnificent, despite the traffic. The street is flanked by a remarkably homogeneous line of old buildings that exhibit almost every type of peccadillo known to the Cotswolds, from wonky mullioned

---

The Levellers

A modern plaque just beside the entrance to Burford church pays tribute to "three **Levellers**, executed and buried in this churchyard, 17th May 1649". Earlier that month, some eight hundred Roundhead soldiers in Cromwell's New Model Army – who had been fighting without pay and who were angry at their leaders' betrayal of the notion that all men possessed equal rights under the law – mutinied. These "Levellers", as they became known (from their desire to level out social inequalities), arrived in Burford on May 14. That night, Cromwell attacked the town with cavalry, seizing 340 of the Levellers and locking them in the church. One, Anthony Sedley, carved his name into the font (it is still visible). After 48 hours of incarceration, the supposed ringleaders – the three men named on the plaque – were dragged out into the churchyard and shot.

Burford now hosts **Levellers Day** (Ⓦ www.levellers.org.uk) on the Saturday closest to May 17 every year, commemorating the Levellers' pre-socialist ideals with music, processions and debates on themes of social justice.

windows and half-timbered facades with bendy beams through to spiky brick chimneys, fancy bow-fronted stone houses, and grand horse-and-carriage gateways. The tourist office (see below) has a free leaflet describing a **walk** around town, but you'd do just as well to take your chances and absorb the fluster of daily life – coach parties browsing at souvenir shops, BMWs disgorging immaculate women outside hair salons or interiors boutiques, country types chatting by family butchers… it's all very Cotswolds.

Arrival, information and accommodation

Of Burford's few regular **bus** services, Stagecoach bus 233 runs about every ninety minutes daily from Witney to the Wychwoods, dropping off on Burford High Street – or there's the Swanbrook bus 853, which stops on the A40 at the top of Burford on a route between Oxford (St Giles), Witney, Northleach and Cheltenham/Gloucester (Mon–Sat 3 daily, 1 on Sun). On Sundays, bus 233 serves Burford from Chipping Norton and Kingham railway station.

Midway down Burford's High Street hill, turn onto Sheep Street to find the **tourist office** (Mon–Sat 9.30am–5.30pm, Nov–Feb closes 4pm; ☎01993 823558, ⓦwww.oxfordshirecotswolds.org), recently awarded with a Green Tourism gong for their efforts to promote sustainable tourism.

BURFORD

EATING & DRINKING

Angel	E
Bay Tree	B
Bull	D
Huffkins	1
Inn for All Seasons	2
Lamb Inn	A

ACCOMMODATION

Angel	E
Bay Tree	B
Bull	D
Burford House	C
Lamb Inn	A
Westview House	F

Lechlade & ▼ Cotswold Wildlife Park   Witney & Oxford ▼

Hotels and B&B

Angel Witney St ☎01993 822714, ⓦwww.the angelatburford.co.uk. Historic inn just off the main High Street, particular renowned for its restaurant (see p.110) but also with three guest rooms decorated in a pleasant version of traditional style. ❹

Bay Tree Sheep St ☎01993 822791, ⓦwww .cotswold-inns-hotels.co.uk. First-class hotel beside the tourist office, occupying a wisteria-clad stone house dating from the sixteenth century. Its twenty-odd rooms, in the main house and a couple of annexes, are done up in a lavish rendition of period style. ❺

Bull High St ☎01993 822220, ⓦwww .bullatburford.co.uk. This venerable old inn on Burford's High Street has been hosting guests for more than three hundred years – Charles II dallied here with Nell Gwynne, as did Lord Nelson with Lady Hamilton. It is known chiefly for its restaurant (see p.110), though also has several generally undemanding, traditionally styled rooms. ❹

Burford House High St ☎01993 823151, ⓦwww.burfordhouse.co.uk. Outstanding choice – a historic eight-room timber-framed townhouse hotel that makes an art of the personal touch. The owners, invariably on hand, are unfailingly courteous and have done a fine job with the interiors, retaining classic features but managing effortlessly to refine and update. Memorably charming and comfortable. **7**

Lamb Inn Sheep St ☎01993 823155, ⓦwww .cotswold-inns-hotels.co.uk. Like the *Bay Tree* very close to the tourist office, this is a tad more

traditional than its neighbour, from the bar's flagstoned floor up. Quality is exceptional, from the seventeen carefully presented guest rooms to the splendid gardens. **6**

Westview House 151 The Hill ☎01993 824723, ⓦwww.westview-house.co.uk. Just uphill from the centre, a top-rated B&B offering two cosy guest rooms at the top of the house. **4**

The Town

From Burford's tourist office, head along Sheep Street to the corner of the sweeping High Street hill. Just here, a Tudor timber-framed building on stone pillars – where traders once paid their tolls – now houses the **Tolsey Museum** (April–Oct Mon–Fri 2–5pm, Sat & Sun 11am–5pm; free), exhibiting town maces, charters and old industrial artefacts.

Turn left and, before you reach the bottom of the hill, where a row of sixteenth-century weavers' cottages stand by **Burford Bridge**, cut through to the right in order to reach the fascinating **St John the Baptist church** (ⓦwww .burfordchurch.org), with architectural bits and pieces surviving from every phase of its construction, beginning with the Normans and ending in the wool boom of the seventeenth century. Very unusually, its clutter of mausoleums, chapels and chantries survived the Reformation. The most impressive **mausoleum** is that of Lawrence Tanfield, James I's Chancellor of the Exchequer, who lies on his canopied table-tomb with his wife, both decked out in their Jacobean finery. Even more striking, however, is the **funerary plaque** of Edmund Harman, Henry VIII's barber and surgeon, stuck to the wall of the nave and sporting four Amazonian figures, the first representation of Native Americans in Britain. It is unlikely that Harman met any, but rather he seems to have been linked to a Spanish company trading with South America. Outside, the **churchyard** is strewn with so-called "bale tombs", unique to the area, their rounded tops reminiscent of a bale of wool.

Eating and drinking

Burford's **dining** is, in the main, posh. Although most of the town's hotels can offer atmospheric restaurants – including the *Bay Tree* and *Lamb Inn* listed on p.109, neither of which will disappoint in terms of ambience or quality – a handful of others stand out. Slightly further afield, you could aim for the *Swan* at Swinbrook (see opposite) or another *Swan* at Southrop (see p.200) – while *Number Four* at Stow (p.183) or *Allium* at Fairford (p.200) are within striking distance. For wholesome deli items, the Foxbury Farm Shop (p.106) is about three miles southeast, towards Brize Norton.

In town

Angel (see p.109). A fine place to eat, highly regarded for its careful presentation and lively, creative menu – a madeira *jus* enlivening roast chicken, coriander and chilli adding zip to crab linguine, and so on. Mains are £10–18, and their light lunches, of picnic-style nibbles or mezze to share (£11–12), are a treat.

Bull (see p.109). A formal setting for memorable fine dining, grafting French and Mediterranean influences onto local ingredients – such as local pork done three ways in calvados – with particular

emphasis on fish and seafood. The style might be a touch over-fussy for some, but there's no doubting the range and ability on display. Mains £13–17.

Huffkins 98 High St ☎01993 822126, ⓦwww .huffkins.com. Legendary tearoom offering afternoon tea and cakes to remember. Also not a bad stop for lunchtime soup and salad.

Out of town

Inn For All Seasons On A40, three miles west of Burford ☎01451 844324, ⓦwww.innforall seasons.co.uk. Known for its unusually wide range of Devon-sourced fish and seafood, alongside local venison, pork, lamb and so on, this pub restaurant offers a slightly more down-to-earth atmosphere than many places in Burford, marked by an easygoing, unaffected service style. Mains £12–18.

Heading west from Burford, turn to p.187 for Northleach or p.189 for Bibury.

Riverside walks beside Burford

Two particularly lovely **walks** cover terrain on the banks of the River Windrush to either side of Burford; download maps and notes for both at ⓦwww .cotswoldsaonb.org.uk.

West of Burford, for walk 5 ("Great Barrington–Burford"; 5 miles; 2hr) take the Swanbrook bus 853 west along the A40 to the Lodge at **LITTLE BARRINGTON** (ask the driver for the right stop). From here walk down to the Windrush and cross to wander through **GREAT BARRINGTON** before returning to the river and following a lane beside the meadows which eventually joins Sheep Street in Burford.

East of Burford, for walk 9 ("Villages of the Windrush Valley"; 4 miles; 2hr), take bus 853 east to the turning for **ASTHALL**; you approach the village, whose Elizabethan manor house was formerly home to the Mitford sisters, on foot. Over the Windrush, walk on into **SWINBROOK**, where the twelfth-century church of St Mary has a monument showing six members of the Fettiplace family reclining comically on their elbows, the Tudor effigies rigid and stony-faced, their Stuart counterparts stylish and rather camp. Just before the church consider a refreshment stop at the ⚔ *Swan* (☎01993 823339, ⓦwww.theswanswinbrook .co.uk) – tempting, considering its excellent ales, award-winning restaurant and contemporary-rustic interiors; it also has very comfortable hideaway-style rooms (⑤). A stroll further brings you to **WIDFORD**, a deserted hamlet of which only the isolated St Oswalds chapel is left, in the middle of a field (built over a Roman villa), its fourteenth-century murals still discernible inside. A beautiful footpath along the Windrush takes you back into Burford.

A mile or so east of Swinbrook lies **Minster Lovell**, covered on p.105.

South of Burford: towards Lechlade

This is the only part of our "Oxfordshire Cotswolds" section to lie significantly outside the Cotswolds Area of Outstanding Natural Beauty: **south of Burford** the A361 road takes in a handful of attractions on its way towards Lechlade (see p.200) – notably the superb **Kelmscott Manor** close to the Thames, home to William Morris, founder of the Victorian "Arts and Crafts" movement.

Less than three miles south of Burford, the **Cotswold Wildlife Park** (daily 10am–6pm; Oct–Feb closes 5pm; last admission 90min before closing; £11.50; ⓦwww.cotswoldwildlifepark.co.uk) is a massively popular visitor attraction, drawing happy families by the thousand to see zebras and rhinos, gibbons and giant tortoises, lions, penguins and tarantulas – to name a few. Kids have a whale of a time, riding the **miniature train** around the park (April–Oct; £1 extra), petting the goats and letting off steam in the adventure playground. Best make a day of it: bring a picnic and laze the afternoon away on the lawns – but there's not much peace and quiet to be had, either way. Among other events, **penguin-feeding** happens daily (11am & 4pm; Oct–Feb 11am & 3pm).

Around three miles further, the beautiful old honeystone village of **FILKINS** (ⓦwww.filkins.org.uk) lies just off the main road. As well as the small **Swinford Museum** (May–Sept 1st Sun of month 2.30–5pm; free), displaying rural craft and agricultural tools, the village houses the **Cotswold Woollen Weavers** (Mon–Sat 10am–6pm, Sun 2–6pm; ⓦ www.naturalbest.co.uk), a shop, café and small textile museum attached to the studios of this upmarket designer, producing fashion collections in Cotswold wool as well as everyday clothing, rugs and home accessories. Fuelling the Filkins feeling is the amiable *Five Alls* (ⓣ 01367 860553, ⓦ www .fivealls.co.uk; closed Mon lunch, also closed Mon–Fri 3–5.30pm), an unprettified tavern dealing in simple, tasty pub grub (mains £9–16) and proper beer.

Southrop (see p.200) lies a couple of miles west of Filkins.

Kelmscott Manor

Before the A361 comes into Lechlade (see p.200), follow signs left onto country lanes which twist and turn through the water meadows down to the Thames-side hamlet of **KELMSCOTT** (also signed on minor roads from the A4095 south of Clanfield; see p.107). It lies about eight miles from Burford, or three miles from Lechlade or Clanfield.

On the edge of the village, a small, relatively modest Tudor farmhouse was where author and designer **William Morris** created a country home from 1871 to his death in 1896. Its very simplicity is what attracted Morris, who wrote: "This is what I came out to see, this many-gabled old house built by the simple countryfolk of the long-past times, regardless of all the turmoil that was going on in cities and courts…"

Built around 1600 by the Turners, local yeoman farmers, and now known as **Kelmscott Manor** (April–Sept Wed 11am–5pm, plus 1st & 3rd Sat of month

---

William Morris and the Pre-Raphaelites

Socialist, artist, writer and craftsman **William Morris** (1834–1896) had a profound influence on his contemporaries and on subsequent generations. In some respects he was an ally of Karl Marx, railing against the iniquities of private property and the squalor of industrialized society, but – in contrast to Marx – he believed machines enslave the individual, and that people would be liberated only through a sort of communistic, crafts-based economy. His prose/poem story *News from Nowhere* vaguely described his Utopian society, but his main legacy turned out to be the **Arts and Crafts Movement**.

Morris's career as an artist began at Oxford, where he met **Edward Burne-Jones**, who shared his admiration for the arts of the Middle Ages. After graduating they both ended up in London, painting under the direction of Dante Gabriel Rossetti, the leading light of the **Pre-Raphaelites**, a loose grouping of artists intent on regaining the spiritual purity characteristic of art before Raphael and the Renaissance "tainted" the world with humanism. In 1861 Morris founded **Morris & Co** ("The Firm"), whose designs came to embody the ideas of the Arts and Crafts Movement, one of whose basic tenets was formulated by its founder: "Have nothing in your houses that you do not know to be useful or believe to be beautiful." Rossetti and Burne-Jones were among the designers, though Morris's own designs for fabrics, wallpapers and numerous other products were to prove a massive influence in Britain. The Laura Ashley aesthetic is a lineal descendant of Morris's rustic nostalgia.

Not content with his artistic endeavours, in 1890 Morris set up the **Kelmscott Press**, named after (but not located at) his summer home, whose masterpiece was the so-called *Kelmscott Chaucer*, the collected poems of one of the Pre-Raphaelites' greatest heroes, with woodcuts by Burne-Jones. Morris also pioneered interest in the architecture of the Cotswolds and, in response to the Victorian penchant for modernizing churches and cottages, he instigated the **Society for the Protection of Ancient Buildings** (ⓦ www.spab.org.uk), still an active force in preserving the country's architectural heritage.

11am–5pm; £8.50; ☎01367 252486, ⓦwww.kelmscottmanor.org.uk) – though it's not, and never was, a manor house – the house is enhanced by the furniture, fabrics, wallpapers and tapestries created by Morris and his Pre-Raphaelite friends, including Burne-Jones and Rossetti. It could easily fill a pleasant half-day. There is limited space, so admission is by timed ticket; it's wise to call ahead to confirm arrangements.

Inside, knowledgeable guides are stationed in every room. From the entrance passage, turn right into the **Old Hall**, once a dining-room and still with its original table and – flanking the fire – seventeenth-century oak chairs, alongside later chairs made by Morris. Further along, the **White Room** is a beautiful, light space dating from a 1660 extension, with Georgian panelling, a Morris *Millefleurs* tapestry woven in 1925 and, in the neighbouring closet, Rossetti's *Blue Silk Dress* (1868), a swoon-worthy portrait of Morris's wife, Jane. Highlights upstairs – among a delightful array of hanging textiles, portraits, original wallpaper and more – include **William Morris's Bedroom**, his four-poster bed bedecked with a pelmet painstakingly hand-woven with his "Verses for the Bed at Kelmscott" (1891):

> *The wind's on the wold*
> *And the night is a-cold,*
> *And Thames runs chill*
> *Twixt mead and hill…*

Beside is the lovely **Tapestry Room**, Rossetti's studio. Upstairs again, the simple **Attics** remain full of atmosphere; one displays a collection of Morris textiles. You return to the ground-floor **Old Kitchen** and out into the **gardens**. Despite the house's popularity – it's always busy – the charm and atmosphere of Morris's Arts and Crafts aesthetic come through loud and clear: this is a house to be happy in.

No buses go anywhere near Kelmscott. Within the village, you're directed to park in a field, from where it's a pleasant ten-minute **walk** to the house. On the way back you'll pass the *Plough* (☎01367 253543), an attractive old pub that's handy for a pint and a decent enough lunch, though the clientele – nearly all manor visitors – are fairly captive, and the interior, with stuck-down willow branches arching across the flagstoned dining-room, speaks of designer aspirations not met. Eight guest **rooms** (❹) cover the basics. See p.107 for details of a circular five-mile walk between Kelmscott and Radcot.

North of Burford: the Evenlode Valley

Along with its southern neighbour the Windrush, which flows through Burford and Witney, the valley of the **River Evenlode** offers classic Cotswolds scenery. From its source near Moreton-in-Marsh, the river flows southeast through Oxfordshire, joining the Thames above Oxford. Don't expect headline attractions or even very much to do: expect, rather, to lose yourself in the byways, stumble across a village pub or two, take in the views on a countryside walk. You could aim, if you like, for **Kingham** village, on the Oxfordshire-Gloucestershire border, where there's a little cluster of fine country inns, or perhaps **Charlbury**, a touch hillier but closer to the attractions of Woodstock.

The Wychwoods
North of Burford, the A361 climbs out of the Windrush valley, offering views towards the Evenlode before dropping down to a cluster of three neighbouring villages whose names recall the ancient forests of Wychwood which formerly covered this area (more on p.97). Just west of the road is **MILTON-UNDER-WYCHWOOD** – of medieval foundation, like its siblings, and benefiting from a

The Cotswold Line railway

Kingham, Charlbury and a handful of other Evenlode villages are well served by regular trains on the **Cotswold Line**, which forms a link in the main line from London Paddington through Oxford to Evesham, Worcester and Hereford, now operated by First Great Western. Single-track for large sections – though by the time you read this an upgrade may have been completed – it nonetheless survived Beeching's Axe. Today, as well as giving urban visitors easy access to deepest Cotswold countryside, it forms a crucial axis of economic and cultural exchange, connecting small villages to big cities (for mutual benefit) and bringing money into the Cotswolds – not only tourism, but also in terms of rural businesses maintaining access to markets, and wealthy urban commuters being able to live in the country. Arguably, the proximity to London created by the railway has also helped Cotswold ideas, for instance about food quality or the value of rural lifestyles, gain currency nationwide.

Above all, it's beautiful. Other railways may have more natural drama, but few can match the evocative scenery of the forty-minute run beside the Evenlode from Oxford to Moreton. In June 1914, a week before the Great War erupted, poet **Edward Thomas** (1878–1917) was travelling this way when his train made an unscheduled stop at Adlestrop, a hamlet north of Kingham. His poem *Adlestrop* immortalized both the line and this part of the Cotswolds – though British Rail still closed Adlestrop station, regardless, in 1966.

Yes, I remember Adlestrop –
The name, because one afternoon
Of heat the express-train drew up there
Unwontedly. It was late June.

The steam hissed. Someone cleared his throat.
No one left and no one came
On the bare platform. What I saw
Was Adlestrop – only the name

And willows, willow-herb, and grass,
And meadowsweet, and haycocks dry,
No whit less still and lonely fair
Than the high cloudlets in the sky.

And for that minute a blackbird sang
Close by, and round him, mistier,
Farther and farther, all the birds
Of Oxfordshire and Gloucestershire.

lovely six-mile circular walk through Fifield (download details at Ⓦ www .oxfordshirecotswolds.org). Stop here, too, for the **Wychwood Deli** (Ⓦ www .wychwooddeli.co.uk), selling cheeses, pies and all sorts of delicious stuff from around the Cotswolds.

There is, however, more interest in **SHIPTON-UNDER-WYCHWOOD**, directly on the A361. Here, overlooking the village green, the *Shaven Crown* (Ⓣ 01993 830330, Ⓦ www.theshavencrown.co.uk) is purportedly one of the ten oldest pubs in Britain, in operation since at least the fourteenth century – perhaps earlier, since it was originally run by Cistercian monks from the now-demolished abbey at nearby Bruern, founded in 1147. The building is pure theatre, from its mullioned windows to its stone fireplaces and arching gateway. Drop in for a pint, a meal or to **stay**: their eight midrange rooms (❸) are all en suite, with bags of atmosphere. Shipton also sports two other historic pubs, the *Lamb* (☎01993 830465, Ⓦwww.shiptonlamb.co.uk; ❹) – a step up in comfort and luxury – and the simpler *Red Horse* (☎01993 830391, Ⓦwww.theredhorse.co.uk; ❷). Add in a station with two **trains** a day (not Sun), plus good **bus** links on RH Transport bus X8 (not Sun) to/from Kingham, as well as Stagecoach bus 233 to/from Witney (extending to/from Chipping Norton on Sundays), and little Shipton becomes a great choice for a rural break.

Two miles east, **ASCOTT-UNDER-WYCHWOOD** is known for the "**Ascott Martyrs**", sixteen village women who, in 1873, spoke out in support of local labourers sacked for forming a trade union. The women's arrest and imprisonment in Oxford Castle led to rioting and, eventually, a royal pardon from Queen Victoria. More prosaically, Ascott's upscale gastropub-cum-hotel, the *Swan*, closed inexplicably in 2010; at the time of writing it was unclear whether it might ever reopen.

Kingham

When *Country Life* magazine calls you "England's favourite village", it could easily prompt a downward spiral. But for **KINGHAM**, set in the Evenlode Valley between Chipping Norton (the highest town in Oxfordshire) and Stow-on-the-Wold (the highest town in the entire Cotswolds), everything's looking up. Since that accolade, in 2007 – awarded on a range of criteria from architectural merit and natural setting to transport links, community spirit and quality of life – this cheery, noticeably upmarket village has gone from strength to strength. There's still nothing to do here, other than eat well, drink well, walk well and sleep well… but that's the point.

Top of the list is booking ahead for a meal to remember at the superb ⋇*Kingham Plough* (☎01608 658327, Ⓦwww.thekinghamplough.co.uk). The epitome of a Cotswold gastropub, this is one of the county's best **restaurants**, atmospherically housed in an old stone building by the large, open village green, with simple contemporary-country decor and furniture and a service ethic that perfectly blends efficiency and warm informality. Come here for local, seasonal produce of all kinds, expertly prepared (mains £15–25) and served off a short, daily-changing menu (not available Sun eve). They also have seven country-style **rooms** (❹–❺), both in the main house and a newer annexe.

Just down the street, expect a friendly welcome at the *Tollgate* (☎01608 658389, Ⓦwww.thetollgate.com), which occupies a renovated seventeenth-century farmhouse sporting a broad, sun-trap front terrace. The food, though a step down from the competition, is excellent – an accomplished, unfussy take on classic English cuisine (mains £11–16) – while their pleasant, attractive rooms (❹) ooze country character.

Kingham **railway station**, with regular service to/from London, Oxford, Moreton and Worcester, lies a mile from the village centre, beyond the fine Perpendicular tower of **St Andrew's Church**. Railbus X8 (Mon–Sat hourly) or bus 233 (3–4 on Sun) meets arriving trains, running from the station to Kingham village green and Chipping Norton, or the other way to Shipton-under-Wychwood. To get to Burford, Minster Lovell and Witney take the X8 to Milton-under-Wychwood and change there to the 233 (Mon–Sat); on Sundays, the 233 runs direct from Kingham.

Around Kingham

A mile or two north of Kingham, just off the A436 Stow–Chipping Norton road, **DAYLESFORD** village, a few yards inside Gloucestershire, has won nationwide renown for *Daylesford Organic* (☎01608 731700, Ⓦwww.daylesfordorganic.com),

Walks around Kingham

Kingham has loads of **walking** possibilities – not least within the **Foxholes Nature Reserve** (Ⓦwww.bbowt.org.uk), an ancient woodland famed for its spring bluebells. Longer routes abound: download maps and descriptions for many at Ⓦwww.oxfordshirecotswolds.org. Walk 1 is a short **circular route** to/from Kingham Station (3.5 miles; 2hr 30min), exploring the fields around Bledington; a longer option is Walk 4 (9 miles; 5hr), also to/from the station but heading out past Foscot to Bruern, then skirting the Foxholes reserve to Idbury and back via Bledington. Several routes offer walks **from Kingham to Chipping Norton**: most straightforward is Walk 11 (5.5 miles; 3hr), along a stream to Swaleford Bridge and then across the meadows, or you could tackle the circuitous Walk 6 (9 miles; 5hr) which takes in woodland and fields around Adlestrop, Chastleton, Cornwell and Salford.

founded in the 1980s when the local landowning Bamford family converted their farming estates to organic. Fashions caught up, and now Daylesford not only markets its own-brand produce but has a village **shop** (Mon–Wed 9am–5pm, Thurs–Sat 9am–6pm, Sun 10am–4pm) – more like the smartest London food hall, vast, immaculate and expensive – stocking premium deli items of all kinds. It's a rather absorbing glimpse of Chelsea in the Cotswolds, even more so at weekends, with the car park lined by top-end 4WDs. That said, the **café** (closes 30min earlier) remains a very pleasant place for scrambled eggs or afternoon tea, and their lunches – salads, risotto, shepherd's pie – are top-quality, if pricey (mains £10–14). On site, too, are a day spa and cookery school.

Extending the area's appeal, just the other side of Kingham – also yards into Gloucestershire – **BLEDINGTON** hosts another of the Cotswolds' most celebrated rural gastropub/hotels. The sixteenth-century *Kings Head Inn* (℡01608 658365, Ⓦwww.kingsheadinn.net), overlooking the village green, quietly ticks every box. Still the heart of the local community, with regulars supping pints at the spruce but avowedly old-fashioned bar, it doubles up as a restaurant of genuine quality, serving local, ethically sourced food that taps directly into the English country mindset – think potted shrimps, steak-and-ale pie, venison and Cotswold lamb – alongside newer-fangled modern British fusion dishes. The rooms, some floral, some designer-chic, are a snip, whether above the bar or in the courtyard annexe (❹–❺). Note that it's **closed on weekday afternoons** (Mon–Fri 3–6pm).

Or you could veer the other way out of Kingham: a couple of miles along the B4450 Chipping Norton road in tiny **CHURCHILL**, the *Forge* (℡01608 658173, Ⓦwww.cotswolds-accommodation.com; ❸) offers a handful of simpler en-suite rooms in tastefully converted old stone premises, a stroll from the **Churchill and Sarsden Heritage Centre** (Sat & Sun 2–4.30pm; free; Ⓦwww.churchillheritage .org.uk), a local history museum housed in the restored chancel of a now-destroyed medieval church.

Charlbury and around

Midway between Kingham and Woodstock, on the dipping and rising slopes above the Evenlode, the little market town of **CHARLBURY** is another, less posh, halt on the Cotswold rail line. (Oxford trains aside, Charlbury also has the handy Stagecoach **bus** S3, linking hourly to/from Woodstock). Cross the river from the **railway station** (built by Brunel) to reach the **church of St Mary**, part twelfth-and thirteenth-century though, unusually, with the internal layout reversed: since the 1990s, the congregation have chosen to turn their back on the dark chancel and pray westwards instead. From here climb into the narrow, close-set central streets, marked by many eighteenth-century buildings. The *Rose and Crown* (℡01608 810103, Ⓦwww.roseandcrown.charlbury.com) is a real drinkers' pub – fantastic for an ever-changing array of local ales – while the *Bell* (℡01608 810278, Ⓦwww .bellhotel-charlbury.com; ❹) and the *Bull* (℡01608 810689, Ⓦwww.bullinn -charlbury.com; ❸) are both worth investigating for their restaurants and country-style rooms. One mile north of town on the hilly B4022 Enstone road, *Cotswold View* (℡01608 810314, Ⓦwww.cotswoldview.co.uk; April–Oct) is a popular **caravan and camping park**, not least for its **pods** – insulated wooden huts that are an alternative to sleeping under canvas: they're bare inside, so you'll need camping gear. The park also has simple **B&B** (❸).

Stretching southwest from Charlbury is **Cornbury Park**, which encompasses the only substantial surviving part of the ancient Wychwood Forest. The Cornbury estate is privately owned, but go to Ⓦwww.oxfordshire.gov.uk /charlburywalk to download a map and notes for an eight-mile **circular walk** following the only public footpath through the forest.

Every road out of Charlbury offers great driving, especially the B4437 west to the Wychwoods, and the lovely B4022 (see also p.105), climbing south into the Windrush Valley. The B4026 also climbs, north towards Chipping Norton; turn off left to reach **CHADLINGTON**, where the locals clubbed together in 2001 to save the village shop from closure, in the process turning it into one of the area's leading (and *very* un-Daylesford) **farm shops** (Ⓦwww.chadlington.com). On the nearby corner is *Café de la Post* (Ⓦwww.cafedelapost.com), an exotic title for a general store doubling as a tearoom, while down the road the *Tite Inn* (℡01608 676475, Ⓦwww.titeinn.com; closed Mon) makes a comfortable spot for a nice pint and a decent meal.

Chipping Norton

As "Gateway to the Cotswolds" Burford may have a touch of the Cinderellas about it, but it would be unfair to call its northern counterpart **CHIPPING NORTON** an ugly sister. This busy little market town (Ⓦwww.chippingnorton .net), only eight miles east of Stow-on-the-Wold (see p.180) is not the prettiest place in the Cotswolds, but it is flanked to the north and east by one of the least explored and most scenic corners of the region, where the limestone uplands are patterned by long dry-stone walls and sprinkled with tiny stone villages. King John granted a **wool fair** charter to the town in the twelfth century – "chipping" comes from *ceapen*, Old English for market – but it reached its peak three hundred years later, when it acquired many of the stalwart stone buildings that now line up along the sloping **Market Square**.

Also paid for by wealthy wool merchants, **St Mary's Church**, just below the square – and beyond a handsome row of almshouses – looks every inch the

---

Walks around Chipping Norton

Chippy's best **walks** include the **Glyme Valley Way** (Ⓦwww.oxfordshire.gov.uk /glymevalleywalk), sixteen miles to Woodstock – chiefly downhill and walkable in a (long) day. See the website for full details, or you could split it in half (8 miles; 4hr): set out south then bear east to join the River Glyme near Lidstone, continuing through Enstone and across fields to end at Kiddington, from where bus S3 returns you to Chipping Norton. The section from Kiddington into Woodstock is described on p.97. Two **circular walks** to/from Chippy are also worthwhile (both at Ⓦwww .oxfordshirecotswolds.org) – an easy one via Over Norton (2.5 miles) and a more taxing one (6.5 miles) across fields to Salford, Cornwell and back.

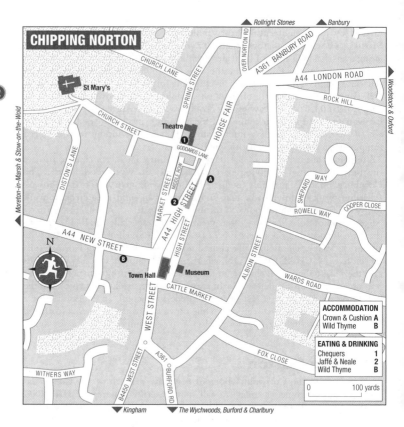

country church, the modesty of its tower offset by the slender windows of its Perpendicular Gothic nave. The vaulted porch is equally striking, not least for the grinning devils and green men that peer down from the roof. By comparison, the interior is rather routine, though the nave is well lit and airy and the east window of the south aisle is a splendid affair, spiralling out from a central tulip; look out also for two superbly carved alabaster table-tombs commemorating sixteenth-century merchants and their wives. Opposite the steps of the Victorian **town hall** on the square, **Chipping Norton Museum** (Easter–Oct Mon–Sat 2–4pm; £1) has a modest but well-assembled collection covering the history of the town from Roman artefacts to World War II memorabilia.

Down in the valley just west of the centre, the **Bliss Tweed Mill** (no public access), built in 1872, recalls the textile mini-boom Chipping Norton enjoyed in the nineteenth century: it's a novel design, with a domed roof and towering, top-heavy chimneystack. Walk a few minutes out along the A44 for a grand view of it; if you drive into town from the west, the same vista opens on your right-hand side.

Practicalities

Several useful **bus** routes converge on Chipping Norton, all stopping on West Street, the continuation of Market Square. Railbus X8 (not Sun) runs regularly from Shipton-under-Wychwood and Kingham station (waiting for arriving trains); on Sundays, bus 233 takes over, with two trips from Witney, Minster

Lovell, Burford, Shipton and Kingham station. The S3 comes from Oxford and Woodstock, and 488 (not Sun) from Banbury and Hook Norton (both Stagecoach), and RH Transport bus X9 (not Sun) from Witney and Charlbury, all with hourly service. Stagecoach bus 50 runs three or four times a day from Stratford via Shipston-on-Stour.

Accommodation isn't widespread: there are forty rooms behind the Georgian facade of the *Crown and Cushion* (℡01608 642533, Ⓦwww.crown-cushion.co .uk; ❹) on the main square, but not all of them are up to snuff. You may do better booking one of the three cosy, stylish rooms at the *Wild Thyme* **restaurant**, just down the hill at 10 New Street (℡01608 645060, Ⓦwww.wildthymerestaurant .co.uk; ❸; closed Mon), whose modern British cuisine is also the best in town – this small, relatively new place has quickly won a reputation for creative, often intriguing food displaying real panache (mains £12–19).

For lighter bites try the little **café** in the wonderful *Jaffé & Neale* independent bookshop on the main square (Ⓦwww.jaffeandneale.co.uk), a real Chippy institution, or sample the atmospheric *Chequers* **pub** (℡01608 644717, Ⓦwww .chequers-pub.com; no food Sun–Tues eve) on Goddards Lane behind the bookshop – an old-fashioned drinkers' local in the front, a bright, airy, family-minded pub restaurant in the back (mains £8–14). Drop in, too, to the Cotswold Deli round the corner (Ⓦwww.cotswolddeli.co.uk or Ⓦwww.cotswoldfood store.co.uk), sister outlet to the one at Longborough (see p.180). Beside *Chequers*, the **theatre** (℡01608 642350, Ⓦwww.chippingnortontheatre.co.uk) offers an unusual dose of culture for a small country town, with drama, music and arthouse cinema.

Chastleton House

Roughly four miles west of Chipping Norton, via the A44 and country lanes – also easily reached from Stow (see p.180) and Moreton (see p.175) – stands **Chastleton House** (Wed–Sat: April–Sept 1–5pm, Oct 1–4pm; £7.85; timed tickets, pre-bookable on ℡01494 755560, Ⓦwww.nationaltrust.org.uk). Built between 1607 and 1612 by Walter Jones, a wealthy wool merchant, this ranks among England's most splendid Jacobean houses, set amid ornamental gardens that include the country's first-ever croquet lawn (croquet's rules were codified here in 1865).

During the Civil War the Joneses were Royalist: they lost most of their wealth to the Cromwellian authorities and remained too poor thereafter to renovate or refurbish. Nothing was done to the house until 1800, when a few repairs were made – and then, virtually nothing since. From the day it was built until 1991, when it was put in the care of the National Trust, the house passed through family hands and was never sold.

Because of this, Chastleton has a special allure. Aside from the architecture, which is sublime, its interiors seem stuck in time, with unwashed upholstery, unpolished wood panelling and miscellaneous clutter clogging some of the corners. This dishevelled air is a credit to the National Trust, who wisely decided to stick to the "lived-in" look. Chastleton seems to have escaped history, claiming no connection to any major events or noteworthy people who might have been tempted to alter it. It feels less like a stately home than a time machine.

The tone is set by the first room, the **Great Hall**, entered through a carved oak screen: the soot marks above the fireplace remain unscrubbed, for a start. The hall's oak table is as old as the house. Other highlights include the **Great Chamber** upstairs, with an elaborate chimneypiece and moulded ceiling, and the hugely impressive **Long Gallery** at the top of the house, barrel-vaulted with an ornate plasterwork ceiling. Head down into the basement for the atmospheric **Old**

Kitchen and adjacent **Beer Cellar**, featuring the longest ladder you're ever likely to see, sixty feet in length and made in 1805 to facilitate gutter-clearing. Leave time to stroll the wonderful **topiary garden**.

The Rollright Stones

Driving west from Chipping Norton along the A44, it only takes a few minutes to reach the signed country lane that leads off to the right to the **Rollright Stones** (ⓦwww.rollrightstones.co.uk), a scattering of megalithic monuments in the fields either side. The eerie array consists of large natural stones moved here – no one is sure why – plus several burial chambers and barrows. The largest is the **King's Men**, comprising over seventy irregularly spaced stones forming a circle thirty metres in diameter, one of the most important such monuments in the country. Signed just off the lane, it's also the easiest to find. The circle gets its name from a legend about a witch who turned a king and his army (of unknown identity) into these gnarled rocks to stop them invading England. Across the lane (which marks the Oxfordshire-Warwickshire border) stands the **King's Stone** monolith, offering pensive views across the countryside, while a third group – dubbed the **Whispering Knights** – lie a short walk southeast of the King's Men on the field margin. The site is open and unstaffed; drop £1 into the honesty box as an admission fee. Roughly a mile east of the site, the **Wyatts Farm Shop** (☎01608 684835, ⓦwww.wyattsgardencentre.co.uk) has books and leaflets about the stones, as well as a café.

Just west of Chastleton and Rollright lies **Moreton-in-Marsh**, covered on p.175.

Hook Norton and around

Signposted a few miles off the A361 Chipping Norton–Banbury road, **HOOK NORTON** is one of the prettier villages in the area, its high street flanked by thatched cottages. Aim first for the **church**, with an impressively tall Perpendicular tower; inside, the early-Norman stone **font** features clear carvings of the pagan signs of the zodiac. Signed at the east end of the village is **Hook Norton Pottery** (Mon–Sat 9am–5pm; ⓦwww.hooknortonpottery.co.uk), with a small shop attached, but the main draw is **Hook Norton Brewery**, dating from 1849 and still fully-functioning – many say "Hooky" beers are Oxfordshire's best. There's an on-site shop and small **museum** (Mon–Sat 9.30am–4.30pm) but you'd do better to time your visit for a two-hour **brewery tour** (Mon–Fri 9.30am, 11am & 2pm, Sat 10.30am & 1.30pm; £9.50; ☎01608 730384, ⓦwww.hooknortonbrewery.co.uk), which shows the brewing process, explains more about the company and the village and ends with free samples. Advance booking is essential. The hourly Stagecoach bus 488 (not Sun) between Chipping Norton and Banbury stops in Hook Norton.

As you'd imagine, **beer** is important hereabouts. Just outside the brewery is the *Pear Tree* (☎01608 737482, ⓦwww.hooky-pubs.co.uk), as good a place to start as any, while the ⚔ *Sun Inn* (☎01608 737570, ⓦwww.the-suninn.co.uk), opposite the church, has a great atmosphere, complete with inglenook fireplace, oak beams and stone flags.

Three pubs near the village are also worth making a beeline for. The wonderfully named *Gate Hangs High* (☎01608 737387, ⓦwww.thegatehangshigh.com) stands alone at a country crossroads on the Sibford road; it's a lovely old pub, in 2010 under new management who are aiming to revive its gastronomic fortunes. Just north, in tranquil **SIBFORD GOWER**, the ⚔ *Wykham Arms* (☎01295

Cotswold food

The Cotswolds is foodie heaven. Few regions of Britain have embraced the Rick Stein/Jamie Oliver/River Cottage-inspired contemporary food revolution with more enthusiasm. Wherever you go, you'll find restaurants serving fresh, seasonal, locally sourced food that is also often organic or ethically produced, along with farm shops, farmers' markets, independent specialist delis and food shops galore. At a time when the old rural ways have changed forever, food has become the clearest, most resonant way to celebrate Cotswold culture.

Cotswold specialities

Predominantly an agricultural area, the Cotswolds is crammed with culinary specialities, best purchased at a local farm shop or **farmers' market** (see p.27).

Farms across the region produce **organic fruit** and **veg**, as well as ethically farmed meat: Old Spot is a traditional Gloucestershire breed of pig which makes its way onto many menus, and the **Real Boar Company** (ⓦwww.therealboar.co.uk) is one of England's few producers of charcuterie from boar, farmed ethically on the Cotswold fringes. Bibury and Donnington both have trout farms, while Upton Smokery (ⓦwww.uptonsmokery.co.uk) produce a range of local smoked **fish** and **game**.

Home Farm, on the Prince of Wales's Highgrove estate outside Tetbury, supplies many ingredients for HRH's nationally distributed **Duchy Originals** organic range (ⓦwww.duchyoriginals.com), including pork for the hams and sausages, grain for the biscuits and barley for ale. R-Oil (ⓦwww.r-oil.co.uk) and Cotswold Gold (ⓦwww.cotswoldgold.co.uk) produce cold-pressed **extra virgin rapeseed oil** as an alternative to imported olive oil.

For something sweet, try a **Banbury cake** – a flat, currant-filled pastry, similar to an Eccles cake; they've been baked and sold in the town for at least five hundred years, but bittersweet **Oxford marmalade** has, regrettably, not been manufactured in Oxford for many years. Local ice cream comes from, among others, the **Cotswold Ice Cream Company** (ⓦwww.cotswoldicecream.net), **Winstones** (ⓦwww.winstonesicecream.co.uk) and **Spot Loggins** (ⓦwww.spotloggins.com) – while, to accompany, there's sticky toffee pudding from the **Cotswold Pudding Company** (ⓦwww.cotswoldpuddingcompany.co.uk).

Organic vegetables ▲

Bibury Trout Farm ▲

Banbury cakes ▼

Cotswolds ice cream ▼

Cotswold cheeses

The Cotswolds excels in cheese — more than a hundred varieties are produced across the region, often on small local farms. Crudges, near Kingham, is one acclaimed artisan producer; for others, see Ⓦwww .specialistcheesemakers.co.uk. Crudges also work with rock musician and celebrity Cotswolds cheesemaker Alex James, though James's award-winning cheeses (Ⓦwww .evenlodepartnership.co.uk) are, in truth, made far away — his mild Blue Monday in Scotland and soft goats' cheeses Little Wallop and Farleigh Wallop in Somerset.

Double Gloucester is produced nationwide. Its crumblier cousin Single Gloucester is rarer, made only from Gloucester cattle milked in Gloucestershire; producers include Ⓦwww .smartsgloucestercheese.com and Ⓦwww .godsellscheese.com. Creamy Oxford Blue is made — oddly — at a Stilton dairy in Derbyshire but matured and distributed by the Oxford Blue Cheese Company (Ⓦwww .oxfordfinefood.com). Gorsehill Abbey (Ⓦwww.gorsehillabbey.co.uk) are known for their Camembert-like St Eadburgha, while the Windrush Valley dairy and Cerney Cheese produce outstanding goats' cheese. Organic Cotswold Brie comes from Simon Weaver near Lower Slaughter (Ⓦwww.simonweaver.net).

▲ Single Gloucester cheese

▼ Gloucester Old Spot pigs

▼ Cotswold apples

Juicy fruit

Another Cotswold success story is fruit juice. Bensons pure apple juice (Ⓦwww .bensonsapplejuice.co.uk) is widely sold; smaller producers include Hayles Fruit Farm (Ⓦwww.hayles-fruit-farm .co.uk) alongside cordials by Five Valleys (Ⓦwww.fivevalleyscordials .co.uk).

Cotswold beer

Artisan brewing has become very popular: Britain now has more breweries than at any time since World War II – and the Cotswolds keeps pace.

▸▸ **Hook Norton** (Ⓦwww.hooknorton brewery.co.uk) has four main ales – Hooky Dark, fruity Old Hooky, malted Hooky Bitter and pale Hooky Gold – supplemented by a welter of seasonal and special-edition beers.

▸▸ **Donnington** (Ⓦwww.donnington -brewery.com) is a family firm based near Stow-on-the-Wold and produces amber "BB" and malty "SBA" bitters. The same family also runs Arkell's Brewery, a bigger concern based in Swindon (Ⓦwww.arkells.com).

▸▸ **Wychwood** (Ⓦwww.wychwood.co .uk) – now owned by Marston's, a national company – brews the flavourful Hobgoblin, alongside speciality beers such as Bah Humbug and The Dog's Bollocks, and also runs Brakspear (Ⓦwww.brakspear-beers .co.uk), known for its organic Oxford Gold.

▸▸ The **Cotswold Brewing Company** (Ⓦwww.cotswoldbrewingcompany.com) produces a range of award-winning, European-style lagers, sold in pubs and restaurants across the region.

You could also try…

Ⓦwww.battledownbrewery.com
Ⓦwww.cotswoldbrewery.co.uk
Ⓦwww.halfpennybrewery.co.uk
Ⓦwww.nailsworth-brewery.co.uk
Ⓦwww.northcotswoldbrewery.co.uk
Ⓦwww.thepatriotbrewery.co.uk
Ⓦwww.puritybrewing.com
Ⓦwww.shotoverbrewing.com
Ⓦwww.stanwaybrewery.com
Ⓦwww.stroudbrewery.co.uk

Riverside pub, Lechlade ▲

Hook Norton beer ▼

Hook Norton brewery ▼

788808, Ⓦ www.wykhamarms.co.uk) already leads the pack in that regard – a seventeenth-century village inn serving outstanding seasonal, local food in its distinctly upscale interior (mains £10–16), renowned in particular for its Sunday roasts. In the other direction, plumb on the A361 beside **SWERFORD**, the *Masons Arms* (Ⓣ 01608 683212, Ⓦ www.masons-arms.com) has also gained recognition for its ethically sourced food, serving a stylish, upmarket pub version of fine dining (mains around £14).

Great Tew

In a region which has beautiful villages and fine old pubs coming out of its ears, **GREAT TEW**, about five miles east of Chipping Norton via the A361 and B4022, takes the biscuit. Not strictly in the Cotswolds, it nonetheless has Cotswold character aplenty, its thatched cottages and honey-coloured stone houses weaving around grassy hillocks with woodland on all sides. Here also is the idyllic, locally renowned ⚑ *Falkland Arms* (Ⓣ 01608 683653, Ⓦ www .falklandarms.co.uk), which rotates guest beers in addition to its Wadworth cask ales, and sells a fine selection of single malts, herbal wines, snuff and clay pipes you can fill with tobacco for a smoke in the flower-filled garden. Little has changed in the flagstone-floored **bar** since the sixteenth century, although the snug is now a small **dining room** serving homemade food (mains from £9). It's also a popular place to **stay**: there are five rooms (❸), sympathetically renovated and attractively furnished.

North Oxfordshire

Although Chipping Norton, Woodstock and other destinations covered above fall into the northern part of Oxfordshire, the tourist entity of **NORTH OXFORD-SHIRE** restricts itself to the market town of **Banbury**, the sleepier dormitory town of **Bicester** and the villages between them, including cosy **Deddington** and nearby **Lower Heyford**, which gives access to walks and narrowboat holidays on the **Oxford Canal**. This is a lovely bit of the country for those who like to be at one remove from the hubbub. It has much of the Cotswolds' beauty, with rolling hills, honeystone villages, ancient churches and, in **Broughton Castle**, one of England's most romantic stately homes, but it stands well outside the Cotswolds proper, so consequently has nothing to live up to – prices are lower, restaurants less fancy, hotels trying less hard to wow. With the M40 motorway running through, and a host of A roads converging on Banbury, you could do worse than base yourself here for a series of day-trips into more prestigious Cotswolds countryside further west.

Banbury

Although it officially plays the county's second fiddle to Oxford, **BANBURY** has never had much to do with its highfalutin neighbour. Indeed, for the last couple of centuries at least, this hardworking, unpretentious place has instead preferred to think of itself as the focus of "**Banburyshire**", an informal network of villages and rural farming communities in the town's immediate orbit which includes parts of the adjacent counties of Northamptonshire and Warwickshire but which pays little heed to the goings-on further south. Banbury is also unusually diverse, with significant populations of Poles – you'll see several Polish delis around town – and Pakistanis, almost all the latter originating from one small district of Kashmir. In

Broughton, Shipston & B ◀   ◀ Stratford, Edgehill & Upton House

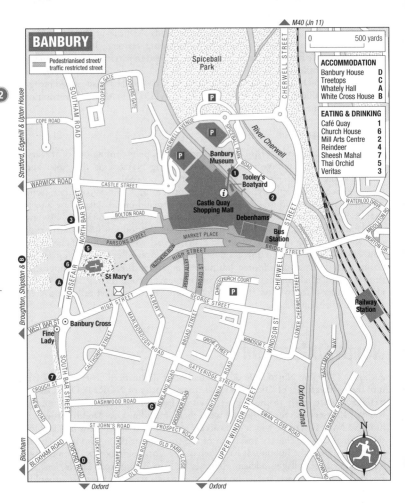

BANBURY

0 ─── 500 yards

Pedestrianised street/
traffic restricted street

Spiceball
Park

River Cherwell

ACCOMMODATION

Banbury House	D
Treetops	C
Whately Hall	A
White Cross House	B

EATING & DRINKING

Café Quay	1
Church House	6
Mill Arts Centre	2
Reindeer	4
Sheesh Mahal	7
Thai Orchid	5
Veritas	3

CHERWELL STREET

SOUTHAM ROAD

COOPERS GATE
COOPERS GATE

COPE ROAD

CHERWELL AVENUE

SPICEBALL PARK ROAD

WARWICK ROAD

CASTLE STREET

Banbury
Museum

Tooley's
Boatyard

WATERLOO DRIVE

NORTH BAR STREET

BOLTON ROAD

Castle Quay
Shopping Mall

Debenhams

Bus
Station

MERTON DR

MIDDLETON RD

PARSONS STREET

MARKET PLACE

BUTCHERS ROW

HIGH STREET

BRIDGE STREET

St Mary's

PEPPER ALLEY

BROAD ST

CHRISTCHURCH COURT

CHERWELL STREET

LOWER CHERWELL STREET

**Railway
Station**

HORSEFAIR

HIGH STREET

ALBERT ST

GEORGE STREET

WINDSOR ST

HASLEMERE WAY

WEST BAR ST
Fine
Lady

Banbury Cross

MARLBOROUGH ROAD

BROAD STREET

GROVE STREET

WINDSOR ST

Oxford Canal

N

SOUTH BAR STREET

CALTHORPE STREET

GATTERIDGE STREET

NEWLAND ROAD

BRITANNIA ROAD

UPPER WINDSOR STREET

SWAN CLOSE ROAD

TRAMWAY ROAD

RIGHTON RD

CROUCH ST

DASHWOOD ROAD

PROSPECT ROAD

OLD PARR CLOSE

NEW ROAD

ST JOHN'S ROAD

LUCKY LANE

CALTHORPE ROAD

OLD PARR ROAD

Bloxham ◀

BLOXHAM ROAD

OXFORD ROAD

▼ Oxford   ▼ Oxford

mindset, preoccupations and accent, this is more of a Midlands town than a Cotswolds one.

Banbury has a long history: **Iron Age** and **Roman** settlements, exploiting a ford across the River Cherwell, were developed under a **Saxon** chieftain named Banna (thus "Banna's burgh"). The town appears in the **Domesday Book** (1086) as "Banesberie". In 1642, Banbury played a key role in the early stages of the **Civil War**, caught between Royalist and Parliamentary forces: it is said that Oliver Cromwell planned the Battle of Edgehill (see p.129) in the back room of the town's *Reindeer* inn. Banbury's twelfth-century **castle** was demolished soon afterwards, the stones used to rebuild the town. Later prosperity arrived with the **canals** in the 1770s, the **railways** in the 1850s and the **motorway** in 1990, but in typically unsentimental fashion, for much of the last century Banbury was known best for hosting the largest cattle market in Europe, livestock being driven into town *en masse* – and often on the hoof – from as far afield as Scotland. The cattle market closed in 1998, though Banbury still thinks big: Britain's entire supply of

Kenco originates here, from the **world's largest coffee factory**. As you drive into town, keep your windows open: you may first sniff the aroma of roasting coffee, perhaps followed by the mouthwatering scents of fresh-baked bread (from the huge Fine Lady bakery) and melting chocolate (from the industrial chocolatiers Barry Callebaut) – a very continental combination of smells wreathing what is, in truth, a pretty ordinary market town.

Arrival, information and accommodation

Banbury is two miles off the M40 at junction 11. Coming **by car** from Oxford, the A4260 via Kidlington and Deddington is a nicer, if slower, drive (roughly 22 miles). Other main routes are from Chipping Norton (A361) and Stratford-upon-Avon (A422). The **railway station**, with frequent services from London Marylebone, Reading, Oxford and Birmingham (New Street and Moor Street) – more details on p.19 – is five minutes' walk east of the town centre via Bridge Street; the station has no bus links, so you have to walk or take a **taxi**. The **bus station** is behind Debenhams off Bridge Street: aside from National Express coaches from Heathrow, Birmingham and further afield, principal local services include the 50A (not Sun) from Stratford via Shipston, the 59/59A from Oxford via Deddington and the 488 (not Sun) from Chipping Norton (all Stagecoach), as well as the 269/270 (not Sun) from Stratford via Kineton and 577 (once on Sat) from Moreton-in-Marsh (both Johnsons).

Ride a cock horse to Banbury Cross

Banbury is well known in both Britain and America for a popular song or nursery **rhyme**:

> Ride a cock horse
> To Banbury Cross
> To see a fine lady upon a white horse
> With rings on her fingers
> And bells on her toes
> She shall have music wherever she goes.

The rhyme was first printed in 1744, but was almost certainly known long before that, probably in several different versions. Its meaning is hard to pin down. Some say "a fine lady" was in fact "a Fiennes lady" – that is, traveller **Celia Fiennes** (1642–1741), sister of the third Viscount Saye and Sele of Broughton Castle (see p.129), the first woman known to have visited every county of England; her memoirs recounting epic horse-rides from Newcastle to Cornwall in the 1680s and 1690s are still in print. Others link the "fine lady" to Lady Godiva, Elizabeth I or even pagan fertility festivals worshipping the goddess of the Earth.

As for "**cock horse**", Banbury Museum offers three explanations – first, that it was another name for a child's hobby horse (a good enough excuse for Banbury to stage a **Hobby Horse Festival** every July; ⓦ www.hobbyhorsefestival.co.uk); or that it refers to riding a horse "a-cock", where a lady would ride side-saddle behind a gentleman on the same animal; or – most plausibly – that a "cock horse" was an extra horse that helped coaches tackle steep slopes: in the eighteenth century, as the London to Banbury coach stopped at the bottom of Stanmore Hill in Middlesex for a fifth horse to be attached, the local children would chorus "Ride a cock horse to Banbury Cross".

But it's all rather hazy. Marry this with the fact that the original Banbury Cross is no more (see p.125), and – as usual with folk rhymes – you're left with not much other than a pretty song.

Banbury's **tourist office** (Mon, Tues, Thurs & Fri 8.45am–5.15pm, Wed 10am–5.15pm, Sat 9.30am–5pm; ℡01295 753752, ⊛www.visitnorthoxfordshire .com) is inconveniently located inside the Castle Quay shopping mall. It's very well stocked with leaflets, maps and books, and staff can book accommodation for the whole region, as well as advise about the plentiful **self-catering** options nearby. There's some good **accommodation** in the centre, a choice of budget chain motels on the outskirts (see p.25) and more options in the villages.

In town

Banbury House Oxford Rd ℡01295 259361, ⊛www.banburyhouse.co.uk. A "Best Western" hotel occupying a row of Georgian townhouses a short walk (uphill) from the centre. There's not much style inside, but it's a comfortable enough place to rest your head. Smoking rooms are available, and they also run serviced apartments for rent nearby. **④**

Treetops 28 Dashwood Rd ℡01295 254444, ⊛www.treetopsbanbury.co.uk. Decent, high-quality B&B in an Edwardian house on a hilly street just behind the town centre, run by a friendly local couple, with four en-suite doubles and a small single. **③**

Whately Hall 17 Horsefair ℡01295 253261, ⊛www.mercure.com. This hotel certainly looks the part – a fine seventeenth-century frontage in honeyed Cotswold stone stretching along a tree-shaded main street through the centre of town, right by Banbury Cross, and with its own resident ghost (Father Bernard, a Catholic priest who was the victim of a practical joke in 1687, died of fright and has restlessly roamed ever since). A good deal of character survives within, too, with plenty of oak panelling and a lovely enclosed rear garden, though the bedrooms lose the plot slightly – aiming for a mix of corporate chic and floral country house, but let down by some tired fittings. Prices reflect the three-star rating. **③**–**④**

🏃 **White Cross House** 7 Broughton Rd ℡01295 277932, ⊛www.bedbreakfast banbury.co.uk. Very good B&B in a big old Victorian house 3min walk from Banbury Cross, offering a choice of sprucely presented twin rooms, all en suite. Breakfast is notably good, with Fairtrade and locally sourced ingredients. Great value. **②**–**③**

Out of town

Cartwright Aynho ℡01869 811885, ⊛www .cartwright-hotel.co.uk. Upmarket boutique-style village hotel, six miles southeast of Banbury (and just over the Northants border) in Aynho's

sixteenth-century former coaching inn. Expect full-on contemporary chic in each of the 21 bedrooms, though some of the rooms are a touch small: it's worth paying a little extra for an "executive" double. There's seasonal, local food in the oak-beamed restaurant, well-kept ales in the bar and (most importantly) a warm welcome. **⑤**

Uplands House Upton ℡01295 678663, ⊛www .cotswolds-uplands.co.uk. Charming rural guesthouse, rated five stars, in a lovely location six miles northwest of Banbury opposite Upton House (see p.129), a few yards inside Warwickshire. The three en-suite double rooms are all done up in traditional style, though noticeably upscale – a four-poster bed in one, a Chinese-style mirror in another – with views over the beautiful rear gardens. **④**–**⑤**

Wormleighton Hall Wormleighton ℡01295 770234, ⊛www.wormleightonhall.com. A working farm in this Warwickshire village just off the A423, eight miles north of Banbury, reached down a long, tree-lined drive: the location is very secluded, with long views over the fields. Guest accommodation is fitted out to four-star standard, with rooms in a converted barn as well as the main house. **④**

Wroxton House Wroxton ℡01295 730777, ⊛www.wroxtonhousehotel.com. Part of the "Best Western" group, this three-star village hotel occupies a seventeenth-century thatched inn four miles west of Banbury. It's a reliable choice, taking in 32 rooms with simple, modern decor, including some in thatched outbuildings, and a genial brand of service that mixes efficiency with informality. **③**–**④**

Camping

Anita's Mollington ℡01295 750731. Decent caravan and camping site just off the A423 about three miles north of Banbury, within walking distance of the village pub and also offering self-catering accommodation.

Bo Peep Aynho Rd, Adderbury ℡01295 810605, ⊛www.bo-peep.co.uk. Well-equipped four-star site a couple of miles south of Banbury near woodland off the A4260. Open April–Oct.

The Town

124

With the site of Banbury's medieval castle now occupied by the **Castle Quay shopping mall**, start a stroll about town in the paved **Market Place** alongside, which has a couple of sixteenth- and seventeenth-century facades surviving in what is essentially still a Saxon layout, with one street entering (from the east) and two streets exiting (to the west). In the northern corner, the Neoclassical frontage of the old corn exchange, opened in 1857, now gives into the mall; just in front, a plaque set into the pavement marks the location of Banbury's original **High Cross**, demolished by order of the Puritan town authorities on July 26, 1600. Inside the mall, turn left to find the **tourist office**, which doubles as the entrance for the **Banbury Museum** (Mon–Sat 10am–5pm; free; Ⓦwww.cherwell.gov.uk /banburymuseum), a well-presented little collection showcasing the town's history, including a medieval cannon, Victorian textiles and views over the adjacent **Tooley's Boatyard**, a narrowboat workshop on the Oxford Canal in continuous use since 1778; the yard runs its own **guided tours** (Easter–Oct Sat 3pm; £5.50; 1hr; Ⓦwww.tooleysboatyard.co.uk), which include a short boat trip.

Back out on the Market Place, follow pedestrianized Parsons Street west to pass beneath the overhanging sign for the **Reindeer Inn** (see p.126), which still has its old wooden gates, marked with the date 1570. Legend has it that Oliver Cromwell held a council of war in the *Reindeer*'s ornate **Globe Room** just before the Battle of Edgehill in 1642, and returned afterwards, possibly to try Royalist suspects, more plausibly to plan the two sieges of Royalist-held Banbury Castle (1644 and 1646). The room's oak panelling was sold in 1912, to local outrage, only returning in the 1960s after its chance discovery in a London warehouse.

Opposite the pub, lanes dog-leg up to **St Mary's Church**, consecrated in 1797 on the site of a collapsed Gothic predecessor and reminiscent of Wren's London churches, with its pepperpot tower and Classical portico. The bright, painted interior and stained glass are Victorian, while a stone outside recalls *Gulliver's Travels* (1726), in which Jonathan Swift claimed to have "observed in the churchyard at Banbury several tombs and monuments of the Gullivers". The ones he saw have now gone, but Gulliver is an old Banbury name: to the left of the stone, for instance, stands the grave of one Samuel Gulliver, died 1828.

St Mary's fronts **Horsefair**, an elegant street marked by the Jacobean facade of the *Whately Hall Hotel* opposite. Barely 100m to the left rises **Banbury Cross**, installed in 1859 to commemorate the wedding of Queen Victoria's eldest daughter to a Prussian prince. It's a dour slice of Neo-Gothic, yet stands in a significant location, where roads from Oxford, Warwick and the Cotswolds (Shipston-on-Stour) meet Banbury's **High Street**. Follow the last of these back down into the town, passing on the right the sixteenth-century frontage of S.H. Jones, a local wine merchant. Just after you re-enter the pedestrianized shopping zone, on the left ironwork figures of livestock hang above the entrance to **Butcher's Row**, an alley which formerly held the town's meat market and now

Banbury to Bath: the Cross-Cotswold Pathway

Banbury is the starting point for the 86-mile **Cross-Cotswold Pathway**, part of the longer, coast-to-coast Macmillan Way (Ⓦwww.macmillanway.org). The pathway runs more or less parallel to the Cotswold Way national trail (see p.32), but further east: starting in Banbury it heads west to Epwell, then turns southwest to Stow and onwards past Cirencester and Castle Combe to Box, from where a link heads into Bath. Full details are in a dedicated guidebook published by the Macmillan Way Association (£5), available on the website. If you're feeling fit, you could combine the Cross-Cotswold Pathway with a turn at Bath onto the Cotswold Way, for the week-long walk north along the ridge to Chipping Campden (see p.154), from where the 21-mile **Cotswold Link** returns you to Banbury – the whole circuit forms an epic 217-mile trek dubbed the **Cotswold Round**.

offers a whisper of atmosphere amid all the retail therapy for the short stroll back into the Market Place.

Eating and drinking

Banbury's **restaurants** match its personality – unsentimental. The best-known delicacy is **Banbury cakes** (ⓦwww.banburycakes.co.uk), oval currant-filled pastries rather like Eccles cakes, but all the historic bakeries which once made and sold them have been pulled down. Only a handful of docile tearooms still oblige, notably *Banesberie* on Butcher's Row and *Café Quay* (reviewed below). Otherwise, the town's strong Kashmiri community has given rise to unusually good curry houses: Parsons Street, in particular, is shoulder-to-shoulder with them.

But, with one or two exceptions, it's all fairly make-do: if you're looking for real quality you'd do better to head out to one of the **villages**. Some nearby options are listed below, or – within a fifteen-minute radius by car – consider the excellent *Inn at Farnborough* (see p.128), the *Crown & Tuns* in Deddington (p.131), the *Wykham Arms* in Sibford Gower (p.120) or the *Masons Arms* on the Chipping Norton road (p.121).

In town

Café Quay Opposite Tooley's Boatyard ☎01295 270444. The only place in town where you can have a coffee and a bun on the waterside, with seating both indoors and on a canal-front terrace. Accessible from Banbury Museum as well as from the canal towpath.

Church House 2 North Bar ☎01295 262292. Lovely-looking old building in Cotswold stone opposite St Mary's Church, originally the church hall, now a pub and brasserie. The food is ordinary – jacket potatoes and baguettes at lunch, steaks and salads in the evening – but come for the interior, a lofty space with a 45-foot curved ceiling: it feels a bit like supping a pint in a cathedral.

Mill Arts Centre Spiceball Park ☎01295 252050, ⓦwww.themillartscentre.co.uk. Local theatre and music venue in a former mill beside the canal lock in the middle of town, whose café-bar is a relaxed and friendly spot for refreshments whether or not you're interested in a show. In among the comedy acts and tribute bands, the centre hosts an acoustic folk club (Wed 8.30pm; £6; ⓦwww.rideacockhorse.co.uk) and regular bar gigs and jam sessions by local musicians (Sun 3pm & Thurs 8pm; free).

Reindeer 47 Parsons St ☎01295 264031, ⓦwww.hooky-pubs.co.uk. Banbury's oldest and best pub – also signed as the *Old Reindeer*, *Ye Olde Reine Deer*, and variations – a sixteenth-century gem that's full of history (see p.125) and offers well-cared-for local Hook Norton ales in a quiet, congenial ambience.

Sheesh Mahal 43 South Bar ☎01295 266489, ⓦwww.sheeshmahalbanbury.co.uk. Best of Banbury's many Indian restaurants, occupying an old town house beside Banbury Cross and offering light, carefully spiced dishes and genial, if rather shy, service. Mains £8–13. Evenings only.

Thai Orchid 56 North Bar ☎01295 270833, ⓦwww.thaigroup.co.uk. A Banbury institution for 25 years, with a cramped interior of extravagantly carved wood and its own fish-pond, serving exquisite Thai food at a lunchtime buffet and – better – à la carte in the evenings. All the classics are present on an encyclopedic menu, the spicing of the soups and curries is perfectly authentic and though service can be a bit perfunctory this is still a reliable choice. Mains £9–15.

Veritas 13 North Bar ☎01295 224890, ⓦwww.veritaswinebars.com. Banbury's classiest restaurant, whose inspired owners have managed to create a fresh, attractive, genuinely welcoming haven of good food in uninspiring surroundings. Their £5 "Crunch Lunch" deals are unbeatable value – fish and chips or chicken kebabs done with style and finesse, matching the style of their à la carte menu: familiar favourites such as goat's cheese starter, haddock fish cakes or braised shoulder of lamb prepared with care (tasty sauces, innovative touches, nothing too fancy) and presented artfully. With mains costing £11–25 (most around £14), it's not cheap, but with service this genial, alongside excellent wines, you may not care.

Out of town

Black Boy Inn Milton ☎01295 722111, ⓦwww.blackboyinn.com. Fine restaurant within a sixteenth-century pub in this easily missed village three miles south of Banbury: dine in the oak-beamed bar – old, but still done up rather tastefully – or opt for the conservatory dining-room. The food is modern British, with innovative touches here and there – Gressingham duck with honey-soy noodles, local pork and redcurrant sausages, pan-seared ling (similar to cod), and so forth. Mains £10–20, with weekly changing set menus available.

Fox Farthinghoe ☎01295 713965, ⓦwww .foxatfarthinghoe.co.uk. Bright and breezy renovated pub in a tiny Northamptonshire village five miles east of Banbury. There are no surprises on the menu – sirloin steak, chicken kiev, beer-battered haddock, all using locally sourced produce where possible – but the attraction is the locals-only feel, the busy, friendly ambience and the distinctly afford-able prices. It's all rather fun. Mains £9–18. Food not served Sunday eve. While you're in Farthinghoe, drop by the excellent *Limes Farm* shop and tearoom (closed Mon; ⓦwww.limes-farm.com) for fresh-baked loaves, farm-made chutneys and more.

Moon & Sixpence Hanwell ☎01295 730544, ⓦwww.themoonandsixpencehanwell.com. Pleasant old pub in this village on Banbury's northwestern fringe, only a couple of miles out, presenting fine dining to savour. The focus is squarely on classic British cuisine with an upmarket edge – for example, home-made venison, pork and chicken sausage, served as a starter with caramelized apples, or oven-roasted breast of guinea fowl stuffed with a herb mousse. Vegetarian dishes are available, best requested when booking (which is essential). À la carte mains cost £16–20, or a two-course set menu (Mon–Thurs) is £12 – and they also offer more affordable "pub classics" (Sun–Fri) such as fish and chips, steak and kidney pudding, ham and eggs, and so on, for £9–10 each.

Listings

Bookshops Waterstones is in the Castle Quay mall – or have a browse at Books & Ink, a second-hand bookshop at 4 White Lion Walk (ⓦwww .booksandink.co.uk).
Hospital See p.36.
Markets General market on Market Place (Thurs & Sat 9am–4pm; ⓦwww.sketts.co.uk). For farmers' markets, see box, p.89.

Pharmacy Boots in Castle Quay mall ☎01295 262015.
Police station Warwick Rd ☎0845 850 5505.
Post office 57 High St.
Taxis There are taxi ranks at the railway station, Banbury Cross and opposite Debenhams. Otherwise try Castle Cars (☎01295 270011, ⓦwww.castlecarsbanbury.co.uk) or Cherwell Cars (☎01295 265555, ⓦwww.cherwellcars.co.uk).

Sulgrave Manor

Eight miles northeast of Banbury in the Northamptonshire village of **SULGRAVE**, a successful wool merchant named **Lawrence Washington** – twice mayor of Northampton – built a manor house in the 1540s on land he had recently purchased from the Crown. A fine example of Elizabethan domestic architecture, the house slowly fell into disrepair over the centuries and would probably have been demolished but for the work of historians in the 1880s, who determined that Lawrence's great-great-grandson John had emigrated to Virginia in 1656 – and that John's great-grandson was none other than **George Washington** (1732–99), first president of the United States. By the turn of the twentieth century, with politicians and philanthropists on both sides of the Atlantic searching for ways to celebrate the centenary of the 1814 Treaty of Ghent, which had established peace between Britain and America, **Sulgrave Manor** was purchased to act as a focus for the "special relationship". The house was opened to the public in 1921 and is still held in trust for the peoples of both countries: the Union Jack and Stars and Stripes fly side-by-side, and this is one of the few places in the English countryside to stage a full-blown Fourth of July ceremonial party.

The manor is open for **guided tours** only (May–Oct Tues–Thurs 2.30pm & 4pm, Sat & Sun 12.30pm, 2.30pm & 4pm; Aug also Tues–Thurs 12.30pm; April open Sat & Sun only; £6.55; ⓦwww.sulgravemanor.org.uk). It's not a big house but the tours last an hour and a quarter: the guides are excellent, bringing the place alive with anecdotes, tales of family life and plenty of colourful context. Above the main door you'll see the Washington coat of arms – three stars and two stripes. (The family originated in County Durham: they adopted the name "De

Llama trekking

For an unusual take on the Banburyshire countryside, **Catanger Llamas** (T01327 860808, Wwww.llamatrekking.co.uk), based at Weedon Lois near Sulgrave, can offer anything from a two-hour stroll with llamas (£95 for two people) up to a full-day trek along old drovers' paths (£170 for two people including picnic lunch; April–Oct only). A pre-walk briefing on how to handle – and, if necessary, placate – your llama is, fortunately, included, and you also get the chance to visit the farm shop to buy llama-wool rugs and hats.

Wessyngton" in the twelfth century following their purchase of the Saxon-era estates around what is now Washington in Tyne and Wear.) Inside, you're led through the Great Hall, an oak-panelled music parlour, the fully-equipped kitchens, a lofty bedchamber, and more, amid plenty of Washingtoniana, including original portraits and memorabilia: the mix of Tudor architectural interest and American historical interest is very engaging. Special **children's tours** (May–Oct Sat 1.45pm; £3.15 per child, accompanying adults free) focus on what life was like for Lawrence Washington's eleven offspring back in the 1540s.

The giftshop, café and **gardens** open half an hour earlier than the manor and remain open until 5.15pm (last entry 4pm) – while a stroll down the road stands the *Star* (T01295 760389, Wwww.thestarinnsulgrave.com), an ancient Hook Norton **pub** with good beer, decent food and four simple en-suite **bedrooms** (❸). Sulgrave lies off the B4525: to get there from Banbury, follow signs for Northampton then, after about four miles, look out for a turnoff left signed for the manor, directly in front of a speed camera.

Cropredy and around

Four miles north of Banbury, peaceful **CROPREDY** was the scene of a major, if inconclusive, Civil War battle in 1644, when Roundheads prevented Royalist forces from crossing a bridge over the River Cherwell, but suffered significant losses in the process. You can download a map and notes for the interesting **Battlefield Walk** around the village (4.5 miles) at Wwww.cherwell.gov.uk. Although the village gained a railway station in 1852 and lost it again in 1956, it has remained a landmark on the Oxford Canal for three hundred years: much of the walk follows the towpath.

There are three excellent reasons to head this way on a detour between Banbury and Stratford. The first is the *Red Lion* in Cropredy village (T01295 750224, Wwww.redlioncropredy.co.uk), a beautiful old thatched pub known locally for its ales and family-friendly atmosphere. Just up the road, the *Carpenters Arms* in tiny **LOWER BODDINGTON** (T01327 260451, Wwww.thecarpentersarms.co.uk) is a Hook Norton pub under new management in late 2010: their food is unusually good – and unusually affordable (mains £6.50–10).

Best of all, just off the A423 in **FARNBOROUGH**, six miles north of Banbury, is the ⚔ *Inn at Farnborough* (T01295 690615, Wwww.innatfarnborough.co.uk), a rural restaurant of the highest quality. The inn has kept its eighteenth-century looks outside, but has been transformed with a contemporary styled interior of rich colours and eye-catching decor, and truly outstanding food. Mains (£11–18) blend a modern British approach – spring lamb with mint peas, seared liver with pancetta and balsamic onions – with innovative touches, such as sautéed monkfish with chorizo or mushroom ravioli with parmesan cream. Many cheaper dishes and affordable set menus (£11 for two courses) are available; watch out, too, for special deals, such as half-price offers before 7pm.

The **Three Counties Ride** is an easy round-trip **cycle route** from Cropredy which passes through Lower Boddington and Farnborough on quiet roads and country lanes: the full ride is 17 miles (about 4hr), but several shortcuts are possible. See ⓦ www.cherwell.gov.uk or pick up a leaflet at Banbury tourist office. Beware that Cropredy and the surrounding area are swamped annually in mid-August by **Fairport's Cropredy Convention** (ⓦ www.fairportconvention .com), a weekend music festival held near the village that always features 1970s rock/folk supremos Fairport Convention.

Edgehill and Upton House

Driving on the A422 from Banbury past **WROXTON**, whose handsome Jacobean abbey (ⓦ www.wroxtonabbey.org) is now a college for American students, there suddenly comes a point where the road drops off a cliff. The 700-foot scarp known, with good reason, as **Edgehill**, offers suddenly spectacular views out over the flatlands of Warwickshire – and was also the scene of the first pitched battle of the English Civil War, on October 23, 1642. Royalist armies, camped on top of the hill and threatening the garrison at Banbury, were confronted by Roundhead troops halted down below at Kineton on a relief march towards Banbury from Warwick. The battle, which took place in the fields south of Kineton, was inconclusive: much of the Parliamentarian infantry fled, but the Royalist cavalry broke ranks in pursuit and were driven back themselves. By nightfall, about a thousand men were dead, with more than twice that number wounded – and the war itself rumbled on for several more years. The battlefield is now mostly off-limits, owned by the Ministry of Defence, but the tales live on at the fine *Castle Inn* (☎ 01295 670255, ⓦ www.castleinnedgehill.com), occupying a crenellated tower beside **RATLEY** village that was built in 1742 to mark the battle's centenary.

A mile away, beside the A422 at the top of the slope, stands **Upton House** (March–Oct daily except Thurs 1–5pm; £8.18; ☎ 01295 670266, ⓦ www.national trust.org.uk), built in 1695 and remarkable for the collection of **fine art** assembled by Walter Samuel, 2nd Viscount Bearsted (1882–1948), whose father founded the Shell oil company. It's an unusual experience, this far out in the country, to be taking in works by El Greco (his *El Espolio* is a highlight), Gainsborough, Reynolds, Stubbs and others – memorably, too, a pair of typically vivid London scenes by Hogarth, *Morning* and *Night*. Make time for the wonderful red and silver Art Deco bathroom, and the collection of Shell Oil memorabilia on the top floor. Half-hour **"taster" tours** of the house operate before formal opening (same days 11.15am, 11.55am & 12.35pm; free) – and the splendid 1930s-style **gardens** (same days from 11am) are worth a stroll. Johnsons **bus** 269 (not Sun) stops near the house twice a day between Banbury and Stratford. Turn to p.149 for an account of Compton Verney, another splendid country-house art gallery nearby.

Broughton Castle

Roughly three miles southwest of Banbury, just off the B4035 near the village of **BROUGHTON**, stands one of England's most photogenic stately homes. **Broughton Castle** (May to mid-Sept Wed & Sun 2–5pm; July & Aug also Thurs; £7; ⓦ www.broughtoncastle.com) isn't a castle at all – rather, it is a chiefly fourteenth-century manor house, in its own substantial grounds behind a battlemented gatehouse and surrounded by a broad moat. Built in golden Cotswold stone, embraced by lawns, water, topiary and a fragrant rose garden, and set amid its own wooded valley, it is nothing short of enchanting.

The house has been in the same family since being purchased by William of Wykeham in 1377: the current owners – Nathaniel Fiennes (born 1920) and his wife, the 21st **Lord and Lady Saye and Sele** – still occupy private apartments in the east wing. As well as public tours and other interests, the family makes good money from film producers: Broughton Castle has starred in, to name a couple of blockbusters, *Shakespeare in Love* and *The Madness of King George*, as well as numerous TV costume dramas. Lord Saye (he tends to drop the "and Sele") is second cousin to the explorer Sir Ranulph Fiennes and third cousin once removed to the actors Ralph and Joseph Fiennes.

Approaching the house is just about the most romantic part of all, making your way over the moat bridge and through the fourteenth-century fortified gatehouse to be confronted by the main facade, with its near-symmetrical sets of tall windows and chimney-stacks. Some of the windows on the west (right-hand) side are, in fact, false, filled in at some point and then repainted for effect.

Inside Broughton Castle

You enter at the **Great Hall**, a broad, light space of bare stone walls festooned with family portraits, suits of armour and medieval weaponry beneath a sixteenth-century plastered ceiling. Stout furniture in red plush has been drawn around the stone fireplace. As you stand by the door, on your right are some standing pikes: the hollow-sounding wall beside them was built by the set designers of *Shakespeare in Love* to conceal some pipework, and left as a memento. Less romantically, the orange carpet, with its vaguely heraldic design, is a relic of the Morecambe and Wise 1975 Christmas special, when Eric and Ernie filmed a song-and-dance number here with Diana Rigg.

Guides will direct you through the **Groined Passage**, its fourteenth-century vaulting in pristine condition, past a spiral staircase to the family's **Dining Room**, also vaulted, featuring beautiful sixteenth-century double-linenfold panelling in oak. You continue upstairs to the **Long Gallery**, remodelled in the 1760s, holding porcelain, marble busts and much portraiture; rooms off it include the **King's Chamber**, its elegant oak bed, made by a local designer in 1992, suiting the lively French chimneypiece of 1554 rather well. Before you go back downstairs to the splendid Tudor **Oak Room** and out to the **gardens**, make your way upstairs again: as well as an exit onto the **roof**, offering breathtaking views over the moat and park, up here is perhaps the house's most interesting nook, the **Council Chamber**, a small, plain hideaway once described as "a room which hath no ears". From 1629 to 1640, a string of notable figures from the Roundhead opposition to Charles I plotted up here in secret, courtesy of their Puritan host, William Fiennes, 8th Baron Saye and Sele – nicknamed "Old Subtlety" for his political shrewdness. Little from that time survives, other than atmosphere.

The interiors are only one reason to visit. In truth, the best of the house is outside: absorbing the views and the history over a quiet cup of tea on the lawns (the stables house a small **café**), and then exploring the dream-like **rose garden**, allows your imagination even freer rein than touring the neatly presented interior. A gardens-only admission fee of £3 excludes entry to the house.

Around Broughton Castle

Access to the fourteenth-century **Broughton Church** (same hours as house), located beside the castle gatehouse, is free. Lopsided inside at first glance, with only a nave and south aisle, it is known for its family monuments, which include ten **hatchments**, diamond-framed coats of arms common from the mid-seventeenth to mid-nineteenth centuries which were created to display the genealogy of a deceased nobleman. A leaflet by the door explains them in detail.

Back up the lane in Broughton village, alongside the castle turnoff stands the *Saye and Sele Arms* (☎01295 263348, ⓦwww.sayeandselearms.co.uk), a lovely old

pub with bags of atmosphere, good beer and decent food (no food Sun eve). Alternatively, head a few miles down the road to Sibford Gower for the *Wykham Arms* (see p.120).

Bloxham

From Banbury Cross, the elegant, tree-lined South Bar road heads up the hill to become the Oxford road (A4260) running south towards Deddington. Partway up, turn off right to join the A361 towards Chipping Norton. Once free of Banbury, you'll pass a marked left turn for the **Wykham Park Farm Shop** (Ⓦ www.wykhampark.co.uk), one of the best in the area, before heading through **BLOXHAM**, a village dominated by, first, the Victorian buildings of Bloxham School and then reputedly the tallest church tower in the county, soaring 198 feet above **St Mary's Church** at the top of the village and visible from miles around. The tower, like the church, is fourteenth-century, though St Mary's also has a Norman doorway and fragments of medieval wall-paintings above the chancel – as well as Victorian stained glass by William Morris and Edward Burne-Jones. Alongside is the village **museum** (Easter–Oct Sat & Sun 2.30–5.30pm; 50p), with changing exhibits on local themes, while set back from the village green stands the *Joiners Arms* (Ⓣ 01295 720223, Ⓦ www.thejoinersarms.com), a roomy old pub with a good reputation. A mile or so east, in **MILTON**, is the fine *Black Boy Inn*, reviewed on p.126. The A361 road through Bloxham continues towards Hook Norton (see p.120) and Chipping Norton (p.117).

Deddington

Around six miles south of Banbury on the A4260 Oxford road, served by Stagecoach bus 59 and 59A towards Oxford, **DEDDINGTON** is a graceful little town, with a fine seventeenth-century church – look for the Gothic vaulting in the north porch – which also boasts one of the area's best (and best-loved) monthly **farmers' markets**; details on p.89. On the Market Place, *Foodies* is a cheery little deli and tearoom – but the real gastronomic highlight is the *Crown and Tuns* on the main road (Ⓣ 01869 337371, Ⓦ www.puddingface.com; closed Mon lunch, food also not served Sun eve). This cheery Hook Norton pub has been updated inside to double as a great local **restaurant**: they specialize in pies, huge ones, made fresh to order. The usual culprits are all present – beef and ale, pork and cider, chicken and mushroom – aided by less common options (venison with gin, salmon, pigeon) and veggie versions (potato and mushroom with tarragon, for instance). They cost around £10–12 and will keep you going for the rest of the day.

Bicester Village

Don't be misled by the name. Lying just east of the M40 junction 9 – easily reached from Banbury and Oxford – **Bicester Village** (Mon–Sat 10am–8pm, Sun 10am–6pm; slightly shorter hours in lower seasons; Ⓦ www.bicestervillage.com) isn't a village at all. A self-contained zone beside the humdrum little town of Bicester, this is, rather, an open-air, extremely swanky "outlet mall", packed with luxury fashion and homeware boutiques selling last season's stock at up to sixty percent off – think Polo Ralph Lauren, Versace, Gucci, Armani, Bulgari, D&G and so forth. Among the dining options on-site is a *Carluccio's*. Parking is plentiful but you could get there best by **train**: Bicester Town station is within walking distance; a shuttle bus runs to the mall from Bicester North station.

Along the Oxford Canal

Shadowing the River Cherwell for most of the way between Banbury and Oxford, the **Oxford Canal** offers some pleasant walking and benefits from **rail** access: trains on the Oxford Canal Line, run by First Great Western, stop at three canalside villages between Oxford and Banbury. Circular and station-to-station walks include the quiet route (4.5 miles) from **TACKLEY** station to **HEYFORD** station. The latter is located directly alongside **Lower Heyford wharf**, headquarters for Oxfordshire Narrowboats (☏ 01869 340348, Ⓦ www.oxfordshire-narrow boats.co.uk), who can book holidays and short breaks on board traditional narrowboats, as well as offering **boat rental** (£115–179/day, depending on the season) and **cycle rental** (£15/day). *Kizzies*, a little **café** by the wharf, does teas and light lunches. A **circular walk** (7 miles) is waymarked from Heyford station to Middle Aston and back along the towpath, and a shorter two-mile waymarked route covers both Lower and **UPPER HEYFORD**, the latter with the *Barley Mow* **pub** (☏ 01869 232300), located alongside what was once RAF Upper Heyford – subsequently one of the US bases where nuclear-armed Cruise missiles were deployed in the 1980s. The base, now decommissioned, is a business estate, though the missile bunkers are still visible.

In woodlands a mile west of Lower Heyford stands handsome **Rousham House** (daily 10am–4.30pm; £5; Ⓦ www.rousham.org). The house itself – built in 1635 – is off-limits, but the gardens are the attraction, largely unaltered from their initial landscaping by William Kent early in the eighteenth century, featuring terraces, cascades, ponds, Gothic follies and a walled garden. Buses on the Stagecoach 59/59A Banbury–Oxford route drop off nearby.

Kidlington (see p.91) and Woodstock (p.94) are a few miles south.

Stratford and the north Cotswolds

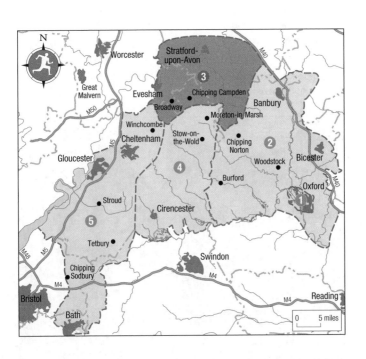

CHAPTER 3   # Highlights

* **Stratford-upon-Avon**
  Shakespeariana aside, this
  old market town can still
  charm with good food and
  world-class theatre.
  See p.136

* **Compton Verney** A modern,
  inspiring art gallery set in a
  fine country house outside
  Stratford. See p.149

* **Ebrington** Thatched cottages,
  peace and quiet and a
  great pub in this charming
  backwater village. See p.153

* **Chipping Campden** Simply
  one of the loveliest of all

Cotswold towns. Unmissable.
See p.154

* **Kiftsgate Court Gardens**
  Bewitching displays of
  roses at this lesser-known
  hillside stately home.
  See p.160

* **Broadway** A leading light of
  Cotswold tourism – certainly
  a pretty place but also
  perhaps a touch too busy.
  See p.161

* **Stanton** Quietly magnificent
  honeystone village, bypassed
  by most visitors. See p.167

▲ Stratford-upon-Avon

3

Stratford and the north Cotswolds

The northern third of this book's coverage takes in a swathe of diverse terrain across four counties. Anchoring the region, at its northernmost limit, **Stratford-upon-Avon** has gained worldwide fame for its associations with England's national poet, **William Shakespeare** – historical (Shakespeare was born here), architectural (the city centre is full of Elizabethan and Jacobean frontages) and cultural (Stratford's Royal Shakespeare Company puts on world-class productions year-round). Whether you base yourself in Stratford, or visit for the day – despite the crowds – you shouldn't miss it.

Stratford, though, lies a good ten miles north of what's normally considered as the Cotswolds. To the southeast, gentle hills line the Warwickshire-Oxfordshire border, offering views out over the flatlands of the Feldon which envelop the little-regarded market town of **Shipston-on-Stour**. There's some pleasant walking and cycling hereabouts, but of more interest are purpose-designed visitor attractions on the minor roads between Stratford and Banbury, most notably the unusually good fine-art collections and exhibitions at **Compton Verney**.

It's southwest of Stratford, on the Warwickshire-Gloucestershire border, that the Cotswolds begins in earnest. Dizzyingly attractive gardens at **Hidcote** and **Kiftsgate** prelude what is perhaps the finest Cotswold village anywhere in this book: for many people, visitors and locals alike, **Chipping Campden** *is* the Cotswolds. Minor villages nearby, notably **Stanton**, remain almost impossibly picturesque – though over-celebrated destinations such as **Broadway** suffer slightly in comparison. Just beyond, though tangential to the region, Worcestershire's **Vale of Evesham** offers low-key diversion from Broadway's overplayed hand.

Trying to draw borders within the Cotswolds, other than topographical ones, is doomed to be inaccurate. In this chapter we've halted coverage short of

Farmers' markets

- **Evesham** 4th Fri of month 9.30am–3.30pm.
- **Stratford** 1st & 3rd Sat of month 9am–2pm Ⓦ www.sketts.co.uk.
Dates may change around Christmas and New Year. See also Ⓦ www.farmers markets.net.

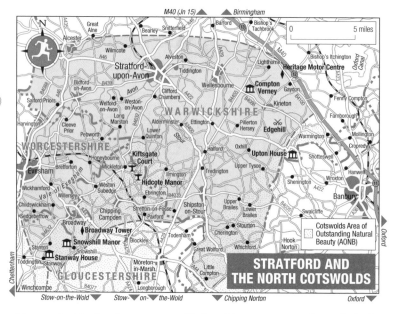

Moreton-in-Marsh – but some would place Moreton as an archetypal north Cotswolds town. Others would say that's not far enough, and the "north Cotswolds" should also include Stow-on-the-Wold and maybe Winchcombe as well. In this book, though, Moreton and Stow are covered in our **Central Cotswolds** chapter, which begins on p.171 – and Winchcombe is on p.208.

Stratford-upon-Avon

Despite its worldwide fame, **STRATFORD-UPON-AVON** is at heart an unassuming market town with an unexceptional pedigree. Its first settlers forded, and later bridged, the River Avon, and developed commercial links with the farmers who tilled the surrounding flatlands. A charter for Stratford's weekly market – a tradition continued to this day – was granted in the twelfth century, and the town later became an important stopping-off point for stagecoaches between London, Oxford and the north. Like all such places, Stratford had its clearly defined class system and within this typical milieu John and Mary **Shakespeare** occupied the middle rank, and would have been forgotten long ago had their third child, **William**, not turned out to be the greatest writer ever to use the English language.

A consequence of their good fortune is that this picturesque little town is nowadays all but smothered by package-tourist hype: in summer at least, its central streets groan under the weight of thousands of tourists, all of them seemingly trying to get into the **Birthplace Museum** at the same time. Don't let that deter you: Stratford still has the ability to surprise and delight, whether in the excellence of some of its restaurants, the gentle river views beside **Holy Trinity Church** or, most notably, in the world-class drama on offer from the **Royal Shakespeare Company**. Although the revamped **Royal Shakespeare Theatre**, opened in 2011, is a beauty, its smaller neighbour the **Swan** is, perhaps, even better: watching Shakespeare (or anything else) in this Elizabethan-style wooden galleried theatre, actors – often household names – performing virtually within touching distance, is a quintessentially memorable Stratford experience. Book well ahead for it.

Arrival

Stratford lies about an hour's **drive** from both Oxford and Cheltenham. If you're driving via the M40, the easiest access from the south is via junction 15 – but from the north, exit instead at junction 16 and approach through **HENLEY-IN-ARDEN**, where a famous tearoom on the high street which serves locally made ice cream makes for an enticing stop-off (Ⓦ www.henleyicecream.org.uk).

Stratford's **park and ride** (Mon–Sat 7.30am–7.30pm; April–Sept also Sun 9.30am–7.30pm; Ⓣ 01564 797070, Ⓦ www.parkandride.net) is located about a mile north of the town centre at Bishopton, where the A46 meets the A3400. Parking is **free**, and Johnsons bus 222 (£1.50; discounts for families) runs every 10 to 15 minutes to Wood Street (for the Birthplace) and Bridge Street (for the theatres). The last bus back is about 7pm. Otherwise, the often busy town-centre **car parks** cost about £6 for half a day or £20 for 24 hours. Some hotels provide parking for guests.

Stratford's sleepy **railway station** is on the western edge of town, ten minutes' walk from the centre. Chiltern Railways run trains about every two hours from

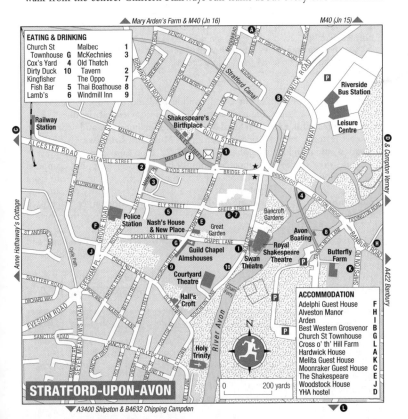

EATING & DRINKING

Church St Townhouse	G	Malbec	1
Cox's Yard	4	McKechnies	3
Dirty Duck	10	Old Thatch Tavern	2
Kingfisher Fish Bar	5	The Oppo	7
Lamb's	6	Thai Boathouse	8
		Windmill Inn	9

ACCOMMODATION

Adelphi Guest House	F
Alveston Manor	H
Arden	I
Best Western Grosvenor	B
Church St Townhouse	G
Cross o' th' Hill Farm	L
Hardwick House	A
Melita Guest House	K
Moonraker Guest House	C
The Shakespeare	E
Woodstock House	J
YHA hostel	D

Mary Arden's Farm & M40 (Jn 16)　　*M40 (Jn 15)*

Railway Station
Riverside Bus Station
Leisure Centre
Shakespeare's Birthplace
Police Station
Nash's House & New Place
Great Garden
Guild Chapel Almshouses
Courtyard Theatre
Hall's Croft
Bancroft Gardens
Avon Boating
Royal Shakespeare Theatre
Swan Theatre
Butterfly Farm
Holy Trinity

Anne Hathaway's Cottage

D & Compton Verney
A422 Banbury

N
0   200 yards

STRATFORD-UPON-AVON

A3400 Shipston & B4632 Chipping Campden

137

Shakespeare: a life

Other than the plays and sonnets he left behind – and even their authorship is disputed – very little about the life of England's national poet can be pinned down with certainty. From civic archives, it is known that on April 26, 1564, **John Shakespeare** – described variously as a glove-maker, a butcher or a merchant in wool or corn – and his wife, **Mary** (née **Arden**), baptized their son, **William**, at Holy Trinity Church in Stratford. It's presumed that the boy was born in Stratford in the few days beforehand, but the date and location are unknown; it has long, though, been an irresistible temptation to place the birth three days earlier, on the feast day of St George, patron saint of England (April 23), in the Shakespeare family house which survives on Henley Street. William went to a local grammar school and, at the age of 18, married **Anne Hathaway**, a local woman almost eight years his senior. The marriage was a rushed affair: less than six months later, Anne gave birth to a daughter, Susanna, followed in 1585 by twins, Hamnet (who died at the age of 11) and Judith.

The trail then goes cold until 1592, by which time Shakespeare was in London, earning a high-profile reputation as a playwright and actor, drawing royal attention from Elizabeth I and, after 1603, her successor James I. His output in the 1590s and 1600s was extraordinary: 38 plays appeared in barely a decade. By 1597 he was clearly a wealthy man, purchasing New Place, an imposing mansion in central Stratford for himself and his family, even while maintaining a house in London. He also invested in the construction of London's Globe Theatre in 1599, where many of his greatest plays were first performed, including *Hamlet*, *Othello* and *King Lear*.

After around 1606 Shakespeare's writing tailed off and he seems to have retired from literary life, spending more time in Stratford than in London. He died on or about his 52nd birthday, on April 23, 1616, and is buried in Holy Trinity Church.

Those are the bare bones – and, in truth, they are of little interest. What Shakespeare did or didn't do hardly matters at all, considering the quality of what he wrote.

London Marylebone via Banbury, and London Midland has hourly trains from Birmingham Moor Street. On both routes Stratford is the end of the line.

Buses are plentiful, except on Sundays. All the following arrive and depart from the lower (eastern) end of Bridge Street. From **Moreton**, **Broadway**, **Chipping Campden** and **Mickleton**, Johnsons bus 21/22 (not Sun) runs about every 90 minutes – or there's Hedgehog community bus H3 from Chipping Campden and Mickleton (Tues, Wed & Sat once; Fri 3 times). Stagecoach bus 50 runs from **Chipping Norton** via **Shipston** four times a day, more frequently on Sundays. From **Banbury**, take Johnsons bus 269/270 (not Sun) via Kineton, or Stagecoach bus 50A (not Sun) via Shipston; they're fairly irregular, but together form a roughly hourly service. Otherwise, half-hourly Stagecoach bus 28/28A/29 (not Sun) or the less regular Sundays-only Diamond bus 166 arrive from **Evesham**; and Johnsons bus 23/23A (not Sun) runs five times a day from Whichford, Shipston and intervening villages.

If you're coming direct from Oxford or Cheltenham, the train is a bit long-winded: your best bet may be a National Express **long-distance coach**, all of

A Cotswolds day-trip by bus from Stratford

If you're based in Stratford, it's straightforward to use Johnsons bus 21/22 (not Sun) for a Cotswolds **day-trip by bus**. A departure around 9am would give you a couple of hours mid-morning in either Broadway or Blockley, depending on your taste, from either of which you can be in Chipping Campden for lunch, returning to Stratford around 6 or 7pm.

which pull into the **Riverside bus station**, on the east side of the town centre, off Bridgeway.

Information and tours

At time of writing, Stratford's **tourist office** was in a state of flux. The private company that ran it for many years under the brand-name "Shakespeare Country" went bust in early 2010. The council hurriedly cobbled together a replacement, but it's starting from scratch and has few resources. At the time of writing, there was an official **tourist information centre** at 62 Henley Street (daily 10am–4pm; ℡01789 264293, ⍉www.discover-stratford.com) – but its future was uncertain. Meanwhile, a separate private concern has bought the Shakespeare Country website (⍉www.shakespeare-country.co.uk) and continues to promote the town and region – but despite the official look of the site, it is now entirely for profit. Other commercial websites include ⍉www.visitstratforduponavon.co.uk, www.shakespeares-stratford.com, www.stratford-upon-avon.co.uk and www.notjustshakespeare.com.

Every day of the year a **guided walk** (Mon–Wed 11am, Thurs–Sun 2pm; £5; ⍉www.stratfordtownwalk.co.uk) departs from the fountain in Bancroft Gardens on Waterside, opposite Sheep Street, covering all points of interest around town in an entertaining two-hour stroll. The same guides also do a **ghost walk** (Mon, Thurs & Fri 7.30pm; £5), starting from the same place.

Stratford Bike Hire (℡07711 776340, ⍉www.stratfordbikehire.com) have **bikes for rent** from £13 a day (or £7 for a half-day), including helmet, locks and repair kit – and they will deliver and collect free of charge within a radius of six miles around Stratford. Child bikes and trailers are available, and they also offer discounts on admission to all five Shakespeare properties. Staff can supply details of the self-guided **Shakespeare Trail**, a nine-mile circular bike tour from Stratford which visits the three Shakespeare houses in town before heading out on the canal towpath to Wilmcote for Mary Arden's Farm and back on minor roads to Shottery for Anne Hathaway's Cottage, then returning to Stratford. With a brisk pace, you could just about squeeze the circuit, including visits to each house, into a half-day.

Tours by bus, boat and train

City Sightseeing runs a one-hour **bus tour** (April–Oct every 15–30mins; first bus 9.30am, last bus Aug 5.30pm, May–July & Sept 5pm, April & Oct 4pm; ⍉www.city-sightseeing.com), which starts on Bridgefoot and has ten stops around the town centre, plus stops at Anne Hathaway's Cottage and Mary Arden's Farm before returning. A hop-on-hop-off ticket is £11.50 (valid 24hr) or £17 (valid 48hr); the latter also covers travel on the "Heart of Warwickshire" bus – see the box on p.140 for details. Family discounts are available, and they also sell good-value **combination tickets** for other attractions, including the Shakespeare properties and river cruises; the website explains further.

For **boat trips** on the Avon, Bancroft Cruisers runs a continuous cycle of 45-minute **cruises** (April–Oct daily 10.30am–5.30pm; £5; ℡01789 269669, ⍉www.bancroftcruisers.co.uk) from their landing-stage on the east side of Clopton Bridge. Avon Boating has half-hour cruises (same hours; £4.50; ℡01789 267073, ⍉www.avon-boating.co.uk) starting from Bancroft Gardens near the Royal Shakespeare Theatre. For both, there's no need to book: just turn up and board. Avon Boating also rents **rowing boats**, punts and canoes (£4/hr) and small motor boats (£25/hr).

The **Shakespeare Express** (℡0121 708 4960, ⍉www.shakespeareexpress.com), a historic steam-train excursion between Stratford and Birmingham Snow

"Heart of Warwickshire" bus

The City Sightseeing "Heart of Warwickshire" **bus** is an unusually convenient and good-value way to access attractions in the countryside around Stratford during the summer months – a real boon if you're reliant on public transport. It starts from Bridgefoot, in Stratford town centre, and runs four times a day (late May, June & most of July Sat & Sun only; late-July to early-Sept daily) on a loop taking 1 hour 20 minutes which includes stops at the YHA hostel in Alveston, Compton Verney (see p.149), the Heritage Motor Centre (see p.150), Warwick Castle, and points in between. A hop-on-hop-off **ticket** costs £9.50 (valid 24hr) or £17 (valid 48hr); the latter also covers travel on City Sightseeing's Stratford bus tour, outlined on p.139. In addition, you receive vouchers for discounted admission to Compton Verney, the Heritage Motor Centre and other attractions, and your ticket is also valid on local bus services.

Hill, runs every Sunday in summer (July to early Sept). From Stratford, the best option is the leisurely return trip to/from Birmingham (2hr 30mins), which costs £20 in Standard Class (£17.50 if booked ahead) or £48.50 in Premier Class; the latter includes lunch served onboard.

Accommodation

With the quantity of visitors passing through, Stratford is understandably replete with **accommodation** options – but the flipside of that particular coin is that quality standards aren't always focused on encouraging repeat business. There are lots of chain hotels offering bland interiors, impersonal service and ho-hum food – obvious ones, in hulking modern blocks, but also secret ones, hidden away behind alluringly half-timbered facades in the town centre, or masquerading as country houses on the approach roads into Stratford. Looks may deceive. That said, things are looking up: widespread redevelopment in 2010, and the relaunch of the RSC theatres in 2011, are noticeably pushing up standards. Note that in the peak summer months and during the **Shakespeare's birthday** celebrations around April 23 (W www.shakespeares birthday.org.uk), it's pretty much essential to **book ahead**.

Hotels

Alveston Manor Clopton Bridge ☏ 0844 879 9138, W www.macdonaldhotels.co.uk. Although chiefly a business hotel, this chain property can double as an undemanding leisure option, offering a wide choice of traditionally styled rooms. The convenience of the location, set back in private grounds away from the tourist maelstrom, but only a short stroll over the river from the town centre, may be a deciding factor. Free parking. ❹

Arden Waterside ☏ 01789 298682, W www .theardenhotelstratford.com. Owned by the RSC and located in prime central position, directly opposite the theatres, this modern hotel opened in 2010 – and with 45 rooms, it just about scrapes the coveted "boutique" tag. Expect contemporary elegance throughout, from spacious suites with luxurious fabrics and marble bathrooms to the Champagne Bar and waterfront brasserie.

Very posh, very formal – yet booking ahead could net a discounted deal. Sister property to the *Kings* hotel in Chipping Campden. ❺

Best Western Grosvenor Warwick Rd ☏ 01789 269213, W www.bwgh.co.uk. Close to the canal, just a couple of minutes' walk from the town centre, this modest, modern hotel occupies a row of good-looking, two-storey Georgian houses. Interiors are crisp and unfussy and there's ample parking at the back. ❸

Church Street Townhouse 16 Church St ☏ 01789 262222, W www.churchstreet townhouse.com. A pretty little independent boutique hotel opened in 2010 in two adjacent buildings in the town centre – one dating from 1768, with a Victorian facade and high ceilings, the other of seventeenth-century origin with gnarled oak beams. The lobby and reception decor may be a touch glitzy for some, but the twelve bedrooms are more restrained – nonetheless with super-kingsize beds, feature headboards, rainfall showers and complimentary port and shortbread in every room. Minimum two-night stay Fri & Sat. The owners – two sharp Stratford businesswomen – know the value of good service: expect a warm welcome. ❹

The Shakespeare Chapel St ☎01789 294997, 🖥www.mercure.com. Now part of a chain, this distinctive old hotel bang in the centre of town, with its mullioned windows and half-timbered Tudor facade, is one of Stratford's best known. The interior has retained its low beams and open fires in a fairly successful amalgamation of old and new, and the corporate atmosphere – though present in the public areas and most of the rooms – isn't quite as intrusive as at many of its competitors. Plump, if you can, for a four-poster suite. Parking £10/day. ❹

B&Bs

In town

Adelphi Guest House 39 Grove Rd ☎01789 204469, 🖥www.adelphi-guesthouse.com. Relaxed, cosy B&B in a good-looking Victorian townhouse a short walk from the centre. The owners have accumulated all sorts of interesting bric-à-brac – from vintage theatre posters to ornate lamp stands – and the six guest rooms are all en suite. The best room, which comes complete with a four-poster bed and views, is in the attic. Delicious home-cooked breakfasts too. ❸

Hardwick House 1 Avenue Rd ☎01789 204307, 🖥www.hardwickstratford.co.uk. Decent, well-kept B&B run by a former professional cricketer, with fresh, contemporary-styled bedrooms and good breakfasts. Located over the canal, a short walk north of the centre. Unusually good value. ❷–❸

Melita Guest House 37 Shipston Rd ☎01789 292432, 🖥www.melitaguesthouse.co.uk. High quality B&B in a big old Victorian house a few minutes' walk over the river from the town centre. Twelve bedrooms, including two garden rooms at the back, are spacious and well-appointed. ❸

Moonraker Guest House 40 Alcester Rd ☎01789 268774, 🖥www.moonrakerhouse.com. This well maintained place, in a large suburban house, has seven en-suite guest rooms, each decorated in smart modern-meets-period style (canopied beds, mini-chandeliers and so forth). Great breakfasts, too – either full English or vegetarian. Just beyond the railway station, about 900 yards west of the centre. ❸

Woodstock House 30 Grove Rd ☎01789 299881, 🖥www.woodstock-house.co.uk. A smart and neatly kept B&B 5min walk west of the centre. It has five comfortable bedrooms, all en suite, decorated in frilly modern style. ❷

Out of town

Bell Alderminster ☎01789 450414, 🖥www.thebellald.co.uk. Renovated eighteenth-century coaching inn in this village five miles south of Stratford on the A3400 (and far from the crowds). There's a good deal of atmosphere in the bar, while the four guest rooms have been done up well, in an appealingly flamboyant, upmarket contemporary style – plump for the top-floor suite and you get oak beams and a free-standing bath. Convenient for both Stratford and Shipston. ❹–❺

Cross o' th' Hill Farm Clifford Lane ☎01789 204738, 🖥www.cross-o-th-hill-farm.com. Once you've mastered the name, this is a lovely, quiet B&B option, at a farm located up a lane off the Shipston Road only a mile or two southeast of the town centre, easily walkable. The atmosphere is quiet, rural and relaxed, set amid meadows and pasture, and the interior style matches up – easygoing contemporary, with a minimum of clutter, while the food is either home-grown or sourced locally. No credit cards. ❹

Hostel and camping

Hostel

Stratford YHA hostel Hemmingford House, Alveston ☎0845 371 9661, 🖥www.yha.org.uk. Fine hostel occupying a rambling Georgian mansion on the edge of the pretty village of Alveston, two miles east of Stratford on the B4086. It has dorm beds (around £16–19) plus doubles and family rooms, some of which are en suite, as well as laundry, cycle rental, parking, kitchen facilities and cut-price breakfasts and evening meals. Get there best on foot or by bike: cross the Clopton Bridge and follow Tiddington Road out of town. Alternatively the Stratford–Leamington buses 15 (not Sun), 18 (not Sun) and 18A stop outside, as does the Stratford–Banbury bus 269 (not Sun) and the "Heart of Warwickshire" bus (see box, p.140). ❶

Campsite

Stratford Touring Park Stratford Racecourse, Luddington Rd ☎01789 201063, 🖥www.stratfordtouringpark.com. Decent, well-kept caravan and camping site by the racecourse, a couple of miles southwest of the town centre. Closed Nov–March.

The Town

Spreading back from the River Avon, Stratford's **town centre** is flat and compact, filling out a simple gridiron just two blocks deep and four blocks long. Broadly, the main drags are Bridge Street, Wood Street and High Street (all shopping), Sheep Street (restaurants) and pedestrianized Henley Street (terrace cafés and Shakespeariana). All of the town's key attractions are dotted around the centre, including the extraordinarily popular **Shakespeare's Birthplace**, as well as **Hall's Croft** and **Nash's House/New Place**, all three of which are managed by the Shakespeare Birthplace Trust (see box below). The other star turns are set amid gardens on the banks of the Avon – the theatres of the **Royal Shakespeare Company** (RSC) in the centre and, further south, **Holy Trinity Church**, where Shakespeare lies buried. In addition, aside from a couple of other town diversions, there are two outlying Shakespearean properties to north and west: **Anne Hathaway's Cottage** in Shottery and **Mary Arden's Farm** in Wilmcote.

Clopton Bridge and Bancroft Gardens

Spanning the Avon at more or less the point where a ford in Saxon times gave rise to the town's name, the multi-arched **Clopton Bridge** – paid for by Hugh Clopton, a Stratford boy who became Lord Mayor of London in 1491 – has carried traffic for more than five hundred years. It is still the main entry into Stratford from the east and south; pedestrians use the car-free **Tramway Bridge** alongside, which offers views of the nesting ducks and swans on midriver islands to left and right. Both lead to the canal basin, terminus of the Stratford Canal, a 25-mile link to the Avon from the Grand Union Canal further north which was completed in 1816 just before the arrival of the railways. The basin is usually packed with narrowboats – many on permanent moorings as cafés or mini-galleries – and all around are the lawns of the waterside **Bancroft Gardens**, a popular place to stroll or relax on the **grass** with an ice cream. By the bridge is the finely sculpted **Gower Memorial** of 1888 – a seated Shakespeare surrounded by characters from his plays – while near the middle of the park stands the elaborately spiky **Swan Fountain**, unveiled in 1996.

From here, two streets storm up into the centre of town: **Sheep Street** dead ahead, or parallel to the right is **Bridge Street**, lined with eighteenth-century facades – once coaching inns, now high-street stores.

Royal Shakespeare Theatre and around

Gazing down on Bancroft Gardens from the south stands the newly rebuilt **Royal Shakespeare Theatre**. There was no theatre in Stratford in Shakespeare's day; the first hometown drama festival in his honour was held only in 1769, more than 150 years after his death, at the behest of London-based actor-manager David Garrick.

Tickets for the Shakespeare houses

There are **five historic houses** connected with Shakespeare that are open to the public in and around Stratford. Three are in the town centre – the Birthplace, Hall's Croft and Nash's House/New Place – with Anne Hathaway's Cottage and Mary Arden's Farm on the outskirts. All five are owned and run by the **Shakespeare Birthplace Trust** (℡01789 204016, ⊛www.shakespeare.org.uk). Tickets are not available for individual properties. Instead, you have to buy a pass for all five (£19) or for the three in the town centre (£12.50). Discounts apply for families. Either buy direct from the trust – in person at any of the five houses, or online – or look out for discount deals in combination with tickets for other attractions around town, such as the City Sightseeing tour bus (see p.139) or river cruises.

Thereafter, the idea of building a permanent home in which to perform Shakespeare's works slowly gained momentum, and finally, in 1879, the Shakespeare Memorial Theatre was opened on land donated by local beer baron Charles Flower. After fire destroyed it in 1926, architect Elisabeth Scott won a competition to design a replacement; her cinema-like red-brick edifice, opened in 1932 and though elegant in parts, was later widely criticized as unsuitable. Scott's design separated actors from audience with a broad proscenium arch that shunted the action back into the bowels of the building; in addition, the auditorium layout was such that people in the highest levels of the circle were seated a hundred feet or more from the stage. Cast and crew complained the backstage areas were cramped, the public complained there were too few toilets, and so on. In the end, the building – which includes the adjacent **Swan Theatre**, created in the 1980s with a galleried Elizabethan-style wooden interior for staging "in-the-round" productions – was closed in 2007 for a complete rebuild. At the time of writing its replacement had not been unveiled, but when you visit you can expect the slickest of modern theatres behind the curving 1930s facade (the only element of Scott's building to survive), with a thrust stage bringing the actors and audience much closer together, vastly improved facilities linking the RST and the Swan for the first time, a landmark brick-built tower rising to one side, a rooftop restaurant and more. Historical flummery notwithstanding, Stratford's biggest draw is **world-class theatre**: if you do nothing else here, watch a play. See the box on p.144 for ticket information.

Beyond the theatre, stroll on along Waterside past the famous *Dirty Duck* pub – or on the lovely riverside footpath through the Avonbank Gardens – to where a quaint little **chain ferry** (50p) shuttles across the river to more gardens on the other bank. Continue walking on the same side to reach Holy Trinity Church, location of Shakespeare's grave (see p.145).

Shakespeare's Birthplace
Top of everyone's bardic itinerary is **Shakespeare's Birthplace** (daily: July & Aug 9am–6pm, April–June & Sept–Oct 9am–5pm, Nov–March 10am–4pm; see the box opposite for ticket info), located a five-minute walk from Bancroft Gardens, halfway along pedestrianized **Henley Street**. You enter via a modern visitor centre, whose displays poke into every corner of Shakespeare's life and times, making the most of what little hard evidence there is, filled out with clips from famous films and performances of Shakespeare's plays over the years.

Next door stands the heavily restored, half-timbered building where the great man was purportedly born – actually two dwellings knocked into one. The northern, much smaller and later part was the house of Joan, Shakespeare's sister, and it adjoins the main family home, which was bought by John Shakespeare in 1556 and today looks something like it would have done then. It includes a glover's workshop, where Shakespeare's father beavered away (though some claim that he was a wool merchant or a butcher), and a bedroom done up as a sixteenth-century birthing room, with cradle, washing-tub and toys – despite the fact that it is not certain that Shakespeare was even born in this building. The house has been attracting visitors for centuries regardless and upstairs one of the old mullioned windows, now displayed in a glass cabinet, bears the **scratch-mark signatures** of some of them, including Thomas Carlyle and Walter Scott.

You exit into the lovely **gardens**, where costumed actors perform excerpts from some of the more famous plays.

Nash's House and New Place
Stroll back along Henley Street and turn right at the small roundabout to walk along **High Street**, lined picturesquely with Tudor buildings but shamelessly

The Royal Shakespeare Company

One of the world's leading theatre companies, the **Royal Shakespeare Company** (℡0844 800 1110, ⓦwww.rsc.org.uk) had its roots in the Victorian ideal of a permanent troupe of actors based in Stratford, but the concept only came to fruition in the 1950s under the artistic directorship of Anthony Quayle and then Peter Hall. Today the company works on a repertory system: you could stay in Stratford for a few days and see three or four different plays – all Shakespeare if you like, but the RSC also produces work by Shakespeare's contemporaries as well as new writing and even the occasional musical.

The RSC has three stages in Stratford. The **Royal Shakespeare Theatre** and the **Swan Theatre** – both newly reopened in 2011 after rebuilding works – stand beside each other on the banks of the Avon. A stroll away along Waterside is the **Courtyard Theatre**, which served as the main venue during the RST's rebuild; however it was only ever intended to be temporary and during 2012 is likely to be converted into a studio space, similar to the "Other Place" studio it replaced on the same site.

Tickets for all productions go on sale months in advance, with prices ranging from around £12 for restricted-view seats at off-peak times to more than £50 for the best seats in the house on weekend evenings. Buy online, on the phone or in person. Young people aged 16–25 qualify for £5 tickets at all performances, and there are also discounted tickets available for people over 60. Occasionally, students and those under 25 or over 60 can pick up **standby tickets** in person on the day of performance – and it's always worth asking at the theatre about **returns** – but don't bet on it. Always plan ahead.

devoted to modern commerce, with familiar brand-names on both sides. Partway down on the right, beside the crooked *Garrick Inn*, stands **Harvard House**, an elaborate half-timbered building which may be flying the Stars and Stripes: John Harvard, grandson of the original owners, studied at Cambridge University before emigrating to America in 1637 and founding a seat of learning in Cambridge, Massachusetts which still bears his name. The house (administered by the Birthplace Trust) formerly held the **Museum of British Pewter**, but was closed at the time of writing with no plans for reopening.

Over the crossing with Sheep Street, High Street becomes **Chapel Street**, with the Guild Chapel in view dead ahead. Along here on the left is another Birthplace Trust property, **Nash's House and New Place** (daily: July & Aug 10am–6pm, April–June & Sept–Oct 10am–5pm, Nov–March 11am–4pm; see the box on p.142 for ticket info). Once the property of Thomas Nash, first husband of Shakespeare's granddaughter, Elizabeth Hall, the house's ground floor is kitted out with a pleasant assortment of period furnishings. Upstairs, one display provides a potted history of Stratford, including a scattering of archeological bits and pieces, and another focuses on the house with a cabinet of wood-carvings made from the **mulberry tree** that once stood outside. Reputedly planted by Shakespeare, the tree was chopped down in the 1750s by the owner, a certain Reverend Francis Gastrell, who was fed up with all the tourists. An enterprising woodcarver bought the wood and carved Shakespearean mementoes from it – hence the carvings in the cabinet. The adjacent **gardens** contain the foundations of **New Place**, Shakespeare's last residence, which was demolished by the same Reverend Gastrell, but for different reasons: he was in bitter dispute with the town council over taxation. The foundations have prompted all sorts of speculation and queries that may be resolved by the archeological dig currently under way there. Alongside, the **Great Garden of New Place**, with lawns, flowerbeds and yew hedges, has been taken over by the archeological teams; until the dig is completed – unlikely for a few years yet – it is closed to the public in summer, but reopens in winter, reached by its own entrance round the corner on Chapel Lane (Oct–April daily about 11am–3.45pm or so; free).

The Guild Chapel and around

Across from Nash's House stands the fifteenth-century **Guild Chapel**, whose chunky tower and sturdy stonework shelter a plain, though atmospheric interior enlivened by some simple stained-glass windows and elaborate **wall-paintings** above the chancel arch; they survived the Reformation under whitewash and were rediscovered in 1804 – but then virtually erased by ill-conceived "renovations". Only faint outlines survive today and it's almost impossible to tell what's what, though Ⓦwww.thearnott.com shows a computer rendering of them in their original glory. Outside the chapel, the adjoining **King Edward VI Grammar School**, where it's assumed Shakespeare was educated, incorporates a creaky line of photogenic fifteenth-century **almshouses** running along the south side of Church Street.

Hall's Croft

Continue past the almshouses and turn left onto **Old Town** for Stratford's most impressive medieval house, **Hall's Croft** (daily: April–Oct 10am–5pm, Nov–March 11am–4pm; see the box on p.142 for ticket info). The former home of Shakespeare's elder daughter, Susanna, and her doctor husband, John Hall, the immaculately maintained Croft, with its beamed ceilings and rickety rooms, holds a good-looking medley of period furniture and – mostly upstairs – a fascinating display on **Elizabethan medicine**. Hall established something of a reputation for his medical know-how and after his death some of his case notes were published in a volume entitled *Select Observations on English Bodies*. You can peruse extracts from Hall's book – noting that Joan Chidkin of Southam "gave two vomits and two stools" after being "troubled with trembling of the arms and thighs" – and then suffer vicariously at the displays of eye-watering forceps and other implements. The best view of the building itself is at the back, in the neat walled garden.

Holy Trinity Church

By the war memorial at the foot of Old Town, Southern Lane heads left along the river back to the theatres, while a footpath leads to **Holy Trinity Church** (April–Sept Mon–Sat 8.30am–6pm, Sun 12.30–5pm; March & Oct Mon–Sat 9am–5pm, Sun 12.30–5pm; Nov–Feb Mon–Sat 9am–4pm, Sun 12.30–5pm; free; Ⓦwww .stratford-upon-avon.org), whose mellow, honey-coloured stonework dates from the thirteenth century. Enhanced by its riverside setting and flanked by the yews and weeping willows of its graveyard, the dignified proportions of this quintessentially English church are the result of several centuries of chopping and changing, culminating in the replacement of the original wooden spire with today's stone version in 1763. Inside, the nave is flanked by a fine set of stained-glass windows, some of which are medieval, and bathed in light from the clerestory windows up above. Quite unusually, you'll see that the nave is built on a slight skew from the line of the chancel – supposedly to represent Christ's inclined head on the cross. In the north aisle, beside the transept, is the **Clopton Chapel**, where the large wall-tomb of George Carew is a Renaissance extravagance decorated with military insignia appropriate to his job as master of ordnance to James I. But poor old George is long forgotten – unlike William Shakespeare, who lies buried in the **chancel** (£1.50), his remains overseen by a sedate and studious memorial plaque and effigy added seven years after his death.

Butterfly Farm

Of the many other tourist attractions around Stratford – a brass-rubbing centre or wizardry show here, a Tudor museum or multimedia Shakespeare experience there – the loveliest, and the one most likely to appeal to parents and Tudor'd-out children alike, is the **Butterfly Farm**, just on the south side of the river on Swan's Nest Lane (daily from 10am; last entry April–Sept 5.30pm, March & Oct 4.30pm, Feb & Nov 4pm, Dec & Jan 3.30pm; £5.95; ⓦwww.butterflyfarm .co.uk). More than 250 species of tropical butterfly roam a huge landscaped greenhouse, along with parrots and a South American iguana. Also explore the caterpillar room, "insect city" and "arachnoland", complete with black widows and tarantulas.

Anne Hathaway's Cottage

Just over a mile west of the centre in the well-heeled suburb of **SHOTTERY** stands **Anne Hathaway's Cottage** (daily: April–Oct 9am–5pm, Nov–March 10am–4pm; see the box on p.142 for ticket info), Anne's home before she married Shakespeare in 1582. The cottage – actually an old farmhouse – is an immaculately maintained, half-timbered affair with a thatched roof and quaint little chimneys, its interior displaying a comely combination of period furniture, including a finely carved four-poster bed. The garden is splendid too, crowded with bursting blooms in the summertime. The adjacent orchard and **Shakespeare Tree Garden** features a scattering of modern sculptures and more than forty trees and shrubs mentioned in the plays, each with a plaque bearing the appropriate quotation. Although the City Sightseeing bus tour (see p.139) can drop you here, the most agreeable way to arrive is on foot from the town centre via the signposted **path** from Evesham Place, at the south end of Rother Street.

Mary Arden's Farm

The final piece in the Shakespeare properties jigsaw is **Mary Arden's Farm** (April–Oct daily 10am–5pm; see the box on p.142 for ticket info), three miles northwest of the town centre in the village of **WILMCOTE**. Mary was Shakespeare's mother and the only unmarried daughter of her father, Robert, at the time of his death in 1556. Unusually for the period, Mary inherited the house and land, thus becoming one of the neighbourhood's most eligible women – John Shakespeare, eager for self-improvement, married her within a year. The site covers several acres, taking in the Arden house, a well-furnished example of an Elizabethan farmhouse, as well as neighbouring Palmer's Farm, outbuildings, nature trails and fields where longhorn cattle and Cotswold sheep graze.

Stratford farmers' market and food festival

Shakespeariana aside, Stratford is renowned locally – and across the region – for its excellent **farmers' market** (ⓦwww.sketts.co.uk), held on the **first and third Saturdays** of every month on **Rother Street**, by the American Fountain at the junction with Wood Street. It's a friendly, jovial glimpse of real life amid all the tourism, and a key point of regional contact – the most northerly market for brewers, bakers and cheesemakers from Oxfordshire and Gloucestershire and, similarly, the southernmost market for producers from Birmingham and the West Midlands. Stallholders start setting up at breakfast time, and the market runs from 9am until about 1 or 2pm, drawing in shoppers from as far afield as Coventry, Banbury and Worcester: best get there early. Look out, also, for late September's **Stratford Food Festival** (ⓦwww .stratfordfoodfestival.co.uk), with speciality markets, talks and live entertainment running across a long weekend.

Costumed re-enactments of what life on a Tudor farm might have been like enhance your wanderings. There is free parking onsite, and the City Sightseeing tour bus (see p.139) passes this way.

Eating and drinking

Stratford is accustomed to feeding and watering thousands of visitors, so finding refreshment is never difficult. The problem is that many places are geared up to serve the day-tripper as rapidly as possible – not a recipe for much gastronomic delight. That said, there is a scattering of notable **restaurants**, several of which have been catering to theatre-goers for many years, though you'd have to look hard to find menus varying from the familiar staples of lamb, chicken, steaks and pasta. Almost every restaurant in the centre (Sheep Street is lined with them) offers a **pre-theatre menu** between 5pm and 7pm, with prices for two courses hovering around £11–13. A handful of the town centre's **pubs** and **cafés** are worth recommending – and if you're in Stratford at the right time, don't miss the twice-monthly **farmers' market** (see box opposite).

Restaurants and cafés

Church Street Townhouse 16 Church St ☎01789 262222, ⊛www.churchstreettownhouse .co.uk. Newcomer on the scene, opened in 2010 (see "Hotels" p.140), offering well-priced, high-quality food sourced locally wherever possible and presented with style, in a cheery, informal dining room that is far enough back into the town centre to catch more locals than theatre-goers. Mains £11–16.

Kingfisher Fish Bar 13 Ely St ☎01789 292513. The best fish-and-chip shop in town. Takeaway and sit-down available – and only 5min walk from the theatres. Closed Sun.

Lamb's 12 Sheep St ☎01789 292554, ⊛www.lambsrestaurant.co.uk. Smart and appealing restaurant with a solid reputation serving a mouth-watering range of stylish English and continental dishes in antique premises – beamed ceilings and so forth. Daily specials at around £9, other main courses £11–16. Closed Mon lunch.

Malbec 6 Union St ☎01789 269106, ⊛www .malbecrestaurant.co.uk. Smart and intimate bistro-style restaurant serving top-quality seafood and meat dishes, often with a Mediterranean slant. The emphasis is on local, seasonal ingredients, served off a short menu. Mains £14–22. Closed Sun & Mon.

McKechnies 37 Rother St ☎01789 299575, ⊛www.mckechnies-cafe.co.uk. Great little independent daytime-only café beside the Market Place offering what's been voted as the best coffee in Stratford, as well as hearty all-day breakfasts and light lunches.

The Oppo 13 Sheep St ☎01789 269980, ⊛www.theoppo.co.uk. Universally shortened to "The Oppo" from its full name, *The Opposition Bistro*. Serves international cuisine in a busy but amiable atmosphere in pleasant old premises next door to (and with the same owners as) *Lamb's*. It's generally a lighter, easier-going option than its neighbour, with some slightly more adventurous options: dishes of the day, chalked up on a board inside, are good value at around £8, otherwise mains are £11–15. Closed Sun lunch.

Thai Boathouse Swan's Nest Lane ☎01789 297733, ⊛www.thaigroup.co.uk. Informal, much-loved restaurant occupying an old boathouse on the river's edge just over the bridge from the town centre, serving up exquisite Thai specialities in a pleasant ambience – book ahead for a window table. Mains are £8–15 or go for a multi-course set menu (£20–26 per person). Closed Sat lunch.

Pubs

Cox's Yard Bridgefoot ☎01789 404600, ⊛www .coxsyard.co.uk. Lively pub and music venue housed in a nineteenth-century former timber warehouse on the riverside. It's open during the day too, with a coffee shop, tearoom and "family pub" doing ice creams and food (most mains £8–10), but the main draw is live music and/or comedy most nights. Very un-Shakespearean.

Dirty Duck 53 Waterside ☎01789 297312. Properly the *Black Swan*, but this archetypal actors' pub, yards from the theatres and stuffed to the gunwales every night with a vocal entourage of RSC employees and hangers-on, was playfully rechristened decades – possibly centuries – ago. Ales are served up in somewhat spartan, wood-panelled premises and there's a terrace for

hot-weather drinking. A long menu encompasses pork sausages, beef and ale pie, fish and chips, steaks, and the like; the food wins no awards, but it's decent enough and well priced (mains £7–14). **Old Thatch Tavern** 23 Greenhill St, corner of Market Place ☎01789 295216. Popular, comfortable pub – the only thatched building left in central Stratford – with low-beamed ceilings and a good range of beers that attracts a mixed crew of tourists and locals.
Windmill Inn Church St ☎01789 297687. Four-hundred-year-old pub with rabbit-warren rooms and low-beamed ceilings. Dodge the menu in favour of one of Stratford's best pints of Flowers ale.

Listings

Bookshops Waterstones is on High St, or drop into the Shakespeare Bookshop on Henley St, run by the Birthplace Trust (ⓦ www.shakespeare.org.uk).
Hospital See p.36.
Markets General market on Rother St (Fri 9am–4pm; ⓦ www.sketts.co.uk). For farmers markets, see box, p.146.
Pharmacy Boots, 11 Bridge St ☎01789 268424.

Police station Rother St ☎01789 414111, ⓦ www.warwickshire.police.uk.
Post office 2 Henley St.
Taxis There are taxi ranks at the railway station, Bridge Street and elsewhere around town. Otherwise try 007 Stratford Taxis (☎01789 414007, ⓦ www.007stratfordtaxis.co.uk) or Main Taxis (☎01789 414514, ⓦ www.maintaxis.co.uk).

Around Stratford

Many of the attractions **around Stratford** lie beyond the remit of a Cotswolds guide, most notably magnificent Warwick Castle, eight miles northeast, and a clutch of stately homes spread all around. West of Stratford the B439 leads to **Evesham** (covered on p.169) – stop off on the way at the lovely old *Bell* in **WELFORD-ON-AVON** (☎01789 750353, ⓦ www.thebellwelford.co.uk) – while south of Stratford, several routes offer interest on journeys towards Oxfordshire or into the Cotswolds proper, particularly if you're looking for wet-weather diversions. Top choice is the superb art gallery at **Compton Verney**, aided and abetted by the **Heritage Motor Centre** nearby – both lying midway between Stratford and Banbury – while routes towards the old market town of Shipston-on-Stour introduce some quiet old villages on the Cotswolds fringe.

Cycling around Stratford

The fairly flat countryside around Stratford is ideal for **cycling**. See p.139 for details of Stratford Bike Hire. One easy way to start is with the regular leisure rides through the nearby countryside run by local cycling club **Shakespokes** (ⓦ www.shakespokes.org.uk), usually departing on Sundays at 9.30am from the American Fountain on Rother Street: they request temporary club membership of 50p. A five-mile stretch of disused railway between Stratford and Long Marston is now the **Stratford Greenway** (the Stratford Bike Hire website has details), a surfaced path for walkers and cyclists with *Carriages Café* (ⓦ www.carriagescafe.co.uk), an old converted railway carriage, offering refreshments partway along at Milcote. At Long Marston, you can turn round and retrace your route, or continue onwards to make a day of it – the Greenway forms part of the Sustrans **National Route 5**, which runs on for 25 miles through Shipston to Banbury, from where trains bring you back to Stratford. Alternatively, you could combine the Greenway with village routes back to Stratford to form a roughly 12-mile circuit – details at ⓦ www.warwickshire.gov.uk/cycling. Also check with **Cotswold Cycling Tours** (☎01789 721108, ⓦ www.cycling-tours.org.uk), based in Lower Quinton south of Stratford, for ideas about countryside rides up to Chipping Campden.

From Stratford the quickest route into the Cotswolds is the B4632 via Mickleton (see p.161), which lies at the foot of the scarp within easy reach of Broadway and Chipping Campden. On the way, near **UPPER QUINTON**, you'll pass the **Lower Clopton farm shop** (closed Sun & Mon; ☎01386 438236, ⓦwww .lowerclopton.co.uk) – impressively well stocked, also with short nature trails leading up to a scenic picnic area on Meon Hill.

South towards Shipston

South of Stratford, the A3400 Oxford road scoots across what is known as the **Feldon**. The name derives from an Old English term referring to land cleared for agriculture: this flattish farming country, ideal for pasturing livestock, fills much of southeast Warwickshire, very distinct from its counterpart – the forest of Arden, referred to by Shakespeare – which covers the northwest of the county, beyond Stratford.

Heading past **ALDERMINSTER**, which has the *Bell* inn (see p.141), you'll see signs for the *Ettington Park Hotel* (☎0845 072 7454, ⓦwww.handpicked.co.uk; ⑥), a fancy affair, and, nearby, the rather more wonderful **Talton Mill farm shop** and deli (closed Sun afternoon; ☎01789 459140, ⓦwww.talton-mill.co.uk), selling a range of local foods and condiments.

Shortly after, the A3400 meets the A429 Roman road **Fosse Way** (see p.175) on its arrow-straight trajectory from Leicester to Cirencester. Less than a mile to the left (north) lies **HALFORD**. Almost everybody thunders through, bound for the motorway, but you could stop off at the locally renowned *Halford Bridge* (☎01789 748217, ⓦwww.thehalfordbridge.co.uk), a sixteenth-century coaching inn on the A429 updated with pleasant interiors, good food and classy B&B (④). Lanes behind the inn lead down into Halford village – tranquil, picturesque and lined with fine old cottages. Here, Halford's old manor house, which has clung onto its Tudor facade, is now also a great option for B&B (☎01789 740264, ⓦwww .oldmanor-halford.co.uk; ④) – very tastefully laid out, with antiques in the three guest rooms and landscaped gardens. The nearby church, with elements of Romanesque and Norman design, a Gothic font and pre-Raphaelite stained glass, is bewitchingly still. Just to the east, the village pub in **OXHILL**, the *Peacock* (closed Mon lunch; ☎01295 688060, ⓦwww.thepeacockoxhill.co.uk), has won awards for the quality of its food, almost all of which is sourced from local suppliers.

South on the A3400, the rather over-neat village of **TREDINGTON** clusters around the tall spire of **St Gregory's Church**, which retains parts of the narrow windows of its Saxon predecessor high up above the nave, though most is fourteenth century. A mile or so south a turning towards the estate village of **HONINGTON**, built around the grand seventeenth-century Honington Hall (no public access), crosses the River Stour at an elegant old limestone **bridge** of the same date, listed as an ancient monument. A mile further south is Shipston (see p.151).

Compton Verney

Two roads run between Stratford and Banbury. The A422 is more direct, whizzing across the Feldon before climbing the Cotswolds scarp near Edgehill and passing the rather splendid **Upton House** stately home and gallery (see p.129) on the Warwickshire-Oxfordshire border. The slower route from Stratford is the B4086 past Alveston and Wellesbourne; immediately after crossing the B4455 Fosse Way, nine miles from Stratford, signs mark **COMPTON VERNEY**, a surprising – and wonderful – oasis of fine art in the depths of open country, well worth an excursion.

From the (free) car park it's a short stroll through beautiful wooded grounds and across a fine Capability Brown-designed bridge, guarded by four lead sphinxes, to **Compton Verney house** (late March to mid-Dec Tues–Sun 11am–5pm; £8; Ⓦwww.comptonverney.org.uk). Cars can drop off directly at the house. Originally built in the 1440s as the manor for an adjacent village, now gone, the house was extensively remodelled in the 1760s by Scottish architect **Robert Adam**. The owner who commissioned Adam, John Peyto Verney, also brought in **Capability Brown** to landscape the grounds. The family later fell on hard times, and eventually sold up in 1921; the house decayed quietly until purchased by a trust in 1993 with the express purpose of opening it to the public as an art gallery.

Theirs is a splendid achievement. The house itself – an imposing U-shaped mansion amid tree-shaded, lakeside lawns – has been beautifully restored: the galleries are light and airy, notes and artistic interpretation are excellent and there's a cycle of world-class **temporary shows** throughout the year – previous highlights have included Turner, Francis Bacon and Surrealism. The **permanent collection** starts on the ground floor with scenes from seventeenth- and eighteenth-century Naples, medieval German works and a room of British portraits. Upstairs are the Chinese galleries, with Neolithic pottery alongside colourful Ming-dynasty enamel and gilt, while the top floor is given over to a delightful collection of **British folk art** – teapots, shop signs, portraits of favourite livestock and scenes of everyday life from bare-knuckle boxing to tooth-pulling.

Even if art isn't your thing, pay £1 at the gallery for a **grounds–only ticket** and you can wander among the lime trees, cedars, yew and Wellingtonia, and stroll through a coppice to an **icehouse** (currently under renovation). A free audioguide, which is also downloadable at the gallery website, describes the grounds. Alternatively, it's free to enter the house for lunch at the award-winning **restaurant** – risotto with local goat cheese, black pudding and watercress salad, grilled sea-bass, and so forth (mains £7–10).

Compton Verney is served by Johnsons **bus** 269 (not Sun) twice a day between Stratford and Banbury – note that the more frequent 270 takes a different route – and the "Heart of Warwickshire" bus, detailed on p.140.

Heritage Motor Centre

From Compton Verney it's a short drive to the old village of **KINETON** – site of the Battle of Edgehill (see p.129) – and then via a minor road to **GAYDON**, directly beside junction 12 off the M40. Signs direct you a mile north on the B4100 to the **Heritage Motor Centre** (daily 10am–5pm; £9; Ⓦwww.heritage-motor-centre.co.uk), also reachable on the "Heart of Warwickshire" bus (see p.140) from Stratford. A purpose-designed showroom occupying one corner of an old RAF base, whose runways now serve as a test track for Jaguar Land Rover's research team based alongside (regrettably off-limits and concealed behind embankments, though you can hear the roar), this is an impressively laid-out evocation of the British car industry. The display floor includes a time-line of vehicles from 1896 to the present, with highly polished examples from each period, as well as groups of Land Rovers, sports cars of various marques, rally cars and so on, along with notes and video screens. At bank holidays and over the summer (dates on the website), an outdoor track hosts petrol-driven go-karts (£6 extra), as well as electric cars for the under-8s (£3 extra) – and there's the chance to experience offroad 4x4 driving over rough terrain (£6 extra).

The centre is a magnet for classic car enthusiasts, staging many rallies over the summer; if you've caught the bug, contact The Open Road (☎0845 070 5142,

@www.theopenroad.co.uk), a firm based near Gaydon which specializes in **classic car rental** – anything from an MGB roadster (£145/day) up to a 1970 Jaguar E-Type (£360/day).

The north Cotswolds

Taking in the northernmost fringes of the Cotswolds Area of Outstanding Natural Beauty (@www.cotswoldsaonb.org.uk), the terrain between Stratford and Moreton-in-Marsh – what we've termed the **NORTH COTSWOLDS** – covers what you might call the good, the bad and the ugly. The "good" is **Chipping Campden**, the region's single most beautiful destination, an array of honeystone Jacobean gables set against forested hills which single-handedly ticks every Cotswold box, while retaining full command of poise and dignity. Other, smaller cohorts such as **Stanton** or **Ebrington** and the modest gardens at **Kiftsgate**, along with some fine **walks**, add memorable breadth. The "bad" might be Campden's near-neighbour, **Broadway** – heartwarming, historically significant and undoubtedly beautiful, but unrelentingly given over to peak-season tourism. As for the last on the list, "ugly" is going too far, but even the most ardent devotee of **Shipston-on-Stour** wouldn't claim it as the fairest of beauties; nonetheless it and its hinterland can give access to landscapes and rural culture that are every bit as enticing as the classic names to those on a long, slow journey of discovery.

Shipston-on-Stour

Purists will snort to see **SHIPSTON-ON-STOUR** (@www.shipstononline.org) even mentioned under a Cotswolds heading: not only is it in Warwickshire (not a Cotswolds county, according to some), but it lies in flatlands between the hills and also lacks the appearance and atmosphere of its Cotswold near-neighbours such as Moreton-in-Marsh (see p.175), eight miles south, and Chipping Campden (see p.154), the same distance west. On the other hand, if that doesn't bother you, this genial old town could make for a pleasant diversion away from the crowds. Shipston's unpretentious mood is set by its name, derived from the Saxon term *Scepwaeisctune*, or "Sheep-Wash Town": this is where local farmers gathered to dip their livestock in the river.

Sheltered beside a meeting-point of roads from four points of the compass, Shipston's little **High Street** is boxed in at both ends, giving it a cosy, enclosed ambience; erase the supermarkets and it could almost be Trumpton. Two coaching inns survive here – dodge the Georgian-fronted *White Bear* in favour of the *George* (☎01608 661453, @www.georgehotelshipston.com; ❸), attractively renovated in boutique designer style, an unusually upmarket place to drink, eat and sleep. You can download an entertaining podcast of a town **walk** at @www.talkingthewalk.co.uk – then lose yourself in the little tangle of lanes off the High Street. Even aside from Sheldons, wine merchants of venerable vintage who offer **tours** of their Victorian cellars on New Street with wine-tastings (from £15; @www.bennettsfinewines.com), Shipston is home to a surprising number of independent businesses: galleries, crafts outlets, haberdashers and, above all, delis. Sample local **cheeses** at Taylors, 29 High Street (@www.taylorsofshipston.co.uk), award-winning **pork pies** at Rightons butchers, 16 Sheep Street (@www.rightonsofshipston.co.uk), and drop into the cheery 🌿 **Taste of the Country**, 2 Market Place (@www.tasteofthecountry.co.uk), which sells a wide range of local foods and fresh-baked breads – it would take a will of iron to glimpse the pile of homemade jam tarts in their window and walk on by. Round the corner rises

St Edmund's Church, of ancient foundation but rebuilt in 1855, a step from the *Horseshoe*, 6 Church Street (☎01608 662190, ⓦwww.horseshoeshipston.com), a seventeenth-century coaching inn that still knows how to pull a pint.

East of Shipston

The B4035 climbs east from Shipston on its way to Banbury, fourteen miles distant. Three or so miles out of town you pass through the twin villages of the Brailes (ⓦwww.brailesvillage.co.uk) – first neat **UPPER BRAILES** and then, almost contiguous, **LOWER BRAILES**, dominated by the church of **St George**, dubbed the "Cathedral of the Feldon". It's a magnificent sight, set back behind an Edwardian lychgate, largely thirteenth- and fourteenth-century, with high clerestory windows, an elaborate Gothic east window and, unusually, three *sedilia* (medieval stone seats for officiating priests) surviving against the south wall of the chancel. East of Brailes, the road continues over Gallow Hill before eventually bumping its way down to Broughton Castle (see p.129) on the edge of Banbury.

The "**Cotswold and Feldon Cycle Route**" (map and notes downloadable at ⓦwww.cotswoldsaonb.org.uk) links Shipston and Lower Brailes in a mostly flat fourteen-mile circuit which initially heads south to **CHERINGTON**, where the modest *Cherington Arms* (☎01608 686233) not only serves its own Cherington Ale but is also making a name for itself as a **music venue**, hosting live bands on alternate Monday nights – check gig lists at ⓦwww.oxfordblues.info and ⓦwww.myspace .com/timportermusic. The cycle route continues to Brailes and between the fields back to Shipston, while an optional extra seven-mile loop (which includes some hill-climbs) heads out from Cherington via **WHICHFORD**, notable for its **pottery** (ⓦwww.whichfordpottery.com) as well as the fine old Hook Norton pub *The Norman Knight* (closed Mon lunch; ☎01608 684621, ⓦwww.thenorman knight.co.uk), overlooking the large, attractively unkempt village green.

From Whichford, it's about three miles to the *Gate Hangs High* pub (see p.120) outside **Hook Norton**, even less to the **Rollright Stones** (see p.120). In the other direction is **Great Wolford** (see p.179), on the approach to Moreton-in-Marsh.

West of Shipston

West of Shipston, once you cross the "Portobello Crossroads" – where the B4035 meets the A429 Fosse Way – you re-enter classic Cotswolds territory. The main draw hereabouts is, of course, Chipping Campden (see p.154) but before you cross

---

Shipston and its villages by bus

The Stagecoach **buses 50/50A** follow a useful route between Stratford, Shipston and Banbury/Chipping Norton. With a bit of planning, you could use a sequence of departures on **bus 50A** (Mon–Sat every 2hr; no service on Sun) to leave Stratford around 9am, have a couple of hours in Shipston, stop off in Lower Brailes for the church and for lunch at the *George Inn* opposite (☎01608 685223, ⓦwww.thegeorgeatbrailes .co.uk), move on again – visiting Broughton for the castle, if you match their opening days (see p.129), or Sibford Gower for a village stroll and a pint at the *Wykham Arms* (see p.120) – and finish up in Banbury (see p.121) at around 5 or 6pm. Stay overnight in Banbury, or jump on an evening train back to Stratford. The less regular Johnsons bus 23/23A is another option between Stratford, Shipston and Brailes. Alternatively, use the same route or **bus 50** (Mon–Sat 4 daily, 6 on Sun) from Stratford to Shipston, for a slow morning and lunch, and then move on that afternoon on bus 50 direct to Chipping Norton (see p.117) where you could stay – or change buses for, say, Kingham or Woodstock. All these routes also operate in reverse.

the Warwickshire-Gloucestershire border you could detour south a mile or so to **STRETTON-ON-FOSSE** (ⓦ www.strettononfosse.co.uk), a quiet village declared a conservation area for its historic Cotswold-stone cottages, where the *Plough* (Ⓣ01608 661053), a friendly old pub with beer mugs hanging from the beams, does decent food.

An unusual place for an excellent **restaurant** is the petrol station on the A429 between the Portobello crossroads and the Stretton turn – here stands *Cotswold Spice* (open evenings only, also Sun lunch; Ⓣ01608 661920, ⓦ www.cotswold spice.co.uk). Once a *Little Chef*, this is now a rather stylish contemporary Indian restaurant, much loved by the locals for the service and the food, both excellent. Plump for any of the usual curry-house suspects, or splash out on one of their fusion options: buttered salmon tikka, mustard sea-bass or ginger lamb with lemon chilli rice, to name a few. Mains are £7–14; check for frequent special offers. Just south is the Ditchford Mill farm shop (see p.180) and Moreton-in-Marsh.

A few miles north of Stretton, picturesque **ILMINGTON** (ⓦ www.ilmington .org.uk), purportedly the highest village in Warwickshire, clusters around the lovely old church of **St Mary**, with its Norman belltower, oak pews carved by twentieth-century English furniture-maker Robert Thompson and the embroidered **Apple Map**, a copy of medieval maps showing the location of each of the village's orchards. Ilmington still holds **Apple Walks**, most often in October, where villagers gather to view the Apple Map and then ramble the nearby lanes to find each of the 38 apple varieties grown locally. Hidcote (see p.160) lies a couple of miles west.

Ebrington and around

On the approach to Chipping Campden, a trio of Gloucestershire villages off the B4035 could draw you into a detour. A mile or so from Stretton-on-Fosse, **CHARINGWORTH** has fine views over the hills, exploited by the gardens and terraces of *Charingworth Manor Hotel* (Ⓣ01386 593555, ⓦ www.classiclodges.co .uk; ❻) – less grand than it initially appears, with modern rooms that are of a high standard but unremarkable. A mile to the southwest, **PAXFORD**'s *Churchill Arms* (Ⓣ01386 594000, ⓦ www.thechurchillarms.com) raises the stakes significantly in terms both of food quality and overall experience. Located on an almost absurdly photogenic corner in a car-an-hour village, it faces a row of traditional Cotswold cottages – one is the village shop, still with its vintage Hovis sign – while across the way, a Victorian chapel stands perfectly framed before open countryside. The pub itself is renowned for its food – an intelligent, informal take on modern British cooking, with seasonal ingredients sourced locally – while also remaining a decent local at heart, inglenook fireplace and all. It also has a few rooms for B&B (❸). Blockley (see p.179) and Moreton (see p.175) lie just to the south.

Competing on charm terms – and perhaps stealing a march – is **EBRINGTON**, a lovely old thatched village of classic good looks secreted into the folded landscape a mile north of Paxford. Beside the tiny triangular village green stands the heart-warming 🌲 *Ebrington Arms* (closed Mon; Ⓣ01386 593223, ⓦ www .theebringtonarms.co.uk), a seventeenth-century inn that not only was CAMRA's North Cotswold Pub of the Year 2010 (and 2009) but also pops up in the Good Food Guide. Duck the oak beams and antlers on the wall to sup your choice of Cotswold ales in a genial, easygoing atmosphere – log fires in winter, walled garden in summer – or try food that is sophisticated without being pretentious: salmon and dill fishcakes, Gloucester Old Spot pork chops or Cotswold lamb with wild mushrooms (mains £10–16). Three comfortable old rooms (❺), freshly refurbished with modern bathrooms, make for high-quality pub B&B.

Two miles west is Chipping Campden.

Chipping Campden

CHIPPING CAMPDEN, twelve miles south of Stratford, gives a better idea than anywhere else in the Cotswolds as to what a prosperous wool town might have looked like in the seventeenth century. The wonderfully elegant, almost perfectly preserved High Street is hemmed in by ancient houses, whose undulating, weather-beaten roofs jag against each other, above twisted beams and mullioned windows. Its name derives from the Saxon term *campadene*, meaning cultivated valley, and the Old English *ceapen*, or market.

More than being merely picturesque, though, Campden (the name is invariably shortened) is alive with atmosphere. There are coach parties, of course, and urbanite weekenders, and a fair contingent of muddy-booted hill-walkers – but there is also a thriving, rooted local community, some having been here all their lives, many having arrived to tap into a wellspring of creativity which has underpinned the town since the days of the nineteenth-century Arts and Crafts movement (see p.112). **Charles Ashbee**, an Arts and Crafts devotee, relocated the London-based Guild and School of Handicraft here in 1902 and though that venture failed, it bequeathed a legacy of independent artisans in art and design which continues to enrich Campden life. The "**Creative Campden**" website explains more (ⓦ www.creativecampden.co.uk).

Add to that the natural drama of the setting: Campden is perched atop the Cotswold scarp, and from **Dover's Hill**, just on the edge of town, views yawn out over a broad swathe of three counties. The town also marks the northern end-point of the **Cotswold Way** (see p.32), a long-distance path which hugs the high ground all the way to Bath, a hundred miles south.

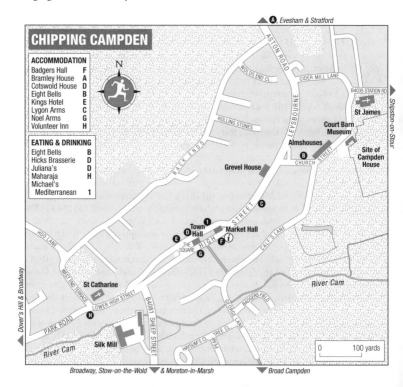

CHIPPING CAMPDEN

Ⓐ, Evesham & Stratford

ACCOMMODATION
Badgers Hall   F
Bramley House   A
Cotswold House   D
Eight Bells   B
Kings Hotel   E
Lygon Arms   C
Noel Arms   G
Volunteer Inn   H

EATING & DRINKING
Eight Bells   B
Hicks Brasserie   D
Juliana's   D
Maharaja   H
Michael's Mediterranean   1

N

ASTON ROAD
WOLDS END CL.
CIDER MILL LANE
B4035 STATION RD
LEYSBOURNE
ROLLING STONES
BACK ENDS
St James
Court Barn Museum
Almshouses
Site of Campden House
Grevel House
CHURCH STREET
HIGH STREET
Town Hall
Market Hall
THE SQUARE
CALF'S LANE
HOO LANE
WEST END TERRACE
St Catharine
LOWER HIGH STREET
B4081 SHEEP STREET
River Cam
Badgers Field
GEORGE LANE
River Cam
PARK ROAD
Silk Mill
HAYSUM'S CL.
TREE CL.

Shipston-on-Stour

Dover's Hill & Broadway

0   100 yards

Broadway, Stow-on-the-Wold ▼ & Moreton-in-Marsh   ▼ Broad Campden

Walking and cycling around Chipping Campden

There's a wealth of **walking and cycling** in the hills and countryside around Chipping Campden. For ideas, maps and guidance, drop into Campden's well-equipped tourist office to pick the brains of its efficient, knowledgeable staff, who can point you in the right direction.

Long-distance walks
Top choice locally is the **Cotswold Way** (see also p.32), which starts (or ends) at Chipping Campden, extending to Broadway, Winchcombe and on south to Bath. The first stage, between Campden and Broadway (6 miles; 4hr), is a great introduction to the walk, with several hilltop viewpoints and bags of Cotswold character. It starts with the walk to Dover's Hill, described on p.158, then heads down through Campden Woods to climb the infamous Fish Hill to Broadway Tower (see p.165), ending with the steep descent into Broadway village (p.161), where there are plenty of accommodation options and – if you time things right – buses to return you to Campden. Chipping Campden is also a midway point on the **Heart of England Way**, with stages linking north down the scarp to Mickleton and Bidford-on-Avon (14 miles) and south over the hills to Bourton-on-the-Water (15 miles) – and it forms one end of the **Cotswold Link**, which facilitates access to the Macmillan Way's Cross-Cotswold Path, 21 miles east at Banbury (see p.125).

Shorter walks
Of the numerous shorter walks around Campden, one of the best starts from the archway of the *Noel Arms* on the High Street, beneath which a trail cuts south to join the road into picturesque **BROAD CAMPDEN** village, a mile or so away in its own valley. To one edge of the village stands the fine old *Bakers Arms* (℡01386 840515), with top-quality local ales and good food. The walk back takes you past Broad Campden's church – the house opposite was converted from a Norman chapel by Charles Ashbee in 1905 – across a stream and between the fields back to Chipping Campden.

Cycling
Cycle Cotswolds (daily 7am–9pm; ℡01789 720193 or 07933 368074, ⌘www.cycle cotswolds.co.uk), based at Chipping Campden's *Volunteer Inn* (see p.156), have 21-speed "Trek" bikes for rent (£10/day or £15 for 24hr), with child bikes and child seats/tag-alongs also available. They offer free delivery and collection within a radius of four miles around Chipping Campden, subject to a minimum order of £20.

Beautiful, inspiring, creative and with a strong sense of its own history, Campden could melt the hardest of hearts. Stay for a night (or a week) – if only to be able to roam in the evening and early morning, when the streets are empty and the golden hues of the stone are at their richest.

Arrival and information
Absurdly, considering the popularity of the place, Chipping Campden has **no buses on Sundays**. The rest of the week, Johnsons bus 21/22 (not Sun) runs about every hour from **Stratford**, **Broadway** and **Moreton** (change at Moreton from Cheltenham), while Henshaw's bus 554 (not Sun) arrives five times a day from **Evesham**. Alternatives are the Hedgehog community bus H3 from Stratford (once on Tues, Wed, Fri & Sat) and H5 from Evesham (once on Thurs). Otherwise, you're left with irregular routes operated by Pulham's: bus 816 from Moreton (once on Tues); bus 608 from **Cheltenham** and Broadway (once on Thurs & Sat); and bus 612 from **Bourton-on-the-Water**, **Stow-on-the-Wold**, Moreton,

Broadway and Evesham (once on Sat). Coming from **Oxford** or London, best catch a **train** to Moreton and change there for a bus or **taxi** (about £25).

The well-equipped **tourist office** (March–Oct daily 9.30am–5pm; Nov–Feb Mon–Thurs 9.30am–1pm, Fri–Sun 9.30am–4pm; T01386 841206, Wwww .campdenonline.org) is bang in the middle of town, on the High Street opposite the Market Hall. The exceptionally knowledgeable and amenable staff (all volunteers) can book **accommodation** on your behalf (£2.50), a useful service in the height of the summer when rooms are in short supply, and have information on all aspects of local life. A **guided town walk** runs once a week in summer (April–Sept Tues 2.30pm; £2), starting from the tourist office.

Accommodation

Chipping Campden's **accommodation** is generally excellent: the high profile of the village and its relatively well-heeled brand of overnight visitor mean that standards are high, with a decent choice to suit most budgets. Many places insist on a two-night minimum stay, especially during the summer peak.

Aside from the places reviewed below, you might also consider a particularly special **self-catering** option: the Landmark Trust (T01628 825925, Wwww .landmarktrust.org.uk) offers the Jacobean banqueting halls of a now-demolished country mansion (see p.158) for holiday rentals. These two small buildings, a step from the church, face each other across the grass of what was the mansion's garden terrace. Even in such an atmospheric place as Campden, they are exceptional. Prices depend on the season, but expect to pay roughly £1500–2000 for 7 nights, or around £1000–1200 for 3 nights.

Hotels & inns

Cotswold House The Square T01386 840330, Wwww.cotswoldhouse.com. On the High Street in the centre of Campden, this plush – perhaps overly plush – hotel occupies an immaculately maintained Regency town house and its older neighbours. Quality is exceptional, both in the main house and the cottages and suites behind: expect mood lighting, underfloor heating, stone baths, free DVDs, six kinds of pillow – the whole nine yards. Their onsite Temple Spa opened in 2010, with a full range of treatments and therapies. ⑧–⑨

Eight Bells Church St T01386 840371, Wwww.eightbellsinn.co.uk. Seven individually done-up bedrooms at this much-loved pub between the High Street and the church. The style is calm – smartly modern without struggling for the designer boutique look – and being at a slight remove from the town centre is a bonus. ④

Kings Hotel The Square T01386 840256, Wwww.kingscampden.co.uk. Super-posh luxury hotel hiding behind an eighteenth-century frontage on the High Street. Lavish contemporary styling, reminiscent of an urban boutique hotel, characterizes the 19 bedrooms, including five extra-special rooms in a renovated cottage, but good offers during the week can make rates surprisingly affordable; prices jump at weekends. Sister to Stratford's *Arden* hotel (see p.140). ⑤–⑥

Lygon Arms High St T01386 840318, Wwww .lygonarms.co.uk. Not to be confused with the venerable top-end *Lygon Arms* in nearby Broadway, this is a decent midrange ex-coaching inn (pronounced "liggon") that's been around for five hundred years or so – though now with rather bland, refurbished rooms that do the job, nothing more. A decent stop-gap. ③–④

Noel Arms High St T01386 840317, Wwww .noelarmshotel.com. Sister property of *Cotswold House*, directly opposite – but considerably more down to earth. Housed in a sixteenth-century former coaching inn, with a traditional wood-panelled bar and log fires, it has 27 bedrooms – pleasant and very comfortable but not flashy. ④

Volunteer Inn Lower High St T01386 840688, Wwww.thevolunteerinn.net. Great budget option at this friendly, outgoing pub and Indian restaurant at the end of the High Street – often used by walkers on the Cotswold Way and cycle enthusiasts (you can rent bikes onsite; see p.155). The nine rooms are modest but perfectly adequate – the only drawback can be noise from the bar, particularly on Friday and Saturday nights. ③

B&Bs

Badgers Hall High St T01386 840839, Wwww .badgershall.co.uk. Popular, atmospheric choice for B&B, in an old stone house on the High Street, above their own tearoom. All the guest rooms are en suite and come complete with period detail – beamed ceilings and so forth; advance bookings are advised. ❹

Bramley House 6 Aston Rd ☎ 01386 840066, ⓦ www.bramleyhouse.co.uk. Fine little B&B in a modern(-ish) Cotswold stone house a few minutes' walk off the High Street – only three guest rooms, all cosy, but the difference comes in the personal touch: great service and locally sourced breakfasts. ❸

The Town

Other attractions aside, Chipping Campden happens to host what might be the single most atmospheric, and emblematic, building in the Cotswolds: the seventeenth-century **Market Hall**. With its uneven floor of worn stones, its simple design – five arches long, two arches wide – its origin as a gift to Campden from the local lord Sir Baptist Hicks, and its physical placement at the centre of village life, this barn-like building in the middle of the High Street, where dairy farmers once sold their wares, summons up more Cotswold ghosts than any number of stately homes or grand gardens. Dawdle here, and make time for slow, aimless strolling along Campden's adjacent **High Street**, past Tudor, Jacobean and the odd Georgian facade, behind which lurk fancy hotels, upscale design boutiques and ordinary shops alike.

Beside the Market Hall, Campden's pint-sized **Town Hall** sports a plaque on one corner marking the start (and end) of the Cotswold Way. A little way further, turn down Sheep Street to reach the ex-**Silk Mill**, which Ashbee took over for the Guild of Handicraft. Today, as well as housing galleries of local art and ceramics, the old building rings with the noise of chisels from the resident stone carvers and hammering from the upstairs workshop of **Hart's** (ⓦ www.hartsilversmiths.co.uk), a silversmith firm which came out to Campden with Ashbee in 1902 and has been based here since. You're free to wander into their workshop – like stepping into an old photograph, with metalworking tools and half-finished pieces strewn everywhere under low ceilings, and staff perched by the windows working by hand on decorative items or jewellery.

The history and work of the Guild, and its leading exponents, is explained at the superb **Court Barn museum** (April–Sept Tues–Sat 10.30am–5.30pm, Sun 11.30am–5.30pm; Oct–March Tues–Sat 11am–4pm, Sun 11.30am–4pm; £3.75; ⓦ www.courtbarn.org.uk). To find it walk up the High Street, past **Grevel House** on the left, Campden's oldest building (built in around 1380), and turn right onto Church Street, itself graced by a magnificent row of seventeenth-century

---

Day-tripping by bus from Chipping Campden

From a base in Chipping Campden, it's possible to use the limited public transport to put together a handful of enticing **day-trips by bus** – not on Sundays, though, when no buses run. Starting from Campden at 9am on Henshaw's bus 554, you could spend a couple of hours mid-morning in Evesham, then take Stagecoach bus 28/28A to be in Stratford for lunch, from where Johnsons bus 21/22 returns you to Campden in late afternoon/early evening. Turn it round to visit Stratford first and, with careful planning, you could add in a stop on bus 554 at Bretforton for an afternoon pint at the *Fleece* (see p.169) before catching the last bus 554 back to Campden around 6pm. On the first and third Saturdays of the month, you could use either of two morning departures on Johnsons bus 21/22 to get you to Stratford in time to browse the excellent farmers' market there (see p.146), returning directly or via Evesham. An alternative itinerary, with less time spent on the road, could involve Johnsons bus 22 to be at Batsford Arboretum (see p.177) a touch after 9am, moving on with Johnsons bus 21 for lunch in Broadway, and returning to Campden on bus 21 in the late afternoon.

almshouses in Cotswold stone. Sited opposite the almshouses, the museum displays the work of Ashbee and eight cohorts, placing it all in context with informative displays and short videos – the bookbinding of Katharine Adams, stained-glass design of Paul Woodroffe, furniture design of Gordon Russell (who has his own museum in Broadway; see p.164), the silver of Hart's and Robert Welch, and more.

A step away, the top end of Church Street is dominated by a splendidly ornate Jacobean gatehouse – but if you peek through the gates, there's nothing there but more or less empty fields. This was the main entrance to an estate created in the 1610s by **Baptist Hicks**, a textile merchant knighted by James I and later Lord Mayor of London. Centred on an imposing three-storey mansion, whose dome was illuminated at night, the estate took in eight acres of formal gardens – but during the Civil War, less than forty years after its construction, Hicks's grandson had the house burnt to the ground rather than allow it to fall into Parliamentarian hands. What survives today, leased by the Landmark Trust (Ⓦwww.landmark trust.org.uk), is the gatehouse, some foundation remnants and a pair of modest banqueting halls (see "Accommodation" p.156); check on the website for details of the 15 or so days a year that the site is open to the public.

A few metres up the hill, approached by an avenue of lime trees, rises **St James' Church** (March–Oct Mon–Sat 10am–5pm, Sun 2–6pm; Nov–Feb Mon–Sat 11am–4pm, Sun 2–4pm; closes 3pm in Dec & Jan; free; Ⓦwww.stjameschurch campden.co.uk). Built in the fifteenth century, the zenith of Campden's wool-trading days, this is the archetypal Cotswold wool church, beneath a magnificent 120-foot tower. Inside, the airy nave is bathed in light from the clerestory windows and there's a delicate and carefully considered balance between height and length. The South Chapel holds the ostentatious **funerary memorial** of the Hicks family, with the fancily carved marble effigies of Sir Baptist and Lady Elizabeth lying on their table-tomb overlooked by the standing figures of their daughter and son-in-law, Edward Noel, who came a fatal cropper fighting the Parliamentarians in the Civil War. The church is also the venue for the prestigious **Chipping Campden Music Festival** (Ⓦwww.campdenmusicfestival.co.uk), held each May.

Dover's Hill

A fine panoramic view rewards those who make the short but severe hike up the first stage of the Cotswold Way north from the town centre to **Dover's Hill**. From the Lower High Street, turn beside St Catharine's church to follow West End Terrace and then Hoo Lane onwards, doglegging along Kingcombe Lane and up onto the hill (which is also accessible on four wheels, with a car park near the summit). The topograph at the highest point, 740 feet above sea level, affords breathtaking vistas extending to the Malvern Hills and beyond. Since 1612 this natural amphitheatre has been the stage for an Olympics of rural sports, though the event was suspended in the mid-nineteenth century just as games like shin-kicking were taking hold. A more civilized version, the **Cotswold Olimpicks** (see opposite), has been staged here annually since 1966 with tug-of-war, falconry and hammer-throwing plus a bit of shin-kicking for old times' sake.

See the walking map and notes at Ⓦwww.cotswoldsaonb.org.uk for how to turn this into a circuit back to Campden (3 miles; 2hr), or how to include **Lynches Wood** just below the summit – carpeted with bluebells in May – to make a longer circuit (4.5 miles; 3hr).

Eating and drinking

Campden has a good range of places to **eat and drink**, most of them attached to one or other of the accommodation places reviewed on p.156 (the exceptions

The Cotswold Olimpicks

Centuries before the revival of the ancient Greek tradition of the Olympic Games – generally recognized to be at Athens in 1896 – the Gloucestershire village of Chipping Campden was staging its own Olympic celebration of athletic prowess. In 1612, local lawyer **Robert Dover** organized a series of competitions on a hilltop site outside Campden (subsequently renamed Dover's Hill in his honour; see opposite) – running, jumping, hammer-throwing, sword-fighting, wrestling, horse-racing and more, partly it seems in order to give the local people something to cheer about, and partly perhaps to select prime athletes for military service in defence of King James, who was an enthusiastic supporter of Dover's enterprise. Within a few years, the games had become known as the "**Olimpicks**", commemorating the Greek tradition, and included music and festivities, games of cards and chess and a grand fireworks display.

After a pause for the Civil War the games rolled on, though largely losing their noble ideals: bottle-throwing grew increasingly popular and wrestling morphed into contests of shin-kicking between opponents in hobnail boots. During the Victorian era, the games drew tens of thousands before their final demise in 1852, when the division of common land meant Dover's Hill passed into private ownership.

Some 76 years later the National Trust bought the hill, hosting a one-off games in 1951 before local enthusiasts revived the tradition in earnest in 1966. Since then the **Cotswold Olimpicks** have been staged annually on Dover's Hill, on a Friday in late May or early June, with a range of competitions including tug-of-war, wrestling and, of course, shin-kicking. Big celebrations are planned for 2012 – the 400th anniversary of the games (and, coincidentally, when London is hosting those other Olympics). Find more information at ⓦ www.olimpickgames.co.uk.

---

below are those listed with full contact details). More excellent dining options lie within easy reach nearby – for example the *Ebrington Arms* in Ebrington (p.153), the *Churchill Arms* in Paxford (p.153), *Three Ways House* in Mickleton (p.161), *Russell's* in Broadway (p.165) and the *Horse and Groom* in Bourton-on-the-Hill (p.178). Otherwise, for a good old-fashioned cup of tea or a reviving espresso, pop into the award-winning *Badgers Hall* tearoom on the High Street or hole up at the *Campden Coffee Company* (ⓦ www.campdencoffeecompany.co.uk), a bright and breezy independent café within the old Silk Mill on Sheep Street.

Restaurants

Eight Bells Inn See p.156. Particularly cosy spot in this charming old stone inn, with a menu encompassing dishes such as pheasant with mushrooms or pork with apricots and chestnuts. Mains are £12–16.

Hicks Brasserie At *Cotswold House* hotel; see p.156. Upmarket brasserie fare in a contemporary setting, featuring high-quality fish and seafood plus meaty mains (£11–18), as well as traditional Sunday lunch and a special steak night on Fridays.

Juliana's At *Cotswold House* hotel; see p.156. Extremely elegant fine-dining restaurant, presenting innovative modern British cuisine in a distinctly cosmopolitan ambience, using locally sourced ingredients wherever possible. Expect at least £50 a head; a multi-course tasting menu is £65, excluding wine. Evenings only. Closed Sun & Mon.

Maharaja Lower High St ☏ 01386 849281, ⓦ www.thevolunteerinn.net. This much-loved midrange Indian restaurant is attached to the *Volunteer Inn* (see "Accommodation" p.156), though run separately from it. The menu takes in all the classics, as well as unusual – and fiery – Bangla-deshi fish and chicken curries, fruity Kashmiri dishes and even venison curry. Mains £8–17.

Michael's Mediterranean High St ☏ 01386 840826, ⓦ www.michaelsmediterranean.co.uk. Warm and welcoming Greek-Cypriot restaurant in an eighteenth-century house on the High Street, focusing – for a refreshing change – on modern Greek and Mediterranean cuisine, featuring an array of mezze starter dishes (hummus, halloumi cheese, kalamari and the like) followed by mains from moussaka and *kleftico* to yoghurt-marinated kebabs and steaks, with *baklava* to finish. Mains £11–21. Closed Sun eve & Mon.

Hidcote Manor Garden

Well signposted down country lanes four miles north of Chipping Campden, beside **HIDCOTE BARTRIM** village – and on the edge of the Cotswold scarp, offering some sweeping views over the Vale of Evesham – **Hidcote Manor Garden** (July & Aug daily 10am–6pm; March–June & Sept–Oct Sat–Wed 10am–6pm, closes 5pm in Oct; restricted opening Sat & Sun only in Nov, early Dec & early March; £8.60; ⓦ www.nationaltrust.org.uk) is often described as one of the greatest gardens of the twentieth century. It was created by Lawrence Johnston, a private and rather enigmatic character, between 1907 and 1930 as a sequence of outdoor "rooms", fully furnished (with plants) and connected by corridors and designed spaces. It's an intriguing concept, executed across a large area, which demands considerable attention: this isn't an attraction to dip in and out of. If gardens are your thing, plan to spend the best part of a day here exploring at leisure, to get under the skin of the place – and to tune out the perambulating crowds.

Hidcote was the first property acquired by the National Trust (in 1947) purely for its garden. They inherited a mature, sophisticated estate which nonetheless eschews many of the usual features associated with such properties. Instead of making the manor a centrepiece from which the garden radiates, Johnston sidelined the house, subtly shifting his garden's focus away from a celebration of human creativity in nature to, rather, a display of natural harmony under human influence. He made no attempt to introduce architecture – no pergolas, summerhouses or stone pathways – other than in the clipping of yew trees and planting of beech avenues to mimic buildings and streets. Aside from a couple of open areas – the **Theatre Lawn** and **Long Walk** – almost every part of Johnston's garden is compact, intimate and intricate, with close, detailed planting. Highlights include the **Red Border**, a sumptuous display in summer of lilies, lobelias, dahlias and more, the **Stilt Garden**, ringed by angular hornbeams, and the **Rose Garden** – but there's lots more. There is, deliberately, no labelling; instead, leaflets describing the planting, and an excellent garden guidebook by Anna Pavord, are available at the ticket desk. Various events run throughout the year, including dawn walks, painting workshops and apple-pressing: check the website for details. A **taxi** from Chipping Campden will cost about £15.

Hidcote Maze

Hidcote Manor's next-door neighbour has devised a neat way to capitalize on the tide of visitors – and generate a bit of extra summer income – by converting one of his corn fields into a **Maize Maze** (mid-July to early Sept daily 10am–6pm; £5; ⓦ www.hidcotemaze.co.uk). Three miles of pathways are created through eight acres of waving foliage in a new design each year (a dragon, a dinosaur, a pharaoh, and so on), and then photographed from the air to hand out as a crib-sheet. At various points you can also climb bridges and observation towers to see the lie of the land, and if all else fails you can call in the "maze master" for a rapid exit. Smaller kids can let off steam at the little play park alongside. It's signposted at a farm gate immediately before the Hidcote Manor car park.

Kiftsgate Court Gardens

If your heart sinks at the prospect of yet another garden, take courage. Located barely half a mile from Hidcote, **Kiftsgate Court Gardens** (Aug Sat–Wed 2–6pm; May–July Sat–Wed noon–6pm; April & Sept Sun, Mon & Wed 2–6pm; £6.50; ⓦ www.kiftsgate.co.uk) sees a fraction of the visitors who pile into its better-known neighbour – and, more to the point, as one plain-spoken admirer put it, "There's not a National Trust teapot in sight." Still privately owned by the granddaughter of Heather Muir, who bought the estate in 1918, this is a simply lovely retreat, perched, like Hidcote, on the very edge of the Cotswold scarp, with breathtaking panoramic views. The house (no public access, apart from a tearoom in one corner) sports a striking Georgian facade with a high Classical portico which originally formed part of Mickleton's manor: in 1887 it was detached, transported up the hill and a new house constructed behind. Around it, Muir and her daughter (and, now, granddaughter, who lives here with her family) created a glorious, low-key garden that is famed, in particular, for its **roses** – lavish, aromatic borders full of them, in numerous varieties, including its own *Rosa filipes* "*Kiftsgate*". Contemporary sculptures dot the grounds, and don't miss the **New Water Garden**, a former tennis court behind clipped yew hedges converted into a Zen-like space for contemplation, featuring a square pool reflecting a small, square island "planted" with 24 gilded bronze philodendron. It is stunning.

Mickleton: the Pudding Club

An old village at the foot of the escarpment below Hidcote, where the B4632 Stratford–Broadway road meets the B4081 zipping down from Chipping Campden, **MICKLETON** is pretty – but not quite pretty enough to merit a stop, were it not for the **Pudding Club** (ⓦwww.puddingclub.com). A bit of gastronomic fun, devised in 1985 to help save traditional British puddings from apparently imminent demise, this once-weekly communal consumption of spotted dick, sticky toffee pudding, syrup sponge and other custard-draped favourites, has gained worldwide fame, hosted – as from day one – at Mickleton's *Three Ways House Hotel* (ⓣ01386 438429, ⓦwww.threewayshousehotel.com; ❻–❼). The hotel, like the village, has charm but isn't quite top-drawer: some rooms, though well equipped and with nice bathroom freebies, are a touch smaller and plainer than you might expect. Plump instead for one of the bigger, cheerier pudding-themed rooms in the Garden Wing. Shortcomings, though, tend to be overshadowed by the genial service – and the puddings. Book well ahead for Pudding Club "meetings" (open to all; £35 per person), which generally happen on Friday evenings: you get a light main course followed by access to the legendary seven-pudding buffet. Strict rules apply: only one pudding at a time, you must finish one pudding before you can get another, and so on. The record, just so you know, is 24 helpings.

Broadway

"Broadway and much of the land about it are the perfection of the old English rural tradition."

Henry James

Wedged into an outlying corner of Worcestershire five miles west of Chipping Campden (and sixteen miles northeast of Cheltenham), **BROADWAY** is a handsome little village at the foot of the steep escarpment that rolls along the western edge of the Cotswolds. It seems likely that the Romans were the first to settle here, but Broadway's zenith was as a stop for stagecoaches plying between London and Worcester. This has defined much of the village's present appearance, its long, broad main street framed by honeystone cottages and former coaching inns shaded beneath chestnut trees. It's undeniably attractive and, like Campden, Broadway can attract more visitors than is comfortable – but unlike its neighbour Broadway feels less able to absorb them. Ordinary, everyday life must exist here somewhere, away from the tearooms, souvenir shops and neatly mown roadside

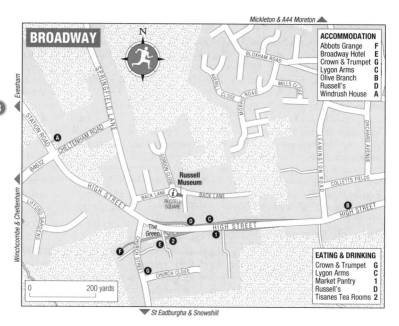

Mickleton & A44 Moreton ▲▲

BROADWAY

N

BLOXHAM ROAD

ACCOMMODATION	
Abbots Grange	F
Broadway Hotel	E
Crown & Trumpet	G
Lygon Arms	C
Olive Branch	B
Russell's	D
Windrush House	A

Russell
Museum

BACK LANE

BACK LANE

HIGH STREET

The
Green

HIGH STREET

CHURCH CLOSE

0   200 yards

EATING & DRINKING	
Crown & Trumpet	G
Lygon Arms	C
Market Pantry	1
Russell's	D
Tisanes Tea Rooms	2

▼ St Eadburgha & Snowshill

lawns, but in truth there's not much sign of it. Stay for a posh meal and/or a comfortable hotel, and for an early-morning stroll while the streets are empty, but then move on.

Arrival and information

As with Chipping Campden (see p.154), Broadway has **no buses on Sundays**. On other days, Castleways bus 606 (not Sun) runs five times a day from **Cheltenham** and **Winchcombe**, Johnsons bus 21 (not Sun) runs four times a day from **Stratford**, **Chipping Campden** and **Moreton**, and Castleways bus 559 (not Sun) runs about every two hours from **Evesham**. Otherwise there are only irregular services: Cresswell's bus 973 from Evesham and Moreton (once on Tues), Pulham's bus 608 (once on Thurs & Sat) from Cheltenham and Chipping Campden and Pulham's bus 612 (once on Sat) from **Bourton-on-the-Water**, **Stow**, Moreton, Chipping Campden and Evesham. By **train**, the closest station is Honeybourne (6 miles), though Moreton (10 miles) and Evesham (8 miles) are about as good; check with the tourist office for taxi information.

The **tourist office** (April–Oct Mon–Sat 10am–5pm, Sun 2–5pm; Feb, March, Nov & Dec closes 4pm; ☎01386 852937, ⓦ www.beautifulbroadway.com) is in the same building as the Russell Museum, on Russell Square behind *Russell's* restaurant. Staff are friendly and knowledgeable, well-equipped with maps and information on the town and surrounding area.

A fine way to get under the skin of the place is with the private **art tours** run on demand by local artist Jeremy Houghton (£20 per person; ⓦ www.broadway arttours.co.uk). **John Singer Sargent**'s *Carnation, Lily, Lily, Rose* (1887), which firmly established his London reputation, was painted in Broadway, at a time when a group of artists and illustrators which included novelist Henry James lived and worked here; Houghton's tours cover places where Sargent and others worked. A local **arts festival** (ⓦ www.broadwayartsfestival.com) ran in 2010 and may become an annual fixture.

Accommodation

You'll find no shortage of lodging possibilities: the tourist office's **accommodation** brochure lists no fewer than 41 establishments in and around the town, even aside from the numerous **self-catering** options – many of which, notably the multi-award-winning Broadway Manor Cottages (Ⓦwww.broadwaymanor -cottages.co.uk), are excellent. That said, Broadway does get extremely busy during the summer peak in particular, and **booking ahead** is always advisable.

Hotels & inns

Broadway Hotel The Green ☏01386 852401, Ⓦwww.cotswold-inns-hotels.co.uk. Fine old hotel perfectly sited on the village green at the busy end of the High Street, originally a sixteenth-century bolthole for the abbots of Pershore and still with period features. Rooms are comfortable, if a touch flowery, and all named after National Hunt champions and Cheltenham Gold Cup stars: depending on your personal situation, you could stay in the "Best Mate" superior double – or the "War of Attrition" twin room. ❺

Crown and Trumpet Church St ☏01386 853202, Ⓦwww.cotswoldholidays.co.uk. Traditional seventeenth-century coaching inn just round the corner off the High Street – and a much-loved option for decent, unpretentious, midrange accommodation, with five simple rooms. A popular choice: book ahead. ❸

Lygon Arms High St ☏01386 852255, Ⓦwww .barcelo-hotels.co.uk. One of the Cotswolds' most famous hotels (pronounced "liggon"), a grand, sprawling coaching inn in classic style – ivy-clad honeystone walls, mullioned windows and all. Known to have been an inn since 1532 (though probably much older: one of the bedrooms has a fourteenth-century fireplace set into its four-feet-thick stone walls), it has long had noble and royal associations, hosting both Charles I (in 1645) and Cromwell (in 1651) in rooms which retain their original panelling and fittings. Called the *White Hart* for most of its history, until renamed in the mid-nineteenth century in honour of local landowner William Lygon, who served under Wellington at Waterloo, it is now owned by the global Barceló chain, though, to their credit, the corporate atmosphere is largely held at bay. Rooms vary from modern styles through to original period suites, all fitted out to an extremely high standard; there's also a spa with swimming pool. ❼–❽

Russell's 20 High St ☏01386 853555, Ⓦwww.russellsofbroadway.co.uk. Outstanding restaurant which also doubles as a relaxed, super-stylish boutique hotel. Just seven rooms are presented with scrupulous attention to detail: mood-lighting enhances feature headboards or walls of exposed stone, textiles set off unusual furniture design, bathrooms host huge stand-alone tubs and showers-for-two, and so forth. A splendid option, unusually keenly priced: book well ahead. ❺–❻

B&Bs

Abbots Grange Church St ☏020 8133 8698, Ⓦwww.abbotsgrange.com. Exceptional B&B in an eye-popping medieval mansion with a venerable history which dates back to the early fourteenth century – and also encompasses Henry James and John Singer Sargent, who lived and worked in the house, among a group of artists and illustrators, in the 1880s. It offers three rooms in what, despite the grandeur, is a private family home – two four-poster rooms and one twin, all with access to the eight-acre grounds (which include a private tennis court and croquet lawn). It's expensive, but entirely unique. ❻–❻

Olive Branch 78 High St ☏01386 853440, Ⓦwww.theolivebranch-broadway.com. Award-winning guesthouse in an old stone house on the upper part of the High Street, out of the fluster. It may be a touch pastel-and-chintz for some tastes, but is otherwise cosy and well run; some rooms have king-size beds and access to the rear garden. ❹

Windrush House Station Rd ☏01386 853577, Ⓦwww.windrushhouse.com. Named Worcestershire's best B&B in 2010, this is another fine guesthouse a step out of town, rather more tasteful than many of the competition, with five stylishly decorated rooms, another excellent breakfast and owners who really know the value of extending a warm welcome. ❹

Out of town

Dormy House Willersey Hill ☏01386 852711, Ⓦwww.dormyhouse.co.uk. Lavish independent four-star country hotel beside the golf club a few miles out of town, on a hillside with great views. Rooms are sleekly modern, with a good deal of style – a fine place to hole up and relax. ❻–❼

Buckland Manor Buckland ☏01386 852626, Ⓦwww.bucklandmanor.com. A couple of miles south of Broadway (and just yards inside

Gloucestershire), this is an extraordinarily opulent country hotel, part of the Relais & Châteaux group. All the details are in order – stone fireplaces, mullioned windows, four-poster beds, cream teas, sweeping views and, as one journalist commented, "bathrooms so big you could live in them". That said, there are only thirteen rooms: this is luxury on a human scale. ⑨

The Town

Broadway is named for its chestnut-lined **High Street**, a wide thoroughfare that previously formed part of the road linking London and Wales, via Worcester. Now blocked at its upper end, on the slopes of Fish Hill – and thankfully bypassed by the A44 – the High Street is still flanked by ex-coaching inns, set back behind broad grass verges. You're likely to enter the village from the west: the B4632 comes in from the A44 roundabout as Station Road, before veering away towards Winchcombe and Cheltenham. At the dog-leg, the High Street enters the village: you'll spot the *Broadway Hotel* on the Green, beside which **Church Street** heads south to Snowshill.

Battle a path between the teashops and take either of a couple of lanes ducking left to reach the signposted **Gordon Russell Museum** (Tues–Sun 11am–5pm; Nov–Feb closes 4pm; closed Jan; £3.50; ⓦwww.gordonrussellmuseum.org), a superbly presented showcase of the work and influence of this noted furniture designer (1892–1980), whose father moved to Broadway in 1904 to run the *Lygon Arms* and whose company, headquartered in the village for sixty years, is still in operation (ⓦwww.hands.co.uk). Housed in a curved building – dubbed locally "The Banana" – which was formerly Russell's workshop, the museum displays drawings, photographs and notebooks alongside videos of interviews with Russell, but the glory of it is the collection of original Russell furniture. It's gorgeous work, ranging from Arts and Crafts to 1930s modernism and beyond: of particular note are the radio cabinets in the upstairs galleries – intricate, highly polished evocations of an age past.

Otherwise, seeing Broadway is merely a matter of letting your feet lead you onward. The further you get up the high street, the quieter things become: beyond the Leamington Road turning, which leads back out to the A44, the **Upper High Street** – now a cul-de-sac, since the link to the Fish Hill road was blocked – is a lovely place to meander, its fine old houses now mostly residential and free from commerce. The **Cotswold Way** long-distance trail runs the length of the High Street, disappearing off to the right (signposted) partway along the Upper High Street to climb to Broadway Tower (see below).

Walks around Broadway

The countryside around Broadway is packed with good **walking** opportunities. A long, full-day stage of the **Cotswold Way** (12 miles; 7hr) branches southwest to Winchcombe, initially heading towards Buckland before diverting through beech woods to Stanton (see p.167) and then Stanway (p.167) and Hailes (p.207), from any of which you could – with some pre-planning – catch the Castleways bus 606 (not Sun) back to Broadway. There's also a **circular route** (7.5 miles; 4hr 30min) which follows the Cotswold Way, then branches off at Stanton church to return north through Laverton and Buckland, rejoining the Cotswold Way at Broadway Coppice for the last short section back into Broadway. Alternatively a fine circular walk (4 miles; 3hr; downloadable at ⓦwww.cotswoldsaonb.org.uk) heads up to Broadway Tower: starting from Broadway High Street, cutting south across fields to join Coneygree Lane off the Snowshill road, climbing steeply to the tower, then following the Cotswold Way path back down onto Broadway High Street again. Full details, maps and information are at the tourist office.

Walking south from the Green, via Church Street, brings you after a mile or so to Broadway's parish church of **St Eadburgha**, a twelfth-century building over a Saxon foundation – wonderfully tranquil and remote from the fluster of the village centre.

Broadway Tower

Atop Fish Hill, a mile southeast of Broadway village, **Broadway Tower** (daily 10.30am–5pm; shorter hours in bad weather; £4.50; ⓦ www.broadwaytower.co .uk) stands at the second-highest point in the Cotswolds (the highest is Cleeve Hill; p.212). The tower itself, a turreted folly built in 1798, has become an icon of the Cotswolds, perched at more than 1,000 feet above sea level with stupendous views on all sides that purportedly encompass thirteen counties. The Pre-Raphaelite artists of Broadway and Chipping Campden loved it, of course – Morris, Burne-Jones, Rossetti and others frequently came up here to take the air and dream of England.

The reality today is a touch more prosaic. Now privately owned, the tower stands alongside a family activity park, comprising an adventure playground, snack bar and picnic area. Inside, the tower's three compact levels now hold displays on the history of the building – but aside from a rather nice topographical model of the Cotswold hills, they're unlikely to inspire. Pay your admission to climb the 71 steps to the roof, for those views.

Eating and drinking

You won't have any trouble finding refreshments in Broadway: aside from browsing the galleries and antiques shops, **eating and drinking** is pretty much all there is to do. Dozens of places oblige, in plain sight packed all around the Green in particular, but – as ever in tourist towns – quality isn't always guaranteed. Shop around, or consider fine alternatives nearby such as *Buckland Manor* (see p.163), *Dormy House* (p.163) or several options in Chipping Campden (p.159).

For picnic supplies or foodie souvenirs, in the absence of a regular **farmers' market** (markets are held only two or three times a year; check dates at the tourist office), you could do worse than pop into either of two excellent local food shops. First is the outstandingly good **Broadway Deli**, 16 High Street (Mon–Sat 8am–5.30pm; ⓦ www.broadwaydeli.co.uk) – which also does lunchtime panini – and second, perhaps surprisingly, is the local supermarket, **Warner's Budgens** (daily 8am–9pm; ⓦ www.warnersbudgens.co.uk), behind the deli on Russell Square. At first glance unremarkable, this is in fact part of a tiny, Cotswolds-only chain of locally run food outlets: alongside all the familiar supermarket brands, it stocks an unusually wide choice of local produce from Gloucestershire, Warwickshire and Worcestershire farms – see the website for details.

Crown and Trumpet See p.163. This cheery, historic local tavern is one of the better watering-holes in town, with decent beers, a lively atmosphere, solid, old-fashioned Sunday roasts and regular sessions of live blues and jazz.

Lygon Arms See p.163. Broadway's famous old hotel hosts easily the most atmospheric dining room in town, the dramatic Jacobean Great Hall, with its oak panelling, minstrels' gallery, open fireplace and barrel-vaulted ceiling. Fortunately, the food matches up – hearty, traditional English cooking of the highest quality. Three-course menu £38. Great Hall closed Sat lunch (though the hotel brasserie is open daily throughout).

Market Pantry 31 High St ⓣ 01386 858318. Pleasant little café offering coffees, freshly baked cakes and light lunches in an easygoing atmosphere of shabby-chic furniture and buzzy conversation.

Russell's See p.163. Far and away the best and most alluring restaurant in – or near – Broadway, with a stylish, contemporary interior and relaxed, efficient service. Take in the classic Modern British menu, featuring produce from the Vale of Evesham and the Cotswolds: local lamb chops with honey-roasted figs, chilli-marinated chicken breast, squid-ink risotto, pan-fried hake on basmati rice, and so on, presented with elegance. Mains £14–22. Closed Sun eve.

Tisanes Tea Rooms 21 The Green ☎01386 853296, ⓦwww.tisanes-tearooms.co.uk. If you're going to indulge in a tearoom, best make it this one – uncompromisingly traditional. No cards. Open for lunch and early evenings. Closed Sun eve.

Childswickham

Two miles west of Broadway, the charmingly named village of **CHILDS-WICKHAM** has less to do with the Cotswolds than the Vale of Evesham (see p.168) – its countryside is flat and its agricultural preoccupations are market gardening and arable. It's nonetheless a pretty place, spread out below the fifteenth-century spire of the originally Norman **church** of St Mary. Stop in for a decent meal at the *Childswickham Inn* (☎01386 852461, ⓦwww.childswickhaminn.co.uk), a family-friendly country pub updated with a stylish brasserie (mains £10–17).

While you're exploring, you might also drop into the family-run **Barnfield Winery and Cider Mill** (ⓦwww.barnfieldcidermill.co.uk), on the Broadway road just outside Childswickham. They're renowned locally for their cider, scrumpy and perry, made onsite using traditional old presses and sold in the mill shop (daily 10am–6pm).

Snowshill

Along the country lane south of Broadway, a mile or so past St Eadburgha's church on the edge of **SNOWSHILL** village, **Snowshill Manor** (March–Oct Wed–Sun noon–5pm; £8.10; ⓦwww.nationaltrust.org.uk) is a good-looking Cotswold manor house holding a trove of exotic curiosities. The architect, craftsman and poet Charles Wade (1883–1956) – inspired as a boy by his grandmother's Chinese cabinet in black and gold lacquer, now on display in the house – spent decades hunting down objects that were not rare or valuable but "of interest as records of various vanished handicrafts". The results of his forays include model carts, boneshaker bicycles, children's prams, wooden toys, beds, beetles, all kinds of musical instruments and other curios; they were crammed into the house, while he himself lived in a cottage in the garden.

It makes for a fascinating rummage through a jumbled mind – rooms across all three floors of the house remain stuffed with all manner of bits and bobs. On the ground floor, the **Turquoise Room** holds Wade's favourite piece, a nineteenth-century wooden model of a Japanese mask-maker. "Grannie's Cabinet" takes pride of place in the **Zenith Room**, while most dramatic is the arrangement of 26 Samurai warriors dating from the seventeenth to the nineteenth centuries in the **Green Room** upstairs. Note that it's a ten-minute walk to reach the house from the car park.

Also of significance is the manor's **garden**, created by Wade in the Arts and Crafts style and now maintained organically, without chemicals. It has been described by gardening expert Monty Don as "overwhelmingly English – soft, subtle and entirely in harmony with the surrounding countryside". All the doors and gates opening onto the garden, and the furniture within it, are painted in "Wade blue", a shade developed by Wade specifically to complement the natural tones of his planting.

Snowshill is also known for its lavender: just outside the village, drop into **Snowshill Lavender** (June–Aug daily 10am–5pm; £2.50; restricted hours and lower prices in winter; ⓦwww.snowshill-lavender.co.uk) to see their 53 acres of fields, browse their fragrant giftshop and scoff lavender scones in the tearoom.

A couple of miles outside Snowshill, within walking distance of the lavender fields, *Snowshill Hill Farm Estate* (☎01386 853959, ⓦwww.broadway-cotswolds .co.uk; ❸) offers great **B&B** on a working farm with sheep and Galloway cattle

STRATFORD AND THE NORTH COTSWOLDS | The north Cotswolds

– only three rooms, all on the ground floor, with locally sourced ingredients for breakfast and an award-winningly warm welcome.

Stanton

The B4632 Cheltenham Road scoots south from Broadway, passing a succession of attractive villages adorning the escarpment on the left. **BUCKLAND** and **LAVERTON** are pretty – but **STANTON**, three miles south of Broadway, takes the biscuit. As unspoilt Cotswold villages go, there are few (if any) better: the entire village is built of warm Cotswold stone, the Norman spired **church of St Michael** is a beauty both inside and out, everywhere you look there are Jacobean gables and mullioned windows and (deliberately) not a shop or a tearoom in sight – it's a stunner.

The only nod to commercialization is the seventeenth-century ⚲ *Mount Inn* (☎01386 584316, ⓦ www.themountinn.co.uk), a walkers' pub hidden away at the top of a steep slope above the village centre, offering spectacular views from its terrace alongside uncomplicated meals (mains £10–13) and fine Donnington ales. Note the pub is closed every afternoon (3–6pm).

From the pub, a lane leads further up Shenberrow Hill to **Stanton Guild-house** (☎01386 584357, ⓦ www.stantonguildhouse.org.uk), perched above the village. Built in the 1960s in inch-perfect traditional style by social worker and proponent of Arts and Crafts philosophy **Mary Osborn**, it operates as a kind of community hub and rural conference centre, hosting spiritual retreats and a regular cycle of weekly classes in skills such as pottery, art, woodwork, furniture restoration and stained glass. The house is generally not open to walk-in visitors, but it is possible to **stay** – either by renting the whole property as a self-catering cottage over the weekend (around £1150 for 3 nights; sleeps up to 15) or, on occasion, by renting rooms on an individual B&B basis. Enquire about arrangements and prices well in advance.

Stanway House and Fountain

A mile south of Stanton, just before you reach the B4077, which cuts east-west between Stow and Tewkesbury, **STANWAY** hamlet is dominated by the presence of **Stanway House** (June–Aug Tues & Thurs 2–5pm; £7, or grounds only £4.50; ⓦ www.stanwayfountain.co.uk) – most prominently its magnificent triple-storied, triple-gabled **gatehouse** in buttery yellow Cotswold stone. A Jacobean manor

---

Walking from Stanton to Snowshill

Numerous fine **walks** pass through or near Stanton. A **circular trail** (6 miles; 4hr 30min; map and notes downloadable at ⓦ www.cotswoldsaonb.org.uk) begins in the village, following the Cotswold Way signposts to climb steeply up Shenberrow Hill, eventually branching off onto a path through quiet Littleworth Wood and down into Snowshill village. From Snowshill you turn west again, climbing to follow another track beside Buckland Wood before rejoining the Cotswold Way to walk south, back up to the edge of Littleworth Wood. From here a minor track offering views west over Stanton and across to the Severn Vale leads you down to the *Mount Inn* and back into Stanton. Shorten the route by eliminating the Snowshill loop and using Little-worth Wood as the furthest point of the circuit (2.5 miles; 2hr 30min).

Castleways **bus 606** (not Sun) runs a couple of times from Broadway High Street in the morning to either Stanton village or the northerly Stanton turn on the B4632, returning (from the Stanton turn) in mid- and late-afternoon. Note that the *Mount Inn* closes at 3pm.

Gloucestershire Warwickshire Steam Railway

Based nominally at **TODDINGTON** – though its station is in fact located east of Toddington beside the roundabout where the B4632 meets the B4077 – the **Gloucestershire Warwickshire Steam Railway** (Ⓣ01242 621405, Ⓦwww.gwsr .com) keeps alive a section of the old Great Western line from Birmingham and Stratford to Bristol, originally opened in 1906 and closed to regular services in 1976. It's a prodigiously successful operation, relying on more than six hundred volunteers and drawing thousands of fare-paying passengers each month. From Toddington, the line runs south to Winchcombe (see p.208) and then on a scenic route down off the Cotswold Edge to a terminus station at Cheltenham Racecourse – though, at the time of writing, a landslide at Gotherington had cut off the final section of track: check the latest information online before you travel.

Trains run pretty much year-round, most frequently in June, July and August, dropping to weekends only in winter (no service Jan & Feb). An adult return fare from Toddington to either Gotherington or Cheltenham Racecourse is £11.

Plans are afoot to extend the line north of Toddington: a section to Laverton may already be open by the time you read this, with Broadway the next major objective (Ⓦwww.broadwayextension.co.uk). Nonetheless it will be many years before the railway – despite its name – actually reaches Warwickshire.

house as splendid as any in the region, it awes from the outside – even if, inside, it's all a bit ramshackle: the limited opening hours are an indication that Lord and Lady Neidpath (the Earl and Countess of Wemyss), whose home this is, are unequivocally not in the museum business. Much of the house's furniture is original, including a 22-foot-long shuffleboard table built in 1620, but there's no literature to help you navigate a path through the distinctly lived-in rooms – the only way is to wander, admiring the well-worn armchairs and family portraits as you go. The main attraction, though, lies outside: Stanway's **water garden**, designed in the 1720s and featuring a canal running on a high terrace with an impressively long cascade, is now home to the **world's tallest gravity fountain** (and the tallest fountain of any kind in Britain), installed in 2004 and driven from a half-million-litre reservoir located 580 feet up in the nearby hills. It's activated twice during the afternoons that the house is open to the public, spouting to 300 feet above the lawns.

Attractions just west and south of Stanway include the Gloucestershire-Warwickshire Railway (see box above) – though Hailes Abbey (see p.207) is a stone's throw away, on the road to nearby Winchcombe (p.208). For coverage of the Guitings and routes east to Stow, turn to p.184.

The Vale of Evesham

A low-lying semicircle of Worcestershire defined by the River Avon, the **Vale of Evesham** – with a history stretching back to the thirteenth-century baron Simon de Montfort – is nonetheless best known for **asparagus**. The area has been a centre of market gardening since the 1950s; today, besides its orchards of apples, cherries and plums, the Vale lies at the heart of the British asparagus industry, hosting thousands of migrant farm workers, most from Eastern Europe, over the spring and summer months. Restaurants all across the region – and beyond, into the Cotswold hills – devise fresh asparagus dishes of all kinds throughout the harvest season of May and June. Watch for festivities around the **British Asparagus Festival** (Ⓦwww.britishasparagusfestival.org), held each spring.

In Cotswold terms the Vale is fairly tangential. Despite some nice walks (and its own Plum Festival in August) Pershore to the northwest is too far-flung. The main focus, inevitably, is the old abbey town of **Evesham**, an easy day-trip from Broadway or Chipping Campden that can provide a refreshing blast of modern-day commerce after all that preserved Cotswold prettiness. Make a circuit of it by stopping in at **Bretforton**, one of the loveliest of the villages.

Evesham

The A44 whisks you past the **Wayside farm shop** (Ⓦwww.waysidefarmshop .co.uk) at Wickhamford into **EVESHAM**, about six miles northwest of Broadway. Protected by a loop of the Avon, the town was once home to a huge Benedictine abbey, founded around 700 AD after a local swineherd, Eof, had a vision of the Virgin Mary (the town's name derives from "Eof's *ham*", or home). The abbey was almost completely destroyed in 1540 during the Dissolution – though what remains is impressive enough.

From pedestrianized **Bridge Street** in the shop-heavy town centre, make your way through to the **Abbey Park**, where stand two churches and the surviving abbey bell tower. First is **All Saints' church** (daily 9.30am–4pm), entered through a Tudor porch, with a Norman arch surviving in the west wall; the interior, though largely Victorian, includes the small sixteenth-century Lichfield Chapel off the south aisle, with some lovely fan-vaulting overhead. Across the lawns – originally where the abbey stood – looms the 110-foot-tall **Bell Tower**, in Perpendicular Gothic style, elaborately carved and sprouting four tall pinnacles; you can walk beneath its central arch out to sloping gardens beyond, from where **boat trips** run on the Avon (April–Oct every 30min 11am–4.30pm; £3; Ⓦwww .handsamboatcompany.co.uk). Back opposite All Saints stands **St Lawrence's church** (same hours), also remodelled in the nineteenth century, though with older parts including, again, a fan-vaulted chapel in the south wall.

A stroll away across the park, located beside the busy north–south **Vine Street** through-road, stands Evesham's oldest building, the fourteenth-century **Almonry Heritage Centre** (Mon–Sat 10am–5pm; March–Oct also Sun 2–5pm; Ⓦwww .almonryevesham.org), which doubles as the **tourist office** (same hours; ☎01386 446944, Ⓦwww.evesham.uk.com). The centre includes a rather good **museum** (£3), hosting displays on the abbey, Saxon burial jewellery and other elements of Evesham's history. A summer-only **guided town walk** (May–Aug Tues 2.30pm; £1; Ⓦwww.eveshamvaletourguides.co.uk) starts from the Almonry.

Abbey aside, Evesham's other claim to fame is as the location of an epic battle in 1265 between **Simon de Montfort** and Prince Edward (later Edward I), which marked the victory of royalist forces over de Montfort's nascent baronial parliament. The site of the clash, a mile or so north of town near Greenhill, now has a **Battlefield Trail** leading across the fields – see Ⓦwww.simondemontfort.org for details of how to walk it. A memorial to de Montfort stands in the abbey park, near the Bell Tower.

Bretforton

Around four miles east of Evesham, just off the B4035 (which goes on to climb to Chipping Campden), **BRETFORTON** is about the prettiest village in the Vale. Its church of **St Leonard** is of Norman foundation, with a fifteenth-century tower, but the reason to come this way is the wonderful old **Fleece Inn** alongside (☎01386 831173, Ⓦwww.thefleeceinn.co.uk). The only pub to be owned by the National Trust, it remained in the same family from around 1400, when it was built as a farmhouse, right through to 1977, when the last owner died. Duck to enter – and keep ducking: the rambling interior, largely unchanged from the fifteenth century, is barely believable, with its bowed beams, tiny old windows, cracked flagstones, high-backed settles, open fires with tin kettles – and, in one of the snugs, a pewter service that was reputedly Cromwell's. The beer is good, even if the meals are more or less unreconstructed pub grub: faggots, a pint of prawns, chicken pie, and so on (mains £8–10). The old courtyard outside is the setting for the annual **Asparagus Auction**, usually held on Bank Holiday Monday at the end of May, when thousands pack in to bid for bundles of the choicest fresh-cut spears.

Bretforton is also known for a couple of innovative small businesses – **Spot Loggins** ice cream (Ⓦwww.spotloggins.com), available at the *Fleece Inn* as well as across the Cotswolds, and the **Little Soap Company** (Ⓣ01386 831379, Ⓦwww .littlesoapcompany.co.uk), whose all-natural products are sold nationwide; they run individual one-day soapmaking courses on demand (£275, includes lunch, refreshments and all equipment).

Honeybourne

A couple of miles east of Bretforton, the rather humdrum village of **HONEY-BOURNE** happens to have a **railway station** on the Cotswold Line railway: trains stop here on routes from Oxford and Moreton-in-Marsh towards Evesham and Worcester – though in sightseeing terms there's not a lot to stop for. Honeybourne has the decent *Ranch* caravan park with pool and play area (Ⓣ01386 830744, Ⓦwww.ranch.co.uk) and there's a small village **pottery** (Ⓣ01386 832855, Ⓦwww.honeybournepots.co.uk).

Mickleton (see p.161) is three and a half miles to the east.

The central
Cotswolds

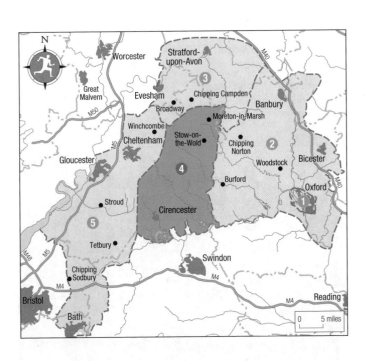

CHAPTER 4 # Highlights

* **Batsford Arboretum** Fine walks in beautiful parkland just outside Moreton. See p.177

* **Blockley** Charming Cotswold village, quiet and attractive. See p.179

* **Cotswold Farm Park** Rare breeds showcased on a working farm. See p.184

* **The Slaughters** Winningly handsome twin villages – great for a luxury retreat. See p.186

* **Northleach** Unspoilt village that merits a detour. See p.187

* **Bibury** One-street riverside village with perhaps the most photographed cottages in England. See p.189

* **Cirencester** The "capital of the Cotswolds" has a grand church, quiet old lanes and good food. See p.191

* **Duntisbourne Rouse** Ancient church in silent countryside. See p.196

* **Fairford** Come for the medieval stained glass – and one of the region's best restaurants. See p.199

▲ Lower Slaughter

The central Cotswolds

4 THE CENTRAL COTSWOLDS

ew main roads cross the Cotswold hills. Two east–west corridors – the A40 and A44 – more or less follow valley contours, linking Oxford with Cheltenham and Evesham respectively, but through history Cotswold topography hasn't lent itself to many easily definable north–south routes. In that regard, not much has changed since the Romans: their **Fosse Way** road – now the **A429** – is still the only north–south artery through the region, cutting a more or less straight line from the wilds of Warwickshire through the **central Cotswolds** to Cirencester and on south towards Bath. This chapter is constructed around a journey along that road.

On its way south, the A429 passes many of the region's most celebrated destinations. **Moreton-in-Marsh** is a placid opener, but by the time you reach **Stow-on-the-Wold**, you're slap bang in the eye of the Cotswold tourism hurricane – a storm which picks up pace a few miles south in **Bourton-on-the-Water**, one of the most visited but perhaps least satisfying of all Cotswold destinations.

As always, head away from the main routes to find the best of the area: **Blockley** village, between Moreton and Chipping Campden, is a beauty, while the high wolds west of Stow are speckled with horsey hamlets flanking the splendid **Cotswold Farm Park** rare-breeds centre, itself only a spit from the famously beautiful twin villages of **Upper** and **Lower Slaughter**.

Once you break free of Bourton and the Slaughters, the pace eases off again. Pretty **Northleach** is thankfully bypassed by both the A40 and A429 at their crossroads, though riverside **Bibury** has become a very popular mid-Cotswolds stop. The southern parts of the region are anchored by the presence of

Farmers' markets

- **Bourton-on-the-Water** 4th Sun of month 9.30am–1pm Ⓦ www.fresh-n-local.co.uk.
- **Cirencester** 2nd & 4th Sat of month 9am–1pm Ⓦ cirencesterfarmersmarket .squarespace.com.
- **Lechlade** 3rd Thurs of month 8.30am–1pm Ⓦ www.fresh-n-local.co.uk.
- **Stow-on-the-Wold** 2nd Thurs of month 9am–1pm Ⓦ www.fresh-n-local.co.uk.
Dates may change around Christmas and New Year. See also Ⓦ www.farmers markets.net.

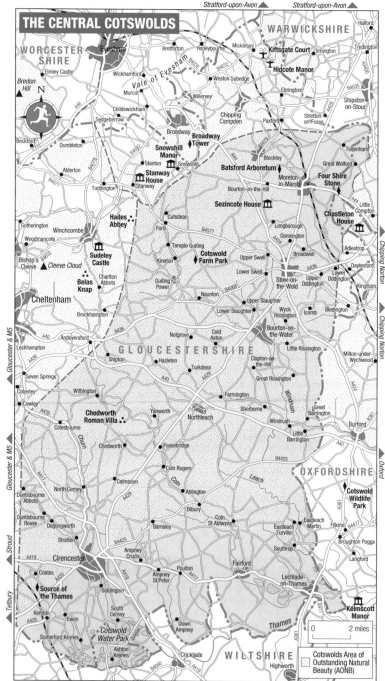

THE CENTRAL COTSWOLDS

Stratford-upon-Avon ▲   Stratford-upon-Avon ▲

WARWICKSHIRE

Halford

WORCESTER-SHIRE

Evesham

Bredon Hill ▲

N

Elmley Castle

Wickhamford

Murcot

Childswickham

Sedgeberrow

Beckford

Dumbleton

Alderton

Brettforton

Honeybourne

Mickleton

Kiftsgate Court

Ilmington

Tredington

Hidcote Manor

Weston Subedge

Ebrington

Shipston-on-Stour

Willersey

Chipping Campden

Paxford

Stretton-on-Fosse

Broadway

Broadway Tower

Snowshill Manor

Stanton

Snowshill

Blockley

Todenham

Batsford Arboretum

Great Wolford

Stanway House

Stanway

Bourton-on-the-Hill

Moreton-in-Marsh

Four Shire Stone

Little Compton

Toddington

Sezincote House

Chastleton House

Cutsdean

Hailes Abbey

Ford

Longborough

Adlestrop

Gotherington

Winchcombe

Woodmancote

Temple Guiting

Donnington

Broadwell

Daylesford

Bishop's Cleeve

Cleeve Cloud ▲

Sudeley Castle

Kineton

Cotswold Farm Park

Upper Swell

Lower Swell

Upper Oddington

Lower Oddington

Kingham

Belas Knap

Charlton Abbots

Guiting Power

Stow-on-the-Wold

Cheltenham

Naunton

Upper Slaughter

Wyck Rissington

Icomb

Bledington

Brockhampton

Lower Slaughter

Bourton-on-the-Water

Notgrove

Cold Aston

Little Rissington

Milton-under-Wychwood

Andoversford

GLOUCESTERSHIRE

Clapton-on-the-Hill

Leckhampton

Shipton

Hazleton

Turkdean

Great Rissington

Seven Springs

Withington

Farmington

Windrush

Coberley

Cowley

Sherborne

Great Barrington

Chedworth Roman Villa

Yanworth

Northleach

Windrush

Burford

Colesbourne

Little Barrington

Chedworth

Fossebridge

Coln Rogers

OXFORDSHIRE

Calmsden

Coln

Leach

North Cerney

Ablington

Cotswold Wildlife Park

Duntisbourne Abbots

Bibury

Duntisbourne Rouse

Coln St Aldwyns

Eastleach Martin

Filkins

Daglingworth

Barnsley

Eastleach Turville

Stratton

Broughton Poggs

Cirencester

Ampney Crucis

Southrop

Langford

Coates

Ampney St Peter

Poulton

Fairford

Lechlade-on-Thames

Source of the Thames

Siddington

Kemble

South Cerney

Down Ampney

Thames

Kelmscott Manor

Ewen

Somerford Keynes

Cotswold Water Park

Ashton Keynes

Cricklade

WILTSHIRE

Highworth

0   2 miles

Cotswolds Area of Outstanding Natural Beauty (AONB)

▼ Swindon   Swindon ▼

Gloucester & M5   Gloucester & M5   Stroud   Tetbury

Chipping Norton   Chipping Norton   Oxford

Cirencester, a lovely, old-fashioned market town which, these days, is the epitome of what has turned Gloucestershire into "Poshtershire" – a polo-playing hideaway on the fringe of classic countryside, yet with speedy links to Cheltenham and London, and now sporting upmarket bars, delis and department stores. It's easy, though, to take what you want and leave the rest behind: Cirencester's Roman museum, for instance, is a cracker, as are the villages of the quiet **Coln Valley** nearby – and humble **Fairford** hosts a restaurant and a church as good as any for miles around.

South along Fosse Way (A429)

Near the Warwickshire village of Halford (see p.149), the arrow-straight Fosse Way leaves the B4455 and joins the **A429** for its journey southwest across the Cotswolds to Cirencester and beyond. Wherever you jump aboard, traffic can be heavy: actual jams are rare, but on summer weekends you may have trouble finding enough of a gap in fast-moving traffic to be able to pull out easily.

Just south of the *Cotswold Spice* restaurant (see p.153), the A429 crosses into Gloucestershire, passing through the centre of **Moreton-in-Marsh**. Shortly after, it skirts **Stow-on-the-Wold** and – south of a split with the A424 Burford road – **Bourton-on-the-Water**, on the way towards **Northleach** and **Cirencester**.

Moreton-in-Marsh

A key transport hub and one of the Cotswolds' more sensible towns, **MORETON-IN-MARSH**, though relatively low-lying – hills rise to east, west and south – isn't in a marsh at all. A now-vanished wetland nearby – a popular spot for local waterfowl – became known as the hen-marsh: it didn't take long for "Moreton Henmarsh" to be mangled into the current formulation. The A429 Fosse Way runs north–south through the town as the High Street, meeting the east–west A44 in the town centre at a dog-leg of mini-roundabouts. Despite a lack of attractions within the town, Moreton has always been an important access point for the countryside and remains so with its **railway station**, served by regular trains on the Cotswold Line direct link between London, Oxford and Worcester (for more on which, see p.22).

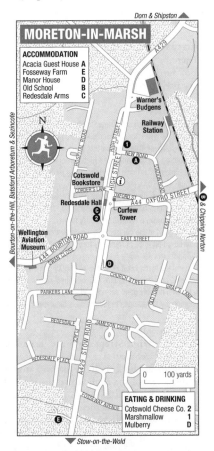

MORETON-IN-MARSH

ACCOMMODATION
Acacia Guest House	A
Fosseway Farm	E
Manor House	D
Old School	B
Redesdale Arms	C

EATING & DRINKING
Cotswold Cheese Co.	2
Marshmallow	1
Mulberry	D

Arrival and information

From the **railway station**, it's a two-minute walk to the High Street; turn left for the **tourist office** (Mon 8.45am–4pm, Tues–Thurs 8.45am–5.15pm, Fri 8.45am–4.45pm, Sat 10am–1pm; Nov–March Sat closes 12.30pm; ☎01608 650881, ⓦwww.cotswolds.com). Local **taxi** firms, who can meet arriving trains to take you to any of the nearby towns or villages, include Moreton Taxis (☎07901 735161, ⓦwww.moretontaxis.co.uk) and Cotswold Taxis (☎07710 117471, ⓦwww.moretontaxis.com).

Buses stop on the High Street: regular routes include Johnsons bus 21/22 (not Sun) to/from **Stratford**, **Chipping Campden**, **Broadway** and **Blockley**, Pulham's "Fosse Link" bus 855 (not Sun) to/from **Stow**, **Bourton-on-the-Water**, **Northleach** and **Cirencester**, and Pulham's bus 801 (May–Sept daily; Oct–April not Sun) to/from Stow, Bourton-on-the-Water and **Cheltenham**. Irregular routes include several operated by Pulham's, including the 612 (once on Sat) to/from Bourton-on-the-Water, Stow, Blockley, Chipping Campden and Broadway, and 817 (twice on Fri) to/from Stow; there's also Johnsons bus 577 (once on Sat) to/from Shipston-on-Stour and Banbury, and the Villager Community bus V4 (once on Wed) from Chipping Norton. You're spoilt for choice on **Tuesday morning**, with lots of extra once-a-week buses arriving for Moreton's **weekly market**, including from Cheltenham, Broadway, Stow, Northleach, Chipping Campden, Charlbury, Kingham, Chipping Norton, Shipston, Banbury, Witney, Burford and elsewhere.

Accommodation

There's a limited choice of decent **accommodation** in town; you'd do better to look further afield. Aside from the places below, investigate Bourton-on-the-Hill (see p.178), Blockley (p.179) or Stow (p.180).

In town

Acacia Guest House 2 New Rd ☎01608 650130, ⓦwww.acaciathecotswolds.co.uk. Simple, decent little B&B on the short street connecting the station to the High Street – very handy for arrivals and departures by train or bus. ❷

Manor House High St ☎01608 650501, ⓦwww.cotswold-inns-hotels.co.uk. Pleasant four-star hotel occupying a sixteenth-century former coaching inn in the centre, with a nice garden centred on an ancient mulberry tree and well-kept, stylish rooms. ❺–❻

Redesdale Arms High St ☎01608 650308, ⓦwww.redesdalearms.com. Relaxed three-star hotel with notably good service and 24 rooms – traditionally styled ones in the main building and

more modern ones (though still not fancy) in the newer rear annexe. ❹–❺

Out of town

Fosseway Farm Stow Rd ☎01608 650503, ⓦwww.fossewayfarm.co.uk. Good-value, traditional farmhouse B&B set back from the A429 a few minutes' walk south of the town centre, also including a large caravan park and campsite. ❷–❸

Old School Little Compton ☎01608 674588, ⓦwww.theoldschoolbedandbreakfast.com. Award-winning, upscale little B&B in this village four miles east of Moreton, offering four rooms in a Victorian schoolhouse that includes beautiful church-style windows in the swanky guest lounge. Hosts are knowledgeable and forthcoming; bedrooms are spacious and thoughtfully kitted out. ❹

The Town

Moreton's **High Street** is a broad, handsome affair, dating from its origins in the thirteenth century as a market town and enhanced with many Jacobean and Georgian facades from its heyday as a stop for London–Worcester coaches. Plumb in the centre of the High Street, the **Redesdale Hall** – dating from 1887, though built in a medieval style – is named for Lord Redesdale, father of the infamous Mitford sisters (among them Nancy, a writer; Diana, wife of British wartime fascist leader Oswald Mosley; and Unity, a close companion of Adolf Hitler), who spent part of their childhood years at Batsford House, just west of Moreton. Nearby, on the corner of Oxford Street, the **Curfew Tower** is Moreton's oldest building, dating from the sixteenth century and once used as the town jail, while opposite, a short stroll west along the Bourton Road brings you to the **Wellington Aviation Museum** (Tues–Sun 10am–12.30pm & 2–5pm; £2; ⓦwww.wellingtonaviation .org), displaying memorabilia from the wartime RAF base located beside Moreton.

Otherwise, it's just a case of ambling around the streets admiring the architecture. Independent shops are well represented on the High Street, not least by the **Cotswold Bookstore** (ⓦwww.twitter.com/cotswoldbooks) and, nearby, the splendidly aromatic **Cotswold Cheese Company** (ⓣ01608 652862, ⓦwww .cotswoldcheesecompany.co.uk). If you're looking for deli items, drop into **Warner's Budgens** at the northern end of the High Street: this supermarket is part of a small Cotswolds-only chain that has won awards for its dedication to local food producers – see also p.165. A mile north of town beside **DORN**, the **Old Farm** shop (Tues & Thurs 9.30am–1pm, Fri 9.30am–6.30pm, Sat 9.30am–5pm; ⓣ01608 650394, ⓦwww.oldfarmdorn.co.uk), stocks a range of local culinary goodies – and also offers camping and B&B (check the website for rates).

If you're around in early September, don't miss the **Moreton Show** (ⓦwww .moretonshow.co.uk), a traditional celebration of local agriculture. Otherwise, book ahead through Rob Ireland Activity Days (ⓣ01386 701683, ⓦwww .robireland.co.uk) or Cotswold Quads (ⓣ01608 650571, ⓦwww.cotswold quads.com) for **archery**, **clay-pigeon shooting** and **quad-biking** at a rural site just north of Moreton.

Eating and drinking

Moreton's best **restaurant** is the *Mulberry*, within the *Manor House Hotel* (see opposite) – a rather posh setting, with muted contemporary styling, serving highly acclaimed modern British cuisine prepared from Cotswold ingredients, such as wild rabbit terrine followed by tenderloin of local pork. Three courses are £39, with good vegetarian options available; there's also an eight-course tasting menu at £50. A simpler choice might be the *Marshmallow*, north along the High Street (ⓣ01608 651536, ⓦwww.marshmallow-tea-restaurant.co.uk), a pleasant tearoom with an outstanding choice of speciality teas – from Gunpowder to Nilgiri – which doubles as a casual restaurant for light meals (mains around £8). Otherwise, make a point of booking for the superb *Horse & Groom* in nearby Bourton-on-the-Hill (see p.178).

For coverage of **Stow-on-the-Wold**, five miles south of Moreton, turn to p.180.

Batsford Arboretum

There's plenty of rural interest just **west of Moreton**, as the hills of the Cotswolds Area of Outstanding Natural Beauty (ⓦwww.cotswoldsaonb.org.uk) rise towards Chipping Campden and the Cotswolds scarp. Accessed directly from the A44 just over a mile west of Moreton – rather than from the quiet village of **BATSFORD** itself, which lies to the north – **Batsford Arboretum** (Feb–Nov daily 9am–6pm, last entry 4.45pm; £6.50; Dec & Jan daily except Wed 9am–4pm, last entry 3pm; £5; ⓦwww.batsarb.co.uk) sprawls delightfully across 56 acres of hilly, south-facing countryside. Originally designed at the end of the nineteenth century by Algernon Mitford, later the first Lord Redesdale, though greatly expanded in the 1950s, its oriental planting and design are enhanced by more than 1,500 tree varieties. In the autumn, Batsford is particularly stunning. Aim first for the waterfall, but also take in the huge Cathedral Lime, a grove of redwoods, reputedly England's largest "handkerchief tree" (*Davidia involucrata*) and the beautiful Peaches Walk. A Japanese rest house offers peaceful views.

Cotswold Falconry Centre

Immediately beside Batsford Arboretum, and reached via the same driveway off the A44, the **Cotswold Falconry Centre** (flying displays daily 11.30am, 1.30pm & 3pm; April–Oct also 4.30pm; £6.50; ⓦ www.cotswold-falconry.co.uk) is home to around a hundred birds of prey, from owls and vultures to hawks, kestrels, eagles and various species of falcon – saker, lanner, aplomado and peregrine. One-hour displays show off the birds' abilities, with plenty of educational info alongside the aerobatic thrills.

Sezincote House

On the south side of the A44, directly opposite the Batsford Arboretum driveway, stands the gate of **Sezincote House** (house and gardens May–Sept Thurs & Fri 2.30–5.30pm, £8; gardens only Jan–Nov Thurs & Fri 2–6pm, £5; ⓦ www .sezincote.co.uk). Built in the few years after 1805, Sezincote – whose name derives from *Cheisnecote*, a blend of French and Old English meaning "home among the oaks" – is remarkable for its exterior, designed by architect Samuel Pepys Cockerell and artist Thomas Daniell in Indian Mogul style. The house sports scalloped peacock-tail arches above the windows, a large "iwan" arch above the main door, a glorious Orangery wing sweeping round to an ornate, pinnacled pavilion and – most prominently – an onion dome atop the main building. Its interiors, though, are less of a draw than the **gardens**, featuring an Indian bridge flanked by Brahmin bulls which preludes lavish planting in a Persian garden and extensive water gardens topped by a Hindu temple.

Bourton House

Alongside Sezincote, a driveway off the A44 gives into the grounds of **Bourton House** (April–Oct Wed–Fri 10am–5pm; £6; ⓦ www.bourtonhouse.com), under new ownership in 2010 and generally less visited than neighbouring attractions. The house – a grand affair – is not open to the public. You approach through the sixteenth-century **tithe barn**, emerging into the flamboyant **garden**, particularly fine in late summer. Past the formal White Garden, an eighteenth-century raised walk offers views over the hills, leading round to the Knot Garden, centred on a basket pond recovered from the 1851 Great Exhibition, and a parterre featuring fanciful topiary. It's all rather lovely.

Bourton-on-the-Hill

Spreading west up the steep A44 from Bourton House and its neighbours, the little village of **BOURTON-ON-THE-HILL** offers a picturesque cluster of cottages wrapped around the handsome church of **St Lawrence**, with wonderful views back over Moreton and the Evenlode valley. Occupying a Georgian building of honey-coloured Cotswold stone at the top of the village, just before the turn to Blockley, is the award-winning ⚶ *Horse and Groom* (closed Sun eve; ☏ 01386 700413, ⓦ www.horseandgroom.info), a free house with a fine reputation locally for good beer, friendly service and – above all – excellent food. It's a calm, civilised pub: interiors are neither self-consciously rustic nor deliberately contemporary. The menu (mains £12–15) changes frequently, taking in pork, lamb and beef sourced from local farmers and seasonal veg filled out with fresh fish and seafood: whatever's cooking, it's worth reserving a table. There are also five appealing rooms (⑤), some with views, one with French doors opening onto the garden. Note that the pub is **closed every afternoon** (3–6pm).

Blockley

Gracing the hills between Moreton and Chipping Campden, **BLOCKLEY** is one of the prettier villages hereabouts, fortunately with roads that are too narrow for large buses to penetrate. A former centre for silk processing – in the late nineteenth century mills kept several hundred people in work here – it's still a prosperous little place, with one notable employer being Britain's biggest manufacturer of motorbike sidecars. Blockley's houses of Cotswold stone, tiered above a rushing brook, are set off by the particularly fine church of **St Peter and St Paul**, originally Norman, its nave lit by three large fifteenth-century windows and sporting a Jacobean pulpit, while one end of the village hosts the charming **Mill Dene Garden** (April–Sept Tues–Fri 10.30am–6pm and first Sat & Sun of month 11am–5.30pm; £5.50; Ⓦ www.milldenegarden.co.uk). Several good **walks** include a circular route of just under five miles which skirts the fields to Batsford village before turning to follow a short stretch of the Monarch's Way – a long-distance path from Staffordshire to Devon – and Heart of England Way back into Blockley.

As tempting a reason to visit, though, is Blockley's **shop** (closed Sun pm; Ⓦ www.blockleyshop.com), owned and run by villagers themselves. It's a cheery spot, and the hub of village life: have a chat with the locals, grab a newspaper and hole up at the **café** alongside for coffee or a light lunch. Blockley's friendly *Great Western Arms* (closed Mon lunch; ☎ 01386 700362, Ⓦ www.greatwesternarms .com) is an uncomplicated venue for an honest pint and simple pub grub (£8–11); the *Crown Inn* (☎ 01386 700245, Ⓦ www.crowninncotswolds.co.uk) is nice enough but its twenty **rooms** (④) are a bit bland. To stay, aim instead for *Lower Brook House* (☎ 01386 700286, Ⓦ www.lowerbrookhouse.co.uk; ⑤–⑥), a lovely B&B occupying a seventeenth-century stone house, with six fresh, individually styled bedrooms.

Johnsons **bus** 21/22 (not Sun) stops more or less hourly between Moreton, Chipping Campden and Stratford. Irregular services include Pulham's bus 608 (once on Thurs) to/from Cheltenham and Pulham's bus 612 (once on Sat) to/from Bourton-on-the-Water and Stow.

A couple of miles north of Blockley stands the acclaimed *Churchill Arms* at **Paxford** (see p.153). Chipping Campden (p.154) and Broadway (p.161) are within easy reach.

East of Moreton

East of Moreton, the A44 soon crosses into Oxfordshire for the brief run towards wonderful Chastleton House (see p.119), the Rollright Stones (p.120) and Chipping Norton (p.117). As it does so, it passes the tall, eighteenth-century **Four Shire Stone**, located alongside the turn towards Great Wolford, which once marked the point where Gloucestershire, Oxfordshire, Warwickshire and Worcestershire touched noses. Today, only the first three still meet here; boundary changes in 1931 transferred Blockley parish, whose ragged borders extended to this point, from Worcestershire to Gloucestershire.

Good pubs are not in short supply: aside from the *Norman Knight* at Whichford (p.152), you could divert to **GREAT WOLFORD** for the much-loved *Fox and Hounds* (☎ 01608 674220, Ⓦ www.thefoxandhoundsinn.com; closed Mon), a sprawling sixteenth-century country inn serving local ales alongside good-value, upmarket modern British staples (mains £12–22), also with three decent guest rooms (③–④). Just north, between **TODENHAM** and the A429, nestling beside the Knee Brook – a tributary of the River Stour – the **Ditchford Mill farm shop** (☎01608 650399, Ⓦwww.simplesuppers.co.uk; closed Mon pm) has won national acclaim for its pork pies. A shade further north lies Stretton-on-Fosse (see p.153).

South of Moreton

South of Bourton-on-the-Hill and Moreton, between the fork of the A424 and A429, **LONGBOROUGH** is perhaps best known hereabouts for the **Cotswold Food Store** (Ⓦwww.cotswoldfoodstore.co.uk), effectively a rather upmarket farm shop on the A424 outside the village, with a wide range of local and organic food – including a great deli counter – and a terrace **café** alongside. The village has its own locally owned shop and café (Ⓦwww.longborough.net) as well as, remarkably, its own opera house, venue every summer for the prestigious **Longborough Festival Opera** (Ⓦwww.lfo.org.uk).

A finstroke away is the **Donnington Trout Farm** (Ⓦwww.donningtontrout .co.uk), supplying fresh and smoked trout to farmers' markets across the region, while **DONNINGTON** village itself hosts the nineteenth-century **Donnington Brewery** (Ⓦwww.donnington-brewery.com), still a family-run concern, whose products you could sup at your leisure at, say, the *Coach and Horses* (☎01451 830325) in Longborough or the award-winning, traditional *Fox Inn* (☎01451 870909) just across the A429 in **BROADWELL** – Donnington pubs, both.

Stow-on-the-Wold

When outsiders want to poke fun at the Cotswolds, they invariably aim first at **STOW-ON-THE-WOLD**. Over the last ten years or so, a succession of metropolitan journalists from the London papers – visiting chiefly to review one or other of the restaurants – have taken delight in tearing strips off Stow for its supposed docility and predictability. *Sunday Times* writer A.A. Gill was apoplectic, dubbing Stow "the worst place in the world" (before going on to declare, apparently seriously, "In Britain all the really innovative food is made in cities. Well, one city. London."). Stow is a symptom of a terrible malaise, comes the bleat. It's ruining the Cotswolds. Why doesn't Stow realize that tearooms and antique shops are nothing to be proud of anymore?

The answer, of course, is that not everybody likes urban culture, and not everybody wants boutique hotels and gastropubs. People don't come to Stow to be thrilled, challenged or intrigued. It's a historic Cotswold market town, busy and largely unprettified: people come to have a pleasant stroll around the old buildings, a leisurely look in the shops and a nice meal. The town delivers on all fronts. A certain breed of narcissistic Londoner may find the place infuriating, but the only reasonable response to that is "diddums".

Arrival, information and accommodation

Perched at 700 feet above sea level, Stow is the highest town in the Cotswolds: eight **roads** from all points of the compass meet here, including the A429 from Moreton and Cirencester, A424 from Broadway and Burford, A436 from Chipping Norton and B4068 from Cheltenham. A taxi from Moreton **railway station**, five miles north, costs £10–12; see p.176 for numbers.

There's a host of **buses**. Regular routes include Pulham's bus 801 (May–Sept daily; Oct–April not Sun) to/from **Cheltenham**, **Bourton-on-the-Water** and **Moreton**, and Pulham's "Fosse Link" bus 855 (not Sun) from **Cirencester**, **Northleach**, Bourton-on-the-Water and Moreton. Irregular services – in addition to those mentioned on p.176 – include three by Pulham's: bus 806 (once on Thurs) from Bourton-on-the-Water, **Shipton-under-Wychwood**, **Chipping Norton**

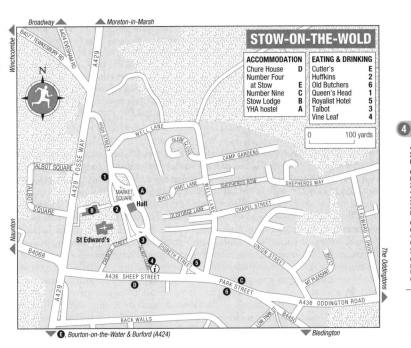

and **Banbury**, bus 810 (once on Thurs) from Cheltenham, Bourton-on-the-Water and **Kingham**, and bus 819 (once on Fri) from **the Guitings**. There's also the Villager Community buses V2 and V4 (both once on Wed) from Chipping Norton, V10 (once on 1st & 3rd Wed of month) from **Winchcombe**, V12 (once on Fri) from Chipping Norton, Kingham, Shipton-under-Wychwood and **Burford**, and V21 (once on Wed) from **Witney** and Burford.

To reach Stow's tiny **tourist office**, at 12 Talbot Court (Mon–Sat 10am–5pm, Sun 11am–4pm; ☎01451 870150, ⓦwww.go-stow.co.uk), duck down the passageway that leads off the main square beside the *Talbot* inn. As well as maps, information and details of good walks in the area, they offer self-guided **audio tours** of the town through ⓦwww.walkingpast.co.uk – downloadable for £5, or complete with iPod rental for £8.

In town

Chure House Lyndhurst Mews, off Sheep St ☎01451 832185, ⓦwww.bedandbreakfast-stowonthewold.co.uk. Nice little B&B in a modern building hidden away off the main road. Rooms are nothing special, but they are comfortable, and both the personal attention and quiet location are a boon. ③–④

Number Nine 9 Park St ☎01451 870333, ⓦwww .number-nine.info. Pleasant old house offering quality B&B just down from the town square. The three bedrooms feature low beams but contemporary styling – and the rates are a bargain. ③

Stow Lodge The Square ☎01451 830485, ⓦwww.stowlodge.com. An eighteenth-century rectory set in its own grounds off the main square, this is a Cotswolds hotel from the old school – antique prints, old bookcases, saggy sofas and all. Run by the same family for over fifty years, it feels it – rooms, service and clientele are very traditional – but there's an idiosyncratic charm to the place nonetheless. ⑤

YHA hostel The Square ☎0845 371 9540, ⓦwww.yha.org.uk. This good-looking Georgian town house on the main square is the Cotswolds' only youth hostel – an excellent choice for a budget stay, with small dorms and a choice of four-bed family rooms as well as kitchen facilities, a garden and a little café. Dorm beds £14–20. Reception closed 10am–5pm. ②

Out of town

🏃 **Number Four at Stow** Fosse Way ☎01451 830297, 🌐www.hotelnumberfour.co.uk. A real find in an unusual location, about a mile south of Stow (and down a steep hill), jammed into the V of the junction between the busy A424 and busier A429. Despite the unromantic setting, this is a very pleasant little country hotel, opened in 2010, family owned and run by two sisters; it's their fourth such venture, hence the name. Inside, road noise is kept to a minimum; most of the time it's barely detectable. Interiors are all very tastefully modern – fabrics and colours work together, and the eighteen bedrooms are simply but stylishly furnished. It's elegant, but not overpowering, and the warm welcome is a breath of fresh air. ❺

The Town

Stow sucks in a disproportionate number of visitors for its size and attractions, which essentially comprise an old **market square** surrounded by seventeenth- and eighteenth-century coaching inns, cafés and antique shops. The square was the scene, on March 21, 1646, of the last battle of the English Civil War, when Royalist armies, routed on a nearby battlefield, were pushed back into the town by victorious Roundheads. The slaughter was such that, legend has it, ducks were seen swimming in the blood: some claim that the lane leading east out of the square, Digbeth Street, is named for "Duck Bath". In quieter times, the narrow walled alleyways, or "tchures", running into the square would have funnelled sheep into the market, which is now dominated by an imposing Victorian **hall**, flanked on one side by a medieval **cross** (though the headstone is a modern replacement) and on the other by a set of stocks (also modern) adorning a small, triangular green.

Behind the square, the church of **St Edward**, with its 88-foot Perpendicular tower, has Norman and Tudor elements, though much in the broad, light interior is Victorian. The churchyard hosts three "bale tombs" of wool merchants – and make sure you stroll around to the photogenic **north porch**, where two yew trees flanking the old wooden door appear to have grown into the stonework.

"Meadows and Mills" is an easy **walk** (4 miles; 2hr 30min) downloadable at 🌐www.cotswoldsaonb.org.uk which heads downhill from Stow across fields to Lower Slaughter (see p.186) and on into Bourton-on-the-Water (p.185). An alternative route, dubbed "From Wold to Water" (6 miles; 3hr) – and also downloadable at the same site – passes through Maugersbury and Icomb before turning to Wyck Rissington and then across water meadows into Bourton.

Eating and drinking

In among its antique shops, butchers and ironmongers, Stow has a couple of fine, upmarket **delis** which stock local produce. People come from miles around for the cheeses at Hamptons, 1 Digbeth Street (☎01451 831733, 🌐www.hamptonsfine foods.co.uk), while a few doors down is Maby's (☎01451 870071, 🌐www.mabys .co.uk), a specialist in wine and olives. The same street also features Miette (☎01451 833543, 🌐www.miette.co.uk), an artisan chocolatier. See p.173 for details of Stow's monthly **farmers' market**.

Stow hosts a clutch of noteworthy **restaurants**. Aside from the options reviewed below, you could also venture slightly further afield to try outstanding places in nearby villages: the *Horse & Groom* at Upper Oddington (see opposite), the restaurants in the Slaughters (p.186), the café at Daylesford (p.115), the *King's Head* in Bledington (p.116) or the *Kingham Plough* (p.115), to name a few.

In town

🏃 **Huffkins** The Square ☎01451 832870, 🌐www.huffkins.com. Legendary Cotswold tearoom – top spot in town for afternoon tea, but also good for snacks and light meals (£6–10).

🏃 **Old Butchers** Park St ☎01451 831700, 🌐www.theoldbutchers.com. Stow's top restaurant, a breezy, debonair take on 21st-century country dining, from its plain walls and exposed brick to the quality of its locally sourced ingredients. Little on the menu (which changes daily) will be a surprise; it's all about the cooking, which is outstanding. Mains roughly £12–18.

Queen's Head The Square ☎01451 830563. Traditional old Donnington pub that provides good beer, good service and a pleasant chatty atmosphere. Food is a level above standard pub grub (mains roughly £9–11).

Royalist Hotel Digbeth St ☎01451 830670, ⓦwww.theroyalisthotel.com. Purportedly the oldest inn in Britain, with parts of the building dated at 947 AD (though the interiors have been freshly modernized). Come for the upmarket *947AD* restaurant, serving superb modern British cuisine (two-course set menu £29), and/or the adjacent, stone-flagged *Eagle & Child* pub, also with a great food menu (mains £13–16).

Talbot The Square ☎01451 870934, ⓦwww .thetalbot.net. Ex-coaching inn on the main square, now a genial middle-of-the-road pub – great for a sociable drink or an uncomplicated meal (mains £9–12).

Vine Leaf 10 Talbot Court ☎01451 832010. Cheery little daytime café-cum-restaurant off the square which does simple food – salads, risotto, homemade burgers (£6–12). Closed alternate Thursdays.

Out of town

Cutler's At *Number Four* hotel, (see opposite). A great choice just south of town – a formal, very grown-up, contemporary styled restaurant serving excellent, upmarket seasonal cuisine: you might find saddle of lamb or sirloin steak on the menu, alongside partridge, lobster or an innovative veg option. Mains roughly £14–20. Closed Sun eve.

For coverage of Stow's busy neighbour **Bourton-on-the-Water**, turn to p.185.

East of Stow

A little way **east of Stow**, the main road splits: to the south, the B4450 loops towards Bledington and Kingham (see p.115), while the A436 continues northeast towards the A44 and the Rollright Stones (p.120). A mile or so out of Stow, signs off the A436 point you to **UPPER ODDINGTON** – one half of a village which is not just split in name. This is the more down-to-earth bit, still with a strong local community who remain justifiably proud of the 🍴 *Horse & Groom* (☎01451 830584, ⓦwww.horseandgroom.uk.com), a bright, hearty country pub updated to include a fine restaurant, showcasing an accomplished, innovative approach to old favourites from salmon poached in white wine to Old Spot pork braised in cider. Mains are £14 to £17 – and don't miss the homemade desserts.

Down the way, **LOWER ODDINGTON** – just that tiny bit closer to swanky Daylesford (see p.115) – is tangibly posher, with a greater proportion of holiday cottages and second homes. Their occupants mosey over to the *Fox Inn* (☎01451 870555, ⓦwww.foxinn.net), a rather more studied take on the traditional country pub, perfectly comfortable and pleasant but with a somehow less engaging atmosphere and less inspiring menu. The contrast is intriguing.

West of Stow

Two roads head **west of Stow**, out onto the open, rolling wolds. The **B4068** cuts southwest towards Cheltenham, passing first through **LOWER SWELL**, where stands the *Golden Ball* (☎01451 833886, ⓦwww.thegoldenball.co.uk), a fine, traditional Donnington pub. Just south of the village is Kirkham Farm, where Simon Weaver produces his famous organic Cotswold Brie (creamery shop open Mon–Fri 9am–5pm; ☎01451 870852, ⓦwww.simonweaver.net). Just to the north, the **B4077** shadows its neighbour initially, passing through **UPPER SWELL** before diverging towards Winchcombe and Tewkesbury.

Both roads pass through horse country: this close to Cheltenham, the villages and countryside host stables galore and many of the pubs are full of stable-hands and jockeys getting the dust out of their throats. On the B4068 in **NAUNTON**, the Victorian *Black Horse* (☎01451 850565) is one example, but for the best-known – and, many say, the best – aim for **FORD**, on the B4077, where you'll see the 𝔛 *Plough Inn* (☎01386 584215, ⓌΘwww.theploughinnatford.co.uk). Located directly beside Jackdaw's Castle, ex-jockey Jonjo O'Neill's training yard, this atmospheric old inn, once voted "Racing Pub of the Year", is bedecked in equestrian memorabilia, saddles and brasses. Stop in for a pint, or a traditional meal in its Georgian-style restaurant extension (mains £11–16). It also has decent B&B rooms (❸) – though bear in mind they will be booked solid during the Cheltenham races. A pleasant **circular walk** (6 miles; 3hr) starts at the pub, heads to **CUTSDEAN** village nearby and follows a back lane to skirt Jackdaw's Castle, picking up the Gloucestershire Way to return to Ford alongside the "gallops".

A couple or so miles west of Ford, the B4077 drops down off the Cotswold Edge, passing near Stanway House (see p.167) and shortly afterwards bumping into the north–south B4632, within spitting distance of Winchcombe (see p.208).

Cotswold Farm Park

In a region bedevilled by "visitor attractions", the **Cotswold Farm Park** (mid-March to early Sept daily 10.30am–5pm; Sept & Oct Sat & Sun only same times; £6.95; Ⓦwww.cotswoldfarmpark.co.uk) stands out. Although aimed squarely at families looking for a fun day out, the park – with its adventure playground, kiddie tractor-driving and maze quest – remains part of a working farm, displaying an authentic, educational atmosphere. It was established in 1971 by farmer Joe Henson to showcase his collection of rare traditional breeds of sheep, pigs, cattle and horses, and is now owned and run by his TV presenter son, Adam. The park occupies a large area, with plenty to see on a wander around (or let the Farm Safari tractor take the strain), including information about the different breeds of farm animals on view, from rare Gloucester cattle and Bagot goats to the ancient Soay breed of sheep, brought here from a Scottish island in the 1960s. Demonstrations take place throughout the season of **lambing** (March & April), **milking** (May–Oct) and **shearing** (May & June). You could also tackle the easy two-mile **wildlife walk** signposted through the adjacent Barton Bushes. There are full restaurant, toilet and picnic facilities onsite.

The farm park lies in the middle of open country east of **KINETON** village – but there is no access from Kineton. Instead take the unnamed minor road that cuts a straight line northwest–southeast between the B4068 and the B4077. Coming from Stow, follow the B4077 for about five miles, then turn left at a signed crossroads. The park is also signed along the Naunton road off the A429, just south of the Bourton-on-the-Water traffic lights. No public transport runs close.

The Guitings

Just west of the Cotswold Farm Park, back roads will take you to the **Guitings** (rhymes with "sightings"). To the north, almost lost in the woods on the banks of the titchy River Windrush, is quiet **TEMPLE GUITING**, named for having been granted in 1120 to the Knights Templar, a group of French Crusaders headquartered at the site of Solomon's temple in Jerusalem. A couple of miles south is its slightly larger twin, **GUITING POWER**, on the slopes above the river. Guiting Power's originally Norman church of **St Michael**, isolated in fields on the southern edge of the village, stands beside the route of the **Warden's Way** (see box opposite). The better of Guiting Power's two pubs, the friendly 𝔛 *Hollow Bottom* (☎01451 850392, Ⓦwww.hollowbottom.com), has decent beer, good food and four handy **rooms** for B&B (❸), with the *Guiting Guest House* (☎01451 850470, Ⓦwww.guitingguesthouse.com; ❹) a four-star alternative. Come in late July and you'll find the **Guiting Festival** (Ⓦwww.guitingfestival.org) in full swing,

Are there any secrets left in the Cotswolds? This is perhaps one of England's most visited rural regions: summer weekends see the three Bs in particular – Burford, Broadway and Bourton-on-the-Water – crammed with holidaymakers. But it's also a big place, and there are plenty of hideaways. Any "best of" list is doomed to failure, since the best of the Cotswolds is often to be found in the unvisited villages and on the nameless back roads – but our ideas for getting off the beaten track should give you a decent start.

Minster Lovell ▲

Walking in the Cotswolds ▼

Some of the classic Cotswold destinations – Chipping Campden, Bibury, the Slaughters, Castle Combe – are undoubtedly worth seeing, but you won't be alone when you visit. Yet countless quieter villages offer atmosphere and Cotswold character in spades. The five named below are a personal choice, as are our selections of B roads, rural hotels and galleries of art or design. For each, we've concentrated on the heart of the Cotswold countryside, deliberately excluding Oxford, Stratford and Cheltenham.

Secret villages

Ebrington p.153: thatched cottages, a lovely pub – and Chipping Campden on the doorstep.

Minchinhampton p.234: quiet, handsome village up on the wild slopes above Stroud.

Minster Lovell p.105: Cotswold charm aplenty in this romantic hideaway.

Sheepscombe p.230: beautiful walks and a great pub, hidden in a steep-sided valley.

Stanton p.167: a historic village sporting classic good looks.

Secret B roads

B4014 Tetbury–Nailsworth: scenic initially, then narrowing for a hairpin journey through deep, dark forest.

B4022 Witney–Charlbury: beautiful drive over the tops from the Windrush to the Evenlode.

B4035 Banbury–Chipping Campden: nice views, interesting villages and a lovely climb to Campden.

B4066 Stroud–Uley: memorable ridge-top drive with views to the Severn.

B4632 Broadway–Cheltenham: gentle canter beneath forested slopes, then climbing through hilly Winchcombe.

Secret hotels (luxury)

Barnsley House, Barnsley p.191: the ultimate in posh country styling.

Calcot Manor, Tetbury p.237: outstanding, family-friendly country-house hotel.

Cotswolds88, Painswick p.230: eye-popping contemporary design.

Cowley Manor, Cowley p.219: top-end designer chic, miles from anywhere.

Lords of the Manor, Upper Slaughter p.186: genteel, upmarket mid-Cotswolds haven.

▲ Looking over Stanton

▼ Barnsley House

Secret hotels (midrange)

Cardynham House, Painswick p.229: flair and comfort in this crooked old house.

Horse & Groom, Bourton-on-the-Hill p.178: great food, great service, great rooms, great location.

King's Head, Bledington p.116: superb gastropub with a sense of style.

New Inn, Coln St Aldwyns p.190: a warm welcome at this lovely old inn.

Rectory, Crudwell p.241: rural character updated for the twenty-first century.

Secret gardens

Kiftsgate p.160: roses and a sense of calm disorder atop the Cotswolds Edge.

Matara p.236: an unusual layout and meditative Asian influence.

▲ Lords of the Manor, Upper Slaughter

▼ Barnsley House gardens

Rousham p.132: one of Monty Don's favourite English gardens, unchanged in 250 years.

Sezincote p.178: lavish Indian and Persian elements combine to great effect in this beautiful waterfall-filled garden.

Sudeley p.210: romantic, evocative gardens, complete with a ruined medieval tithe barn, in this grand old castle.

Secret art

Compton Verney p.149: world-class art gallery occupying a beautiful restored and updated manor house in the Warwickshire countryside showcasing bookbinding, stained glass and jewellery.

Court Barn, Chipping Campden p.157: superb displays on Campden's Arts & Crafts heritage.

Gordon Russell Museum, Broadway p.164: fine museum devoted to this master of British design.

Kelmscott Manor p.112: original Arts & Crafts furniture, textiles and paintings at this isolated house near the Thames that was home to William and Jane Morris.

Upton House p.129: memorable country-house collection of Old Masters.

Compton Verney ▲

Canal narrowboats ▼

Cotswolds canal ▼

Secret canals

Eighteenth-century canal engineers made monumental efforts to link the rivers Severn and Thames. First came the **Stroudwater Navigation** from Framilode to Stroud, followed in 1789 by the **Thames and Severn Canal**, linking Stroud to Lechlade – the highest navigable point on the Thames – via Sapperton Tunnel, once England's longest canal tunnel and still flanked by great pubs (see p.234). After its 1840s heyday, the 36-mile link fell into disrepair; today, the **Cotswold Canals Trust** (Ⓦwww.cotswoldcanals.com) is dredging and renovating to reconnect Stroud – and, eventually, the entire canal – to the national waterways network (Ⓦwww.waterscape.com). Museums in Gloucester (p.223) and Banbury (p.125) showcase canal history.

In the meantime you can still explore the **Oxford Canal**, which links Oxford with Coventry – either on a narrowboat, rentable at Lower Heyford (p.132) and Thrupp (p.92), or on towpath walks around Heyford and Cropredy (p.128).

Guiting Power's village hall managing, somehow, to pull in jazz and classical music performers of world renown. Pulham's **bus** 804 serves Guiting Power to/from Cheltenham once daily Monday to Friday, with an extra service on Tuesdays, Thursdays and Saturdays. Pulham's bus 818/819 runs to/from Bourton and Stow once on Fridays.

Bourton-on-the-Water

BOURTON-ON-THE-WATER, four miles southwest of Stow, stands at the centre of Cotswold tourism. Set just east of the A429 Fosse Way, its old quarter straddles the tiny **River Windrush**: beside the village green – flanked by photogenic Jacobean and Georgian facades in yellow Cotswold stone – five picturesque little **bridges** describe a series of arcs over the shallow water, dappled by shade from overhanging trees. Bourton is lovely, but its proximity to main roads means that it's invariably packed with people: tourist coaches cram in all summer long and the village, inevitably, has changed to accommodate them. The little **High Street**, alongside the green, now concentrates on souvenirs, banks and teashops, interspersed with a few purpose-designed attractions: a Model Village here, a Dragonfly Maze there. You'll find a model railway exhibition, a motoring museum – even a bird park by the river showing off flamingoes and king penguins. Kids might enjoy it, but they might enjoy the Cotswold Farm Park (see opposite), ten minutes' drive away, more.

And if you've come to Bourton seeking Cotswold atmosphere, simply take a seat on the bench in the tranquil churchyard at **WYCK RISSINGTON**, a crowd-free village barely a mile to the northeast. The church itself, largely twelfth- and thirteenth-century – with a plaque on the organ noting that Gustav Holst was organist here in 1892 and 1893 – is entrancing.

Curiously, the Bourton attraction which, on the surface, appears the most contrived is perhaps the most genuinely interesting. The **Cotswold Perfumery** (Mon–Sat 9.30am–5pm, Sun 10.30am–5pm; ☎01451 820698, ⓦwww.cotswold -perfumery.co.uk) isn't just another fancy souvenir shop, but one of Europe's very few manufacturers and retailers of perfume, offering informative **factory tours** (booking essential; £5) of their modest little site, taking in the perfume garden, laboratory and compounding room. They also have one-day **perfumery courses**, covering how to create and blend a fragrance (£125, including lunch and free gifts).

A short walk east of Bourton, the barely-visited **Greystones Farm Nature Reserve** (☎01451 810853, ⓦwww.gloucestershirewildlifetrust.co.uk) is a working organic livestock farm which includes Salmonsbury Meadows, a patchwork of ponds and islands sheltering wildflowers and water birds. Bourton tourist office has details of walks in the area. Otherwise, you can download details of the easy

---

The Warden's Way and Windrush Way

Two paths cross the high wolds west of Stow, both linking Bourton-on-the-Water with Winchcombe (see p.208) – a distance of fourteen miles – and both graded as easy. The **Warden's Way** winds through the villages of Lower and Upper Slaughter, Naunton and Guiting Power before passing through woodland and skirting Sudeley Castle to enter Winchcombe. Its neighbour, the **Windrush Way**, is a lonelier affair, following the river out of Bourton to Harford Farm, then branching west to take a hilltop route to Winchcombe via Hawling and Spoonley Wood. Both can be tackled in either direction: many people choose to combine the two in a circular route, either to/from Bourton or to/from Winchcombe. Pick up information and maps at local tourist offices.

"**Rissington Round**" walk (3.5 miles; 2hr) at Ⓦwww.cotswoldsaonb.org.uk – this starts in **GREAT RISSINGTON** at the pleasant *Lamb Inn* (Ⓣ01451 820388, Ⓦwww.thelambinn.com), reachable from Bourton on Pulham's bus 802 (every 2hr; not Sun), and heads across the fields to **LITTLE RISSINGTON** before descending to skirt a fishing lake on the return to Bourton.

Practicalities

Bourton is served by plenty of **buses**, including those outlined on p.176 and p.180. The cheery, well-equipped **tourist office** (Mon–Fri 9.30am–5pm, Sat 9.30am–5.30pm; Oct–March closes 1hr earlier; Ⓣ01451 820211, Ⓦwww .bourtoninfo.com) stands beside the perfumery, just across the river from the village green. Bourton's monthly **farmers' market** (see p.173) is held on the fourth Sunday of every month at Countrywide Stores on Station Road (Ⓣ01451 820551, Ⓦwww.countrywidefarmers.co.uk).

There's no compelling reason to **stay**. Bourton's only decent hotel is rather pricey: occupying a seventeenth-century building in the village centre, the family-run *Dial House* (Ⓣ01451 822244, Ⓦwww.dialhousehotel.com; ❺–❻) has bags of atmosphere, pleasant gardens and a decent restaurant. All rooms are individually decorated in contemporary style – rich fabrics, sleek bathrooms and careful detailing. There are B&Bs aplenty, but otherwise your best bet is to head up the slopes south of Bourton to titchy **CLAPTON-ON-THE-HILL**, for the gorgeous views and *Clapton Manor* (Ⓣ01451 810202, Ⓦwww.claptonmanor.co.uk; ❹), a picture-perfect Tudor-Jacobean mansion – still a family home – offering two rooms for B&B, grand breakfasts and a wealth of local knowledge.

Two nearby **campsites** are worth a look. On the road towards Clapton Hill, just south of Bourton, is *Field Barn Park* (Ⓣ01451 820434, Ⓦwww.fieldbarnpark .com), a site for the over-30s only – while the small, basic site at *Folly Farm* (Ⓣ01451 820285, Ⓦwww.cotswoldcamping.net) lies two and a half miles west of Bourton off the A436.

The Slaughters

Just across the A429 from Bourton-on-the-Water, the **Slaughters** (as in *slohtre*, Old English for marshy place, cognate with "slough") are much more enticing than their neighbour, though still on the day-trippers' circuit. They take in some of the most celebrated village scenery in the Cotswolds.

First comes **LOWER SLAUGHTER**, a mile or so northwest of Bourton. Here, the River Eye snakes its way through the village, overlooked by a string of immaculate honeystone Cotswold cottages. The village **church of St Mary** blends in well, but in fact it's largely Victorian. There is a small **museum** (and souvenir shop) signposted in a former mill, but once you've done the five-minute stroll through the village you're better off walking up the river valley for an hour or so to **UPPER SLAUGHTER**, another pretty little place tucked in a wooded dell. Its **church of St Peter**, a Saxon foundation rather mucked about with in the 1870s, could entice you to dally.

Beside the church in Upper Slaughter stands ⚶ *Lords of the Manor* (Ⓣ01451 820243, Ⓦwww.lordsofthemanor.com; ❽–❾), a luxurious **hotel** in the old rectory. The building dates from 1649, added to in the nineteenth century. Set grandly in its own park, it screams "traditional country house hotel", but actually presented extremely tastefully – modern, but not overpoweringly contemporary. The 26 rooms are the same: sumptuous without being brash. Clocks tick, the parquet creaks; it's all rather restful. The restaurant is one of the best in the area, awarded a Michelin star (two courses £59).

Down the hill in Lower Slaughter two hotels face off. *Lower Slaughter Manor* (℡01451 820456, Ⓦwww.lowerslaughter.co.uk; ➒) is the posher, a Relais & Châteaux property which plays the country-house-hotel part with a straight bat. Nothing is left to chance here: traditional rooms have a fresh, engaging ambience, contemporary rooms are edgy and faux-urban, all are spacious and elegant. The restaurant follows suit. Just across the road, *Washbourne Court* (℡01451 822143, Ⓦwww.washbournecourt.co.uk; ➑–➒) is an altogether lighter prospect. Still a seventeenth-century building, still in honeyed limestone, it has nonetheless been transformed inside, with contemporary decor, modern art on the walls and a breezy, interested service ethic. Notably family friendly, the hotel has little time for Cotswold stuffiness, offering thirty bedrooms featuring bold modern fabrics and design touches, alongside a fine-dining restaurant (two courses £38) and less formal bar menu (mains £10–17) in the "Scholar's Lounge" – the hotel was once a crammer for Eton College.

From here, Guiting Power (see p.184) lies a couple of miles northwest.

Northleach

Secluded in a shallow depression ten miles southwest of Stow – and the same distance northeast of Cirencester – **NORTHLEACH** is one of the central Cotswolds' more appealing villages. Despite the fact that the A40 Oxford–Cheltenham road and the A429 Fosse Way between Stow and Cirencester cross at a large roundabout just north of the town, virtually no tourist traffic makes its way into the centre.

First stop is the old Georgian prison, now the headquarters of the Cotswolds Conservation Board (Ⓦwww.cotswoldsaonb.org.uk), located beside the traffic lights on the A429 less than a mile south of the A40/A429 roundabout. A door on the right gives into the **prison** (April–Oct Wed–Sun 10am–4pm; free), with interesting displays in the old cells on the history of crime and punishment in Gloucestershire; this leads through to "**Escape to the Cotswolds**" (same hours), an excellent modern visitor centre explaining the work of the conservation board in maintaining the Cotswolds Area of Outstanding Natural Beauty. They double as a mini tourist office, stocking plenty of informative leaflets, and have access to a "rural life" exhibition of old wagons and carts.

From here, West End leads into Northleach, growing ever narrower as it curves into the centre. As you walk the last bit, as long as you were slightly short-sighted and had some luck with the sunshine, you could perhaps for a brief minute imagine yourself in a rather pleasant, self-possessed little town in Bordeaux or the Dordogne, characterized by silvery limestone facades and refreshingly free of commerce. Around the quiet, sloping **Market Place** cluster rows of late-medieval buildings, with more framing the adjoining **Green** – some half-timbered – but the outstanding feature is the handsome Perpendicular **church of St Peter and St Paul**, erected in the fifteenth century at the height of the wool boom. Its porch – suitably ostentatious – is overseen by a set of finely carved corbel heads, while wide clerestory windows light the beautifully proportioned nave. The floor is inlaid with an exceptional collection of **memorial brasses**, marking the tombs of the merchants whose endowments paid for the church. On several, you can make out the woolsacks laid out beneath the owner's feet – a symbol of wealth and power that survives in the House of Lords, where a woolsack is placed on the Lord Chancellor's seat.

Two minutes' walk along the High Street from Market Place is **Keith Harding's World of Mechanical Music** (daily 10am–5pm; £8; Ⓦwww.mechanicalmusic .co.uk), a bewildering one-room collection of antique musical boxes, barrel organs and automata. The entrance fee includes an hour-long demonstration tour, of which the highlight is hearing the likes of Rachmaninov, Gershwin and Paderewski playing their own masterpieces on piano rolls.

Practicalities

Northleach is served by reasonably regular **buses**: Pulham's bus 855 "Fosse Link" (not Sun) to/from Moreton, Stow, Bourton and Cirencester; Swanbrook bus 853 (Mon–Sat 3 daily, 1 on Sun) to/from Gloucester, Cheltenham, Oxford, Witney, Minster Lovell and Burford; Pulham's bus 815 (once on Tues) from Moreton, Stow, Lower Slaughter and Bourton; and Pulham's bus 809 (once on Wed) from Cheltenham.

At the excellent *Wheatsheaf* (ⓣ01451 860244, ⓦwww.cotswoldswheatsheaf.com; ④), a former coaching inn on West End, the old stone exterior has been left intact, but the public areas have been remodelled in a bright modern style softened by period furniture, bookcases and etchings of favourite livestock – this is very much a pub devoted to country pursuits, organizing regular riding, shooting and fishing parties. Its **restaurant** is first-rate, offering traditional English cuisine – roast duck, loin of pork and so forth – with mains around £15. There are nine comfortable, en-suite **guest rooms**. A mile south of town, off the A429, is the simple *Far Peak* **campsite** (ⓣ01285 720858, ⓦwww.farpeakcamping.co.uk).

Otherwise you're left with the unreconstructed old *Red Lion* pub on the Market Place – which, despite the sign, hasn't done B&B for years – a handful of other places in plain view, or the blander *Blades* daytime bistro/café (closed Sun; ⓣ01451 860715, ⓦwww.blades.me.uk), beside the AONB visitor centre in the old prison – good for coffee or a light lunch.

East towards Burford

East of Northleach, the A40 powers towards Burford (see p.108). Before you put your foot down, detour north onto tiny lanes approaching **FARMINGTON**; on the edge of the village look for signs to the wonderful **Cotswold Ice Cream Company** (ⓣ01451 861425, ⓦwww.cotswoldicecream.net), headquartered here at Hill House Farm. You're free to drop in, watch them at work and buy direct (May–Sept Thurs–Sun 10.30am–4.30pm). Further east, past the rather obscure National Trust-owned **Sherborne Estate**, where a seventeenth-century grandstand, **Lodge Park**, is open to the public (mid-March to Oct Fri–Sun 11am–4pm) – and the modest village of **WINDRUSH**, where Pinchpool Farm produces some of the Cotswolds' finest goat's cheese – the last villages inside Gloucestershire are **LITTLE BARRINGTON** and then **GREAT BARRINGTON**. The latter hosts the popular *Fox Inn* (ⓣ01451 844385, ⓦwww.foxinnbarrington.co.uk). See p.111 for details of a **walk** alongside the River Windrush from here into Burford.

Chedworth Roman villa

West of Northleach, a group of widely spaced villages – Turkdean, Hazleton, Notgrove and Cold Aston – offer picturesque meanderings on a looping route northwards towards the Slaughters (p.186) or the Guitings (p.184). Elsewhere, roads west off the A429 show "Roman Villa" signs for a twisting and turning drive along hilly country lanes above the River Coln for three miles or more to reach **Chedworth Roman Villa** (Tues–Sun: April–Oct 10am–5pm, March & Nov 10am–4pm; £6.30; ⓦwww.nationaltrust.org.uk). In the fourth century AD, when this villa was built, it would have been one of the largest country houses in Britain – a giant mansion of fifty rooms or more, arrayed on three sides around a large courtyard, with its own spring, two bath-houses, heated living rooms, and more. Today, you pass first through an interpretation centre before exiting to the open site, which retains a sense of drama: it's not difficult to imagine the grandeur of the house, set in remote countryside. Consolidation work, completed in 2011, showcases the surviving mosaic floors in the dining room along the left side of the grassy courtyard. Further along, in the corner of the site, the spring – probably holy, with a shrine or temple built around it – still flows, flanked by the bath-houses. A Victorian shooting lodge, plonked beside the courtyard, now houses a small museum of finds.

The villa is misleadingly named: **CHEDWORTH** village lies a mile or more south, known for a rather fine **church** with a twelfth-century tower and the *Seven Tuns* (℡01285 720242, ⓦwww.youngs.co.uk), a seventeenth-century pub with a water-wheel outside, bare boards inside and a reputation for good beer. Nearby, at Denfurlong Farm, the **Chedworth Farm Shop** (℡01285 720265, ⓦwww.cotswoldfarmfayre.com) lies just off the main A429 Fosse Way at a point roughly four miles north of Cirencester.

In the other direction from the villa, on the A40 northeast of **COMPTON ABDALE**, the *Puesdown Inn* (℡01451 860262, ⓦwww.puesdown.cotswoldinns.com) is a decent place to whet your whistle and have a bite to eat in congenial if unexciting modern surroundings. The food is reliably good, with seasonal dishes and some less highfalutin options, including pizza. There are comfortable rooms (❸–❹), but they're a touch pricey, not least because of road noise.

South towards Cirencester

Either side of the A40 junction, the arrow-straight A429 takes on rollercoaster aspirations, shooting down one hillside and immediately whizzing straight up the next. About three miles **south of Northleach**, a particularly steep dip, which marks the valley of the River Coln, shelters the **Inn at Fossebridge** (℡01285 720721, ⓦwww.fossebridgeinn.co.uk; ❺), a rather atmospheric three-hundred-year-old coaching inn with eight comfortable, traditionally styled rooms and a lovely back garden offering lakeside strolls. Roads here turn off west to the Roman villa (see opposite) and east into the maze-like Coln Valley (p.190). You could stop at Fossebridge for a meal, or alternatively push on down the A429 a couple of miles south to "Foss Cross" for the locally renowned **Hare & Hounds** (℡01285 720288, ⓦwww.hareandhoundsinn.com). Cirencester is five miles further on, while Fosscross Lane turns off east at the *Hare & Hounds* for the easy drive over the tops to Bibury.

Bibury

Hidden away on the B4425 between Burford and Cirencester, at the point where the road crosses the River Coln, **BIBURY** – like Broadway, Burford and Bourton-on-the-Water – is another of those Cotswold honeypots. Winningly attractive (and famously dubbed "the most beautiful village in England" by Victorian designer William Morris), it draws crowds by the coachload. Yet there's even less to do here than in its alliterative compadres: strolling the village lanes is the thing, but everybody else has had the same idea.

As you come in from the Burford direction, the road takes you down past Bibury's splendid, quiet church of **St Mary** – with Gothic windows, Saxon elements surviving above the chancel arch and a fifteenth-century timber ceiling – to reach the riverbank. Across the way to the left is the focus of all the attention. **Arlington Row**, originally built around 1380 as a wool store, was converted in the seventeenth century into a line of cottages to house weavers working at nearby Arlington Mill. It was this glimpse of hound's-tooth gables, warm yellow stone and wonky windows which stole Morris's heart – and which is now immortalized in the UK passport as an image of England.

To reach Arlington Row from the main road, you have to cross a diminutive patch of boggy meadow known as **Rack Isle** (it's where clothes were once hung on racks to dry). Now protected by the National Trust, the wildflower-strewn isle has several pretty footpaths winding across it to the little bridge over the Coln at the far end – a couple of hundred yards away – where sits **Bibury Trout Farm** (March–Oct Mon–Sat 9am–6pm, Sun 10am–6pm; Nov–Feb Mon–Sat 9am–4pm; £3.75; ⓦ www.biburytroutfarm.co.uk). Unsurprisingly popular, since it's the only paying attraction in a heavily touristed village, the fishery has footpaths leading out across a network of ponds to scenic picnic spots (you can buy fresh and smoked trout in the shop for barbecuing) and also offers a catch-your-own section, with all equipment provided.

Practicalities

Other than to local villages, Bibury's only regular **bus** links are to/from Cirencester, on Cotswold Green bus 860 (Mon–Fri 5 daily), Pulham's bus 865 (once on Sat) and Ebley bus 866 (once on Mon & Thurs). A **taxi** to Bibury from Kemble station (see p.192) is about £25. By the bridge in the village centre stands the *Swan* (ⓣ01285 740695, ⓦwww.swanhotel.co.uk; ❺–❻), decent enough but suffering a bit from hotel-by-numbers – little, other than the setting, truly stands out. At the other end of the village, *Bibury Court* (ⓣ01285 740337, ⓦwww .biburycourt.co.uk; ❻) looks ravishing, a Jacobean mansion to die for. Tranquil in its own grounds, it offers untrammelled peace and quiet: people come, people whisper, people go, and the loudest noise is the church bells. The restaurant is excellent, but the rooms might disappoint – not as elegant, nor as well-appointed as the price might indicate. Two larger rooms, bizarrely, have no en-suite bathroom. In some ways you might do better at the village's only pub, the *Catherine Wheel* (ⓣ01285 740250, ⓦwww.catherinewheel-bibury.co.uk; ❸), which offers four beamed doubles and a modest gastropub menu.

Into the Coln Valley

A thicket of narrow, empty lanes criss-crosses its way north from Bibury back up the Coln valley towards Fossebridge on the A429. Once past **ARLINGTON** and **ABLINGTON**, on Bibury's doorstep, you could aim for tiny **COLN ROGERS**, named for Roger of Gloucester, a twelfth-century knight, and today almost lost in the forest. Here, reached down a track off a back road, stands the **Saxon church** of St Andrew – simple, but resonant with age. With a good map, you could put together a circular walk following tracks through and behind Coln Rogers: it's extraordinary to find a place so scenic, and so quiet, this deep in the heart of the Cotswolds.

Coln St Aldwyns

Aim the other way out of Bibury, and a back road makes short work of the couple of miles south to **COLN ST ALDWYNS**. Down through the village, and just before you cross the river again towards Quenington, on the left stands the sixteenth-century, stone-built 🏛 *New Inn* (ⓣ01285 750651, ⓦwww.new-inn .co.uk; ❾). Out of the hubbub, but not hard to find, and superbly updated to boutique standards, this is a great base from which to explore the whole region, from Cirencester to Northleach, Burford, Fairford, Bibury and everywhere in between. It scores first with its service – genial and switched-on – and next with its **restaurant**, offering contemporary, seasonal cuisine lightened with innovative

Walking around Barnsley and Bibury

A scenic, quiet **walk** (11 miles; 5hr) links a series of trails to cover some rough terrain between Barnsley and Bibury. From the centre of Barnsley, paths head north across Barnsley Park and on, over the fields and across Fosscross Lane to Winson village, alongside Coln Rogers (see opposite) in the wooded Coln Valley. Climb to Lamborough Banks for a great view, then turn south to drop down to Bibury. The return leads on paths behind Arlington to cut southwest across the fields, through Deadlands Copse and back to Barnsley.

touches, such as pan-fried Bibury trout with buttered samphire, pork belly with a red wine sauce or (in autumn) risotto of hare with wild mushrooms. Mains are £16 to £19. Finally, the thirteen **rooms** are outstanding, featuring bold colours, quirky design touches and luxury bathrooms.

Fairford, a couple of miles south, is covered on p.199.

Barnsley

Southwest out of Bibury, the B4425 passes through **BARNSLEY**, once a little-regarded cluster of houses on the Cirencester road, now firmly on the map of five-star Cotswold tourism for the conversion of a country house on the edge of the village into one of the region's swankiest hotels. *Barnsley House* (☎01285 740000, ⓦwww.barnsleyhouse.com; ⑨) occupies a glorious Jacobean mansion – but its style is anything but Jacobean. Inside, you could be in the flashiest of boutique pads: state-of-the-art styling announces that, here, money is no object. The **restaurant** is outstanding (Italian-inspired mains £10–25), there's an onsite **spa** that breathes contemporary minimalism, or you could visit for the spectacular **gardens** alone (daily 10.30am–4.30pm; £7.50 including tea).

For mere mortals, much of this is out of reach. Not so the hotel's other venture. Opposite the hotel gates, Barnsley's village pub has been transformed into – you guessed it – *The Village Pub* (☎01285 740421, ⓦwww.thevillagepub.co.uk), a super-sleek, urban stylist's ironic take on country ways, sporting a *papier-mâché* stag's head above the fireplace, heavy swag curtains, designer settles and pub grub so immaculate it borders on fine dining (mains £12–15). They also have six **rooms** (④–⑤), finished to a superbly high standard. Note that the pub is closed on weekday afternoons (Mon–Thurs 3.30–6pm).

Beyond Barnsley, as the B4425 approaches Cirencester, you'll pass a turn for Abbey Home Farm, location of the **Organic Farm Shop** (closed Mon; ☎01285 640441, ⓦwww.theorganicfarmshop.co.uk), with a wide range of foods, an award-winning café (book for Sunday lunch; £13; veggie and vegan options available) as well as yurts (②), a lakeside cabin and eco-friendly camping.

Cirencester

Plumb astride the A429 nineteen miles southwest of Stow (and a little less southeast of Cheltenham), **CIRENCESTER** is a pleasantly old-fashioned town on the southern fringes of the Cotswolds. It made an early start, when, as Corinium, it became a provincial capital and a centre of trade under the **Romans**. The town flourished for three centuries: its grand forum was one of the largest in northern Europe, and in the province of Britannia Corinium was second in size and importance only to Londinium (London). The **Saxons** put paid to all that, largely destroying the Roman town. The **wool** boom of the Middle Ages saw a revival, and today, with its handsome stone buildings, Cirencester is an affluent little place that lays claim to be capital of the Cotswolds. Come, chiefly, for the outstanding **Roman museum** and the **church** – but also make time to tap into the upmarket food-and-shopping lifestyle that has made Cirencester the unlikely hub of what the media are calling "Poshtershire". Alongside a developing hinterland of quality food producers, the town now has genuinely good **restaurants** – often populated, entertainingly, by a very distinctive breed of ladies who lunch.

Arrival and information

Driving into Cirencester may try your patience. There is a bypass-cum-ring road – but it's less of a ring, more of a lop-sided horseshoe, punctuated by poorly signed roundabouts. As you go round, the A429 and A419 battle for supremacy, with signs for Swindon and Bristol often superseding closer-at-hand destinations. The bypass is itself bypassed by the A417 (which, inconveniently, turns into the A419 at one point). Add to that a fiendish one-way system, and you may wonder what Cirencester has got to hide.

Trains on the London–Swindon–Cheltenham line stop at Kemble station (see p.197), about five miles to the southwest. Two bus routes link Kemble station to Cirencester: Stagecoach bus 881 (not Sun) runs about every two hours, or Pulham's "Fosse Link" bus 855 (not Sun) has three or four services a day. Otherwise, **taxis** meet arriving trains, charging about £10 into Cirencester; local firms include Corinium (☎01285 659331, ⊛www.coriniumtaxis.co.uk) and Kemble (☎01285 800006, ⊛www.taxisofkemble.co.uk).

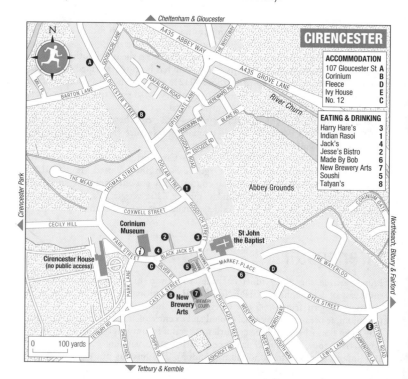

Cirencester is a hub for local **buses**. Regular services include Stagecoach bus 881 (not Sun) to/from **Tetbury**, Pulham's "Fosse Link" bus 855 (not Sun) to/from **Northleach**, **Bourton**, **Stow** and **Moreton**, Cotswold Green bus 28/28A (not Sun) and 54/54A (not Sun) to/from **Stroud**, Stagecoach bus 151 (not Sun) to/from **Cheltenham**, Swanbrook bus 852 (not Sun) to/from **Gloucester**, Cotswold Green bus 860 (Mon–Fri) to/from **Bibury** and **Barnsley**, APL bus 877 (not Sun) to/from **Fairford** and **Lechlade**, and Andybus 93 (not Sun) to/from **Malmesbury** and **Crudwell**. Irregular services abound, including Ebley bus 866 (once on Mon & Thurs) and Pulham's bus 865 (once on Sat) which both run to/from Fossebridge, Coln Rogers, Bibury and Southrop. National Express long-distance **coaches** serve Cirencester direct from central London and Heathrow airport: they are also a useful way to get to and from Cheltenham or Gloucester on a Sunday, when local buses don't run.

Buses stop in the Market Place, a short, signposted walk from the Corinium Museum on Park Street, within which resides the **tourist office** (Mon–Sat 10am–5pm, Sun 2–5pm; Nov–March closes 4pm; ☎01285 654180, Ⓦwww .cotswolds.com & Ⓦwww.cotswold.gov.uk). The Cirencester Civic Society runs **guided walks** in summer (May–Sept Sun 3pm, also June–Aug Wed 2.30pm; 1hr 30min; £2; Ⓦwww.ccsoc.org.uk), starting from the church in Market Place.

Accommodation

For a town with history, location and money on its side, Cirencester's **accommodation** is a touch disappointing: quality is acceptable, but the range is a bit limited. Book well ahead for the places below – or visit from a nearby base at, say, Tetbury (see p.236), Coln St Aldwyns (p.190) or the yurts of Abbey Home Farm (p.191).

Hotels

Corinium 12 Gloucester St ☎01285 659711, Ⓦwww.coriniumhotel.co.uk. Decent three-star family-run hotel on this attractive, narrow street a short walk northwest of the centre. Only fifteen rooms, modestly priced and adequately furnished. ❹

Fleece Market Place ☎01285 658507, Ⓦwww .fleecehotel.co.uk. Rather uninspiring, business-minded three-star – overlook the minor deficiencies in favour of a cheery welcome, historic premises and a central location. ❹

B&Bs

107 Gloucester Street 107 Gloucester St ☎01285 657861, Ⓦwww.107gloucesterstreet .co.uk. Choice B&B in a Georgian house on this narrow street less than 10min walk northwest of the Market Place. Only one double and one twin, tastefully furnished, with a cosy lounge and a friendly welcome. No cards. ❸

Ivy House 2 Victoria Rd ☎01285 656626, Ⓦwww.ivyhousecotswolds.com. Of a string of B&Bs along Victoria Road, this is one of the more attractive options, a high-gabled Victorian house with four en-suite guest rooms, modestly done up. ❸

No. 12 12 Park St ☎01285 640232, Ⓦwww .no12cirencester.co.uk. A stolid Georgian townhouse virtually opposite the museum hides this swanky, very nicely presented B&B-cum-boutique pad. Four rooms, with tasteful, muted colours set off by silks and velvets, have luxury pretensions: a free-standing claw-foot bath here, an antique leather sleigh bed there. ❹

Campsite

Mayfield Park Cheltenham Rd ☎01285 831301, Ⓦwww.mayfieldpark.co.uk. Well-equipped site on the A435 near Perrotts Brook, a couple of miles north of town.

The Town

Cirencester's heart is the delightful, swirling **Market Place**, busy with traffic and commerce, and packed with traders' stalls for the Monday and Friday markets (and the fortnightly Saturday farmers' market; see p.173). An irregular line of eighteenth-century facades along the north side contrasts with the heavier Victorian structures opposite, but the parish church of **St John the Baptist** (daily 10am–5pm; Oct–March closes 4pm; free; ⓦ www.cirenparish.co.uk), built in stages during the fifteenth century, dominates. The flying buttresses that support the tower had to be added when it transpired that the church had been constructed over the filled-in Roman ditch that ran beside Ermin Street, the Gloucester–Silchester road, which passed this way. Its grand three-tiered south **porch**, the largest in England and big enough to function at one time as the town hall, leads to the nave, where slender piers and soaring arches create a superb sense of space, enhanced by clerestory windows that admit a warm light. The church contains much of interest, including a colourful wineglass **pulpit**, carved in stone around 1450 and one of the few pre-Reformation pulpits to have survived in Britain. Set into a display case nearby is the **Boleyn Cup**, a gilded silver goblet made in 1535 for Anne Boleyn. To the left of the chancel, superb fan vaulting hangs overhead in the **chapel of St Catherine**, who appears in a vivid fragment of a fifteenth-century wall painting. You can also climb the **tower** (May–Sept Sat 10am–4pm). Outside, one of the best views of the church is from the **Abbey Grounds**, site of the Saxon abbey demolished in 1539 during the Dissolution, and now a small park skirted by the small River Churn and a fragment of the Roman city wall.

From the Market Place, walk down Black Jack Street to access Cirencester's most handsome quarter, centred on Park, Thomas and Coxwell streets – all of them narrow and lined by stone houses dating mostly from the seventeenth and eighteenth centuries. One of those on Park Street houses the sleek, state-of-the-art **Corinium Museum** (Mon–Sat 10am–5pm, Sun 2–5pm; Nov–March closes 4pm; £4.50; ⓦ www.cotswold.gov.uk), offering the chance for an absorbing couple of hours taking in the town's Celtic, Roman and Saxon heritage. Mosaics abound, including large, floor-sized pavements, there's a trove of Bronze Age gold, an excellent video on Cotswold life in the Iron Age, a reconstruction of a Romano-British garden, and more. Less ancient items include a hoard of silver and gold coins totalling a dizzy £18 that was buried in a lead pipe during the Civil War and unearthed in 1981.

Outside the museum on the right, a yew hedge the height of telegraph poles along Park Street conceals **Cirencester House**, the Earl of Bathurst's residence. At no point can you actually see the building (it's rather plain anyway), but you can stroll the attached three-thousand-acre **park** (daily 8am–5pm; ⓦ www.cirencesterpark.co.uk): head along Park Street and turn left onto **Cecily Hill**, a lovely street which culminates in an eccentric-looking castle – actually a Victorian barracks – beside the park gates at the top end. The park's **polo** grounds (spectators £5; ⓦ www.cirencesterpolo.co.uk) attract some of the country's top players, with games held virtually every afternoon between May and September.

Just south of the Market Place off shop-lined Cricklade Street, the **New Brewery Arts** centre (Mon–Sat 9am–5pm, Sun 10am–4pm; free; ⓦ www.newbreweryarts.org.uk) has more than a dozen resident artists, whose studios you can visit and whose work you can buy.

Eating and drinking

Cirencester has a welter of noteworthy **restaurants** and plenty of **pubs**, the latter aided by the presence on the town's outskirts of the Royal Agricultural College (ⓦ www.rac.ac.uk). Rob Rees, an award-winning chef and local food entrepreneur who goes by the title "The Cotswold Chef" (ⓦ www.thecotswoldchef.com), runs a Food Centre on the college grounds, offering short cookery courses and weekend events; see his website for details. Then there's **Cirencester Cupcakes** on Swan Yard (closed Sun & Mon; ⓦ www.cirencestercupcakes.co.uk), just behind the Market Place, offering artisan-baked goodies fresh from the oven – and the **Chesterton Farm shop** (closed Sun; ☎01285 653003, ⓦwww.chestertonfarm.co.uk) on the town's southern outskirts off Cranhams Lane.

Harry Hare's 3 Gosditch St ☎01285 652375, ⓦwww.harryhares.co.uk. Landmark town-centre restaurant gazing across at the church, just round the corner from the Market Place. Occupying a splendid old building – its neo-Gothic facade concealing what was a thirteenth-century tithe barn, added to in the fifteenth century, still with some original timbers over Roman column bases – this is a classic dining venue for Cirencester's monied set. Choose from the à la carte menu – risotto, Caesar salad, steak, sea bass and so forth (most mains £12–16) – or the lighter brasserie menu (lunch only; two courses £12), both of which change regularly. Alternatively, just drop by for coffee; it's a classy, pleasant experience either way.

Indian Rasoi 14 Dollar St ☎01285 644822, ⓦwww.indianrasoi.org. An up-to-date, contemporary styled restaurant serving probably the best curry in Cirencester (which is not such faint praise as you might imagine). Go for the classic dishes, and especially the mouthwatering choice of lamb curries.

Jack's 44 Black Jack St ☎01285 640888. Attractive little independent daytime café in an old building (and covered alleyway) beside the Corinium Museum – salads, soups, cakes and big cups of coffee. Cash only.

Jesse's Bistro The Stableyard, 14 Black Jack St ☎01285 641497, ⓦwww.jessesbistro.co.uk. Wonderful little hideaway, in a courtyard off the street between the museum and the main square. The speciality here is fish and seafood – as you walk in, you'll get a whiff of the fish counter beside the door, freshly caught beasties whisked over direct from the Cornish coast. The menu changes daily; expect crab salad or *moules marinière*, oven-roasted mackerel or pepper-crusted bream alongside meaty favourites such as rump steak or calves' liver – hearty food, expertly prepared and served with smooth informality. Mains are roughly £11–14. Closed Sun all day & Mon eve.

Made By Bob The Corn Hall, 26 Market Place ☎01285 641818, ⓦwww.foodmadebybob.com. Striking, buzzy daytime café-restaurant just off the main square – very hip, serving outstanding food and snacks in a smart yet casual ambience. Opens for breakfast (Bircher muesli, kippers, eggs benedict, all the way up to a full English), and stays open after lunch for posh afternoon tea. The kitchen is placed centrally: watch the chefs prepare anything from fish soup with gruyère or red pepper tart to grilled squid or ribeye steak, from a daily changing menu (mains £8–17) – or just drop by to the deli section for swanky sandwiches (£4–5), olives, fresh-baked bread and the like. Mon–Sat 7.30am–6.30pm.

New Brewery Arts Café Brewery Court, off Cricklade St ☎01285 657181, ⓦwww.newbreweryarts.org.uk. Pleasant daytime café in this buzzing arts centre – good for a coffee or a light lunch, with some delicious veggie options.

Soushi 12 Castle St ☎01285 641414, ⓦwww.soushi.co.uk. Modest little Japanese restaurant, opened in 2009 and already with a reputation for excellence. As well as sushi platters and bento boxes for lunch, there's a full evening menu of sushi and sashimi, alongside specialities such as chicken skewers, sweet ginger tofu, slow-cooked pork belly, tempura, and more – all very fresh, and authentically prepared by the Japanese chef. Mains £11–17. It's a small place, hidden away down a side-alley: expect good food, rather than lavish atmosphere. Closed Sun & Mon, and Tues eve.

Tatyan's 27 Castle St ☎01285 653529, ⓦwww.tatyans.com. A Chinese restaurant that's something of a legend in these parts, drawing diners from far and wide to sample the acclaimed combination of authentic Chinese food, an unusually enticing list of French wines and a cheerful, relaxed ambience. The menu takes in a host of favourites, with a special emphasis on fish – not many Chinese restaurants feature Cornish lobster baked whole with ginger and spring onions (£28). Most mains £8–16, with set menus from £25 a head. Closed Sun.

Listings

Hospital See p.36.

Markets General market on Market Place (Mon & Fri 9am–3pm; ⓦwww.cirencester.co.uk). For farmers markets, see box, p.173.

Police station The Forum ☎0845 090 1234.

Post office Castle St.

Taxis Local firms include 2&Fro (☎01285 640088, ⓦwww.cirencestertaxis.co.uk) and Home James (☎01285 641339, ⓦwww.homejamestaxi.co.uk).

Around Cirencester

The countryside **around Cirencester** holds plenty of interest. To the north are gardens and an award-winning pub in **North Cerney**, while country lanes lead to a remarkable Saxon church in the **Duntisbournes**. To the west and southwest you could explore nooks and crannies around the source of the **Thames**. South of Cirencester the **Cotswold Water Park** offers family-friendly activities galore. To the east lies **Fairford**, a worthwhile stop on the way towards beautiful Kelmscott Manor. Northeast of Cirencester, scenic Bibury (see p.189) is an easy drive on the road to Burford, while the A429 Fosse Way makes a straight ten-mile run to Northleach (p.187).

North Cerney

If you want to move on quickly to Gloucester or Cheltenham, take the speedy A417 dual carriageway (though expect traffic at the bottleneck around Birdlip). The slower A435 is, however, a more pleasant drive, passing first through **NORTH CERNEY**, home of acclaimed goat's cheese producer Cerney Cheese (no public access; Ⓦwww.cerneycheese.com) and the adjacent **Cerney Gardens** (late Jan to end July Tues, Wed, Fri & Sun 10am–5pm; £4; Ⓦwww.cerneygardens.com). Also in the village is the award-winning *Bathurst Arms* (☎01285 831281, Ⓦwww.bathurstarms.com), a traditional old inn – log fires, wooden beams – updated to high standards in drinking, dining and lodging. Much of the food is sourced from Gloucestershire farms, from Cerney goat's cheese starters to Old Spot pork, Churn Valley venison and Cotswold lamb (mains £12–17), while the eight well-presented rooms (❸–❹) are a bargain. Note that the pub is closed on weekday afternoons in winter (Nov–March Mon–Fri 3–6pm).

Beyond North Cerney, the A435 continues up the valley of the River Churn to Seven Springs, passing near **Cowley Manor** (see p.219) on the way.

The Duntisbournes

Northwest of Cirencester, the hills start to rear up on the approach to Stroud, forming a folded landscape of high tops and deep, damp valleys. Minor roads off the A417 first reach **DAGLINGWORTH** – about a picturesque and unvisited a Cotswold village as you could dream up – before penetrating the narrow valley of the **Duntisbournes**. This succession of tiny communities – barely even hamlets, most of them – includes **MIDDLE DUNTISBOURNE** and **DUNTISBOURNE LEER** before culminating in **DUNTISBOURNE ABBOTS**, with a Norman church overlaid by Victorian restoration and *Five Mile House* (☎01285 821432, Ⓦwww.fivemilehouse.co.uk), an old inn updated inside to a rather classy gastropub. The walk from Cirencester is lovely, roughly five miles altogether.

Before you get there, though, look out for a carved wooden finger-post on the single-track road between Daglingworth and Middle Duntisbourne. This marks the otherwise indiscernible location of **DUNTISBOURNE ROUSE**, neither a village nor a hamlet, but effectively just a church – and a real beauty. Dedicated to St Michael, this tiny country church of Saxon origin stands alone on grassy slopes beside a wood, reached via a lychgate by the roadside. The chancel is Norman, the tower and bells fifteenth-century (with the saddleback top added later), but the power of the place is its age – and its isolation.

Up the road past Duntisbourne Abbots in **WINSTONE**, *Winstone Glebe* (☎01285 821451, Ⓦwww.winstoneglebe.com; ❹) offers traditional B&B in a Georgian village rectory. Misarden Gardens (see p.230) lie across the valley to the west.

Thames Head and around

Southwest of Cirencester, three roads diverge. First the A419 departs west towards Stroud, splitting from the southwest-bound A429, which follows the line of the Fosse Way for a mile or so before itself dividing. The A433 picks up the Roman road towards Tetbury (though it shortly afterwards abandons the ancient route, which reverts to a lonesome track marking the Wiltshire-Gloucestershire border), while the A429 branches south towards Malmesbury, passing first through **KEMBLE**, a mundane little village which happens to have one of the Cotswolds' few main-line **railway stations**, with services to Swindon, Reading and London in one direction, and Stroud, Gloucester and Cheltenham in the other. See p.192 for bus and taxi options to and from here.

There are three main reasons to come this way. Kemble is surrounded by water meadows that are traditionally regarded as the **source of the River Thames**. The congenial *Thames Head Inn* (☎01285 770259, ⓦwww.thamesheadinn.co.uk), on the A433 just by the railway bridge, has made a good living out of folk seeking the river's origins. Bar staff (and a big sketch-map hanging in the pub's porch) can point you onto the short walk of about fifteen minutes from the pub to **THAMES HEAD**, a point by a copse in open fields, where a stone marker declares a shallow depression to be the river's source. However, if you're keen to see flowing water, check at the pub beforehand: Thames Head, confusingly, is often dry (see the box below for more).

Attraction number two is in **EWEN**, about a mile east of Kemble. Here stands the *Wild Duck Inn* (☎01285 770310, ⓦwww.thewildduckinn.co.uk; ⑤), an ivy-clad stone building dating from 1563, set in its own gardens and offering a relaxed take on contemporary country style in both the twelve guest rooms – sleek and individually designed – and the restaurant. Expect warm service and excellent modern British cuisine (most mains £11–17), accompanied by an impressive wine list.

But if that feels a touch too fancy, head out onto the wild back lanes between **COATES** and **TARLTON** villages, off the A433. Signs will lead you to the ⚓ *Tunnel House Inn* (☎01285 770280, ⓦwww.tunnelhouse.com), reachable by car only along a narrow, rutted track which climbs beside the now-defunct Thames & Severn Canal to the grand Georgian "East Portal". This is the point where the canal enters the Sapperton Tunnel – once the longest canal tunnel in Britain – on its way to Sapperton (see p.234) and Stroud. The pub, which stands directly above

---

Head of the river

When you reach **Thames Head** (see above), don't be disappointed if there's no water in sight. The River Thames is fed by groundwater, and the water table rises and falls throughout the year; the Environment Agency continuously tracks the river's source, which shifts along a line of several miles of boggy ground between Thames Head and Ashton Keynes, southeast near Cricklade.

To cast further aspersions, this bit of the river is shorter than the River Churn, which rises at Seven Springs on the Cotswold Edge and flows south through Cirencester to join the Thames near Cricklade. Because Seven Springs flows year-round, and because the distance from Seven Springs to the confluence is over 12 miles longer than from Thames Head to the confluence, many say that the stream rising at Thames Head is, in fact, insignificant and the true Thames rises at Seven Springs. By this reasoning, the Churn should in fact be regarded as the Thames.

But logic is no match for tradition. Thames Head remains the focus of attention – indeed, the marked **Thames Path** (ⓦwww.nationaltrail.co.uk) starts here: walk it direct to the Thames Barrier at Greenwich in southeast London, 184 miles away.

Cotswold Airport

What was once RAF Kemble, an airfield located off the A433 four miles southwest of Cirencester – home for many years to the famous Red Arrows aerobatic display team – has now become **Cotswold Airport** (☏01285 771177, ⓦwww.cotswoldairport .com). It has no scheduled flights and is used only by private jets, but there are occasional public events and air shows. Hangar E2 houses the **Bristol Aero Collection** (Mon 10am–3.30pm; Easter–Oct also Sun same times; £5; ⓦwww.bristolaero .com), a display of civilian and military aircraft, missiles and a mock-up of the Giotto spacecraft, designed to showcase the history of aerospace manufacture at Filton, not far away near Bristol. The intention is eventually to move the collection to Filton, where a Concorde is ready to become the centrepiece of a new air museum.

the portal, feels like a haven, with its vintage memorabilia, fireside sofas, bookshelves and stuffed owl. Nonetheless, and despite the location, it can get busy, with locals and visitors alike arriving for a country pint or a decent pub meal (mains £9–15), or for the basic **camping** available onsite. Stagecoach **bus** 881 (not Sun) stops a short walk away about every two hours on a route between Cirencester, Kemble station, Tarlton and Tetbury.

Two **long-distance paths** pass the *Tunnel House*: the Cirencester–Tetbury stage of the Monarch's Way, and the Macmillan Way (see p.32) en route to Sapperton, but casual walkers could otherwise opt for a post-prandial ramble around the pub on woodland paths above the silted-up canal. The **Cotswold Canals Partnership** (ⓦwww.cotswoldcanalsproject.org) has the long-term goal of reopening this once-thriving link between the Severn and the Thames, but it's long, slow work: they are currently dredging and rebuilding in order to reconnect Stroud to the national waterways network. Reopening the full route to Lechlade is a distant dream.

Cotswold Water Park

Covering an area of forty square miles straddling the Gloucestershire–Wiltshire border, the **Cotswold Water Park** (ⓦwww.waterpark.org) takes in no fewer than 147 lakes. Created over several decades by sand and gravel extraction, the lakes vary widely in size, beauty and accessibility. Some are owned by individuals or clubs, many are given over to second-home developments, but plenty are protected as Sites of Special Scientific Interest: 20,000 waterfowl overwinter here, fourteen of the UK's seventeen species of bat are resident, beavers are monitored as part of a reintroduction project, there are 23 species of dragonfly to find, and so on. Leisure is also big: private operators on several of the lakes offer activities from angling to waterskiing.

Your first port of call should be the **Gateway Centre** (daily 9am–5pm; ☏01793 752413), located beside the B4696 "Spine Road", which is signed off the A419 about four miles southeast of Cirencester – they have full information on the park's facilities, including details of walks in the nature reserves dotted around the lakes, bike rental, kayaking, camping, and more.

Continue on the B4696 towards **SOMERFORD KEYNES** and you'll reach the water park's biggest draw, the **Cotswold Country Park and Beach** (daily 9am–9pm; hours curtailed to 7pm or 5pm in winter; June–Aug weekends £5, weekdays £4, dropping to £2 in winter; ⓦwww.cotswoldcountrypark.com). This cluster of adjacent lakes, set in 70 acres of grounds – which includes the UK's largest inland beach – has kids' activities galore, as well as some quieter corners.

From the Spine Road exit off the A419, if you turn north you'll come to the rather wonderful **Butts Farm Shop** (closed Sat pm, Sun & Mon; ☏01285 862224,

(W) www.thebuttsfarmshop.com). This working farm specializes in rare breeds, and the shop is crammed with home-cured bacon, exotic sausages and pâtés alongside more familiar local produce. The farm itself is also **open for visits** (Tues–Sun 10.30am–5pm; £5; phone to confirm opening (T) 01285 869414), where kids can bottle-feed lambs, milk goats, ride ponies and take a tractor safari.

The Ampneys and Poulton

East of Cirencester, the A417 makes short work of the thirteen miles to Lechlade. Past pretty **AMPNEY CRUCIS**, beside a turnoff to Ampney St Mary in what is termed **AMPNEY ST PETER** (though there are no signs), stands the small *Red Lion* ((T) 01285 851596), one of England's most noteworthy historic pubs. It hasn't been done up in decades but remains entirely free of the usual studied pub character – no horse-brasses or tankards hanging from the beams. This is just two plain rooms in a three-hundred-year old stone cottage – and, remarkably, there's no bar. Instead, the landlord perches on a stool in the corner, pulling pints from two handpumps and passing them over the back of a wooden bench to his customers, who sit together around one table by the fireplace. The other room has the same set-up: a bench around two walls, and one table by the fire. There's no food, and nowhere for loners to hide: the only option is to introduce yourself to the regulars. At the time of writing opening hours were very restricted (Fri & Sat 6–10pm, Sun 12–2pm).

There's a more mainstream pub down the road in **POULTON**, where the *Falcon* (closed Sun eve & Mon; (T) 01285 850878, (W) www.falconinnpoulton.co.uk) came under new management in 2010; expect upmarket dining in a relaxed, family-friendly setting.

From Poulton, back roads cut north for two or three miles to Barnsley (see p.191) and Bibury (p.189), and south the same distance to **DOWN AMPNEY**, birthplace of the composer Ralph Vaughan Williams, also with a strikingly beautiful thirteenth-century church.

Fairford

FAIRFORD, on the River Coln about six miles east of Cirencester, and just a couple of miles south of Coln St Aldwyns (see p.190), has a busy, narrow main road carrying the A417, but is still rather pretty, with a tight dog-leg bridge and ancient, silver-stoned cottages – some half-timbered – lining the street. Once you squeeze into the centre, the broad **Market Place** opens off the A417 (which is here named as London Road or London Street). It's a pleasant, short stroll up the Market Place, past the diminutive Coln Bookshop at 4 High Street, to reach Fairford's main attraction, the elegant **St Mary's Church** (daily 10am–5pm, Oct–March closes 4pm; (W) www.stmaryschurchfairford.org.uk). Built in the 1490s over ancient predecessors, this is a splendid example of Perpendicular Gothic, broad and lofty, constructed around an earlier tower – but it is famed for its unique array of late-medieval **stained glass**. Created in the first decade or so of the sixteenth century by Barnard Flower, glazier to the king (Henry VII), at his workshop in Westminster, the glass survives intact as a complete set of 28 windows. Guides in the church can explain the themes, which include episodes from the life of Christ and depictions of prophets and apostles – look out for Mary's parents apparently cuddling and kissing in the north aisle; St Apollonia, patron saint of dentists, holding forceps and a just-plucked tooth in the south aisle; and the great west window showing the Last Judgement (with, to the right, Cain killing Abel). The choir stalls hide a fine set of **misericords** dating to the early fourteenth century.

Practicalities

APL **bus** 877 (not Sun) runs five times a day to Fairford to/from Cirencester and Lechlade, and there's also Stagecoach bus 74 (not Sun) every couple of hours from Lechlade. Church aside, Fairford has gained recognition for its **food** – most notably the ♣ *Allium* **restaurant**, 1 London Street (closed Sun eve, Mon, & Tues lunch; ☎01285 712200, ⓦwww.alliumfood.co.uk). A squat, rather unprepossessing stone cottage at the foot of the Market Place has been transformed inside to a light, spacious and rather snazzy dining room. Book in advance for lunch or dinner: this is a hugely popular spot, drawing diners from as far afield as London and Cheltenham to sample accomplished, upmarket contemporary British cuisine, served in a relaxed atmosphere. Menus change regularly, focused on seasonal ingredients; choose from the main seasonal menu (two courses £37), a cheaper *table d'hôte* menu (available Wed–Fri lunch plus Wed & Thurs eve; two courses £23), a "pot luck" Tuesday evening menu that may include some new dishes (two courses £23) and pricier tasting menus and other options.

If that's a step too far, *The Bridge* (closed Sun & Mon; ☎01285 712032, ⓦwww.thebridgefairford.com) is a simpler option, with pizzas, pasta, risotto and Italian mains (£9–15), or there's the *7a Coffee Shop* (closed Sat & Sun; ☎01285 712918, ⓦwww.7acoffeeshop.co.uk). Either way, don't leave town without dropping into *Deli Allium* on the Market Place (closed Sun & Mon; ☎01285 711111, ⓦwww.alliumfood.co.uk) for local breads, cheeses and chutneys as well as olives, charcuterie, coffee and more.

Worthwhile **accommodation** within Fairford is limited: opt for the decent B&B *Hathaway* (☎01285 712715, ⓦwww.mini-webs.com/hathaway; ❷–❸). Beware crowds descending for the **Royal International Air Tattoo** (ⓦwww.airtattoo.com), held over a weekend in mid-July at RAF Fairford nearby.

Southrop

Northeast of Fairford, country lanes cross over into the valley of the River Leach for a culinary landmark at **SOUTHROP** (pronounced "sutherop") – the *Swan* (closed Sun eve; ☎01367 850205, ⓦwww.theswanatsouthrop.co.uk). A classic updating of an ivy-swathed seventeenth-century village inn into a landmark country restaurant, this place exudes charm. The bar – kitchen stools, white-painted stonework – is still a locals' retreat, while the restaurant showcases inventive, upmarket, but not overly fussy cooking, with plenty for carnivores to get their teeth into (including local Kelmscott pork) and a good choice of fish and veggie options. Mains are £11–18. Book well ahead. It's a short way from here east to the A361 at Filkins (see p.111), just south of Burford.

Ebley **bus** 866 (once on Mon & Thurs) and Pulham's bus 865 (once on Sat) follow a scenic tour to Southrop from Cirencester, round the countryside via Fossebridge, Coln Rogers, Bibury and Coln St Aldwyns. In addition, the Friday run on APL bus 861 from Cirencester will serve Southrop on request.

Lechlade

Four miles east of Fairford and eight miles south of Burford (p.108), **LECHLADE**, oddly, is a port town. This is the highest navigable stretch of the River Thames and, in the nineteenth-century heyday of the Thames & Severn Canal, Lechlade functioned as a transshipment point for cargo moving between the canal and the river. In truth, though, there's not much left, and the town now labours under the weight of road traffic on the east–west A417 and the north–south A361. They cross by the wedge-shaped **Market Place**, overlooked by the spire of the splendid fifteenth-century church of **St Lawrence** (ⓦwww.stlawrencelechlade.org.uk).

Roam the interior, with its Tudor east window, and then stroll the churchyard, as Shelley did in 1815: his poem *A Summer Evening Churchyard, Lechlade*, is commemorated by a carved stone at the entrance. See p.173 for details of the farmers' market held on the square.

The **Ha'penny Bridge** nearby carries the A361 over the Thames, overlooked by the pleasant *Riverside* pub at Park End Wharf (℡01367 252534, Ⓦwww.arkells .com & Ⓦwww.riverside-lechlade.co.uk), which also has self-drive boats for rent (℡01367 250013, Ⓦwww.cotswoldcruises.co.uk). From here you can follow the Thames Path for the short **walk** west to **INGLESHAM**, where the River Coln and the canal enter (there are plans afoot to restore the lock here – see Ⓦwww .cotswoldcanalsproject.org), or the slightly longer walk east to **St John's Lock**, near where the River Leach enters and marked by an 1854 **statue of Old Father Thames** by Raffaelle Monti which originally stood in London's Crystal Palace, then was moved to Thames Head (see p.197) before ending up here. Half-hour **cruises** run in summer (April–Sept Sat & Sun plus some weekdays 11am–5pm; £3; Ⓦwww.lechladetripboat.co.uk) from the Riverside Park on the south side of the bridge.

By St John's Lock, the *Trout Inn* (℡01367 252313, Ⓦwww.thetroutinn.com) is a busy riverside **pub**, with a programme of live jazz, blues and folk events and decent food (mains £11–16) – but otherwise, there's little to keep you from pressing on to the fascinating **Kelmscott Manor** a couple of miles east (see p.112) and/or the country pubs in and around **Clanfield** (p.107).

5

The west and south Cotswolds

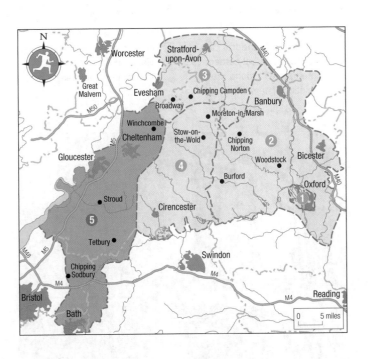

CHAPTER 5

Highlights

* **Winchcombe** Historic walkers' village: a great base for the area, with memorably down-to-earth charm. See p.208

* **Sudeley Castle** Stunning medieval castle, impeccable royal heritage, evocative formal gardens. See p.210

* **Cheltenham** Engaging spa town with an artistic bent. See p.213

* **Gloucester Cathedral** One of England's greatest cathedrals: come to stroll around the magical cloisters. See p.222

* **Painswick** Delightful village of charm and taste, set in hilly Cotswold scenery. See p.228

* **Tetbury** Top choice as a base for the south Cotswolds, offering good shopping, a fine church and great food. See p.236

* **Westonbirt Arboretum** Lose yourself in the natural splendour. See p.239

* **Castle Combe** Perfectly preserved old weavers' village on the Cotswolds' southernmost fringes. See p.244

▲ The Montpellier district, Cheltenham

5

The west and south Cotswolds

D efined by the great escarpment of the Cotswold Edge, which rolls from one end of this chapter to the other, the area we've dubbed the **WEST AND SOUTH COTSWOLDS** encompasses some of the region's most dramatic scenery. From almost any point atop the Edge, panoramic views gaze westwards – perhaps out over Tewkesbury towards the Malverns, or across the Severn Vale and Forest of Dean into Wales. The gently bucolic scenery of the central Cotswolds is here replaced by a tougher landscape, a tougher climate and a tougher history: the valleys around Stroud in particular experienced widespread industrialization during the eighteenth and nineteenth centuries, with hundreds of textile mills and ambitious canal projects.

The high, open wolds west of Stow reach the Cotswold Edge at **Winchcombe**, a small town with a long history that is now a prime base for independent-minded types keen to explore the great outdoors. Winchcombe has become one of the Cotswolds' great walking centres, with footpaths to suit all tastes and abilities enveloping the town – not least the **Cotswold Way**, which shadows the Edge from north to south. Within easy reach of Winchcombe are a magnificent castle at **Sudeley**, a ruined abbey at **Hailes** and the evocative prehistoric burial mound of **Belas Knap**, which squats atop **Cleeve Hill**, the Cotswolds' highest point.

Farmers' markets

- **Cheltenham** 2nd & last Fri of month 9am–3pm ⓦ www.cheltenham.gov.uk.
- **Chipping Sodbury** 2nd Sat & last Thurs of month 9am–1pm ⓦ www.sodburytc.co.uk.
- **Dursley** March–Dec 2nd Sat of month 8.30am–1pm ⓦ www.stroud.gov.uk.
- **Gloucester** Every Fri 9am–3pm ⓦ www.fresh-n-local.co.uk.
- **Malmesbury** 2nd & 4th Sat of month 9am–1pm ⓦ www.wiltshirefarmersmarkets .org.uk.
- **Nailsworth** 4th Sat of month 9am–1pm ⓦ www.stroud.gov.uk.
- **Stroud** Every Sat 9am–2pm ⓦ www.fresh-n-local.co.uk.
- **Winchcombe** 3rd Sat of month 9am–1pm ⓦ www.tewkesburybc.gov.uk.

Dates may change around Christmas and New Year. See also ⓦ www.farmers markets.net – and take a look at ⓦ www.gloucestershirefarmshops.co.uk.

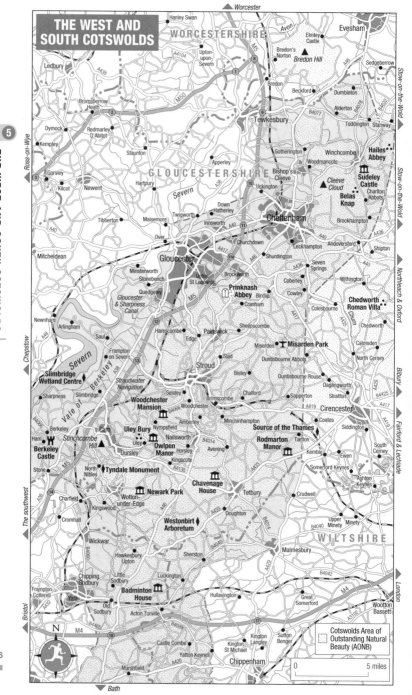

THE WEST AND
SOUTH COTSWOLDS

WORCESTERSHIRE

GLOUCESTERSHIRE

WILTSHIRE

Cotswolds Area of
Outstanding Natural
Beauty (AONB)

0   5 miles

N

Down below, flanking the M5 motorway and serving as a focus for road and rail, are **Cheltenham**, famed for its horse-racing and its Regency architecture, and **Gloucester**, dominated by its breathtaking medieval **cathedral**. Villages along the Severn near Gloucester offer diversions – notably the **Slimbridge** wetland reserve and a fairytale castle at **Berkeley** – or otherwise you could head up again into the nearby hills for some of the loveliest of the Cotswolds' hideaways. **Painswick** is a popular draw, though nearby villages such as **Sheepscombe** and **Slad** remain quiet, despite the latter's literary associations as the home of *Cider with Rosie* author Laurie Lee.

Unsentimental **Stroud** lies at a conjunction of valleys, with near-Alpine landscapes dominating the view: climb to the high commons at **Minchinhampton** to blow the cobwebs away, or aim for scenic drives around **Nailsworth** or along the towering Cotswold Edge near **Uley**, site of more prehistoric burial mounds. **Tetbury**, over towards the Wiltshire border, is another perfect anchorpoint, with a range of high-quality hotels, some outstanding restaurants and attractions nearby which include nature walks within the extraordinary **Westonbirt Arboretum**.

The character of the southernmost tip of the Cotswolds, beyond the likes of Westonbirt and down-to-earth **Wotton-under-Edge**, is markedly different from that further north. Landscapes are flatter, grasses coarser, stonework greyer. Stop in at the market town of **Chipping Sodbury**, or brave the promenading crowds within the photogenic one-street village of **Castle Combe** – but, in truth, by the time you reach the M4, the best of the Cotswolds lies behind you.

The B4632 to Cheltenham

The **B4632** approaching Cheltenham takes in some of the Cotswolds' hilliest terrain. The road starts life in Stratford-upon-Avon (see p.136) before scooting southwest past Mickleton (p.161) and bypassing Broadway (p.161) on a scenic zigzag south beneath the Cotswold Edge. It meets the B4077, coming west from Stow-on-the-Wold (p.180), at a roundabout just outside Stanway (p.167).

Near the roundabout, a section of the old Cheltenham–Stratford rail line which runs this way is now restored as the **Gloucestershire Warwickshire Steam Railway**, covered on p.168. A turning shortly afterwards trundles southeast a mile or two to the remains of the grand Cistercian **Hailes Abbey**, huddled into a fold in the hills. The main draw hereabouts is the rather lovely historic town of **Winchcombe**, now a centre for walkers, which abuts the estate of **Sudeley Castle**, last resting place of Henry VIII's sixth wife and still replete with historic character. Nearby rises **Cleeve Hill**, the highest summit in the Cotswolds, on the fringes of Cheltenham.

Hailes Abbey and around

Hailes Abbey (daily: July & Aug 10am–6pm; April–June & Sept 10am–5pm; Oct 10am–4pm; £4; ⓦ www.nationaltrust.org.uk & ⓦ www.english-heritage .org.uk), signposted just off the B4632 a couple of miles north of Winchcombe, was once one of England's great Cistercian monasteries, founded in the 1240s. Pilgrims came from all over the country to pray before the abbey's phial of Christ's blood – that is until 1538, when, during the Dissolution, the relic was discredited as "honey coloured with saffron". The abbot was forced to surrender the abbey to Henry VIII's commissioners the following year, and shortly thereafter the buildings were demolished.

What survives is chiefly an assortment of foundations, but some cloister arches remain, worn by wind and rain. The grassy ruins may lack drama, but Hailes is still worth visiting for its onsite **museum**, where you can examine thirteenth-century bosses at close quarters, and for **Hailes Church**, just across the road, which is older than the abbey and contains beautiful wall paintings dating from around 1300. Its cartoon-like hunting scene was probably a warning to Sabbath-breakers.

For a touch more atmosphere, follow an old track southeast up the steep hill overlooking the abbey for a mile or so to **FARMCOTE** village, where the tiny **St Faith's church** once hosted pilgrims on their way to or from Hailes, and **Farmcote Herbs** (May–Nov Sat, Sun, Tues & Wed 10.30am–6pm; Oct & Nov closes 4.30pm; Ⓦwww.farmcoteherbs.co.uk) sells herbs, chilli pepper plants and chutneys. Return to the abbey, or continue a couple of miles further across the high wolds to reach the welcoming *Plough Inn* at Ford (see p.184).

On the way – and before you get stuck into the serious climb – you'll pass the **Hayles Fruit Farm** (Ⓣ01242 602123, Ⓦwww.hayles-fruit-farm.co.uk). Located just past the abbey, this working farm is famed chiefly for its apples and pears – and its legendary Badger's Bottom cider, a mainstay at farmers' markets across the Cotswolds. Stop in at the well-stocked **farm shop and tearoom** (daily 9am–5pm), tackle their family-friendly **nature trail** or stay overnight: a year-round **campsite** takes tents and caravans. Farm staff maintain doggedly that their spelling (with a Y) is original, and that it was a meddling bureaucrat in 1936, when English Heritage took over responsibility for the abbey, who decided that Hailes (with an I) looked more decorous. There may be truth in this: railway records show that, as late as 1928, a newly opened station nearby was named for "Hayles Abbey". Then again, medieval spelling was so hit-and-miss it's doubtful the odd vowel made much difference either way.

Winchcombe

About eight miles southwest of Broadway – and nine miles northeast of Cheltenham – **WINCHCOMBE** has a long main street flanked by a fetching medley of limestone and half-timbered buildings, the former pure Cotswolds, the latter more typical of Evesham (which we cover on p.169). It's an unprettified working town which nonetheless holds itself with considerable grace, rooted in an unusually long history and offering engaging attractions to complement beautiful surroundings – notably magnificent **Sudeley Castle** on the outskirts and some fine **walks**. It makes a perfect base to explore this corner of the Cotswolds, within easy reach of Broadway (see p.161), Stow (p.180) and Cheltenham (p.213), but far removed from all of them in pace and outlook.

Arrival, information and accommodation

No buses run on Sundays. Aside from irregular local services, Castleways **bus** 606 (not Sun) serves Winchcombe several times a day on a route to/from Broadway, Stanton and Cheltenham, and Castleways bus 559 (not Sun) stops in once a day to/from Broadway and Evesham. Beside the museum on the High Street, Winchcombe's **tourist office** (April–Oct Mon–Sat 10am–1pm & 2–5pm, Sun 10am–4pm; rest of year Sat & Sun 10am–4pm; Ⓣ01242 602925, Ⓦwww.cotswolds.com & Ⓦwww.winchcombe.co.uk) has plenty of information and maps. With access to the Cotswold Way as well as a host of lesser walks round and about, Winchcombe has set itself up as the **walking** capital of the Cotswolds: the box opposite has some ideas for local walks. Even aside from the beautiful setting, Winchcombe's **accommodation** is a bargain. You can **camp** nearby at Hailes (see above).

In town

Gower House 16 North St ☎01242 602616. Of Winchcombe's many B&Bs, this is a good option, with three comfortable rooms – two en suite – in an attractively modernized seventeenth-century house in the town centre. No credit cards. ❷

Wesley House High St ☎01242 602366, ⓦwww.wesleyhouse.co.uk. Rather classy small hotel wedged into a house where eighteenth-century preacher John Wesley stopped over, featuring five upscale rooms, individually decorated and immaculately presented. ❹

White Hart High St ☎01242 602359, ⓦwww.whitehartwinchcombe.co.uk. A good-looking old inn on the main street with wooden floors and benches to suit its cheerful atmosphere. Eight en-suite rooms are decorated in traditional-meets-folksy manner, and there are also three cheaper "ramblers" rooms with shared bath. ❷–❹

Out of town

Westward at Sudeley Lodge Sudeley ☎01242 604372, ⓦwww.westward-sudeley.co.uk. Splendid family-run B&B in the hunting lodge of Sudeley Castle, built in 1730 and now at the heart of a working farm a mile or so outside Winchcombe. Three rooms, decorated in traditional style, are complemented by a warm welcome, great setting and epic breakfasts. ❹

The Town

With the proximity of the **Stone Age** burial mound Belas Knap (see p.212) and the **Iron Age** hill forts on Cleeve Hill (p.212), the area around Winchcombe was of considerable importance long before the **Romans**. By the eighth century, Winchcombe was capital of the kingdom of **Mercia**, and its **abbey**, centred on the shrine of **St Kenelm**, a ninth-century boy-martyr, long predated Hailes Abbey down the road. **Winchcombeshire** even survived as a full fledged English county for a few years in the eleventh century, before being subsumed into Gloucestershire. Until the Dissolution, when Winchcombe Abbey was completely destroyed, the constant flow of pilgrims helped support the town, which also flourished during the medieval wool boom. One of the grand results was **St Peter's**, Winchcombe's main church, a mainly fifteenth-century structure distinguished by forty alarming gargoyles that ring the exterior. Inside, aside from a bold Jewish Star of David adorning the original painted cover of the seventeenth-century **font** – evidence, it seems, of newfound Protestant zeal to return to the fundamental roots

Walks around Winchcombe

Take a look at the Ordnance Survey Explorer map covering the Cotswolds and you'll find Winchcombe hunched like a spider amid a web of **walking paths** reaching out on all sides. Aside from the **Cotswold Way** – on which we describe a circular route to Belas Knap on p.212 – there's the **Windrush Way** and **Warden's Way** (details on p.185), both connecting Winchcombe to Bourton-on-the-Water; the **Gloucestershire Way** to Stow or Tewkesbury; and two long-distance routes heading north into Worcestershire, the 42-mile **Wychavon Way** and 60-mile **St Kenelm's Way**.

The dedicated walking website ⓦwww.winchcombewelcomeswalkers.com has full information. There you can download details of a circular walk (2 miles; 1hr) from Winchcombe to Sudeley Castle (see p.210) as well as a scenic loop (5 miles; 3hr) through Spoonley Wood, two miles southeast of town. It starts in the same place as the Cotswold Way walk, by the war memorial on Abbey Terrace, opposite Winchcombe's church, but shortly after peels left to cross the grounds of Sudeley Castle and follow the contour of the hill to **Spoonley Wood**, site of a ruined Roman villa with a beautifully preserved **mosaic** *in situ*. From there, strike uphill to a farm track, which you can follow southwest, turning right at Cole's Hill towards abandoned Waterhatch Farm. The path then drops gently down to river level and wends its way back to Winchcombe.

Many other options exist for short, circular walks around town, including a pleasant countryside circuit outlined at ⓦwww.winchcombe.co.uk.

of Christianity – the church's most striking feature is its broad chancel and Victorian east window: the medieval wooden screen which formerly stood in front was removed to the west end of the church in the 1980s, giving the interior unusual airiness.

Otherwise, the best of Winchcombe is sampled wandering the **High Street** and the few streets around. **Castle Street** dips down to cross the trickling River Isbourne – claimed to be the only river in England to flow north for its entire length – on the short stroll to **Sudeley Castle** (see below). The corner with North Street is marked by the Victorian town hall, within which resides the **Winch-combe Folk and Police Museum** (April–Oct Mon–Sat 10am–12.30pm & 2–4.30pm; £1.50; Ⓦ www.winchcombemuseum.org.uk), displaying historical bits and bobs as well as a collection of police memorabilia. The old stocks outside have seven holes, purportedly to enable an infamous one-legged scoundrel of old to get his come-uppance here alongside three pals.

A mile north of the centre, just off the B4632 Broadway road beside **GREET** village, you'll find Winchcombe's station on the preserved Gloucestershire Warwickshire Steam Railway (see box, p.168) right by **Winchcombe Pottery** (Mon–Fri 9am–5pm, Sat 10am–4pm; May–Sept also Sun noon–4pm; Ⓦ www .winchcombepottery.co.uk), a craft enterprise that has been going here since 1926.

Eating and drinking

The 🍴 *White Hart* (see "Accommodation" p.209) doubles up as the best place to **eat**. Its speciality is hearty British cooking, with a focus on sausages in gourmet varieties such as venison and red wine or pork and stilton. Dine in the restaurant (mains £9–16) or at the bar (from £5). *Wesley House*, too, has a traditional restaurant – lamb, pan-roasted halibut, roast guinea fowl and the like (two courses £20) – and a more contemporary styled grill (closed Mon), for ravioli, fishcakes and steak and chips (mains £9–16). Otherwise, pop into *Juri's Tea Room* (closed Mon–Wed; Ⓣ 01242 602469, Ⓦ www.juris-tearoom.co.uk), a daytime **café** serving award-winning cream teas, or slope off for a quiet pint at the old *Plaisterers Arms* (Ⓣ 01242 602358) **pub** near the church. If you're stocking up for a picnic, try the cheery local **deli** Food Fanatics, 11 North Street (Ⓣ 01242 604466, Ⓦ www.food -fanatics.co.uk).

Sudeley Castle

Rising amid a magnificent estate on Winchcombe's southern edge, and surrounded by immaculate gardens, **Sudeley Castle** (April–Oct daily 10.30am–5pm; £7.20; Ⓦ www.sudeleycastle.co.uk) manages to combine ravishing good looks with a long and fascinating history. The Cotswolds may have more than its fair share of stately homes and grand country piles – but this is a genuine beauty. Spare Sudeley an afternoon, at least.

Some history

Sudeley's royal history stretches back before **Domesday**: a Saxon manor house here was **Ethelred the Unready**'s wedding present to his daughter, Goda. The house or castle on the Sudeley site was destroyed during the reign of **Stephen**, though the family lived on: legend has it that **William de Sudeley**, son of the local lord in the early thirteenth century, was one of the four knights who murdered Thomas Becket at Canterbury. The present buildings date chiefly from the mid-fifteenth century, when **Ralph Boteler**, a senior military commander under Henry V and Henry VI, was created the **1st Baron Sudeley** and set about building a castle to befit his status. He nonetheless had precious little time to enjoy what became known as one of the finest properties in England: in 1469, during the Wars of the Roses, the new king **Edward IV** confiscated Sudeley. Boteler never saw it again. **Richard III** was the owner-resident for several years, and in 1535 **Henry VIII** spent a week at Sudeley with Anne Boleyn.

Sudeley's golden age centres on a few years in the 1540s. After Henry VIII died in 1547, **Edward VI** gave the castle to **Sir Thomas Seymour**, brother of Henry's third wife, Jane – and a legendary womanizer. His affair with **Katherine** (or **Catherine**) **Parr**, Henry's sixth and final wife, began as early as 1543; within six months of Henry's death, Seymour and Parr were married. Shortly thereafter they moved into Sudeley with a household numbering more than a hundred, including **Lady Jane Grey**, who was living under Seymour's protection, and Elizabeth Tudor, daughter of Henry VIII by Anne Boleyn. The calm was shortlived: Parr died at Sudeley in 1548 after giving birth to a daughter, Mary (whose subsequent life is a mystery – most historians believe she died young), and the political tide quickly turned against Seymour, who was executed for treason in 1549.

Sudeley remained in the spotlight. **Elizabeth I** stayed for three days in 1592, and during the **Civil War** Sudeley acted as a Royalist garrison, coming under repeated attack and eventually suffering near-demolition. The remains mouldered grandly, attracting the attention of **George III**, who fell down a crumbling flight of stairs on a visit in 1788. Katherine Parr's coffin was rediscovered amid the ruins in 1782, though it wasn't until more than fifty years later that **John and William Dent**, industrialists from Worcester, purchased the derelict estate and began what was, for the time, surprisingly sensitive restoration of the surviving Elizabethan shell. **Emma Dent**, a niece, continued their work, collecting antiques and Tudor furnishings for the castle and engaging in good works for the townsfolk of Winchcombe, which included funding new roads and a public swimming bath. The current owner, **Elizabeth Ashcombe**, wife of the 4th Baron Ashcombe, has lavished energy particularly on the castle **gardens**, which today have become as much of a draw as the castle itself.

Visiting the castle and grounds

From the **visitor centre**, paths lead on circuitous routes through the grounds, past a ruined medieval **tithe barn**, wildflower meadow and herb garden on the approach to the battlemented castle, its tall chimneys rising romantically above the trees. You **enter** via the original fifteenth-century west wing, where a series of rooms are given over to **historical exhibits**, from a collection of replica Tudor

Day-trips by bus from Winchcombe

It's fairly straightforward to put together enticing day-trips into the Cotswolds countryside around Winchcombe by **bus** – though not on a Sunday, when none of these routes operate. From Winchcombe, Castleways bus 606 goes to Broadway (p.161) for a couple of hours' break mid-morning, after which Johnsons bus 21 can take you to Blockley (p.179), Batsford Arboretum (p.177) or Moreton-in-Marsh (p.175) in one direction, or Chipping Campden (p.154) or Stratford-upon-Avon (p.136) in the other. The return journey retraces your steps, though check timetables carefully: on Saturdays, for instance, the Campden/Stratford route doesn't work. As an alternative from Winchcombe, take a morning service on Castleways bus 606 to Cheltenham, from where you can catch Stagecoach bus 46 for an hour or so in Painswick (p.228); bus 46 proceeds to Stroud (p.231), where you switch to Cotswold Green bus 28 to give you a couple of hours in Cirencester (p.191), from where Stagecoach bus 151 heads to Cheltenham in good time for the last Castleways bus 606 back to Winchcombe.

costumes and original lacework to stories of Henry VIII and a lock of Katherine Parr's hair. Drop into the adjacent **coffee shop**, housed in what was formerly the castle kitchens and now bedecked with heraldic banners – but the main reason to visit Sudeley is to spend time outdoors: appreciating the architecture and gardens as you stroll trumps the exhibition rooms ten times over.

Behind the west wing, alongside the towering ruins of the Elizabethan **Banqueting Hall** – left romantically untouched during the Victorian restoration – explore the pretty **Knot Garden** and stroll through a grove of mulberry trees to reach the spectacular **Queen's Garden**, surrounded by yews and filled with summer roses. Alongside, presaged by the **White Garden** – an all-white array of passion flowers, roses, peonies, clematic and spring tulips – stands the Perpendicular Gothic **St Mary's Church**, rebuilt by George Gilbert Scott in 1863; inside, a rather beautiful Victorian tomb marks the final resting-place of Katherine Parr. Beyond, a **pheasantry** holds fifteen endangered species of pheasant from around the world, while in the far corner of the grounds, kids will be rather more entertained by a giant **adventure playground**.

Special **connoisseur tours** (April–Oct Tues, Wed & Thurs 11am, 1pm & 3pm; £12 ticket includes castle and grounds) offer guided visits to the Ashcombes' **private apartments** in the east wing, taking in the castle's grandest rooms, bedecked with Tudor finery as well as artworks by Van Dyck, Rubens and others.

Belas Knap

South of Winchcombe, up on the eastern ridge of Cleeve Hill (see below), the Neolithic long barrow of **Belas Knap** (free; ⓦ www.english-heritage.org.uk) occupies one of the wildest – and highest – spots in the Cotswolds. Dating from around 3000 BC, this is the best-preserved burial chamber in England, stretched out like a strange sleeping beast cloaked in green velvet, more than fifty metres long, twenty metres wide and a touch under five metres high. Its name derives from the Old English *cnaepp*, meaning hilltop, along with, most likely, *bel* meaning beacon, though some theorize a link with the Latin word *bellus* (beautiful).

The best way to get there is to **walk**, undertaking the two-mile climb up the Cotswold Way from Winchcombe. The path strikes off to the right near the entrance to Sudeley Castle; when you reach the country lane at the top, turn right and then left for the ten-minute hike to the barrow. Details of this route incorporated into a circular walk (5.3 miles; 4hr) to/from Winchcombe – also with a shorter variation (3.5 miles; 3hr) – can be downloaded at ⓦ www.cotswoldsaonb .org.uk. It's also possible to **drive** to Belas Knap; heading out of Winchcombe on the B4632, follow signs into a lay-by, then join the steep, narrow Corndean Lane up to a hillside pull-in where you can park for the short walk up to the site.

What you see first is the **false portal** on the north side, set back between two horned prominences – probably designed to put grave-robbers off the scent. Four other entrances around the barrow give into small **burial chambers** that would originally have held several bodies each. The views over the surrounding countryside are exceptional.

For an exhilarating, lonely drive, continue south on Corndean Lane, scuttling over the hills and through dense woods past **CHARLTON ABBOTS** to eventually join the A436 Cheltenham–Stow road near **ANDOVERSFORD**.

Cleeve Hill

Southwest of Winchcombe, the B4632 clings to the shoulders of the Cotswold Edge, offering stupendous views out towards Tewkesbury from the cliff-edge village of **CLEEVE HILL**, named for the expanse of grassed limestone which rears above. This is wild, windswept countryside: when Cheltenham, some 900 feet below, is swathed in valley mists, the great rolling expanse of **Cleeve Common**, atop the ridge and speckled with wildflowers in season, can bask in glittering sunshine, rising to the **highest point in the Cotswolds**. The true summit – at 1,083 feet – is a flattish area at the southern edge of the common; aim instead for the better views from the northern edge around what is dubbed **Cleeve Cloud**, at roughly 1,040 feet, and easily reached by a stiffish walk up from a parking area near the golf course, signed off the B4632. See ⓦwww.cotswoldsaonb.org.uk for downloadable details of the **Cleeve Hill Common Ring**, a circular walk (6 miles; 4hr 30min) from the car park, with a shorter alternative (4 miles; 3hr), that takes in the best of the open hilltops and viewpoints.

At the foot of the hill, and bypassed by the busy A435 four miles north of Cheltenham, **BISHOP'S CLEEVE** is a humdrum little town, though just nearby in **WOODMANCOTE** you could aim for family-run B&B at *Gambles Farm* (ⓣ01242 677719, ⓦwww.gamblesfarm.co.uk; ❷–❸) – bargain rates for what are cosy, well-kept rooms at a busy working stable yard.

Cheltenham

Until the eighteenth century **CHELTENHAM** was like any other Cotswold town, but the discovery of a spring in 1716 transformed it into Britain's most popular **spa**. During Cheltenham's heyday, a century or so later, royalty and nobility descended in droves to take the waters, which were said to cure anything from constipation to worms. The super-rich have since moved onto sunnier climes, but the town has maintained a lively, still rather posh atmosphere, holds lots of good restaurants and shows off some of England's best-preserved Regency architecture.

Having said that, there's not actually a great deal to do. Taking in the grand facades is pleasant, as is dipping in and out of the shops or holing up in one of the luxury spa hotels, but otherwise most visitors head off into the Cotswolds. The exception is if you're here for the **racing** (see box below) or for one of Cheltenham's excellent **arts festivals** (ⓦwww.cheltenhamfestivals.com) – **jazz** (April), **science** (June), **classical music** (July) or **literature** (Oct), or the separately run **folk** festival (Feb; ⓦwww.cheltenhamtownhall.org.uk) – when the town musters fresh interest.

Arrival

Trains from London, Reading, Bristol, Birmingham and all round the UK come into Cheltenham Spa, a surprisingly small two-platform station. The main

---

Cheltenham races

Cheltenham racecourse (ⓣ0844 579 3003, ⓦwww.cheltenham.co.uk), on the north side of town, a ten-minute walk from Pittville Park at the foot of Cleeve Hill, is Britain's main venue for National Hunt racing, also known as "steeplechase" – that is, in which the horses must jump over hurdles or fences. The principal events are the four-day **Festival** in March, which attracts forty thousand people each day, culminating in the famous **Cheltenham Gold Cup**, and the three-day **Open** in November, but there are smaller meetings throughout the season, which runs from late October to early May. For what many say is the best view, with the best atmosphere, book ahead for entry to the pen opposite the main stand, known as Best Mate Enclosure (£10–40, depending on the event).

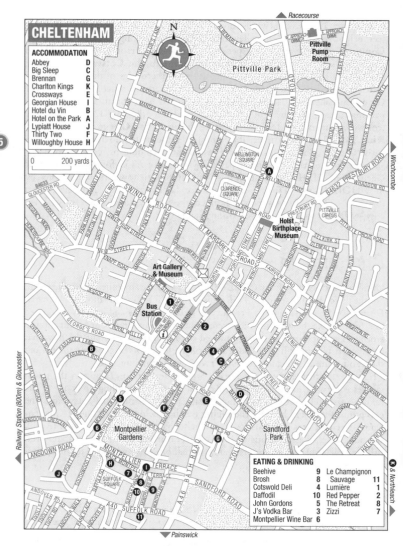

ACCOMMODATION

Abbey	D
Big Sleep	C
Brennan	G
Charlton Kings	K
Crossways	E
Georgian House	I
Hotel du Vin	B
Hotel on the Park	A
Lypiatt House	J
Thirty Two	F
Willoughby House	H

0   200 yards

EATING & DRINKING

Beehive	9	Le Champignon	
Brosh	8	Sauvage	11
Cotswold Deli	4	Lumière	1
Daffodil	10	Red Pepper	2
John Gordons	5	The Retreat	8
J's Vodka Bar	3	Zizzi	7
Montpellier Wine Bar	6		

entrance is on Queen's Road, about three-quarters of a mile west of the city centre, from where the most frequent transport into town is Stagecoach bus D (Mon–Sat every 10min 6am–6pm, then every 30min until 10.45pm, Sun every 30min 8.45am–6.45pm), which drops off on Clarence Street in the centre. A **taxi** is about £5 – or it's a twenty-minute walk.

National Express **coaches** from central London and Heathrow Airport arrive at the **bus station** on Royal Well Road, just behind the city centre: these are also a useful way to get to or from Cirencester on a Sunday, when local buses don't run.

Some **buses** arrive at the Royal Well bus station, but many drop off on the main street, Promenade, nearby. Regular services include bus 46 to/from **Nailsworth**,

Stroud and Painswick, bus 94 to/from Gloucester and bus 151 (not Sun) to/from Cirencester and North Cerney (all Stagecoach); Swanbrook bus 853 to/from Oxford, Witney, Minster Lovell, Burford and Northleach; Castleways bus 606 (not Sun) to/from Broadway, Stanton and Winchcombe; Pulham's bus 801 (May–Sept daily; Oct–April not Sun) to/from Moreton, Stow and Bourton-on-the-Water; Pulham's bus 804 (not Sun) to/from the Guitings; and Swanbrook bus 833 (not Sun) to/from Northleach.

Irregular services include several run by Pulham's: bus 608 (once on Thurs) to/from Chipping Campden, Blockley, Bourton-on-the-Hill and Broadway; bus 809 (once on Wed) to/from Northleach; bus 811 (once on Sat) to/from Chipping Norton, Kingham, Shipton-under-Wychwood and Bourton-on-the-Water, and bus 813 (once on Tues) to/from Moreton; as well as Cotswold Green bus 23 (once on Thurs) to/from Stroud, Slad, Sheepscombe, Bisley and Miserden.

If you're driving, take advantage of Cheltenham's two park and ride facilities (ⓦwww.gloucestershire.gov.uk/parkandride). Arle Court is on the western edge of town by the A40/B4063 roundabout, signposted from the M5 junction 11; parking is free and bus 511 runs into the centre (Mon–Sat every 12min 7.15am–7pm; £2.50 return, additional passengers £1.50 each, children under 14 free). Cheltenham Race Course car park is signposted on the northern edge of town; parking is free and bus D runs into the centre (Mon–Sat every 10min 7.15am–6.45pm; £3 return; park and ride suspended during big race meetings).

Information

Cheltenham's helpful tourist office is in the centre, at 77 Promenade (Mon, Tues & Thurs–Sat 9.30am–5.15pm, Wed 10am–5.15pm; ☏01242 522878, ⓦwww.visitcheltenham.info & ⓦwww.cotswolds.com). After 2012, though, it will move to the new Art Gallery and Museum (see p.216) on Clarence Street. The office takes bookings for guided walking tours of Regency Cheltenham (April–Oct Sat 11.30am, also July & Aug Sun 11.30am; 1hr 30mins; £4) and full-day guided coach tours to destinations all round the Cotswolds (April–Oct Thurs 10.15am; £29).

As well as "Car-Free Cotswolds" leaflets, detailing bus times and routes to/from all major Cotswolds destinations and suggesting day tours to/from Cheltenham by public transport (with exact bus times), the tourist office stocks information on "The Romantic Road", a pair of self-guided countryside driving tours which start and end in Cheltenham. The first (70 miles) describes a route through Winchcombe, Broadway, Chipping Campden, Stow and the Slaughters; the other (90 miles) visits Northleach, Burford, Bibury, Cirencester and Painswick.

Accommodation

Hotels and guest houses abound across the city, many of them in fine Regency houses, and rooms are easy to come by – except during the races and festivals, when you should book weeks in advance. The tourist office offers a free booking service.

By the time you read this, the *Ellenborough Park* luxury hotel (ⓦwww.ellenboroughpark.com), occupying a splendid old manor house north of the centre in Prestbury, near the racecourse, will be open – and, by the looks of it, worth a splash. Alternatively, aim for *Cowley Manor* (see p.219), a remarkable design hotel in rural surroundings only five miles south of Cheltenham.

Hotels

Big Sleep Wellington St ☎01242 696999, ⓦwww.thebigsleephotel.com. Excellent contemporary budget hotel in the centre, with sixty rooms including family rooms and suites, all with a retro designer feel and hi-tech gadgetry but no frills – and, more important, exceptionally low prices. ❷

Charlton Kings London Rd ☎01242 231061, ⓦwww.charltonkingshotel.co.uk. Informal, well-run three-star hotel two miles east of the centre on the A40 – a decent option if you want to leave your car and get a bus into town. Rooms are fresh and spotlessly presented, the food is good and the hands-on owners are charming. Great value. ❹

Hotel du Vin Parabola Rd ☎01242 588450, ⓦwww.hotelduvin.com. Swanky boutique-style hotel in the sought-after Montpellier district, with 49 stylish rooms and suites and a reputation for excellent in facilities, service and cuisine. ❻–❼

Hotel on the Park 38 Evesham Rd ☎01242 518898, ⓦwww.thehoteluk.co.uk. Impressive luxury hotel just north of the centre with twelve individually designed rooms, some doing the Georgian thing to a T, others taking a bolder, more contemporary line. All, though, draw on Cheltenham's spa history to take a pride in their feature bathrooms: you might get an infinity tub, a jacuzzi or an aromatherapy bath, perhaps also with mood-lighting for soothing self-pampering. ❼–❾

Thirty Two 32 Imperial Sq ☎01242 771110, ⓦwww.thirtytwoltd.com. Magnificently stylish contemporary boutique hotel occupying an otherwise anonymous Regency town house overlooking gardens. The location is central but quiet – and the interiors are a wow, from the luxury fabrics to the rainfall showers. ❼–❾

Willoughby House 1 Suffolk Sq ☎01242 522798, ⓦwww.willoughbyhousehotel.co.uk. A handsome Regency building south of the centre, featuring classic traditional styling across its nine rooms along with a sense of old-world charm and opulence. ❻

B&Bs

Abbey 14 Bath Parade ☎01242 516053, ⓦwww.abbeyhotel-cheltenham.com. The thirteen rooms at this centrally located four-star B&B are attractively and individually furnished, with wholesome breakfasts taken overlooking the garden. Friendly service. ❸–❹

Brennan 21 St Luke's Rd ☎01242 525904, ⓦwww.brennanguesthouse.co.uk. Small, simple B&B in a Regency building on a quiet square, with six rooms, none en suite. No credit cards. ❷

Crossways 57 Bath Rd ☎01242/527683, ⓦwww.crosswaysguesthouse.com. Very central, this comfortable Regency house has period trimmings updated with a flavour of contemporary styling, and a choice of well-equipped single, double and triple rooms. ❹

Georgian House 77 Montpellier Terrace ☎01242 515577, ⓦwww.georgianhouse.net. Three fancy bedrooms in a house dating from 1807, quiet, spotless and full of period charm. ❹

Lypiatt House Lypiatt Rd ☎01242 224994, ⓦwww.lypiatt.co.uk. Victorian villa set in its own grounds, with spacious rooms, open fires and a conservatory with a small bar. ❹

The Town

Cheltenham is a town of two halves. Start on the broad **Promenade**, focus of the town centre, which sweeps majestically south from the High Street and is lined with some of Cheltenham's grandest houses and smartest shops (in among a welter of familiar high-street brands). Streets to either side effortlessly keep up appearances: the Ladies' College is a step away, and round the corner on Clarence Street stands the **Cheltenham Art Gallery and Museum** (ⓦwww.cheltenham.artgallery.museum) – closed at the time of writing, but from 2012 due to showcase its outstanding Arts and Crafts collection and social history exhibits in a swanky new architect-designed space on the same site.

A brief stroll north lies the **Holst Birthplace Museum**, 4 Clarence Rd (Feb to mid-Dec Tues–Sat 10am–4pm; £4.50; ⓦwww.holstmuseum.org.uk). Once the home of the composer of *The Planets*, its intimate rooms hold plenty of Holst memorabilia and give a good insight into Victorian family life. Further north along handsome Evesham Road, it's about ten minutes' walk into the **Pittville** district, where a certain Joseph Pitt began work on a grand spa in the 1820s, soon afterwards running out of cash. Most of the area is now parkland, though Pitt did manage to complete the domed **Pump Room** (Wed–Sun 10am–4pm;

ⓦwww.pittvillepumproom.org.uk) before he hit the skids. A lovely Classical structure with an imposing colonnaded facade, it is now used as a concert hall, but you can still sample the **spa waters** from the marble fountain in the main auditorium for free. Very pungent they are too.

But the best of Cheltenham lies in the other direction. From the Promenade, head south past **Imperial Square**, laid out in 1818, whose greenery is surrounded by proud Regency terraces, into the **Montpellier** district. **Montpellier Walk** features a parade of shops sporting Classical-style caryatids – supporting columns carved as female figures – designed in the 1840s, or you could duck one street west onto **Montpellier Street**, a handsome and harmonious row of upscale bars, cafés, beauty parlours and independent boutiques.

Press on south, over the busy main road, and into **"the Suffolks"**, a pleasant residential district of terraces with a buzzy, engaging ambience. It's centred on the large, rather unkempt **Suffolk Square** but also takes in a powwow of interesting shops and restaurants along adjacent **Suffolk Parade**. Even if you're not hungry, be sure to pop into two architectural highlights: the Regency Gothic **church of St James** on Suffolk Square, transformed inside into the *Zizzi* pizza restaurant, and the superb Art Deco **Daffodil** restaurant on Suffolk Parade, occupying what was a cinema, complete with all its glorious 1920s fittings.

Eating and drinking

Cheltenham caters for all tastes and pockets, its **restaurants**, **bars** and **pubs** managing to draw in punters from around the Cotswolds. You'll have no difficulty finding somewhere congenial – though if you're planning to be in town during any of the festivals or big race meetings, you'd do well to book a table in advance.

Restaurants and cafés

Beehive 1–3 Montpellier Villas ☎01242 579443, ⓦwww.thebeehivemontpellier.com. Friendly ambience and great French food in a lofty, atmospheric restaurant above the easygoing pub of the same name. Mains from £13, with a three-course set menu at £20. Reservations advised. Restaurant Wed–Sat eves plus Sun lunch. Bar menu Mon–Sat lunch and eve.

Brosh 8 Suffolk Parade ☎01242 227277, ⓦwww.broshrestaurant.co.uk. Heart-warming and unusual locals' favourite, on this landmark restaurant street, offering a flavour of modern Middle Eastern cuisine. The owners, an Israeli-English couple, use local, Cotswold-sourced ingredients to create intriguing takes on Jewish and Eastern Mediterranean classics, either in the restaurant (mains £16–20) or, just as appealingly, as mezze sampler dishes at the bar – hummus, falafel, shakshuka and a couple of dozen other choices (£2–4 each). Wed–Sat 7–11pm.

Cotswold Deli 34 Rodney Rd ☎01242 577143, ⓦwww.thecotswolddeli.co.uk. Friendly little daytime café and deli in the town centre, offering coffee, wholesome snacks and light lunches (around £5). Closed Sun.

Daffodil 18–20 Suffolk Parade ☎01242 700055, ⓦwww.thedaffodil.com. Eat in the circle bar or auditorium of this breathtakingly designed 1920s Art Deco ex-cinema, where the screen has been replaced with a hubbub of chefs. Great atmosphere and first-class British cuisine (mains £13–22). Live jazz every Mon night. Closed Sun.

Le Champignon Sauvage 24 Suffolk Rd ☎01242 573449, ⓦwww.lechampignonsauvage .co.uk. Cheltenham's highest-rated restaurant, its sensitively updated classic French cuisine awarded two Michelin stars among a welter of other awards and critical acclaim. The ambience is chic and intimate, the presentation immaculately artistic. Two-course set menu £45, three courses £55. Book well ahead. Closed Sun & Mon.

Lumière Clarence Parade ☎01242 222200, ⓦwww.lumiere.cc. Award-winning restaurant showcasing upscale, contemporary, seasonal British food in a genial ambience of informality. Cornish scallops or sexed-up corned beef prelude mains such as Gloucester Old Spot pork done two ways, partridge or local venison. Two-course menus are £36 (or £19 at lunch). Closed Sun, Mon & lunch on Tues.

Red Pepper 13 Regent St ☎01242 253900, ⓦwww.redpeppercheltenham.co.uk. Family-run deli, coffee lounge and bistro in the centre, with a friendly, informal vibe and a wide range of dishes, from pie and mash or fishcake and salad for a light lunch (£6–8) through to rack of lamb, gnocchi or seabass in the evenings (mains £10–13). Closed Sun–Tues eves.

Zizzi St James Church, Suffolk Sq ☎01242 252493, ⓦwww.zizzi.co.uk. Italian chain restaurant, housed spectacularly within a converted Regency Gothic church, complete with stained glass and a soaring interior. The chancel now houses the spotlit open kitchen. Never mind the pizza, enjoy the atmosphere.

Pubs and bars

John Gordons 11 Montpellier Arcade ☎01242 245985, ⓦwww.johngordons .co.uk. This lovely little independent wine bar, hidden off Montpellier's fanciest street, is a breath of fresh air among the more or less generically posh watering holes hereabouts. Drop in ostensibly to pick the brains of the knowledgeable, forthcoming staff about buying wines and whiskies. But then take a seat in the shop or outside in the old Victorian covered arcade to watch the world go by while sampling a glass or two of wine, alongside a plate of charcuterie, cheeses and/or antipasti (£8–12). Every town should have one.

J's Vodka Bar 6 Regent St ☎01242 519512, ⓦwww.jsvodkabar.com. Killer drinks from a range of 24 vodkas, served to the accompaniment of DJs playing house and funk. Closed Sun–Tues.

Montpellier Wine Bar Bayshill Lodge, Montpellier St ☎01242 527774, ⓦwww.montpellierwinebar .com. Stylish wine bar and restaurant with lovely bow-fronted windows. Good breakfasts are also served, and Friday is fish night.

The Retreat 10–11 Suffolk Parade ☎01242 235436, ⓦwww.theretreatwinebar.com. Lively venue which caters to the business fraternity at lunchtimes and a Cheltenham Ladies' College set in the evening. Good lunches too. Closed Sun.

Listings

Hospital See p.36.
Markets For farmers' markets, see box, p.205.
Police station Lansdown Rd ☎0845 090 1234.
Post office 192 High St.
Taxis Try Cheltenham Taxi (☎01242 650250, ⓦwww.cheltenham-taxi.co.uk) or Starline (☎01242 250250, ⓦwww.textbookings.co.uk).

Theatre The Everyman Theatre (☎01242 572573, ⓦwww.everymantheatre.org.uk), in the centre of town on Regent Street, is very active, staging all kinds of productions year-round in a beautiful Victorian auditorium.

South of Cheltenham

South of Cheltenham, the A46 heads to Prinknash (see p.230) and Painswick (p.228), while the **A435** forms the most direct route to Cirencester. A couple of miles beyond Cheltenham's suburbs, it rises to the junction with the east–west A436 at the resonantly named **SEVEN SPRINGS**, where the source of the River Churn – or, some say, the true source of the Thames (see p.197) – is marked, prosaically, by a child-friendly chain pub and a busy double-roundabout intersection.

A few hundred yards south of Seven Springs, follow a minor road west to the tiny village of **COBERLEY**. Around a couple of bends, a sign for Coberley church points mutely at a little huddle of cottages beside an arched gatehouse. Open the gate, or the door beside it, to walk through to the Perpendicular church of **St Giles**, originally – like the cottages, the gatehouse and the cluster of stables and outbuildings around the adjacent courtyard – part of the grand Coberley Hall, built in the thirteenth century but now gone. The church, though, is full of atmosphere; originally Saxon and Norman, largely rebuilt around 1870, it's worth visiting for its south chapel, founded by **Thomas de Berkeley**, a knight who fought at the Battle of Crécy (1346). The chapel still houses Berkeley's tomb alongside that of his wife, Lady Joan and, poignantly, an unnamed child – presumably their daughter. Local folk-history has it that Lady Joan, who outlived Berkeley and married again, was the mother of Dick Whittington, thrice Lord Mayor of London.

In an entirely different vein, the next village south of Coberley, **COWLEY**, conceals the sensational ♣ *Cowley Manor* (☎01242 870900, Ⓦwww.cowleymanor.com; ❾), a country-house hotel set in 55 acres which follows none of the usual rules. It, rather, showcases contemporary chic transplanted to this rural setting: interior clutter has been replaced by long, clean sightlines, fussy fittings superseded by witty, intelligent design. Expect low, square couches, elegant contemporary mood-lighting and guest rooms with curvaceous modern furniture. There's also an onsite spa. Fortunately, the service matches the style – relaxed, switched-on and intelligent. It's ferociously expensive, but if ever a Cotswold hotel merited a splurge, this is the one.

If you can't afford it, drown your sorrows at the stone-flagged *Green Dragon Inn* (☎01242 870271, Ⓦwww.green-dragon-inn.co.uk), just down the road in **COCKLEFORD** – also with its own fresh, charming rooms (❻) and decent food, served in a bar sporting wooden furniture crafted by designer Robert Thompson. Further south, past **COLESBOURNE** – where a ten-acre **garden** (Feb & early March Sat & Sun 1–4.30pm; £6.50; Ⓦwww.colesbournegardens.org.uk) is renowned for its winter displays of snowdrops – you reach North Cerney (see p.196) and then Cirencester (p.191).

East of Cheltenham, the A40 speeds towards **Northleach** (see p.187) and **Burford** (p.108) on its way to **Oxford** (p.45), while the A436 branches off at Andoversford towards **Bourton-on-the-Water** (p.185) and **Stow** (p.180).

Gloucester

For centuries life was good for **GLOUCESTER**, which lies ten miles west of Cheltenham. The Romans chose this spot for a garrison to guard the River Severn and spy on Wales, and later for a *colonia*, or home for retired soldiers – the highest status a provincial Roman town could dream of. Commercial success came with traffic up the Severn, which developed into one of the busiest trade routes in Europe: the city's political importance hit its peak under the Normans, when William the Conqueror was a regular visitor. Gloucester became a religious centre too, as exemplified by the construction of what is now the cathedral, but by the fifteenth century it was on the slide: navigating the Severn this far upstream was so difficult that most trade shifted south to Bristol. In an attempt to reverse the decline, a canal was opened in 1827 to link Gloucester to Sharpness, sixteen miles south on a broader stretch of the Severn. Trade picked up for a time, but it was only a temporary stay of economic execution.

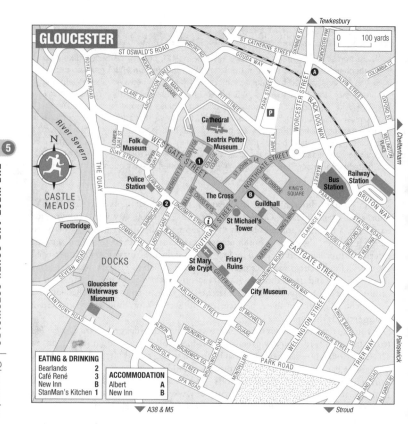

GLOUCESTER

▲ Tewkesbury

0 — 100 yards

ST CATHERINE STREET
SKINNER ST
WORCESTER PAR
ST OSWALD'S ROAD
PRIORY RD
GOUDA WAY
ROYAL OAK ROAD
KINGSHOLM ROAD
ST MARY'S SQUARE
ARCHDEACON STREET
CLARE ST
PITT STREET
PARK STREET
WORCESTER STREET
BLACK DOG WAY
ALVIN STREET
OXFORD ST
COLUMBIA CT
WELLINGTON PLACE

▶ Cheltenham

Cathedral
Beatrix Potter Museum
Folk Museum
WESTGATE STREET
LOWER QUAY STREET
UPPER QUAY STREET
THE QUAY
River Severn
N
CASTLE MEADS
Footbridge
COLLEGE COURT
HARE LA
ST JOHN'S LA
NORTHGATE STREET
KING'S SQUARE
MARKET PARADE
Bus Station
Railway Station
BRUTON WAY
STATION ROAD

P
Police Station
Ⓐ
ⓘ
The Cross
St Michael's Tower
Ⓑ
Guildhall
OSBORNE
CLARENCE ST
RUSSELL STREET
BEDFORD ST
STATION ROAD

DOCKS
COMMERCIAL RD
BARBICAN
LADYBELLGATE ST
BLACKFRIARS
SOUTHGATE STREET
BELL LANE
LONGSMITH STREET
BERKELEY STREET
KINGS CARS
②
③
St Mary de Crypt
Friary Ruins
GREYFRIARS
QUEEN ST
KING'S WALK
EASTGATE STREET

Gloucester Waterways Museum
SEVERN ROAD
LLANTHONY ROAD
PARLIAMENT STREET
City Museum
BRUNSWICK ROAD
HAMPDEN WAY
WELLINGTON STREET
KING'S BARTON ST
ARTHUR STREET
TRIER WAY

▶ Painswick

ALBION ST
BRUNSWICK SQ
BRUNSWICK SQ
ST MICHAEL'S SQUARE
NORFOLK STREET
BRUNSWICK ROAD
MONTPELLIER
PARK ROAD
SPA ROAD
MIDLAND ROAD
ST MARK'S ST

EATING & DRINKING
Bearlands — 2
Café René — 3
New Inn — B
StanMan's Kitchen — 1

ACCOMMODATION
Albert — A
New Inn — B

▼ A38 & M5

▼ Stroud

Today, the **canal** is busy once again, though this time with pleasure boats, and the Victorian **docks** have undergone a facelift, their assorted warehouses turned into offices, apartments, a large antiques centre and the **Gloucester Waterways Museum**, focus of the grand **Tall Ships Festival** (Ⓦwww.gloucestertallships.co .uk). The main reason for coming this way, though, is to see Gloucester's awe-inspiring **cathedral**, and its breathtakingly beautiful fan-vaulted **cloisters**. Visit on a Friday and you could explore one of the region's best **farmers' markets** too.

Arrival

Gloucester is served by **trains** from London and Reading to/from Cheltenham, but the station actually lies off the main line, meaning many fast trains from the Midlands and the Southwest bypass Gloucester (change at Cheltenham Spa for connections). Slow trains stop in on their way to/from Bristol, Cardiff, Worcester and Birmingham. The **station** stands on Bruton Way, a five-minute walk east of the centre.

Directly opposite is the **bus station**. Useful regular services include several on Stagecoach – bus 14/14B to/from **Stroud**, bus 91A (Sun only) to/from **Frampton**, **Slimbridge** and **Berkeley**, bus 93 (not Sun) to/from Stroud and **Nailsworth** and bus 94 to/from **Cheltenham** – supplemented by Swanbrook bus 852 (not Sun) to/ from **Cirencester** and the Duntisbournes, Swanbrook bus 853 to/from **Oxford**, **Witney**, **Minster Lovell**, **Burford** and **Northleach**, Mikes bus 201 (not Sun) to/

Gloucestershire airport

Gloucester's titchy **airport** (℡01452 857700, Ⓦwww.gloucestershireairport.co.uk) lies right beside junction 11 of the M5. It mostly handles private jets, plus a few domestic scheduled flights from Jersey and the Isle of Man aboard regional low-cost carrier Manx2.com. Stagecoach **bus** 94 between Cheltenham and Gloucester stops three-quarter of a mile from the terminal; otherwise, you're reliant on **taxis**. There are plenty of **pleasure flights**, run by the likes of Ⓦwww.tigerairways.co.uk, www.cotswoldaeroclub.com and www.ballooning-network.co.uk.

from **Wotton**, Jackies bus 207 (not Sun) to/from **Berkeley** and Cotswold Green bus 256 (twice on Wed) to/from **Painswick**. National Express **coaches** also arrive here from central London and Heathrow Airport; they're a useful way to get to/from Cirencester on a Sunday, when local buses don't run.

Gloucester has two **park and rides** (Ⓦwww.gloucestershire.gov.uk/parkandride). Just north of the centre by the A38/A417 roundabout is **St Oswalds** (parking £1.50, bus £1.20 return), while a long way south in Quedgeley, off the A38 near M5 junction 12, is **Waterwells** (parking free, bus £2 return). The two are linked every 12–15min by Bennetts bus 507 (Mon–Fri 6.30am–8pm, Sat 7.30am–8pm), which runs from one to the other, dropping off in the city centre and near the Waterways Museum on the way.

Information and accommodation

The **tourist office** is very central at 28 Southgate Street (Mon 10am–5pm, Tues–Sat 9.30am–5pm; July & Aug also Sun 11am–3pm; ℡01452 396572, Ⓦwww.visit gloucester.info & Ⓦwww.cotswolds.com). They have details of self-guided walks on marked routes along the River Severn and Sharpness Canal. Within the city Gloucester Civic Trust (℡01452 526955, Ⓦwww.gloucestercivictrust.org) run two **guided walks** in summer – one from St Michael's Tower in the centre (April–Sept Mon–Sat 11.30am; 1hr 30min; £3), the other from the Waterways Museum around the docks (April–Sept Wed, Sat & Sun 2pm; 1hr 30min; £3). They also have five downloadable **audio trails** (£3.50 each) for self-guided city walks. Rather more entertaining are **Gloucester Ghost Walks**, which run year-round (Wed 8pm, Thurs 6.30pm; £5; ℡07908 552855, Ⓦwww.gloucesterghostwalks.co.uk), starting from the tourist office and led by paranormal investigator Lyn Cinderey.

There's not much reason to **stay**: better accommodation lies outside the city, and you'd best to visit on a day-trip from Cheltenham (see p.213), Painswick (p.228) or further afield. If you're stuck, the fourteenth-century galleried *New Inn*, 16 Northgate Street (℡01452 522177, Ⓦwww.relaxinnz.co.uk; ❷), has 33 pleasant rooms in a convenient central location – though expect swirly carpets in the bar and corporate furniture – or try the *Albert*, 56 Worcester Street (℡01452 502081, Ⓦwww.alberthotel.com; ❸), a nineteenth-century town house with adequate B&B.

The City

Gloucester lies on the east bank of the Severn, its centre spread around a curve in the river. The city clusters around Northgate, Southgate, Eastgate and Westgate streets, all Roman roads; where they meet is dubbed the **Cross**, though no cross stands there. This is the location of the Friday **farmers' market**, overlooked by **St Michael's Tower**, all that's left of a fifteenth-century church – the tower now houses a heritage information centre for Gloucester Civic Trust, who run guided walks from here (see p.221). Gloucester's main shopping area lies east of the Northgate–Southgate axis, while the **cathedral** and **docks** are the focus of interest to the west.

Gloucester Cathedral

The superb condition of **Gloucester Cathedral** (daily 7.30am–6pm; free; Ⓦ www.gloucestercathedral.org.uk) is striking in a city that has lost so much of its history; this one building still keeps seven masons in full-time employment. The Saxons founded an abbey here, and four centuries later, Benedictine monks arrived intent on building their own church. Work began in 1089. As a place of worship it shot to importance after the murder of Edward II at Berkeley Castle (see p.227) in 1327: Gloucester took his body and the king's shrine became a major place of pilgrimage. The money generated helped finance the conversion of the church into England's first and greatest example of the **Perpendicular style**, crowned by a magnificent 225-foot tower. Henry VIII recognized the church's prestige by conferring the status of cathedral.

Beneath the fourteenth- and fifteenth-century reconstructions, some Norman aspects remain, best seen in the **nave**, which is flanked by sturdy pillars and arches adorned with immaculate zigzag carvings. Only when you reach the choir and transepts can you see how skilfully the new church was built inside the old, the Norman masonry hidden beneath the finer lines of the Perpendicular panelling and tracery. The **choir** has exceptional fourteenth-century misericords, and also provides the best vantage point for admiring the **east window**, completed in around 1350 and – at almost 80 feet tall – the largest medieval window in Britain. Beneath it, to the left (as you're facing the east window) is the **tomb of Edward II** in alabaster and marble. In the nearby **Lady Chapel**, delicate carved tracery holds a breathtaking patchwork of stained-glass windows. In the **south ambulatory**, the tomb of Robert, duke of Normandy – eldest son of William the Conqueror – forms a painted wooden effigy dating from around 1290 (though Robert died in 1134). Dressed as a Crusader, he lies in a curious pose: his crossed arms and legs signify his length of military service.

The innovative nature of the cathedral's design is also evident in the beautiful **cloisters**, completed in 1367 and featuring the first fan vaulting in the country; the intricate quality of the work is outdone only by Henry VII's Chapel in Westminster Abbey, which it inspired. Take time to explore, not least to find the monks' **lavatorium** on the north side, a communal washing area with a long stone

---

Cheese Rolling at Cooper's Hill

Amid woodland near **BROCKWORTH**, roughly four miles southeast of Gloucester – and six miles southwest of Cheltenham – rises **Cooper's Hill**, a vertiginous grassy slope which has been the site of an annual **Cheese Rolling Festival** (Ⓦ www.cheese-rolling.co.uk) for, some say, hundreds of years. On the last Monday in May, at noon, officials launch a round of Double Gloucester cheese down the hill – whereupon dozens of intrepid (mostly drunk) souls run down after it, to the accompaniment of much revelry from assembled onlookers. Whoever reaches the bottom first wins the cheese; second and third place win small cash prizes. In case you're tempted to take part, have a look at the website for images of just how steep Cooper's Hill is: it's not quite ninety degrees, but it might as well be. The resulting string of hospitalizations among competitors has resulted in the race often being banned; the 2010 event was officially cancelled – though cheeses were still rolled and people still ran – and, at the time of writing, the future of the "festival" remains uncertain.

basin. The cloisters were used to represent the corridors of Hogwart's School of Witchcraft and Wizardry in the *Harry Potter* films.

Back inside, the **north transept** serves as the entrance to the **upstairs galleries** (April–Oct Mon–Fri 10.30am–4pm, Sat 10.30am–3.30pm; £2) where an exhibition explains the east window and allows you to view it at close quarters; in the **Whispering Gallery** you can pick up the tiniest sounds from across the vaulting. The fee also grants access to the **treasury**, of minor interest. You can climb the **tower** for exceptional views (Wed–Fri 2.30pm, Sat 1.30pm & 2.30pm; also Mon & Tues in school hols 2.30pm; £3).

Around the city centre

The cathedral grounds lie alongside **Westgate Street**, the quietest and most pleasant of the city's four main thoroughfares – an odd mix of fast food outlets and pound shops with independent businesses and lively locally run cafés. One of the cottages on College Court, a lane between Westgate Street and the cathedral, was the workshop of John Pritchard, a Victorian **tailor** who was commissioned to make a new suit of clothes for the mayor. During the job, he returned one Monday morning to find the suit completed, apart from one buttonhole which bore a note reading "no more twist". Pritchard ascribed the miracle to fairies, though in truth two drunken employees had slept off their Saturday night excesses in the workshop rather than going home, and were then too embarrassed to be seen in the street by Sunday churchgoers, so stayed and worked. The bones of the story caught author Beatrix Potter's imagination when she visited in 1897; she sketched another, more picturesque house a few doors down to serve as the location for her children's story *The Tailor of Gloucester* – and that building is now a **Beatrix Potter Museum and Shop** (Mon–Sat 10am–5pm, Sun noon–5pm; free; ⓦ www.tailor-of-gloucester .org.uk), with lots of Peter Rabbit trinkets for sale and a small room of Victorian memorabilia. Out on Westgate Street, just beyond the pedestrian zone to the west at no. 103 is the **Gloucester Folk Museum** (Tues–Sat 10am–5pm; free; ⓦ www .gloucester.gov.uk/folkmuseum), with displays on social history filling three floors of a handsome Tudor and Jacobean building.

From humdrum **Southgate Street**, beside the chiefly fourteenth-century St Mary de Crypt church, **Greyfriars** lane leads southeast, past the gaunt, half-forgotten ruins of a Franciscan friary – founded here in 1231 and now just a looming, skeletal ruin among the modern developments – and beside the covered market to reach Brunswick Road, where a Victorian building houses the **City Museum** (Tues–Sat 10am–5pm; free; ⓦ www.gloucester.gov.uk/citymuseum). The diverting archeological collection includes a decorative bronze mirror dating to about 50 AD and an exquisite set of twelfth-century bone and antler playing pieces – the Gloucester Tables Set – bearing designs representing everything from the signs of the zodiac to biblical stories.

Gloucester Docks

Roughly a third of a mile southwest of the city centre, **Gloucester Docks** holds fourteen **warehouses** built for storing grain following the opening of the Sharpness canal to the River Severn in 1827. Most have been turned into offices and shops, but there's still a good deal of atmosphere. The southernmost Llanthony Warehouse is now occupied by the **Gloucester Waterways Museum** (daily: July & Aug 10.30am–5pm; rest of year 11am–4pm; £4.25; ⓦ www .gloucesterwaterwaysmuseum.org.uk), which delves into every nook and cranny of the area's watery history, from the engineering of the locks to the lives of the horses that trod the towpaths, along with plenty of interactive displays. Out from the main building you can also practise "walking the wall" in the time-honoured manner of boatmen, who propelled their narrowboats through the tunnels by their feet, and explore the boats themselves moored up along the quayside. There are also regular **boat trips** out onto the Sharpness canal, with commentary (May–Aug daily noon, 1.30 & 2.30pm; April, Sept & Oct Sat & Sun only; 45mins; £4.75) as well as a programme of longer **cruises** (book in advance; roughly £14–25 per person) – all-day excursions to Tewkesbury or Sharpness, or shorter lunchtime or afternoon jaunts out to Saul Junction (see p.226), generally with onboard meals included. Don't mistake the docks for "Gloucester Quays", a retail and entertainment complex adjacent to the south.

North of the centre

About two miles north of Gloucester, off the A38 near **TWIGWORTH**, eighteenth-century Wallsworth Hall is now home to the **Nature in Art gallery** (Tues–Sun 10am–5pm; £4.75; Ⓦ www.nature-in-art.org.uk). Dedicated exclusively to artistic portrayals of the natural world in all disciplines – from painting to decorative and applied arts – it includes a Byzantine mosaic alongside Lalique glassware, and works by Picasso beside Royal Doulton china, as well as a changing series of temporary exhibits by contemporary artists and craftspeople. Stagecoach bus 71 (not Sun) from Gloucester bus station drops off nearby.

Eating and drinking

Gloucester's best **cafés and restaurants** are all within spitting distance of the Cross. Top choice for coffees and light lunches is ⋇ *StanMan's Kitchen*, 42 Westgate Street (closed Sun; ⓣ 01452 412237, Ⓦ www.stanmanskitchen.co.uk), a cheery café and deli (named after the owners' young son Stan) which sells loads of tasty local specialities, from fresh-baked bread to Gloucestershire cheeses and charcuterie, homemade cakes and Cotswolds ice cream. It's generally packed. Alternatively, there are well-prepared British and European dishes at *Bearlands*, a smart **restaurant** on Longsmith Street (closed Sun & Mon; ⓣ 01452 419966, Ⓦ www .bearlandsrestaurant.co.uk), where a two-course set meal is £25. Pop in to take a look at the medieval galleried *New Inn* on Northgate Street (see "Accommodation", p.221) – but then slope off to the lively, fancifully decorated *Café René* **pub** instead, beside Greyfriars off Southgate Street (ⓣ 01452 309340, Ⓦ www.caferene .co.uk). It serves decent burgers and other more substantial dishes, including great Sunday barbecues in summer, and also hosts live blues, jazz and acoustic **music** in the cellar bar (Thurs–Sun).

As a footnote, just west of the city in **OVER**, the Over Farm Market (ⓣ 01452 521014, Ⓦ www.overfarmmarket.co.uk) has been named best **farm shop** in the region and is a leading light in the Gloucestershire Farm Shops movement (Ⓦ www.gloucestershirefarmshops.co.uk). Expect a heavenly range of local cheeses, fruit, veg, breads, cakes, meat and beer.

Listings

Hospital See p.36.

Markets Country Market, Northgate Hall, St Johns Lane (Thurs 8.30am–12.30pm; Ⓦ www.gloucester countrymarket.co.uk). For farmers' markets, see box, p.205.

Police station Longsmith St ⓣ 0845 090 1234.

Post office Kings Square.

Sport Gloucester's highly rated – and well supported – rugby union team (ⓣ 0871 871 8781,

Ⓦ www.gloucesterrugby.co.uk) plays at Kingsholm Stadium, a short walk north of the centre on Kingsholm Rd. Tickets cost from £18 standing or £28 seated.

Taxis Try Gloucester Taxi (ⓣ 01452 341341, Ⓦ www.gloucester-taxi.co.uk) or Associated (ⓣ 01452 311700, Ⓦ www.associatedtaxis gloucester.co.uk).

The Vale of Berkeley

Flanking the M5 southwest of Gloucester, and tucked between the Cotswold Edge and the River Severn, the **Vale of Berkeley** is somewhat tangential to a Cotswolds holiday, but hosts a sprinkling of noteworthy sights that might draw you down to the marshy ground beside the river. Best known is the **Slimbridge Wetland Centre**, an internationally renowned wildlife reserve with tons of activities alongside its core attraction of birdwatching. **Berkeley Castle**, scene of medieval regicide, is another highlight, as is a scattering of quiet pubs and byways in the Severn-side villages – notably an outstanding seafood restaurant in far-flung **Arlingham**. Dursley and Wotton, though nominally part of the Vale, are covered later on in this chapter (see p.242 & p.243 respectively).

Frampton-on-Severn

Along the A38 about nine miles southwest of Gloucester, near junction 13 of the M5, a turning marks the B4071's departure north onto a peninsula framed by an oxbow of the River Severn. The first village you come to, off to the left, is **FRAMPTON-ON-SEVERN**, a pretty place of Georgian and Tudor houses draped around what is purportedly the longest village green in England – effectively an open meadow, some 22 acres in area. Whet your whistle first at the rather refined *Bell* (℡01452 740346, ⓦwww.thebellatframpton.co.uk; ❸–❹), at the top end of the green, and by the time you reach the other end you'll be grateful for refreshment at the *Three Horseshoes* (℡01452 740463), a beer-drinkers' local. Hidden away behind gates midway along the green is Frampton Court (℡01452 740267, ⓦwww.framptoncourtestate.co.uk; ❺), an eighteenth-century mansion set in a groomed estate that is open for occasional tours and upscale B&B. Otherwise, keep going beyond the *Three Horseshoes* and, at the end, turn right towards the river to reach the isolated **church** of St Mary, consecrated in 1315 and beautifully tranquil; its lead Romanesque font is

> ### The Severn Bore
>
> The Severn Estuary has the second-highest tidal range in the world (after the Bay of Fundy in Nova Scotia), its water levels varying by an extraordinary fifteen metres or more. During the highest tides, the rising water is funnelled up the narrowing river with ever-increasing force, forming a foaming wave up to two metres high known as the **Severn Bore**. It's an obvious draw for river-surfers, but also attracts crowds of onlookers, both for the rush of the bore and the transformation of a calm river into a torrent which appears to flow upstream for an hour or more after the bore itself has passed. Connoisseurs have identified a number of prime viewpoints along the Severn near Gloucester. The best is on the west bank at **MINSTERWORTH**, where the *Severn Bore Inn* (℡01452 750318) offers parking and a good vantage point. A decent alternative on the east bank is at **STONEBENCH**, but the narrow lanes here are often crowded with vehicles, making access difficult; further downstream, the *Old Passage* at **ARLINGHAM** (see p.226), though not a tip-top location (it stands on a broad curve), is a good second-best – and they host highly acclaimed "Bore Breakfasts" on the mornings that the wave rushes past.
>
> Exact timings for different viewpoints are published a year in advance by the Environment Agency (ⓦwww.environment-agency.gov.uk) and enthusiast websites such as ⓦwww.severn-bore.co.uk. Each bore is given a star-rating on the basis of its likely height and speed: four- and five-star events (meaning a tidal range above five metres) tend to occur most frequently in spring and autumn.

probably older than the church. Back along the street, the *True Heart* (℡ 01452 740504, Ⓦ www.thetrueheart.co.uk; ❹) does decent family-run B&B in a quiet Georgian cottage.

Saul and Arlingham

North of the Frampton turn, the B4071 crosses the Gloucester and Sharpness Canal, immediately afterwards bending right to enter **SAUL** village. Follow signs through the village to find **Saul Junction**, the point where the Stroudwater Navigation, a canal built in the 1770s from Framilode (on the Severn nearby) east to Stroud, was crossed in 1827 by the newfangled Gloucester and Sharpness Canal. The Stroudwater, long fallen into disrepair, is now the subject of intensive restoration efforts by the Cotswold Canals Trust (Ⓦ www.cotswoldcanalsproject .org). The junction-point, dotted with pleasure craft, has a good deal of atmosphere, especially in the misty mornings: you could walk from here to the Severn at Framilode, then make a loop back past Fretherne to settle in for lunch at the Frampton *Bell* (see p.225).

A hut on the towpath at Saul Junction houses the **Canal Heritage Centre** (Sat 12.30–5pm, Sun 10am–5pm; ℡ 07854 026504, Ⓦ www.cotswoldcanals.com), offering information, light refreshments and **boat trips** to and fro, which operate on demand (call ahead for prices).

Back on the "main" road, if you keep going straight, you'll eventually come to **ARLINGHAM**, where the *Red Lion* (℡ 01452 740700, Ⓦ www.redlionarlingham .co.uk) is the hub of village life and has details of walks through the muddy countryside. The main reason to come out this far, though, lies further down the road, on the banks of the Severn gazing across to Newnham church, dramatically perched on the cliffs opposite. Here stands the 🍴 *Old Passage* (℡ 01452 740547, Ⓦ www.theoldpassage.com), a classy, award-winning **restaurant** specializing in immaculately presented fish and seafood: fresh lobster (Welsh or Cornish), oysters, crab, mussels and more, interspersed with seasonal dishes – including meat and vegetarian options – and market-fresh fish. Mains are £17–20, but there is a lunch menu (Tues–Fri) of £15 for two courses. Book well ahead for their three pretty, simply furnished **rooms** (❾).

Note that the restaurant is **closed** on Sunday evenings and Mondays, as well as every afternoon (2.30–6.45pm).

Slimbridge Wetland Centre

Heading south along the A38 past **CAMBRIDGE** (pronounced as it looks – the village has a bridge over the River Cam), a roundabout marks the turn down towards the Severn for **SLIMBRIDGE** and the neighbouring **Slimbridge Wetland Centre** (daily 9.30am–5.30pm; Nov–March closes 5pm; £8.86; Ⓦ www.wwt.org.uk/slimbridge). This was the first Wildfowl and Wetlands Trust reserve, founded in 1946 by naturalist Peter Scott. Its primary purpose is to study and protect the numerous resident and migratory species of ducks, geese and swans – but within its three square kilometres it also has a large area open to the public. The quantity (and quality) of stuff you can do here is impressive, from boat rides and Land Rover safaris to canoeing, birdwatching and loads of educational play activities for children. There are guided walks, late-afternoon commentaries in the winter months as migratory swans come into land, tours of the heated Tropical House, and more, all detailed on the website. Come early; stay late.

Berkeley

Bolingbroke: How far is it, my lord, to Berkeley now?
Northumberland: Believe me, noble lord,
I am a stranger here in Gloucestershire:
These high wild hills and rough uneven ways
Draws out our miles, and makes them wearisome.

Shakespeare, *Richard II*

He could have just said "not far". Off the A38 about fifteen miles south of Gloucester, secluded within a swathe of meadows and gardens beside the little village of **BERKELEY**, looms the grandly impressive presence of **Berkeley Castle** (June–Aug Sun–Thurs 11am–5.30pm; April, May, Sept & Oct Sun & Thurs same hours; £7.50; Ⓦ www.berkeley-castle.com). The stronghold has a turreted medieval look, its twelfth-century austerity softened by its gradual transformation into a family home (the Berkeleys have been in residence here for almost 900 years). The interior is packed with mementoes of its long history, including its grisliest moment when, in 1327, **Edward II** was murdered here – purportedly by a red-hot poker thrust into his backside. You can view the cell where the event took place, along with dungeons, dining room, kitchen, picture gallery and the Great Hall, with its painted sixteenth-century wooden screen. It's a hugely impressive historical jaunt, liberally scattered with portraiture and antique furniture, Brussels tapestries in the Morning Room and beer barrels in the cellar. Outside, the grounds include a **Butterfly House**, with British and exotic examples flying freely.

Within easy walking distance of the castle, in Berkeley village itself, stands the excellent **Edward Jenner Museum** (June–Aug daily 12.30–5.30pm; April, May & Sept Tues–Sat 12.30–5.30pm, Sun noon–5.30pm; Oct Sun noon–5.30pm; £4.80; Ⓦ www.jennermuseum.com). Jenner, who discovered the principle of **vaccination**, was born in Berkeley in 1749; after studying in London, he returned here in 1772 to practise as a doctor and conduct his experiments. The museum occupies his former house, the Chantry, with rooms devoted both to Jenner's work and also to well-designed displays on modern stories of vaccination.

For a refreshment stop nearby, follow the narrow High Street south for less than a mile to **HAM** and the *Salutation Inn* (closed Mon lunch; Ⓣ 01453 810284, Ⓦ www .salutationinn.biz) an unpretentious garden **pub** that knows its beer and has a modest food menu. It's easy to put together a circular walk of about two hours from Berkeley to Ham and the Severn. Where the B4066 Berkeley road meets the main A38, you'll spot the Puddleditch **farm shop** (closed Sun; Ⓣ 01453 810816, Ⓦ www.puddleditch farmshop.co.uk), specializing in homemade cakes and Gloucestershire cheeses.

The south Cotswolds

Encompassing a ribbon of undulating terrain from the busy roads coming down off the Cotswold Edge into Cheltenham and Gloucester virtually as far as Bath, the **SOUTH COTSWOLDS** hold some of the region's best-loved countryside – as well as some of its most memorable hideaways. Things get off to a cracking start at **Painswick**, a village of legendary beauty high above Gloucester, beside which a web of narrow lanes feed into the **Slad valley**, as gloriously evocative today as when *Cider with Rosie* author Laurie Lee walked out one midsummer morning in 1934 from his home village of **Slad** to seek his fortune. Roads and rivers cascade down to **Stroud**, once a minor powerhouse of the Industrial Revolution, though today the money has moved out into the villages: **Bisley**, **Minchinhampton**, **Nailsworth** and their neighbours lie in – or must be reached via – high, impenetrable valleys which are virtually Alpine in character, and which have consequently shielded their hosts from the worst depradations of development.

Moving south, **Tetbury** is something of a last hurrah for the Cotswolds, ticking all the right boxes – countryside, churches, hotels, restaurants, delis – and given an extra shimmer of poshness by the proximity of Prince Charles's Highgrove estate, a polo club, lots of big houses, some upscale country inns and the fabulous **Westonbirt Arboretum**.

South again and, although you're still in the Cotswolds, character and mood shift irrevocably: landscapes are plainer and less grandly open, and that characteristically golden yellow Cotswold limestone is slowly replaced by a silvery, greyer variety – nice, but not the same. Either side of the M4, aim for **Chipping Sodbury** and **Castle Combe**, the former an old market town, the latter a one-street village frequently claimed to be England's prettiest.

Painswick

Heading south from either Cheltenham or Gloucester, most people thump down the M5 bound for Bristol and/or Bath. Aim instead for **PAINSWICK**, a congenial old wool town seven miles southeast of Gloucester, or ten miles from Cheltenham, and almost 500 feet up on a south-facing hillside. Ancient buildings jostle for space on its narrow, steep streets tumbling down off the regrettably busy A46.

The relatively easy access means that Painswick can see promenading crowds in season, but its charm survives more or less intact: take your time to stroll through the **churchyard**, where 99 **yew trees**, trimmed into bulbous lollipops, surround a fine collection of seventeenth- and eighteenth-century table tombs. And there are, apparently, exactly 99: the Devil himself, so storytellers say, brings death every time someone has tried to plant a hundredth. When every parish in the Gloucester diocese was given a yew tree to mark the millennium in 2000, eyes rolled in Painswick; the hapless tree was nonetheless planted – and remains healthy. Seven years later, though, one of the older yews toppled, implacably restoring the numerological balance. The **church** itself (daily 9.30am–6pm; Nov–March closes 4pm) is a Perpendicular beauty, though nothing remains of the pre-existing building mentioned in the Domesday Book. On the Sunday following September 19 each year, Painswick hosts the **clypping ceremony**, derived from an Anglo-Saxon word meaning to clasp or embrace: the village children process around the churchyard with flowers in their hair, then join hands to encircle the church and sing a special hymn, amid much festivity.

Otherwise, just stroll Painswick's half-dozen streets to sample the atmosphere. At the foot of ancient Bisley Street, flanked by mostly fourteenth-century buildings, you could drop into the **Gloucestershire Guild of Craftsmen** (Tues–Sat 10am–5pm; Ⓦwww.guildcrafts.org.uk), a centre for promoting contemporary design, with a gallery and shop.

Painswick Rococo Garden

Painswick's most promoted attraction – and a genuine one-off, unlike any other Cotswold garden – is the **Rococo Garden** (mid-Jan to end Oct daily 11am–5pm; £6; Ⓦwww.rococogarden.co.uk), occupying most of the grounds of the privately owned eighteenth-century Painswick House, located about half a mile north of the village up the B4073 Gloucester road. Created in the 1730s in a deep valley behind the house by Benjamin Hyett, son of the original owner, the garden lay overgrown and abandoned for many years until restoration in the 1970s, thanks to a painting commissioned by Hyett in 1748 which showed the garden in its original form. This is England's only example of Rococo garden design, a short-lived

Walks around Painswick

Despite – or because of – the steep hills, there are some fine walks near Painswick, which lies plumb on the Cotswold Way. The Painswick tourist office has details of a leg-stretching **circular walk** (7 miles; 4hr) which heads north out of the village and up onto the Cotswold Way to panoramic vistas atop **Painswick Beacon** (929ft) clear into Wales, Shropshire and down to the Severn Estuary, before swinging around between farms to **EDGE** and back up into Painswick. Another route leads southeast out of the village down Tibbiwell Lane, across the Painswick Stream and up Greenhouse Lane on the other side to reach the ridge-top at **Bull's Cross**, on the B4070 road, which offers views out over **SLAD** (see p.231) and the Slad valley beyond. From Bull's Cross, pick a path north or south to descend back into the Painswick valley again.

An alternative circular **walk** (4 miles; 3hr) which takes in Cooper's Hill – site of the famous cheese-rolling festival (see p.222) – starts from **CRANHAM** village, a couple of miles north of Painswick, reached on Cotswold Green bus 256 (twice on Wed) from Gloucester and Painswick, or Pulham's bus 232 (once on Mon) from Cheltenham. It plunges straight into the ancient beech woods, climbing to join the Cotswold Way for the scenic stretch to the top of Cooper's Hill before descending on a path back to Cranham – where the traditional *Black Horse* (℡01452 812217) is on hand for refreshment and decent meals; the pub garden is lovely. Download details of the walk at Ⓦwww.cotswoldsaonb.org.uk. The composer **Gustav Holst**, who stayed for a while in Cranham, often walked these paths; when he set Christina Rossetti's poem *In The Bleak Midwinter* to music for a hymnal published in 1906, he named his tune *Cranham*. The familiar melody is the perfect mental accompaniment for a chilly Christmas walk in Cranham Woods.

The website of the Rococo Garden (see opposite) also offers downloadable details of several walks in and around Painswick.

fashion typified by a mix of formal geometrical shapes and more naturalistic, curving lines. In among the planting, expect to see statues and odd little follies, not least the spiked, curving **Exedra**, overlooking the diamond-shaped kitchen garden. For the best vistas, walk around anticlockwise. Winter is particularly special, with vast banks of snowdrops carpeting the slopes in February and March.

Practicalities

The hourly Stagecoach **bus** 46 links Painswick with Cheltenham, Stroud and Nailsworth – on Sundays too – while Cotswold Green bus 256 runs to/from Gloucester twice on Wednesdays only. Painswick's summer-only **tourist office** (April–Oct Mon–Fri 10am–4pm, Sat 10am–1pm; ℡01452 813552, Ⓦwww.visitthecotswolds.org.uk & Ⓦwww.cotswolds.com) was, at the time of writing, temporarily housed upstairs in the titchy Town Hall, beside the church; phone ahead to see if it's moved when you visit.

A lovely **hotel** is ⚜ *Cardynham House* on Tibbiwell Street (℡01452 814006, Ⓦwww.cardynham.co.uk; ❸–❹), which has nine modern themed rooms, most with four-posters, charmingly presented within a fifteenth-century building. The adjacent bistro (closed Sun eve & Mon), run by an outgoing Romanian couple, is a great place for simple, well-cooked **food**. Just up the street is *Olivas* (℡01452 814774), a Mediterranean deli and daytime café that has delicious tapas-style light lunches, while opposite the church, *St Michaels* (closed Mon & Tues; ℡01452 814555, Ⓦwww.stmichaelsrestaurant.co.uk) is an upscale, rather posh restaurant serving French-influenced cuisine (two-course menu £28, or £15 at lunchtime) and also offering classy rooms (❹) for B&B.

Painswick's trump card, though, is the extraordinary *Cotswolds88* on Kemps Lane (☎01452 813688, ⓦwww.cotswolds88.com; ❼–❾), a glamorous design hotel crowbarred into the eighteenth-century vicarage. If it feels like a Soho boudoir inside, there's a reason: the hotel is owned by London design guru Marchella De Angelis, who is into – among other things – numerology (hence the deeply significant "88" tag) and interiors that are either daringly avant-garde or tiresomely garish, depending on your taste. Expect chrome statues, psychedelic lighting, zebra-striped chaises longues, wallpaper that is not merely bold but reckless and a cool service ethic which, remarkably, manages to blend genuine warmth with a rather enticing dash of contempt. Stay, eat, drink, smile – this is a playful bolthole to savour.

Prinknash

A couple of miles north of Painswick on the A46 Cheltenham road, signs point down off the hill to **Prinknash Abbey** (ⓦwww.prinknashabbey.org.uk). Prinknash – pronounced, bizarrely, *prinnidge* – is a functioning community of twelve Benedictine monks, who live in a sixteenth-century manor house below the car park which is off-limits to general visitors, as is the incongruous 1972 tower block which served as the monks' residence until 2008. Stop in at the modern **visitor centre** (Wed–Sun 10am–4pm) for an earnest cup of tea and to sample the atmosphere – but otherwise head off down a signed lane to the separately run **Prinknash Bird and Deer Park** (daily 10am–5pm; Nov–March closes 4pm; £6.50; ⓦwww.thebirdpark.com), a great rural retreat for families, with fallow deer, donkeys, bird-feeding and country paths to explore.

Sheepscombe

Follow the Painswick Stream to its source and you come to **SHEEPSCOMBE**, tucked away off the B4070 amid beech woods at the head of the valley. This hidden, barely visited village sports classic Cotswold good looks and an isolation which has served it well: the lanes in and out are barely wide enough for a single car, yet the views yawn out over open countryside. As if by magic, it also lays claim to one of the Cotswolds' best-loved pubs. The 🍴 *Butchers Arms* (☎01452 812113, ⓦwww .butchers-arms.co.uk) simply gets everything right – beer, atmosphere, welcome, food… it's all spot on, neither fancy nor dour. To stretch your legs, wander down through the village and over to the still, silent **church** of St John the Apostle, built in 1819, when the now-gone Sheepscombe mill supported twice the population the village has today. Few corners of the Cotswolds hold such resonance.

Sheepscombe (and Slad and Miserden) are served by Cotswold Green **bus** 23, which runs once on Thursday mornings from Stroud to Cheltenham, returning the same way that afternoon.

Miserden

Over the ridges a couple of miles east of Sheepscombe – and past **WHITEWAY**, where a group of activists bought land in 1898 to establish an anarchist commune which still survives, with shared facilities and no property deeds – stands **MISERDEN**. Poised above the valley of the River Frome near its source, the peaceful village offers access to **Miserden Park Gardens** (April–Sept Tues–Thurs 10am–4.30pm; £4; ⓦwww.miserdenestate.co.uk). The mismatch in spelling is, apparently, accurate: the village has an E, the gardens and manor house have an A, though nobody is sure why – and both are pronounced the same anyway. Up here, at over 800 feet in elevation, breezes can be a little fresh, but the topiary remains immaculate and the borders unruffled. Warm your cockles at the eighteenth-century *Carpenters Arms* (℡01285 821283) in the village. Sapperton (p.234) lies a few miles south, while narrow, steep lanes cross the valley and over to the Duntisbournes (see p.196), marking a **watershed**: on the ridge's western side, moisture drains into the Frome and thence to the Atlantic, while the eastern side drains to the Churn and the North Sea.

Slad

From **BIRDLIP**, a popular viewpoint up on the escarpment beside the A417, four or five miles east of Gloucester, the B4070 winds a scenic, undulating route southwest towards Stroud. Past turns for Sheepscombe (see opposite), the road dips to scoot along the western slope of the Slad valley. **SLAD** itself, a little village strung out along and below the road, with a steep hillside behind, enjoys tumbling vistas down to the Slad Brook and beyond. This was the home for many years at the beginning and end of his life of **Laurie Lee**, author of the famous childhood memoir *Cider with Rosie* (see box below).

Walks aside – there are plenty: an easy four-mile route circumnavigates the village from Bull's Cross on the ridge above, coming down to the brook, past the quarries and back up to the ridge again – Slad's most obvious draw is the *Woolpack* pub (℡01452 813429) on the main road. Lee's haunt for decades, it remains unrenovated, a simple stone cottage of an inn, with thick walls, small windows and outside toilets. The beer (from the Uley brewery the other side of Stroud) suits the yawning views from the little terrace to a T, and decent food, a step above usual pub fare, adds to the allure. Before you move on, you might pay a visit to Lee's last resting-place, in the graveyard of the Holy Trinity **church**, on the slopes opposite the pub. As it says on his stone, "He lies in the valley he loved."

Stroud

A couple of miles south of Slad, the B4070, the A46 from Painswick and half a dozen other roads from all directions slip into the humdrum market town of **STROUD**, once the centre of the local cloth industry, now famed chiefly for its **farmers' market**.

There are, in truth, few reasons to stop in Stroud: the best of this part of the Cotswolds lies chiefly in the countryside of the **Five Valleys** surrounding the town – the Painswick Valley and Slad Valley to the north, the Toadsmoor Valley and Frome Valley to the east (the latter also known as the "Golden Valley";

Laurie Lee in Slad

Laurie Lee is acclaimed as one of Britain's best twentieth-century writers. Born in Stroud in June 1914, he was raised by his mother in a Slad cottage; his father had left for London during World War I and never returned. Lee's most famous work *Cider with Rosie*, published in 1959 and often still given as a set text in schools, describes his childhood in Slad, evoking the atmosphere of the isolated rural village – before the appearance of cars – in beautifully vivid, engaging language. At the age of twenty, Lee left Slad for London and then travelled for four years through Spain, an experience recalled decades later in his masterpiece of travel writing *As I Walked Out One Midsummer Morning* (1969) and in *A Moment of War* (1991), a starkly affecting memoir of his time as a volunteer in the Spanish Civil War. Lee produced many other narrative books, essays and collections of poetry, yet seemed little taken with the London literary establishment. On the proceeds of *Cider with Rosie* he chose to buy a cottage in Slad, where he returned with his wife Kathy in the 1960s, remaining until his death in 1997.

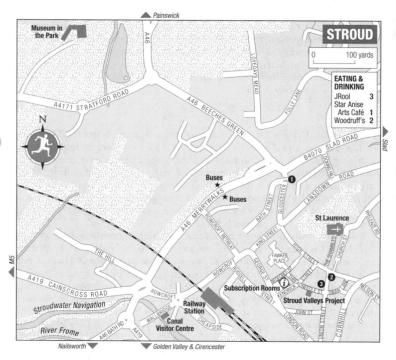

see opposite) and the Nailsworth Valley to the south (p.235). This topography of rushing streams, deep, narrow gorges and high common land for grazing sheep spurred the eighteenth- and nineteenth-century construction of textile mills galore, which in turn led to feats of engineering that transformed Stroud into a hub first for canal transport between the Severn and the Thames and, later, the railway. Stroud's legacy of textile excellence is celebrated at the **Museum in the Park**, in Stratford Park (Tues–Fri 10am–5pm, Sat & Sun 11am–5pm; Aug also Mon 10am–5pm; Oct–March closes 4pm; free; Ⓦwww.museuminthepark.org.uk), with historical displays and a roster of changing temporary exhibitions on art and design.

Nowadays Stroud is big on independent shops and markets. Leading the pack is the Saturday **farmers' market** (see p.205), a weekly jamboree of forty or fifty stallholders which fills the central streets, alongside music and impromptu happenings. In a similar vein, the Shambles, a medieval arcaded lane beside the church, hosts the **Shambles Market** (Ⓦwww.shamblesmarketstroud.co.uk) every Friday and Saturday – anything from books to cheese. You could also drop into the **Stroud Valleys Project** shop, 8 Threadneedle St (Ⓦwww.stroudvalleysproject .org), the front for a charity supporting environmentally sustainable businesses in the nearby villages, or any of a clutch of thriving, unbranded local shops, cafés and delis dotted through the town centre.

Practicalities

Make your way from Stroud's **railway station** – on the London–Cheltenham line – up through the steep streets of the busy town centre to the late-Regency **Subscription Rooms** on George Street. Now a modest concert venue, the building also hosts the **tourist office** (Mon–Sat 10am–5pm; ☏01453 760960, Ⓦwww.visitthecotswolds.org.uk & Ⓦwww.cotswolds.com). Among their racks of material are route descriptions for a series of walks through nearby villages and towpath strolls west along the Stroudwater Navigation **canal**, which begins at Wallbridge just behind the station.

If you're using public transport to get around, you may find yourself switching **buses** in Stroud. Most stop on Merrywalks, the main street west of the centre. Principal regular services include several operated by Stagecoach: bus 14/14B to/from **Gloucester**, bus 93 (not Sun) to/from Gloucester and **Nailsworth**, bus 46 to/from **Cheltenham** and Nailsworth, bus 20 (not Sun) to/from **Dursley**, bus 40 (not Sun) to/from **Wotton** and Nailsworth, and bus 26 (not Sun) to/from **Brimscombe** and **France Lynch**. Cotswold Green operate bus 54/54A (not Sun) to/from **Cirencester**, bus 29/29A (not Sun) to/from **Tetbury** and **Minchinhampton**, bus 28/28A (not Sun) to/from Cirencester, Minchinhampton and **Rodborough Common**, bus 25 (not Sun) to/from **Bisley** and bus 23 (once on Thurs) to/from **Slad**, **Sheepscombe** and **Miserden**.

For **eating**, *Woodruff's*, 24 High Street (℡01453 759195, ⓦwww.woodruffs organiccafe.co.uk) was Britain's first organic **café**, and remains a chatty, friendly place for a healthy, locally sourced lunch. Round the corner is the relaxed bistro *JRool*, 12 Union Street (closed Sun eve & Mon eve; ℡01453 767123, ⓦwww .jrool.co.uk), while a stroll away at the bottom of Gloucester Street, you could sample the lively buzz – and decent food – at the ✲ *Star Anise Arts Café* (closed Sun–Fri eve; ℡01453 840021, ⓦwww.staraniseartscafe.com), which is also one of the supporters of the characteristically community-minded **Stroud Pound** initiative (ⓦwww.stroudpound.org.uk), a local currency scheme that aims to help refloat the local economy through charitable support.

Roads head out from Stroud in all directions. To the north are **Painswick** (see p.228) and **Slad** (p.231). To the west it's a short drive to the **Vale of Berkeley** (p.225), while southwest is the glorious ridgetop B4066 **towards Uley** (p.241). To the south is **Nailsworth** (p.235), below the heights around **Minchinhampton** (p.234), while to the east lies the "**Golden Valley**" (see below) on the route to **Cirencester** (p.191).

East of Stroud: the Golden Valley

Hemmed in by high slopes on both sides, the A419 and the railway line head **east of Stroud** into the valley of the **River Frome**, named the "**Golden Valley**" – so locals claim – by Queen Victoria when gazing through her train window; on an autumn afternoon, when low sunshine lights up the wooded slopes, aflame with colour, it's not hard to see her point. The seven miles to Sapperton, where the railway and the Thames and Severn Canal both duck into tunnels beneath the hills, at one time hosted 150 mills processing Cotswold wool and other textiles for distribution around the Empire. Now the canal is long-disused (see ⓦwww.cotswold canalsproject.org for plans to revive it) and the villages are mostly quiet – but still virtually inaccessible, clinging to the forested slopes with only the narrowest of lanes to connect them.

CHALFORD, the main settlement, was known as "Little Switzerland": its Alpine slopes are speckled with mill-workers' cottages and threaded by a Lilliputian High Street barely wide enough to fit one car. Walk, instead, to find the distinctive **Round House** – a circular cottage that is still lived in – and to view the Arts and Crafts fittings in **Christ Church** on the main road. **FRANCE LYNCH** on the slopes above, named for exiled Huguenot weavers who settled here in the eighteenth century, is home to the *King's Head* (℡01453 882225, ⓦwww.kings headfrancelynch.co.uk), an award-winning local with good beer and decent food, while beside Chalford you could take shelter in Turkoman-style yurts on *Westley Farm* (☎01285 760262, ⓦwww.cotswoldyurts.co.uk), kitted out to luxury standards and bookable over the summer months for a minimum of three nights; the website has details.

Find a route via the lanes above Chalford to reach pretty **BISLEY**, dominated by the spire of All Saints' Church and centred on the *Bear Inn* (☎01452 770265, ⓦwww.bisleybear.co.uk), a rather lovely updated village pub, with one spick-and-span room for B&B (❸). Walking routes from the pub lead into the quiet, beech-filled **Toadsmoor Valley**.

At the upper end of the Golden Valley, **SAPPERTON** marks the "West Portal" of the canal tunnel (the "East Portal" is near Coates; see p.197). Two locally renowned pubs are worth heading this way for. The *Daneway Inn* (closed Mon eve; ☎01285 760297, ⓦwww.thedaneway.com) is a fine drinkers' pub near the portal. Slightly removed, in Sapperton village, the *Bell* (☎01285 760298, ⓦwww.food atthebell.co.uk) is known best for its **food**, well-presented modern British cooking in a cheerful, easygoing setting (mains £13–18). Book ahead if you can.

Minchinhampton and around

Gazing down on Stroud from between the Frome and the Nailsworth Stream, vertiginous slopes reach up to **Rodborough Common** and, adjacent to the south, **Minchinhampton Common**, 600 acres of wildflower-speckled limestone meadow which, in large part, are protected by the National Trust. Things can get a little wild and woolly up here: the commons are gloriously exposed, much loved by walkers, kite-flyers and other determined cobweb-blowers.

MINCHINHAMPTON itself is quite a find, a village of considerable character, with its handsome **High Street** culminating in the seventeenth-century **Market House**, raised on pillars to protect one-time stallholders beneath. Across the way, Holy Trinity **church** – of ancient foundation but rebuilt in 1842 – looks rather emasculated: its unsafe spire was pulled down in 1863 and a makeshift coronet hastily erected to preserve the stumpy half-tower's dignity. Beside the Market House, Minchinhampton's wonderfully named Woefuldane organic dairy has a **farm shop** (closed Sat pm, Sun & Mon; ☎01453 886855, ⓦwww.woefuldane organics.co.uk): drop in to snaffle one or two of their award-winning artisan cheeses, if nothing else. A few doors down stands *Sophie's* **restaurant**, 20 High Street (☎01453 885188, ⓦwww.sophiesrestaurant.co.uk), a highly respected, informal venue for mid-priced French country cooking and fine choices of French wines. Beware their curious hours – open for morning coffee and lunch on weekdays (Tues–Fri 9.15am–2pm) and in the evenings on selected Saturdays only; the website has details. Always book ahead. Two hundred metres east of the High Street, off Tetbury Street, is **Tobacconist Farm** (Wed–Fri 10am–6pm, Sat 10am–4pm; ☎01453 883534, ⓦwww.tobacconistfarm.co.uk), with farm visits for children as well as another great farm shop.

To **stay** up here, you could try the *Burleigh Court Hotel* (☎01453 883804, ⓦwww.burleighcourthotel.co.uk; ❻), a rather stiff – but very quiet – country house property hidden on the slopes just below Minchinhampton. A livelier choice lies across at the far (northern) side of the common: walk there direct, or make a short detour around the western ridge via nearby **AMBERLEY** for liquid and/or culinary refreshment at the cheery *Black Horse* (☎01453 872556, ⓦwww .blackhorseamberley.co.uk), with a terrace offering stupendous views. Where Minchinhampton Common becomes Rodborough Common, at the top of the winding Bear Hill road stands the castle-like *Bear of Rodborough* (☎01453 878522, ⓦwww.bearofrodborough.info; ❺–❻), a stout, traditional hotel – part of the

Cotswolds Inns and Hotels group – offering stout, traditional rooms: expect a sense of history overlaid with lots of dark, polished wood. Just over the way, on the eastern slopes of Rodborough Common, **Winstones** (℡01453 873270, Ⓦwww.winstonesicecream.co.uk) have been making ice cream locally since 1925; today, as well as supplying cafés and restaurants all over the Cotswolds, they still sell direct from their shop counter all year round.

Nailsworth

Set down in a forested valley below Minchinhampton, about four miles south of Stroud via the A46, **NAILSWORTH** once hummed to the activity of thirteen textile mills. Most are now refurbished as modern business estates, though **Dunkirk Mill**, complete with its twelve-foot water wheel, and **Gigg Mill** are occasionally accessible to the public on open days; timings and arrangements are publicized by the Stroudwater Textile Trust (Ⓦwww.stroud-textile.org.uk).

With its wooded surroundings and easygoing air, Nailsworth is a rather attractive little place. Drop into the **tourist office** (Mon–Fri 9.30am–5pm, Sat 9.30am–1pm; ℡01453 839222, Ⓦwww.visitthecotswolds.org.uk & Ⓦwww.cotswolds.com), located by the roundabout at the bottom of the main drag, Fountain Street, for a chat and a bit of local insight before setting off to discover – well, not much. There's a late-Victorian church, an ironmonger, a crafts shop, the Yellow-Lighted Bookshop. What matters here is **food**: Nailsworth has a reputation for culinary quality as well as diversity, and its **restaurants** draw people from far and wide. We review a selection below, some of which include **accommodation**. Look out, too, for the monthly **farmers' market** (see p.205).

Eating and drinking

Egypt Mill Bridge St ℡01453 833449, Ⓦwww.egyptmill.com. A charmingly renovated textile mill beside the River Frome in the town centre. The name recalls notorious eighteenth-century mill-owner Nathaniel Webb, who drove his workers so hard they nicknamed him Pharaoh and his mill Egypt. The days of bondage are thankfully past; now what you'll find is a cheerful clutter of memorabilia adorning a quirky, informal restaurant. Expect interesting approaches to familiar dishes: wild mushroom stroganoff with cognac, pork with black pudding, and the like. Mains are £12–16, but there are frequent cut-price offers, especially at lunchtime. This is also Nailsworth's most congenial hotel, with a choice of fresh, unfussy rooms in the main building or larger alternatives in the adjacent Mill House annexe. ❹–❺

Hobbs House 4 George St ℡01453 839396, Ⓦwww.hobbshousebakery.co.uk. Legendary Cotswold artisan baker, established in 1920 in Chipping Sodbury and now with outlets around the area, including this wonderful little bakery shop and bistro overlooking a free-flowing stream beside the street. It's great for coffee and light lunches, emphasizing British traditional dishes that are cooked with style from ingredients sourced locally. Mains £11–17. Mon–Sat 8am–3pm, plus Thurs–Sat 6.30–9.30pm.

Olive Tree 28 George St ℡01453 834802, Ⓦwww.theolivetree-nailsworth.com. Cheery little café-restaurant with a menu of Italian-cum-Mediterranean salads and light bites that covers familiar pizza/pasta ground while also venturing into moussaka and Moroccan stews (mains £10–12). Mon–Sat 8.30am–4pm, plus Thurs–Sat 6.30–9.30pm.

Passage to India Old Market ℡01453 834063. More than a simple curry house, this Indian restaurant has a gold-standard reputation, drawing diners from as far afield as Bath and Bristol for its perfectly authentic, perfectly cooked range of curries. Most mains are around the £11–13 mark.

Wild Garlic 3 Cossack Sq ℡01453 832615, Ⓦwww.wild-garlic.co.uk. Highly regarded restaurant serving imaginative food rooted in local flavours and traditions. The menu is short, but quality of cooking, presentation and service are tip-top. Closed Sun eve, Mon, Tues lunch. Also with three rooms for B&B. ❸

Williams Food Hall 3 Fountain St ℡01453 832240, Ⓦwww.williamsfoodhall.co.uk. This avowedly upscale deli-cum-fish market-cum-oyster bar opposite the tourist office is an impressive discovery. The smell of the sea hits you as soon as you step over the threshold, and their breakfasts (from 7.30am) and lunches are sensational – fishy specialities interspersed with posh takes on hearty English classics (mains £9–18). Daytimes only. Closed Sun.

Out of town

Weighbridge Inn Avening Rd ☎ 01453 832520, ⓦ www.2in1pub.co.uk. A mile or so east of Nailsworth on the B4014, in the depths of the forest by a bridge, this old pub has reinvented itself with a very simple culinary idea: the "2 in 1 pie". Hefty pies, baked in the bowl, are split fifty-fifty – you choose a filling for one side (steak and mushroom, perhaps, or pork and bacon in stilton sauce) and the chef supplies homemade cauliflower cheese for the other side. Pies range from £12.50 to £14, with smaller options available – and there's also a menu of familiar pub grub.

Tetbury

With Prince Charles's Highgrove estate on one side, his Duchy Home Farm on the other, and Princess Anne's Gatcombe Park estate just up the road near Avening, **TETBURY**'s claim to fame may be as the Cotswolds' most royal town – but, in truth, this attractive, engaging place has plenty going for it with or without the Windsors. Set on the Cotswold fringes, a mile or two from the Wiltshire border, Tetbury's combination of scenic countryside, a broad choice of accommodation, attractions both historic and – in the form of **Westonbirt Arboretum** – natural, plus good shopping and excellent food make this one of the best places in this entire chunk of the Cotswolds to hole up and chew the cud. It's also crammed with antique shops, and is undeniably posh: every August sees the **Festival of British Eventing** (ⓦ www.gatcombe-horse .co.uk), but then arrive on the last Monday in May for the **Woolsack Races** (ⓦ www.tetburywoolsack .co.uk) and you'll find local toughs hauling great lumpy sacks through the streets in front of cheering crowds, a dotty hangover from medieval days of wool wealth.

Map of Tetbury showing:

EATING & DRINKING
Chef's Table	1
House of Cheese	3
Hobbs House Bakery	4
The Ormond	B
Priory Inn	A
Quayles	2
Snooty Fox	E

ACCOMMODATION
The Close	D
Oak House No.1	C
The Ormond	B
Priory Inn	A
Snooty Fox	E
Talboys House	F

Arrival, information and accommodation

Trains on the London–Swindon–Cheltenham line stop at Kemble station (see p.197), about seven miles to the northeast. Stagecoach **bus** 881 (not Sun) runs about every two hours from the station to Tetbury, on a route from Cirencester. Otherwise, **taxis** meet arriving trains, charging about £18 into Tetbury; local firms include Corinium (☎01285 659331, ⓦwww.coriniumtaxis.co.uk) and Kemble (☎01285 800006, ⓦwww.taxisofkemble.co.uk). Tetbury is also served by Cotswold Green bus 29 (not Sun) to/from Stroud and Minchinhampton and Wessex Connect bus 620 (not Sun) to/from Bath and Chipping Sodbury.

Tetbury's **tourist office**, 33 Church Street (March–Oct Mon–Sat 10am–4pm; Nov–Feb Mon–Sat 11am–2pm; ☎01666 503552, ⓦwww.visittetbury.co.uk & ⓦwww.cotswolds.com), has encyclopedic quantities of information on attractions and services, including tours of Duchy Home Farm and wine- or cheese-tasting excursions to nearby farms. There's a wealth of high-quality **accommodation**, both in the centre and easily accessible in the nearby countryside.

In town

The Close Long St ☎01666 502272, ⓦwww .theclose-hotel.com. A grand old sixteenth-century house, whose fifteen bedrooms exude classic good taste and quality, with just enough of a contemporary zing to keep things interesting without falling into the trap of designer edginess. ⑤–⑥

Oak House No. 1 The Chipping ☎01666 505741, ⓦwww.oakhouseno1.com. Eye-popping superposh B&B in this centrally located Georgian town house. Just three suites are available, furnished with antiques and state-of-the-art contemporary bathrooms, and the public areas wow with opulent settings of designer art and one-off modern furniture. ⑦–⑧

The Ormond 23 Long St ☎01666 505690, ⓦwww.theormond.co.uk. Good-value threestar hotel in the centre of town, with a briskly engaging style of service and rooms which sport more taste and humour than you might expect for either the price, the location or the town. ④

Priory Inn London Rd ☎01666 502251, ⓦwww.theprioryinn.co.uk. Excellent familyfriendly hotel on the edge of the centre – bright, breezy and cheerful. The fourteen rooms are neutral and unfussy, focusing on comfort rather than fripperies and refreshingly free of the desire to impress. ⑤

Snooty Fox Market Place ☎01666 502436, ⓦwww.snooty-fox.co.uk. Traditional old coaching inn in the centre of town, renamed by a former owner who was snubbed by the local hunt. These days it's been thoroughly updated: the buzzy, outgoing atmosphere is rather engaging, a nod to the traditional here, a touch of playful japery there. Nothing surprises, but this is a reassuringly safe pair of hands. ④–⑤

Talboys House Church St ☎01666 503597, ⓦwww.talboyshouse.com. Seventeenth-century town house originally built for a wealthy wool merchant, with rooms lavishly themed along Indian lines, using swags of Kashmiri fabrics and prints of Hindu gods. ④

Out of town

Calcot Manor 4 miles west of Tetbury ☎01666 890391, ⓦwww.calcotmanor.com. Stylish, relaxed, efficient, friendly – it's hard to know where to begin with what is widely acknowledged as one of the best hotels in England. Located by the A4135/A46 crossroads, in an expansive 220 acres of grounds, its 35 rooms are each individually designed, with smaller ones in the main farmhouse and larger options – including family rooms – ranged around the adjacent courtyard. Nothing is too much trouble, yet, unlike at its sister property *Barnsley House* (see p.191), there's no hint of slightly amused detachment: staff are fully engaged with every guest and every concern, busting a gut to make sure it all goes just as you'd want. ⑨

Hare and Hounds 3 miles southwest of Tetbury ☎01666 881000, ⓦwww.hareand houndshotel.com. A fine, traditional country house hotel on the A433 just short of Westonbirt, offering a fresh, competent approach to four-star accommodation – nothing out of place and all bases covered. It's undoubtedly a cut above Tetbury's in-town hotels, and the quiet of the countryside location is lovely. Member of the Cotswold Inns and Hotels group. ⑤

Whatley Manor 4 miles south of Tetbury, near Easton Grey ☎01666 822888, ⓦwww.whatley manor.com. A thoroughly upmarket, unabashedly lavish country hotel, set around a cobbled courtyard and offering a rare blend of warmth in design and a lack of pretension. Its 23 rooms and suites are fitted out to an exceptionally high standard – and, at this slight remove from the main touring zones of the Cotswolds, benefiting from an agreeably local feel. Member of the Relais & Châteaux group. ⑨

The town and around

Directly across the road from the tourist office rises Tetbury's **church** – curiously dedicated to both St Mary the Virgin and St Mary Magdalen. You enter beneath the tower, its spire soaring to 186 feet; this was the only survival from a pre-existing church, demolished in 1777. The new church which resulted, completed in 1781, is acclaimed as one of the country's finest examples of **Georgian Gothic**: the view along the nave, with its dark box pews, candle chandeliers, slender wooden columns and enormous windows, is nothing short of breathtaking. The cloister-like ambulatory on the north side adds another dimension of eighteenth-century elegance.

Following Church Street north past the independent Yellow-Lighted Bookshop at no. 21 (Ⓦwww.yellow-lightedbookshop.co.uk) brings you to the main cross-roads, overlooked by the *Snooty Fox* inn and marked by the pillared, seventeenth-century **Market House**, which still hosts a general market every Wednesday and Saturday morning. From here, Tetbury's main drag, the aptly named **Long Street**, heads away to the northwest, lined with shops and hotels, including the **Highgrove Shop** at no. 10 (Ⓦwww.highgroveshop.com) – stocking only homeware and gift items – and, in the old courthouse at no. 63, the **Tetbury Heritage Centre** (Mon–Fri 10am–3pm; free), chiefly dedicated to displays on the history of policing.

Highgrove, home of Prince Charles, lies about a mile southwest of Tetbury off the A433 in **DOUGHTON**; tours of the **gardens** – led, needless to say, by a guide rather than HRH himself – operate in the summer (April–Oct; £16.50; book by phone ℡020 7766 7310, Ⓦwww.highgrovegardens.com). There's a waiting list of several weeks. In the other direction from Tetbury, turn off the A433 London road to follow Cherington Lane north: a few hundred yards along you come to **Duchy Home Farm**, where Charles first experimented with organic farming on a large scale in the 1980s. It still operates as the leading source of produce for the Duchy Originals brand – drop into their Veg Shed **farm shop** (Wed, Fri & Sat 8am–5pm; ℡01666 503507) to pick up the freshest of organic ingredients.

A couple of stately homes lie in the Tetbury countryside. Further along the A433 towards Cirencester you'll reach **Rodmarton Manor** (May–Sept Wed & Sat 2–5pm; £8; Ⓦwww.rodmarton-manor.co.uk), designed by Arts and Crafts devotee Ernest Barnsley and completed in 1929 using local materials and skilled craft workers. As well as the house – crammed with original Arts and Crafts furniture – the gardens are a noteworthy attraction. On minor roads a couple of miles northwest of Tetbury, **Chavenage House** (May–Sept Thurs & Sun 2–5pm; £7; Ⓦwww.chavenage.com) is a captivatingly beautiful Elizabethan house, still lived in as a family home and a regular star in TV costume dramas from *Lark Rise to Candleford* to *Tess of the D'Urbervilles*.

Eating and drinking

Like Cirencester, Stow and one or two other Cotswold locations, Tetbury has a reputation for excellence in **eating and drinking**: the town hosts a clutch of fine restaurants, with several country inns and hotels nearby adding to the choice. As well as the options reviewed below, the *Potting Shed* at Crudwell (see p.241), *Wild Duck* at Ewen (p.197) and places in Nailsworth (p.235) are all within easy reach. Tetbury's September **Food and Drink Festival** (Ⓦwww.tetbury fooddrinkfestival.com) sees a host of foodie events over a long weekend, the family-run Bow-in-the-Cloud **vineyard** (℡01666 823040, Ⓦwww.bowinthe cloud.co.uk) near Malmesbury offers regular **wine-tasting** events – and then there are the **delis** about town, from House of Cheese, 13 Church Street (closed

Sun & Mon; ☎01666 502865, ⓦwww.houseofcheese.co.uk), and Hobbs House Bakery, 18 Church Street (closed Sun; ☎01666 504533, ⓦwww.hobbshouse bakery.co.uk) to Quayles, 1 Long Street (☎01666 505151, ⓦwww.quayles .co.uk), akin to a ritzy London food hall in its variety and quality.

In town

Chef's Table 49 Long St ☎01666 504466, ⓦwww.thechefstable.co.uk. Combination of a daytime deli, which doubles as a café, and the upstairs bistro, open for lunch and dinner, which is focused on an open kitchen. Come for the freshest of French-influenced rustic dishes, whipped up from whatever's arrived at the deli and chalked up daily on a board (mains £8–13) – or book ahead for their cookery day courses (£130) and cook your own lunch. Closed Sun, Mon eve & Tues eve.

The Ormond See "Accommodation" p.237. This award-winning restaurant focuses squarely on local suppliers, with an inventive range of classic, hearty dishes – think honey-roast ham, steak and ale pie or juniper duck with sausage – presented with style. It is, however, far from formal: good food and intelligent service mark it out. Mains £10–18.

Priory Inn See "Accommodation" p.237. This cheerful, family-friendly spot emphasizes local credentials: ninety percent of their ingredients are sourced within thirty miles of Tetbury. In this case, though, it's less of an issue, since – although the mains of Gloucester pork or Bibury trout are excellent (£11–18) – the house speciality is wood-fired pizza (£7–10): they still manage to work in Double Gloucester and local bacon as toppings, but, as far as pizza is concerned, hang the ethics and go for flavour.

Snooty Fox See "Accommodation" p.237. Pleasant, accommodating atmosphere in this popular inn, where uncomplicated cooking is presented decently and charged moderately. Mains £10–21.

Out of town

Calcot Manor See "Accommodation" p.237. This outstanding country hotel has two dining options. The posher is the *Conservatory* restaurant (mains £17–26), specializing in fish and shellfish – artfully done but less engaging than the adjacent *Gumstool Inn*, a rather bogus version of a country pub but nonetheless with much of the same food though priced considerably lower (mains £10–17), alongside a welter of upscale pub favourites, from fish pie to sausage and mash.

Hare and Hounds See "Accommodation" p.237. Another place with two options – but this time, if you're prepared to push the boat out, the extremely good *Beaufort Restaurant* is a sound choice, with a solid reputation among the regulars from the Beaufort Polo Club next door. Expect a small menu of carefully selected ingredients, explained and enhanced by the outstanding wait staff, and top-notch presentation. Two courses are £29. The *Jack Hare's Bar* alongside plays the "restaurant food in a pub setting" trick to perfection (mains £12–18).

Trouble House 3 miles northeast of Tetbury ☎01666 502206, ⓦwww.troublehousetetbury .co.uk. Intriguingly named old country pub on the A433 Cirencester road, now an upmarket restaurant with a reputation for inventiveness, perhaps mixing fish with chorizo or offering bhajis as a starter. The atmosphere is calm and easygoing: all the effort goes into the cooking. Definitely worth booking. Mains £13–15. Closed Sun eve & Mon.

Westonbirt Arboretum

A little over three miles southwest of Tetbury via the A433, just before the village of **WESTONBIRT**, lies **Westonbirt: The National Arboretum** (Mon–Fri 9am to dusk, Sat & Sun 8am to dusk; £6–10 depending on season; ⓦwww.forestry .gov.uk/westonbirt). Wessex Connect **bus** 620 (not Sun) from Tetbury drops off at the entrance. Everything about the place relies on superlatives, from its role as protector of some of the oldest, biggest and rarest trees in the world to the display of natural colours it puts on in autumn, when even superlatives are insufficient. With 17 miles of paths to roam, across 600 acres and between 16,000 trees, the best advice is to make a day of it. There's plenty to do, including **self-guided trails**, prepared by staff for each season, **guided walks** (Easter–Oct Sat & Sun 2pm; free; book ahead on ☎01666 880147), lots for kids and families, the annual **Festival of the Tree** (last week of Aug), which features wood sculpting and workshops, the canine-friendly **Dog Days** weekend every February, and more.

Malmesbury

The small Wiltshire hill town of **MALMESBURY** lies on the periphery of the Cotswolds, five miles southeast of Tetbury (and twelve miles south of Cirencester). It may have lost most of its good looks with a rash of modern development, but there's no gainsaying the stirring beauty of its partly ruinous Norman abbey.

The **High Street** begins at the bottom of the hill by the old silk mills and heads north across the river and up past a jagged row of ancient cottages on its way to the octagonal **Market Cross**, built around 1490 to provide shelter from the rain and now the venue for the fortnightly **farmers' market** (see p.205). Nearby, the eighteenth-century **Tolsey Gate** leads through to the **abbey** (daily 10am–5pm; Nov–March closes 4pm; free; Ⓦwww.malmesburyabbey.info), which was once a rich and powerful Benedictine monastery. The first abbey burnt down in about 1050, the second was roughed up during the Dissolution, but the beautiful Norman **nave** of the abbey church has survived, its south porch sporting a multitude of exquisite if badly worn Romanesque figures. Three bands of figures surround the doorway, depicting scenes from the Creation, the Old Testament and the life of Christ, while inside the porch the apostles and Christ are carved in a fine deep relief – stately figures in flowing folds surmounted by a flying angel. The tympanum shows Christ on a rainbow, supported by gracefully gymnastic angels. Within the main body of the church, the pale stone brings a dramatic freshness, particularly to the carving of the nave arches (look out for the Norman beak-heads) and of the clerestory. To the left of the high altar, the pulpit virtually hides the **tomb of King Athelstan**, grandson of Alfred the Great and the first Saxon to be recognized as king of England; the tomb, however, is empty and the location of the king's body is unknown. Malmesbury's local celebrities include **Eilmer the Monk**, who in 1005 attempted to fly from the abbey tower with the aid of wings: he limped for the rest of his life, but won immortal fame as the "flying monk".

Beside the abbey, the splendid **Abbey House Gardens** (mid-March to end Oct daily 11am–5.30pm; £6.50; Ⓦwww.abbeyhousegardens.co.uk) have gained popularity as the home of the TV-featured "Naked Gardeners"; they offer a few "clothes optional" visiting days each year, detailed on the website.

Practicalities

Buses to Malmesbury from Cotswold destinations are limited to the Andybus 93 (not Sun) to/from **Cirencester** and **Crudwell** and Cotswold Green bus 278 (once on Wed & Fri) to/from **Tetbury**. They stop on Cross Hayes, round the corner from the Market Cross, right by the **tourist office** (Mon–Thurs 9am–4.50pm, Fri 9am–4.20pm, Easter–Sept also Sat 10am–4pm; Ⓣ01666 823748, Ⓦwww.malmesbury.gov.uk & Ⓦwww.visitwiltshire.co.uk), which shares the entrance for the **Athelstan Museum** (daily 10.30am–4.30pm; free; Ⓦwww.athelstanmuseum.org.uk), an engaging and well-presented local history collection.

Stop in at the *Smoking Dog* on the High Street (Ⓣ01666 825823) – despite the weird name, it's a fine old drinkers' **pub** with decent food. There's no real reason to **stay**, though the *Old Bell* in Abbey Row (Ⓣ01666 822344, Ⓦwww.oldbellhotel.co.uk; ⑤) provides a strong incentive: originally built as a guest house for the abbey, it has loads of atmosphere, strikingly modernized rooms and a good **restaurant**. Note that if you're visiting on the last weekend in July, the mammoth **WOMAD** music festival (Ⓦwww.womad.org) attracts over 80,000 people to Charlton Park, a mile northeast of Malmesbury off the B4040: be prepared for traffic delays and diversions.

Crudwell

Four miles north of Malmesbury on the A429 Cirencester road, and easily reached on back roads east of Tetbury, **CRUDWELL** is an unremarkable village made remarkable by the success of its ⚥ *Potting Shed Pub* (℡01666 577833, Ⓦwww .thepottingshedpub.com). A gently contemporary conversion of an old village boozer, this is now one of the leading rural **restaurants** in the Cotswolds, awarded a fistful of gongs which include National Dining Pub of the Year 2011. All the gloominess of its old low-beamed interior has been banished, with light Shaker-style wood panelling to the bar, clutter-free flagstones underfoot and an eponymous *faux*-potting shed extension, sporting artfully placed garden paraphernalia under a high pitched ceiling. Aside from knowing how to pull a proper pint, they've also brought a whiff of panache to country pub dining: their chips are triple-cooked, their autumn burger made from local pheasant, their mash laced with basil, their cod served with chorizo and lemon fondant potato. Mains are £13–19, a snip considering the quality. Book well in advance, at lunch or dinner.

Adding to Crudwell's newfound allure, just across the road is the sister business, the splendid ⚥ *Rectory* **hotel** (℡01666 577194, Ⓦwww.therectoryhotel.com; ⑤–⑥), a twelve-bedroom country house that delivers comfort and quiet without attempting to spring surprises – other than in the tea menu, which lists eleven varieties from Lahloo smokey to Darjeeling second flush.

Five miles north of Crudwell brings you to Kemble station (see p.197) and Ewen (p.197), with Cirencester (p.191) a couple of miles further.

From Stroud to Uley

Southwest of Stroud, the **B4066** cuts a glorious route along the Cotswold Edge, worth driving simply for the sake of it. As you climb away from the Frome valley, **SELSLEY** – or, specifically, the saddleback tower of its glorious Arts and Crafts **church** of All Saints (Ⓦwww.allsaintsselsley.org.uk) – hoves into view, the church adorned with stained glass by William Morris. Further up, on a left-hand curve, a signed turn leads left down a track to a valley-side car park. This is the closest you can drive to **Woodchester Mansion** (Ⓦwww.woodchestermansion .org.uk), a rather spooky Victorian Gothic house in a hidden valley which was left part-built in 1873 and never completed. It can be visited only on selected **open days**, as publicized on the website – effectively weekends in summer plus some other days in spring and autumn. Parking is free; admission to the house costs £5.50. However, the only access is on foot from the car park – a walk of about a mile down the hillside – or with the free shuttle, which runs on open days. Note that Woodchester village lies several miles away on the A46, from where there is no access. Around the mansion stretches **Woodchester Park** (Ⓦwww.national trust.org.uk), with some silent walks beside a string of five lakes.

Walks around Selsley and Uley

Two easy **circular walks** using part of the Cotswold Way – and both downloadable at Ⓦwww.cotswoldsaonb.org.uk – offer scenic routes flanking this bit of the B4066. The first (5 miles; 4hr) begins at **KING'S STANLEY**, reached from Stroud and Gloucester on bus 14, and heads up straight away onto Selsley Common, offering grand views over the Severn. After a pause in Selsley village, the path drops down for a towpath walk along the Stroudwater canal before the return to King's Stanley. The second route (4 miles; 3hr 30min) begins at the *Old Crown* in **ULEY** (see p.242), climbing steeply to Uley Bury and then out onto Cam Long Down for more all-round panoramic views before circling back to the bury and down into Uley again.

The same turning off the B4066 marks a minor road to **NYMPSFIELD**, a rather pretty village, unused to visitors; hole up for a while in the *Rose and Crown* (℡01453 860240) or branch off on Tinkley Lane for the *Thistledown Environmental Centre* (℡01453 860420, Ⓦwww.thistledown.org.uk), to explore their eco-conservation schemes (daily 10am–5.30pm; £3.50) or spend the night at their **organic campsite**, accessible by car.

Back on the B4066, just past the Nympsfield turn is a layby for the **Coaley Peak viewpoint**, the first of several along this stretch offering vistas out over the Severn Vale. Here is also the Neolithic burial mound **Nympsfield Long Barrow**, while just further along the road is the **Uley Long Barrow**, also known as **Hetty Pegler's Tump** (after a seventeenth-century landowner, and currently off-limits for renovation work; Ⓦwww.english-heritage.org.uk). A bit further, before the road drops down off the ridge, to one side rises the mound of **Uley Bury**, among the largest Iron Age hill-forts in Britain. Fences prevent you from clambering on top of the bury, but you can walk around the edge – about two miles in total – and take in some staggering views. The atmosphere peaks on a winter's day, when bracing winds blow across the ridge while mist gathers in the valley below.

Six miles out of Stroud, the B4066 finally drops down into **ULEY**, whose village **church** lords it over the small green and *Old Crown* pub (℡01453 860502, Ⓦwww.theoldcrownuley.co.uk) – a fine place to sup a local Uley ale (Ⓦwww.uleybrewery.com). Beside the pub, Fiery Lane branches down through dense woods to reach **OWLPEN**, home of the superb Arts and Crafts **Owlpen Manor** (Ⓦwww.owlpen.com), closed at the time of writing, with a projected reopening date in 2012.

From Uley, the B4066 continues its anticlimactic descent into Dursley.

Dursley and North Nibley

Tucked into a fold of the Cotswold escarpment, the valley-floor town of **DURSLEY** doesn't have much to say for itself. A couple of old buildings and a grand church in its centre are overshadowed by humdrum modern commerce, fuelled by Dursley's location astride a network of main roads, including the A4135 from Tetbury, which links to the Gloucester–Bristol A38. Slimbridge (see p.226) and Berkeley (p.227) lie two or three miles west. The Cotswold Way passes through and, in truth, so should you. One thing might hold you back, though. Dursley's *Old Spot Inn* (℡01453 542870, Ⓦwww.oldspotinn.co.uk) has won a barrelful of awards, not least National Pub of the Year, for the quality of its beer and its determinedly unreconstructed interior: an ordinary old fireplace, bookcase in the corner, plain tile floor, and so on. Hunt it out for a pint to savour: it's hidden away on Hill Road, off Dursley's main street.

Soaring above Dursley and its adjoining neighbour **CAM** is **Stinchcombe Hill**, famed as the westernmost point of the Cotswolds; struggle up to the scenic golf course on the top, or follow the wiggly B4060 as it circumnavigates the hill. Once you've come around you'll spot on a shoulder of the hills ahead what looks like a tall obelisk. This is the 111-foot **Tyndale Monument**, built in 1866 to commemorate William Tyndale, the first person to translate the Bible into English, who was born around these parts in about 1490. Paths lead up to it from **NORTH NIBLEY** at its base, and you can normally enter to climb the interior staircase for exceptional views from the top. Paths around the summit – short, steep ones and longer, gentler ones – lead back to North Nibley.

Below North Nibley, the slenderest, tightest of lanes drops down into the valley, signposted to **WATERLEY BOTTOM**. It's a difficult drive: the lane forks several times without warning (and without signposts) and there are few passing places.

It's worth studying the OS map as you go, in order to find the seriously well-hidden *New Inn* (☎01453 543659) among orchards on the valley floor, another top-rated country pub.

Wotton-under-Edge

The B4060 coils around to enter **WOTTON-UNDER-EDGE**, passing first the cheery, well-stocked **Wotton Farm Shop** (☎01453 521546, ⓦwww .wottonfarmshop.co.uk). Wotton itself, crammed beneath high slopes, makes for a picturesque diversion: **Long Street**, as well as ordinary shops and banks, has some good-looking old buildings. Turn left onto **Market Street** to reach the **Heritage Centre**, which doubles as the **tourist office** (Tues–Fri 10am–1pm & 2–4.45pm, Sat 10am–1pm; Nov–March Tues–Fri closes 4pm; ☎01453 521541, ⓦwww.wottonheritage.com & ⓦwww.visitthecotswolds.org.uk), on the corner of the Chipping market square. The same building, entered from Market Street, houses the **Electric Picture House** (ⓦwww.wottoneph.co.uk), a popular art-house cinema run by Wotton volunteers: taking the weight off for a couple of hours in front of a flickering screen is, oddly, a great way to support the local economy.

A gentle **walk** of four and half miles leads down from the Chipping on signed paths southwest to **KINGSWOOD** village, where a grand sixteenth-century gatehouse (ⓦwww.english-heritage.org.uk) is the only remnant of a demolished Cistercian abbey. Paths lead on through the fields in a circuit back to Wotton. To the southeast of town near **OZLEWORTH** stands the Tudor hunting lodge **Newark Park** (June–Oct Wed, Thurs, Sat & Sun 11am–5pm; March–May Wed & Thurs only; £5.65; ⓦwww.nationaltrust.org.uk & www.michaelclaydon .co.uk), reached from Wotton on a rising and falling **circular walk** (6.5 miles; 5hr; downloadable at ⓦwww.cotswoldsaonb.org.uk) that also takes in a chunk of the Cotswold Way.

To the Sodburys

South of Wotton, where the A46 and A433 meet, **HAWKESBURY UPTON** stands out for the seventeenth-century *Beaufort Arms* (☎01454 238217, ⓦwww .beaufortarms.com), a fine old pub whose name highlights the presence, a mile south, of **BADMINTON** village, famed for its April horse trials (ⓦwww .badminton-horse.co.uk) and the adjacent **Badminton House**, residence of the dukes of Beaufort for more than three hundred years (but closed to the public).

Further south on the A46, a turn-off west drops down to **CHIPPING SODBURY**, a pleasant, busy market town with a long history: its name is Saxon, deriving from "Soppa's burg" (though no record survives of who Soppa was), prefixed by *ceapen*, meaning market. The **High Street** is purportedly one of the widest in England, formerly flanked by market stalls. Partway along, beside the centrally placed **clock tower**, is the **tourist office** (mid-March to end Oct Mon–Sat 10am–5pm; ☎01454 888686, ⓦwww.visitchippingsodbury.com & ⓦwww .cotswolds.com), well stocked with maps and leaflets. The clock tower is also the location of Sodbury's twice-monthly **farmers' market** (see p.205). Further east, **Broad Street** has a number of handsome facades; a Tudor house survives on nearby Hatters Lane. On Horse Street, past the post office, an eighteenth-century **milestone** marks the distance of 108 miles to Hyde Park Corner in London. A fine town-house **B&B** is *Moda House*, 1 High Street (☎01454 312135, ⓦwww .modahouse.co.uk; ❹), with eleven comfortable rooms.

The tourist office has details of a twenty-mile **cycle ride** through the nearby countryside to **WICKWAR** and back, or you could head less than a mile east to

OLD SODBURY, a silent residential village topped by the ancient **church** of St John the Baptist: a Saxon-style T-shaped stone in the external east wall, carved with four rounded crosses, suggests that the church's knoll has been a place of worship for many centuries, if not millennia. It's got bags of atmosphere. Andybus 41 (not Sun) and Wessex Connect bus 620 (not Sun) make the short run between Sodburys. A **circular walk** (2.5 miles; 2hr) from the church runs north along the Cotswold Way to **LITTLE SODBURY** and back across the fields; download details at Ⓦ www.cotswoldsaonb.org.uk.

Castle Combe

East of the Sodburys, the B4039 sidles south over the M4, from where signposted back lanes give access to **CASTLE COMBE** (Ⓦ www.castle-combe.com), a remarkable (but often very crowded) medieval village which has almost entirely kept its looks. The lower village – the part of interest – forms a single, narrow street, with nowhere to park and not much space to get through; if you're driving, the best advice is to leave your car in the free car park just off the B4039 and walk the few minutes down the hill.

On the way you'll pass the village **museum** (Easter–Oct Sun 2–5pm; free; Ⓦ www.museum.castle-combe.com), a modest local history collection. First sight of the village is the multi-gabled Dower House, built around 1700. Then you come down to the titchy main square, marked by the medieval **Market Cross**, its square tiled roof supported on four thick stone pillars. The view down the main street is exceptional: although evidence of 21st-century life does exist (road markings, signs, a bus stop), Castle Combe's appearance has changed little in 500 years. It shares a Cotswold history: the Bybrook stream, which is the village's *raison d'être*, at one time ran three textile mills – most of Castle Combe's houses are weavers' cottages. Off to the right is the **church** of St Andrew, an unusually grand wool church which shelters the tomb of Walter de Dunstanville, a Crusading knight (and Baron of Castle Combe) who died in 1270. The Norman **castle** for which the village is named survives only as barely discernible foundations, now out of bounds on a hilltop golf course. Up on top, too, is **Castle Combe Circuit** (Ⓦ www.castlecombecircuit.co.uk) – essentially the perimeter track of an old airfield – which hosts various rally and touring car championships, as well as have-a-go track day events.

Practicalities

By the Market Cross, the *White Hart* (☎ 01249 782295) is a medieval half-timbered **inn** which, centuries on, still focuses on beer. Directly opposite, the *Castle Inn* (☎ 01249 783030, Ⓦ www.castle-inn.info; ⑤) is a posh choice for **dining** (mains £16–20), also with lovely **rooms**; it goes without saying that the best times to explore the village and surrounding valleyside paths are morning and evening, before or after the bulk of visitors roam. See the locals' website Ⓦ www.castle -combe.com for details of other accommodation.

Bath, last stop on the Cotswold Way, lies about ten miles to the south.

Contexts

Contexts

Books

T he Cotswolds are awash with opportunities for **further reading** – indeed, in a region so famous for its beauty, it can be a relief to exercise a different set of muscles by reading about the place rather than relying solely on appearances. The few choices below are not intended to form a comprehensive bibliography. Rather, they are a selection of some easily accessible, broadly representative titles; those with the 🏃 symbol are particularly recommended.

Cotswold **memoirs** from the early and middle years of the last century abound, but most are now out of print. We haven't touched on the many widely known titles that mention the Cotswolds within a larger frame of reference, such as Bill Bryson's *Notes from a Small Island* or Simon Jenkins' *England's Thousand Best Churches*. Of the dozens of **walking guides** – both commercially produced books and smaller, often self-published pamphlets (which you'll find for sale in local tourist offices) – we've picked out a noteworthy handful. We've also included a small selection of books which could serve as an introduction to **Oxford**.

A word about purchasing: we've tried, here and there throughout the guide, to draw attention to **independent bookshops** that survive in towns and – sometimes – villages across the region. Although it's easy to buy books and maps online, or at chain bookstores in larger towns, try to hunt down a locally owned bookshop instead: these places offer a degree of expertise and local knowledge that can far outstrip the competition – not to mention stock that may include titles of local interest that are difficult or impossible to find elsewhere. See ⓦ www.localbook shops.co.uk for listings.

Oxford

James Attlee *Isolarion: a Different Oxford Journey*. Intriguing sidelong glance at Oxford constructed around a route along the busy, unpretentious Cowley Road: rather than medieval architecture and dreaming spires, this is more about pubs and street culture, woven around a meditation on the meaning of place.

Colin Dexter The *Inspector Morse* series. Traditional crime writing which brilliantly evokes the atmosphere and daily life of Oxford. Any of the thirteen novels in the series – from *Last Bus to Woodstock* (1975) through to *The Remorseful Day* (1999) – alongside a handful of short stories published separately, offers identifiable Oxford settings, as Dexter constructs superb plots centred on his famously prickly detective. The TV series (1987–2000; ⓦ www.inspectormorse .co.uk), starring John Thaw, ran for

33 episodes, not all of which were based on Dexter's work.

🏃 **Jan Morris** *Oxford*. A classic account of the city by one of Britain's most distinguished travel writers, first published in 1965. Also seek out her anthology of almost a thousand years of writing on the university, published as *The Oxford Book of Oxford*.

🏃 **Philip Pullman** *Northern Lights; The Subtle Knife; The Amber Spyglass*. Hugely entertaining and thought-provoking novels, set partly in Oxford – though an Oxford from a slightly other world. Brought together as a trilogy under the title *His Dark Materials*.

Geoffrey Tyack *Oxford: an Architectural Guide*. Accomplished, broad-brush approach to understanding the city's architecture, in a chronological format from the eleventh century to the present day.

Jenny Woolf *The Mystery of Lewis Carroll: Understanding the Author of Alice in Wonderland*. Detailed biography of Carroll, delving deep into his private life in Oxford – and notably unearthing his previously undiscovered bank accounts. Fascinating stuff.

The Cotswolds

Fiction

Jane Bailey *Tommy Glover's Sketch of Heaven*. Beautifully written evocation of Cotswold village life during World War II, as Kitty, an eight-year-old London evacuee, tries to adjust. Follow this with Bailey's *Mad Joy*, another wartime Cotswold yarn.

Jilly Cooper *Riders*. The first – and most famous – of the *Rutshire Chronicles* series of racy blockbuster paperbacks, partly set in the Cotswolds countryside (Cooper lives in Bisley, near Stroud). The plot is constructed around a feud between two showjumpers, but it doesn't really matter: as one reviewer neatly put it, "Sex and horses – who could ask for more?".

Katie Fforde *Flora's Lot*. One of the best-known novelists at work in the Cotswolds today, Fforde frequently draws on rural life to inform and enrich her unique brand of comic romantic fiction – not least in this light, charming tale of a townie who tries to rejuvenate a country antiques business.

History and background

Jane Bingham *The Cotswolds: A Cultural History*. Inspiring, fascinating analysis of what the Cotswolds has meant to insiders and outsiders alike over centuries, using analysis of literary and artistic sources – and a deep understanding of the place – to shed unusually clear light.

William Fiennes *The Music Room*. Beautifully written memoir, placing the author's childhood, growing up at the moated Jacobean mansion Broughton Castle near Banbury, alongside the family drama of his epileptic, increasingly violent brother. A moving, memorable read.

Laurie Lee *Cider with Rosie*. The archetypal Cotswold tale, a memoir of the author's childhood in Slad, just north of Stroud, in the years after World War I – vivid, lyrical and utterly absorbing. Essential reading.

J.B. Priestley *English Journey*. Minor gem of early travel writing, as Priestley travels around England in 1933, beautifully describing Burford, the Slaughters, Bourton-on-the-Water and elsewhere and – even then – decrying the tide of tearooms and urban day-trippers.

Rob Rees *The Cotswold Chef: a Year in Recipes and Landscapes*. Slim volume packed with seasonal recipes by Rees (see also p.27), a chef and tireless advocate for Cotswold food producers.

Ivor Smith *Memoirs of a Cotswold Vet*. Herriot-style account of life in a small veterinary practice over the years 1972 to 2001, laced with humour, insight and colourful characters.

Ian Walthew *A Place in My Country: In Search of a Rural Dream*. An urban writer ups sticks to a Cotswold village. It's a familiar format, but this is a book which breaks the mould: the author not only deftly describes the country characters around him, but begins to empathize with them, as an image emerges of a rural economy decimated by wealthy outsiders and a rural culture relentlessly undermined by a national preoccupation with all things urban.

Rev. F.E. Witts *The Diary of a Cotswold Parson*. The day-to-day doings of Reverend Witts of Upper Slaughter covering the period 1820 to 1852, as he commutes daily to Gloucester and observes the building boom in Cheltenham.

Nature and walking guides

Anthony Burton *Cotswold Way*. The official National Trail guide for the Cotswold Way, complete with Ordnance Survey mapping. Of the many other books on the path, the most diverting is Mark Richards' *The Cotswold Way*, the first-ever guide (published in 1973, when Richards was a full-time Cotswold farmer, and subsequently updated): its route descriptions are supplemented with a wealth of local knowledge and Wainwright-style pen-and-ink drawings.

Iain Main, Dave Pearce & Tim Hutton *Birds of the Cotswolds: a New Breeding Atlas*. Updated guide to the region's bird life, taking into account habitat changes since the 1980s and featuring maps and photos.

Nicholas Mander *Country Houses of the Cotswolds*. A lavishly illustrated account of more than thirty of the region's grandest houses, drawn from the archives of *Country Life* magazine.

Helen Peacocke *Paws Under the Table: 40 Dog-Friendly Pubs and Walks from Oxford to the Cotswolds*. Does what it says on the tin.

Tony Russell *The Cotswolds' Finest Gardens*. The former head forester at Westonbirt Arboretum – now a BBC gardening regular – describes sixty of the region's best publicly accessible gardens, alongside an array of colour photos.

C

CONTEXTS | Books

Small print and
Index

A Rough Guide to Rough Guides

Published in 1982, the first Rough Guide – to Greece – was a student scheme that became a publishing phenomenon. Mark Ellingham, a recent graduate in English from Bristol University, had been travelling in Greece the previous summer and couldn't find the right guidebook. With a small group of friends he wrote his own guide, combining a highly contemporary, journalistic style with a thoroughly practical approach to travellers' needs.

The immediate success of the book spawned a series that rapidly covered dozens of destinations. And, in addition to impecunious backpackers, Rough Guides soon acquired a much broader and older readership that relished the guides' wit and inquisitiveness as much as their enthusiastic, critical approach and value-for-money ethos.

These days, Rough Guides include recommendations from shoestring to luxury and cover more than 200 destinations around the globe, including almost every country in the Americas and Europe, more than half of Africa and most of Asia and Australasia. Our ever-growing team of authors and photographers is spread all over the world, particularly in Europe, the US and Australia.

In the early 1990s, Rough Guides branched out of travel, with the publication of Rough Guides to World Music, Classical Music and the Internet. All three have become benchmark titles in their fields, spearheading the publication of a wide range of books under the Rough Guide name.

Including the travel series, Rough Guides now number more than 350 titles, covering: phrasebooks, waterproof maps, music guides from Opera to Heavy Metal, reference works as diverse as Conspiracy Theories and Shakespeare, and popular culture books from iPods to Poker. Rough Guides also produce a series of more than 120 World Music CDs in partnership with World Music Network.

Visit www.roughguides.com to see our latest publications.

Rough Guide credits

Text editor: Lucy White
Layout: Umesh Aggarwal
Cartography: Ed Wright
Picture editor: Nicole Newman
Production: Erika Pepe
Proofreader: Helen Castell
Cover design: Nicole Newman, Dan May
Photographer: Chloë Roberts
Editorial: **London** Andy Turner, Keith Drew,
Edward Aves, Alice Park, Jo Kirby, James Smart,
Natasha Foges, Róisín Cameron, James Rice,
Emma Beatson, Emma Gibbs, Kathryn Lane,
Monica Woods, Mani Ramaswamy, Harry Wilson,
Lucy Cowie, Lara Kavanagh, Alison Roberts,
Eleanor Aldridge, Ian Blenkinsop, Joe Staines,
Matthew Milton, Tracy Hopkins; **Delhi** Madhavi
Singh, Jalpreen Kaur Chhatwal, Jubbi Francis
Design & Pictures: **London** Scott Stickland,
Dan May, Diana Jarvis, Mark Thomas,
Sarah Cummins, Emily Taylor; **Delhi** Ajay Verma,
Jessica Subramanian, Ankur Guha, Pradeep
Thapliyal, Sachin Tanwar, Anita Singh, Nikhil
Agarwal, Sachin Gupta
Production: Rebecca Short, Liz Cherry,
Louise Daly
Cartography: **London** Katie Lloyd-Jones;
Delhi Rajesh Chhibber, Ashutosh Bharti, Rajesh
Mishra, Animesh Pathak, Jasbir Sandhu, Swati
Handoo, Deshpal Dabas, Lokamata Sahu
Marketing, Publicity & roughguides.com:
Liz Statham
Digital Travel Publisher: Peter Buckley
Reference Director: Andrew Lockett
Operations Coordinator: Becky Doyle
Publishing Director (Travel): Clare Currie
Commercial Manager: Gino Magnotta
Managing Director: John Duhigg

Publishing information

This first edition published May 2011 by
Rough Guides Ltd,
80 Strand, London WC2R 0RL
11, Community Centre, Panchsheel Park,
New Delhi 110017, India

Distributed by the Penguin Group

Penguin Books Ltd,
80 Strand, London WC2R 0RL

Penguin Group (USA)
375 Hudson Street, NY 10014, USA

Penguin Group (Australia)
250 Camberwell Road, Camberwell,
Victoria 3124, Australia

Penguin Group (NZ)
67 Apollo Drive, Mairangi Bay, Auckland 1310,
New Zealand

Rough Guides is represented in Canada by
Tourmaline Editions Inc. 662 King Street West,
Suite 304, Toronto, Ontario M5V 1M7

Cover concept by Peter Dyer.

Typeset in Bembo and Helvetica to an original
design by Henry Iles.

Printed in Singapore
© Matthew Teller 2011
Maps © Rough Guides

264pp includes index
A catalogue record for this book is available from
the British Library
ISBN: 978-1-84836-604-6

The publishers and authors have done their
best to ensure the accuracy and currency of
all the information in **The Rough Guide to
the Cotswolds**, however, they can accept no
responsibility for any loss, injury, or inconvenience
sustained by any traveller as a result of
information or advice contained in the guide.

1   3   5   7   9   8   6   4   2

Help us update

We've gone to a lot of effort to ensure that the first
edition of **The Rough Guide to the Cotswolds**
is accurate and up-to-date. However, things
change – places get "discovered", opening hours
are notoriously fickle, restaurants and rooms raise
prices or lower standards. If you feel we've got it
wrong or left something out, we'd like to know, and
if you can remember the address, the price, the
hours, the phone number, so much the better.

Please send your comments with the subject
line "**Rough Guide the Cotswolds Update**"
to ©mail@uk.roughguides.com. We'll credit all
contributions and send a copy of the next edition
(or any other Rough Guide if you prefer) for the
very best emails.

Find more travel information, connect with
fellow travellers and book your trip on ⓦwww
.roughguides.com

Acknowledgements

The author would like to thank all those in and around the Cotswolds who were so forthcoming with ideas, tips, news, advice and generosity. In particular, the indefatigable and hugely supportive Chris Dee of Cotswolds Tourism; Hayley Beer at Oxfordshire Cotswolds; Jo Butler, Heather Armitage and Digna Martinez in Oxford, and my wonderful Oxford guide Elizabeth Hudson-Evans; Tania Aspinall, Jackie Fallon and Peter Ward-Brown in Stratford; Isobel Milne in Cirencester; Tony Fisher at the Cotswold Farm Park; Jill Bewley at the Cotswold Water Park; Rob Rees; PRs, press officers and visitor relations staff at museums, attractions, hotels and restaurants all round the region (forgive the general approach: space won't allow me to thank everyone individually); and last but definitely not least, staff at TICs and VICs across the Cotswolds, who do a magnificent, often under-appreciated frontline job every day helping people make the most of this wonderful part of the world.

At Rough Guides, huge thanks to my editor Lucy White, who has done a truly exceptional job bringing this book to life. Patient, insightful, deft and sharp, Lucy is a pleasure to work with. Thank you, too, to Ed Wright for fine cartography, Umesh Aggarwal for spot-on setting; Nicole Newman and Chloë Roberts for hard work on the pics; and Jo Kirby for getting the ball off the ground (and keeping it rolling).

Finally thanks to the marvellous Kedi Simpson; to Phil Lee for big-picture generosity; to Clare Taylor up the road; and, as always, to Hannah for everything.

SMALL PRINT

Photo credits

All photos © Rough Guides except the following:

Full page
Bourton-on-the-Water pub © Photolibrary

Introduction
Duntisbourne Abbots springtime © Photolibrary
A summer punt jam under Magdalen Bridge in Oxford © Photolibrary

Things not to miss
01 Sudeley Castle © Photolibrary
02 Walkers on the Cotswold Way footpath, Stanway village © David Hughes/Super Stock
04 *The Kingham Plough* © courtesy of *The Kingham Plough*
08 Blenheim Palace, Woodstock © Super Stock

09 Chipping Campden © Steven Vidler/Corbis
10 Lower Slaughter © Mike Kemp/Corbis
15 Hertford College, Oxford © Jean Brooks/ Super Stock
16 Painswick © David Noton/Getty

Secret Cotswolds colour section
Broadway Tower © Steven Vidler/Corbis
Minster Lovell © Super Stock
The Mount Inn at Stanton © Mike Kemp/Corbis
Barnsley House © courtesy of Barnsley House
Lords of the Manor © courtesy of *Lords of the Manor*
The Rectory © courtesy of *The Rectory*

Index

Map entries are in colour.

A

A&E 36
Abbey Home Farm 191
Abbey House Gardens
.... 240
Ablington 190
accommodation 24
activity holidays 34
Adlestrop 114
airports 20
Alderminster 149
ales, local ..... see *Cotswold
  Food* colour section
Allium restaurant 200
Amberley 234
Ampney Crucis 199
Ampney St Peter 199
Andoversford 212
antiques 35
Area of Outstanding Natural
  Beauty 39
Arlingham 226
Arlington Row 189
arrival 19
Arts & Crafts 112
Ascott-under-Wychwood
.... 115
Ashton Keynes 197
asparagus 168
Asthall 111
Aston 107
ATMs 37
Avening 236

B

B roads, top 5 ...see *Secret
  Cotswolds* colour section
B&Bs 25
backpackers 26
Badminton 243
Bampton 106
Banbury 121–127
Banbury 122
bank holidays 38
banks 37
Barnsley 191
Barringtons, the 111, 188
Batsford Arboretum 177
beach 198

Beatrix Potter 223
bed and breakfast 25
beer festivals 29
beers, local ... see *Cotswold
  Food* colour section
Belas Knap 212
Berkeley 227
Bibury 189
Bicester Village 131
bikes 24, 32
Binsey 85
Bird Park, Prinknash 230
Birmingham Airport 20
Bishop's Cleeve 213
Bisley 234
Bladon 101
Blanc, Raymond 91
Bledington 116
Blenheim Palace ... 98–103
Bletchingdon 94
Blockley 179
Bloxham 131
Boddington, Lower 128
Bodleian Library 64
booking rooms 24
books 247
bookshops, independent
.... 247
Bourton House 178
Bourton-on-the-Hill 178
Bourton-on-the-Water ... 185
Brailes, the 152
Bretforton 169
breweries ...... see *Cotswold
  Food* colour section
Brightwell Vineyard 91
Bristol Aero Collection .. 198
Bristol Airport 20
Brize Norton 106
Broad Campden 155
Broadway 161–166
Broadway 162
Broadway Tower 165
Broadwell 180
Brockworth 222
Broughton Castle 129
BST 38
Buckland 163
budgeting 35
Bull's Cross 229
Burford 108
Burford 109
bus museum, Oxford 95
buses 23

business hours 37
Butts Farm 198

C

Calcot Manor 237
Cam 242
Cambridge (Glos) 226
campervans 23
camping 26
canals .... see *Secret
  Cotswolds* colour section
car rental 23
caravans 26
cards, credit 37
cashback 37
Castle Combe 244
casualty 36
celebrities 8
cellphones 38
Central Cotswolds
.... 173–205
Central Cotswolds 174
Cerney Gardens 196
Chadlington 117
Chalford 233
Charingworth 153
Charlbury 116
Charlton Abbots 212
Charlton-on-Otmoor 93
Chastleton House 119
Chavenage House 238
Chedworth 189
Chedworth Roman Villa
.... 188
cheese-rolling 222
cheeses, local .... see
  Cotswold Food colour
  section
CHELTENHAM 213–218
Cheltenham 214
  accommodation 215
  arrival 213
  art gallery 216
  B&Bs 216
  bars 218
  buses 214
  cafés 217
  coaches 214
  Daffodil, the 217
  Devil's Chimney 219
  eating 217
  Everyman Theatre 218

festivals 213
folk festival 213
gallery, art....................... 216
Gold Cup........................... 213
history 213
Holst Birthplace Museum
.... 216
horse-racing...................... 213
hotels 215
Imperial Square................. 217
information, tourist............ 215
jazz festival 213
Leckhampton Hill.............. 219
literature festival.............. 213
Montpellier 217
museum 216
music festival 213
park and ride..................... 215
Pittville Pump Room 216
police................................ 218
public transport................. 213
pubs 218
races 213
rail station 213
restaurants 217
science festival 213
Suffolks, the..................... 217
taxis.................................. 218
theatre.............................. 218
tourist office 215
tours 215
trains 213
transport, public............... 213
walks, nearby.................... 219
walks, guided.................... 215
wine.................................. 218
chemists 36
Cherington........................ 152
Chesterton Farm 195
children............................ 40
Childswickham 166
Chimney........................... 107
chip and pin 37
Chipping Campden
.... 154–159
Chipping Campden 154
Chipping Norton............ 117
Chipping Norton............ 118
Chipping Sodbury 243
Churchill (Oxon)............. 116
Churchill, Winston 101
Churn, River 197
Cider with Rosie 231
circus, Giffords 40
Cirencester.......... 191–195
Cirencester 192
Clanfield 107
Clapton-on-the-Hill........ 186
Cleeve Cloud.................. 213
Cleeve Hill 212
coaches........................... 19
Coates 197
Coberley 218

Cockleford 219
Colesbourne 219
Coln Rogers 190
Coln St Aldwyns........... 190
Compton Abdale 189
Compton Verney 149
Confessor's Way 92
Cooper's Hill 222
Corinium Museum 194
Cornbury Park 117
costs............................... 35
Cotswold Airport 198
Cotswold Canals Trust
......see *Secret Cotswolds*
colour section
Cotswold Chef, the 27
Cotswold Country Park &
Beach 198
Cotswold Edge................ 6
Cotswold Falconry Centre
.... 178
Cotswold Farm Park 184
Cotswold Ice Cream Co
.... 188
Cotswold Line Railway
.... 114
Cotswold Link path 125,
155
Cotswold Lion 6
Cotswold Olimpicks 159
Cotswold Perfumery..... 185
Cotswold Round 32
Cotswold Spice 153
Cotswold Water Park ... 198
Cotswold Way 32
Cotswold Wildlife Park
.... 111
Cotswolds AONB 39
Cotswolds Conservation
Board 39
Cotswolds map 4
Cotswolds Tourism......... 39
Cotswolds, central
.... 173–205
Cotswolds, central 174
Cotswolds, north
.... 151–168
Cotswolds, north 136
Cotswolds, Oxfordshire
.... 108–121
Cotswolds, Oxfordshire
.... 90
Cotswolds, south
.... 227–244
Cotswolds, south 206
Cotswolds, west
.... 205–227
Cotswolds, west.......... 206
Cotswolds88 hotel........ 230

cottages........................... 26
Country Park & Beach
.... 198
Covered Market, Oxford
.... 72
Cowley (Glos) 219
Cowley (Oxon)................ 45
Cowley Manor 219
Cranham......................... 229
Crazy Bear 91
credit cards 37
crime............................... 36
Cropredy......................... 128
Cross-Cotswold Pathway
.... 125
Crudwell 241
currency.......................... 37
Cutsdean 184
cycling 24, 32

D

Daglingworth 196
Daylesford 115
Deddington.................... 131
Devil's Chimney............. 219
Ditchford Mill 180
doctors 36
Donnington.................... 180
Dorchester.................... 91
Dorn............................... 177
Doughton....................... 238
Dover's Hill 158
Down Ampney.............. 199
driving...................... 19, 23
Duchy Home Farm 238
Duntisbourne Rouse..... 196
Duntisbournes, the....... 196
Dursley 242

E

East End 105
East Midlands Airport.....20
eating and drinking........27,
see *Cotswold Food*
colour section
Ebrington 153
Edge 229
Edgehill, battle of 129
electricity 36
emergency numbers....... 38
emergency, medical 36
English Heritage 35
Enjoy England 39

Evenlode, River 113
Evesham 169
Ewen 197
exchange 37
Eynsham 104

F

Fairford 199
families 40
farm shops 27
Farmcote 208
farmers' markets 27
Farmington 188
Farnborough 128
Farthinghoe 127
Feldon, the 149
ferries 21
festivals 29
Filkins 111
Five Valleys 231
Fleece Inn 169
flight arrival 20
food and drink 27,
    see *Cotswold Food*
    colour section
food festivals 29
food, local ..... see *Cotswold
    Food* colour section
Ford 184
Foss Cross 189
Fosse Way 175
Fossebridge 189
Four Shire Stone 179
Foxbury Farm 106
Frampton-on-Severn 225
France Lynch 233
Frome Valley 233
further reading 247

G

galleries, top 5 ... see *Secret
    Cotswolds* colour section
gardens, top 5 ... see *Secret
    Cotswolds* colour section
Gatcombe Park 236
Gatwick Airport 20
Gaydon 150
getting around 21
getting there 19
Giffords Circus 40
GLOUCESTER 219–224
Gloucester 220
    accommodation 221
airport 221
arrival 220
B&B 221
Beatrix Potter 223
boat trips 224
Brockworth 222
buses 220
cafés 224
cathedral 222
cheese-rolling 222
City Museum 223
Cooper's Hill 222
Cross, the 221
cruises 224
docks 223
eating 224
farmers' market 221
Folk Museum 223
gallery, Nature in Art 224
ghost walks 221
Gloucester Cathedral 222
Gloucester Docks 223
Greyfriars 223
Harry Potter 223
history 219
hotels 221
information, tourist 221
market 221
Nature in Art gallery 224
Over 224
park and ride 221
police 224
Potter, Beatrix 223
pubs 224
rail station 220
restaurants 224
rugby 224
St Michael's Tower 221
Tailor of Gloucester 223
Tall Ships Festival 220
taxis 224
tourist office 221
tours 221
trains 220
Twigworth 224
walks, guided 221
Waterways Museum 223
Gloucester Cathedral
    222
Gloucestershire Airport
    221
Gloucestershire
    Warwickshire Steam
    Railway 168
Gloucestershire Way 32
Glyme Valley Way 97
GMT 38
Golden Valley 233
GPs 36
Great Barrington ... 111, 188
Great Milton 91
Great Rissington 186
Great Tew 121
Great Wolford 179
Greet 210

guesthouses 25
Guiting Power 184

H

Hailes Abbey 207
Halford 149
Ham 227
Hampton Poyle 94
Hanborough 95
Hanwell 127
Harry Potter 53, 75, 223
Hawkesbury Upton 243
Hayles Fruit Farm 208
health insurance 36
Heathrow Airport 20
Henley-in-Arden 137
Heritage Motor Centre ... 150
Hetty Pegler's Tump 242
Heyford 132
Hidcote Manor 160
Highgrove 238
holiday companies 34
holidays, public 38
Honeybourne 170
Honington 149
Hook Norton 120
horse-racing 213
hospitals 36
hostels 26
hotels 25

I

Ilmington 153
information, tourist 39
Inglesham 201
Inn at Fossebridge 189
inns 25
Inspector Morse 53, 85,
    247
insurance 36
Islip 92

J

Jericho 80

K

Kelmscott Manor 112

Kemble 197
Kiddington 97, 117
Kidlington 91
kids 40
Kiftsgate Court 160
Kineton (Glos) 184
Kineton (Warks) 150
King's Stanley 241
Kingham 115
Kingscote 236
Kingswood 243
Kirtlington 93

L

Lechlade 200
Leckhampton Hill 219
Lee, Laurie 231
Levellers, the 108
Little Barrington 111, 188
Little Rissington 186
Little Sodbury 244
llama trekking 128
Lodge Park 188
London 20
Long Hanborough 95
Longborough 180
Lords of the Manor 186
Lower Boddington 128
Lower Brailes 152
Lower Clopton 149
Lower Heyford 132
Lower Oddington 183
Lower Slaughter 186
Lower Swell 183
Luton Airport 20
Lygon Arms 163

M

Macmillan Way 32
mail 37
Malmesbury 240
Manoir aux Quat'Saisons
.... 91
map of Cotswolds 4
maps 37
markets 27
marmalade, Oxford ...... see Cotswold Food colour section
Matara garden 236
Mickleton 161
Milton 131

Milton-under-Wychwood
.... 113
Minchinhampton 234
Minster Lovell 105
Minsterworth 225
Misarden Park 230
Miserden 230
mobile phones 38
money 37
Moreton-in-Marsh 175
Moreton-in-Marsh 175
Morris, William 112
motorhomes 24
motorway access 19
Murcott 93
music festivals 30
music, classical 30

N

Nailsworth 235
narrowboats ...... see Secret Cotswolds colour section
National Hunt racing 213
National Rail Enquiries
.... 21
national trails 32
National Trust 35
Naunton 183
Newark Park 243
North Cerney 196
North Cotswolds
.... 151–168
North Cotswolds 136
North Leigh Roman Villa 105
North Nibley 242
North Oxfordshire
.... 121–132
Northleach 187
Nympsfield 242

O

Oddingtons, the 183
Old Sodbury 244
Olimpicks, Cotswold 159
opening hours 37
Ordnance Survey 37
Organic Farm Shop 191
organic food 27
OS maps 37
Otmoor 93
Over 224
Owlpen Manor 242
OXFORD 45–86

Oxford, greater 46
Oxford, city centre... 50–51
Oxford, central 60
  accommodation 55–58
  Addison's Walk 70
  airport 49
  Alice in Wonderland 75, 76
  All Souls College 67
  Antony Gormley sculpture
  61
  arrival 48
  Ashmolean Museum 78
  B&Bs 55
  backpackers 58
  Balliol College 61
  bars 84
  Bate Collection of Musical
    Instruments 76
  Bath Place 65
  Bear, the 73
  bicycles 54
  Binsey 85
  Blackbird Leys 46
  Blackwell's 61
  boat rental 70
  boat trips 70
  Bodleian Library 64
  Botanic Garden 69
  Brasenose College 66
  Bridge of Sighs 65
  Broad Street 61
  Broad Walk 69
  bus museum 95
  buses 55
  cafés 81
  camping 58
  Canal, Oxford 132
  Carfax 73
  Carroll, Lewis 75
  castle, Oxford 77
  cathedral 75
  Catte Street 65
  Cherwell, River 77
  Christ Church College 74
  Christ Church Meadow 76
  Clarendon Building 64
  clubs 86
  coaches 49
  colleges 58
  Cornmarket 77
  Corpus Christi College 68
  Covered Market 72
  Cowley Road 81
  cruises 70
  cycling 54
  Daily Info 52
  Dead Man's Walk 69
  Divinity School 64
  drinking 84
  driving 49
  Eagle & Child, the 78
  eating 81
  Emperors, the 63
  Exeter College 72
  farmers' markets 45
  Folly Bridge 76
  Frideswide 47

INDEX

gallery, Christ Church......... 76
George Street..................... 78
ghost walks....................... 53
Gloucester Green.............. 78
Gordouli, the 63
Great Clarendon Street...... 80
Halley, Edmund................. 65
Harry Potter.................. 53, 75
Henry VIII........................... 47
Hertford College................ 65
High Street 71
High, The........................... 71
history 46
History of Science museum
.... 63
hostels............................... 58
hotels 55
information, tourist............. 52
Inspector Morse........... 53, 85
Isis..................................... 77
Jericho 80
Jesus College 72
Jewish heritage................. 80
Keble College.................... 79
Lamb & Flag, the................ 85
Lincoln College 72
Little Clarendon Street....... 80
Magdalen College.............. 69
markets 45
Martyrs' Memorial............. 63
May Day celebrations 69
Merton College 68
Merton Grove 69
Merton Street..................... 68
Mitre, the............................ 72
Modern Art Oxford............. 73
Morris, William 48
Museum, Ashmolean 78
Museum, History of Science
.... 63
Museum, Natural History
.... 79
Museum, Oxford................. 73
Museum, Pitt Rivers........... 79
music venues 86
music, classical.................. 86
Natural History Museum 79
New College....................... 65
Newman, Cardinal 48
Oriel College 68
Oxfam 61
Oxford Brookes University
.... 48
Oxford Bus Museum........... 95
Oxford Canal..................... 132
Oxford Castle Unlocked 77
Oxford Castle..................... 77
Oxford Cathedral 75
Oxford Martyrs................... 47
Oxford Movement.............. 48
Oxford Museum 73
Oxford Union 78
park and ride..................... 49
parking 55
Pear Tree 52
Pembroke College 73
Perch, the........................... 85

Pitt Rivers Museum............ 79
police................................. 86
porter's lodge 61
public transport.................. 48
pubs 84
punting 70
Queen's College................. 71
Radcliffe Camera 66
rail station 48
Redbridge 52
restaurants 81–84
Rhodes Building................. 68
rickshaws 54
ring road............................. 49
rowing 77
Ruskin College 80
St Edmund Hall.................. 71
St John's College............... 78
St Mary the Virgin 67
St Michael's Street............. 77
St Michael-at-the-Northgate
.... 78
St Scholastica Day Riot 47
Seacourt............................. 52
self-catering 55
Sheldonian Theatre............ 63
student halls....................... 56
subfusc 71
synagogue.......................... 80
taxis................................... 86
tearooms 81
Thames, River 77
theatres 86
Thornhill 52
TIC..................................... 52
Tom Quad 74
Tom Tower.......................... 75
tourist office 52
tours 52
trains 48
transport, public................. 48
Trinity College 63
Trout, the............................ 85
Turf Tavern........................ 65
Turl Street........................... 72
University Church............... 67
University College 71
university rooms................. 56
Wadham College................ 80
walking tours...................... 52
Walton Street..................... 80
Water Eaton 52
Wolvercote 85
youth hostels...................... 58
Oxford marmalade .... see
    Cotswold Food colour
    section
Oxfordshire 90
Oxfordshire Cotswolds
.... 108–121
Oxfordshire, North
.... 121–132
Oxhill.............................. 149
Ozleworth 243

P

Painswick 228
park and ride 23
parking........................... 23
Parr, Katherine............. 211
passports....................... 36
Paxford 153
pharmacies.................... 36
phones........................... 38
police............................ 36
post offices.................... 37
Potter, Beatrix.............. 223
Potting Shed, the 241
Poulton 199
Pre-Raphaelites............ 112
Prinknash Abbey 230
public holidays 38
public transport 21
Pudding Club, the 161
Puddleditch Farm......... 227
Puesdown Inn.............. 189

R

racing, National Hunt ...213
Radcot Bridge 107
rail routes................. 19, 22
railway, steam.............. 168
Ramsden 105
rapeseed oil................... see
    Cotswold Food colour
    section
Ratley 129
reading, further............ 247
Ride a cock horse 123
Rissingtons, the............ 186
Rococo Garden 228
Rodborough Common
.... 234
Rodmarton Manor 238
Rollright Stones........... 120
Romantic Road 215
Rousham House........... 132
Royal Agricultural College
.... 194
Royal Mail..................... 37
Royal Shakespeare
    Company (RSC)......... 144
rugby 224

S

St Eadburgha 165

Sapperton......................234
Sarsden 116
Saul 226
Saul Junction.................226
seasons 8
self-catering...................26
Selsley 241
service charges 39
Seven Springs 218
Severn Bore..................225
Sezincote House 178
Shakespeare, William ...138
Sheepscombe 230
Sherborne.....................188
Shipston-on-Stour........151
Shipton-under-Wychwood
.................................114
shopping........................35
Shottery........................146
Sibford Gower 120
Slad 231
Slaughters, the 186
Slimbridge Wetland Centre
.................................226
Snowshill Manor...........166
Sodburys, the...............243
Somerford Keynes........198
Source of the Thames
.................................197
Southrop.......................200
Spoonley Wood............209
sports 32
Stadhampton...................91
Stansted Airport 20
Stanton.........................167
Stanway House 167
steam railway 168
steeplechase 213
Stinchcombe Hill 242
Stonebench 225
Stones, Rollright...........120
Stow-on-the-Wold
............................180–183
Stow-on-the-Wold.......181
Stratford and the north
Cotswolds.................136
Stratford Greenway 148
STRATFORD-UPON-
AVON................136–148
Stratford-upon-Avon ...137
accommodation 140
almshouses......................145
Anne Hathaway's Cottage
....146
arrival...............................137
B&Bs................................141
Bancroft Gardens.............142
bars 147
bicycles..................139, 148
Birthplace, Shakespeare's
....143

boat trips...........................139
buses 138
Butterfly Farm 146
cafés..................................147
camping 141
church, Holy Trinity 145
Clopton Bridge..................142
cruises...............................139
cycling......................139, 148
Dirty Duck, the 147
eating................................147
farmers' market.................146
grave of Shakespeare......145
Guild Chapel 145
Hall's Croft 145
Harvard House 144
history 136
Holy Trinity Church............145
hostel 141
hotels 140
information, tourist............139
market................................146
Mary Arden's Farm...........146
Nash's House....................143
New Place..........................143
park and ride.....................137
parking 137
police.................................148
public transport.................137
pubs 147
rail station 137
restaurants 147
Royal Shakespeare Company
....144
Royal Shakespeare Theatre
....142
Shakespeare's Birthplace
....143
Shakespeare's grave........145
Shakespeare's tomb 145
Shottery.............................146
Stratford Greenway...........148
Swan Theatre....................143
taxis...................................148
tearooms 147
theatre...............................142
tomb of Shakespeare.......145
tourist office 139
tours 139
trains 137
transport, public...............137
walks, guided....................139
Wilmcote............................146
youth hostel 141
Stretton-on-Fosse 153
Stroud...........................231
Stroud 232
Stroudwater Navigation
......see *Secret Cotswolds*
colour section
student halls 26
Sudeley Castle 210
Sulgrave Manor 127
Swells, the 183
Swerford 121
Swinbrook 111

Swinford Bridge............104

T

Tackley..........................132
Tadpole Bridge 107
Tailor of Gloucester 223
Tall Ships Festival........220
Talton Mill 149
Tarlton...........................197
telephones.......................38
Temple Guiting 184
Tetbury.................236–239
Tetbury 236
Thames and Severn Canal
......see *Secret Cotswolds*
colour section
Thames Head 197
Thames Path 32, 197
Thames, source of........197
Thomas, Edward 114
Thrupp (Oxon) 92
TICs 40
time zone.........................38
tipping 39
Toadsmoor Valley 234
Tobacconist Farm.........234
Toddington 168
Todenham.....................179
Toot Baldon 91
tourist information 39
train routes 19, 22
transport, public............21
travel insurance 36
Traveline 21
travellers with disabilities
.................................40
travelling with children....40
Tredington.....................149
Trouble House 239
Tunnel House Inn..........197
Twigworth 224
Tyndale Monument.......242

U

Uley 242
Uley Bury......................242
university halls................26
Upper Braides................152
Upper Heyford...............132
Upper Oddington 183
Upper Quinton..............149
Upper Slaughter 186
Upper Swell..................183

Upton House 129
UTC 39

V

Vale of Berkeley 225
Vale of Evesham 168
VICs 40
visas 36
VisitBritain 39

W

walking 32
walking holidays 34
Warden's Way 185
Washington, George 127
Water Park, Cotswold ... 198

Waterley Bottom 242
Welford-on-Avon 148
Westonbirt Arboretum
.... 239
Weston-on-the-Green 94
Whatley Manor 237
Whichford 152
Whiteoak Green 105
Whiteway 230
Wickwar 243
Widford 111
Willersey Hill 163
Wilmcote 146
Winchcombe 208
Windrush 188
Windrush Way 185
Winstone 196
Witney 103
wolds 7
Wolvercote 85
Woodchester Mansion
.... 241

Woodmancote 213
Woodstock 94–98
Woodstock 95
wool churches 6
Woolpack, the 231
Wotton-under-Edge 243
Wroxton 129
Wychwood Brewery 104
Wychwood Project 97
Wychwood Way 97
Wychwoods, the 113
Wyck Rissington 185
Wykham Park Farm 131

Y

youth hostels 26

INDEX

Map symbols

maps are listed in the full index using coloured text

– · – ·	County boundary	⊙	Statue
– – –	Chapter boundary	★	Bus stop
⬤⑫	Motorway & junction number	▲	Peak
═══	Main road	⚔	Campsite
═══	Minor road	🏛	Stately home
▬▬▬	Pedestrianized street	♛	Castle
▬●▬	Railway	∴	Ancient ruins/ archeological site
- - - - -	Footpath	✕	Battle site
— —	Ferry route	⊥	Gardens
———	River	⌂	Abbey
———	Canal	✡	Synagogue
▨	Water	⊠	Public entrance (Oxford college)
⊐⊏	Bridge/ tunnel entrance	▬	Building
♦	Point of interest	⊣⊢	Church
ⓘ	Tourist information	⊡	Christian cemetery
⊠	Post office	▨	Park/gardens/ open land (town maps)
🅿	Parking	▨	Area of Outstanding Natural Beauty (AONB) (chapter maps)
⊞	Hospital		

MAP SYMBOLS

Contains Ordnance Survey data © Crown copyright and database right 2011

So now we've told you about the things not to miss, the best places to stay, the top restaurants, the liveliest bars and the most spectacular sights, it only seems fair to tell you about the best travel insurance around

WorldNomads.com
keep travelling safely

Recommended by Rough Guides